From Shakespeare to Joyce

FROM
SHAKESPEARE
TO JOYCE

Authors and Critics; Literature and Life

ELMER EDGAR STOLL

FREDERICK UNGAR PUBLISHING CO.
NEW YORK

To

W. SOMERSET MAUGHAM

Dramatist, Novelist, Critic,
Lover of Life and Art

Acknowledgments

THE PUBLISHER and the author wish to thank publishers for permission to quote from their books as follows:

Messrs. Dodd, Mead and Company, Chesterton's *Charles Dickens* (1906) and *Fancies vs. Fads* (1923) and Gissing's *Charles Dickens* (1904); Messrs. Henry Holt and Company, New York, Quiller-Couch's *Shakespeare's Workmanship* (1917); Messrs. The Macmillan Company, New York, Yeats's *Essays* (1924); Messrs. Longmans, Green and Company, New York, Bailey's *Shakespeare* (1929); New Directions, Norfolk, Connecticut, Levin's *James Joyce* (1941); Charles Scribner's Sons, New York, Stevenson's Critical Essays, South Seas Edition, Vol. XIII; and the Cambridge University Press, the Harvard University Press, and the University of Minnesota Press for permission to quote from *Art and Artifice in Shakespeare* (1933), *Shakespeare and Other Masters* (1940), and *Poets and Playwrights* (1929), by the present writer.

Preface and Prelude

THE ESSAYS or studies in this collection, traversing so wide a field, are, necessarily, rather independent and self-contained. The reader of a discussion of Milton, near the end of the book, cannot fairly be expected to have read, in order, all the preceding ones, from Shakespeare to Joyce. Consequently, though by cross reference I have endeavored to reduce it, there is some repetition. For the point of view is identical: that a work of art does not (miraculously) change as the criticism changes,[1] that there is meaning (either sense or a consistent nonsense) in poetry (or it isn't poetry), that there is truth in criticism (or it isn't criticism), and that the criterion for this is the conscious or unconscious intention of the author. As in my previous writings, I have endeavored to hold by Pope's principles in the verses I have repeatedly echoed:

> A perfect Judge will read each work of Wit
> With the same spirit that its author writ.
>
> In every work regard the writer's end . . .

[1] This fantasy of the impressionist critics has lately been given the sanction of the learned, by Professors Lovejoy, Boas, and Teeter, *Journal of the History of Ideas* (1940), January, p. 11, and April, pp. 207-25.

And while the point of view is kept, certain ideas recur, particularly those involved in Milton's definition of poetry as simple, sensuous, and passionate, and the doctrine that the greatest poetry or drama is (more or less) for all men and not a puzzle for any.

A miscellany, however, needs, with many people, some defending. And it is natural to demand of a book unity and symmetry, a fullness and completeness of presentation. But though without these the book in itself may suffer, the truth, at the same time, may not so much; want of truth being, as I have suggested, the chief and crying fault of criticism. The best ideas that a man has are those which come to him; the worst, those he goes after or works out to fit in with those which have arrived. And these to fit or fill in are often the worst of any, the result of his making too much of his godsends or windfalls. As Bacon said, in words to which I am attached: "The human understanding, when it has once adopted an opinion . . . draws all things else to support and agree with it." For as he had said already: "The human understanding is of its own nature prone to suppose the existence of more order and regularity in the world than it finds." So that, in the complete and thorough discussion of a subject or topic, there is the danger of attaining proportions in the book at the expense of the proportions of reality.

No doubt in turning, as here is done, from subject to subject, from author to author, the writer may be disturbing the proportions of reality as much. These may suffer from an *idée fixe,* which imposes itself on everything. But that is still more likely to happen if he is working out a scheme or system, tracing a development in evolution, or proving a source or an influence. By Mr. Eliot's "comparison and analysis, the chief tools of the critic," as applied to authors often far apart in time and place and without discernible connection, one is less likely to be putting pressure upon the facts. That conclusion, in any case, is more in keeping with my premise: to the man with fixed ideas the fruitful new ones seldom come, or cannot.

And in the criticism of English literature, especially that of Shakespeare, there may be a particular advantage in such want of system or program. Unlike Corneille, Racine, and (in a measure) Molière, not only Shakespeare but also most other great English poets have themselves had no system or program, no definite, ordered critical rules or principles. They have not even proceeded from any formulated abstract conception, whether philosophical or artistic, or realized it in practice. Shakespeare has no thesis or teaching, no *ars poetica,* either, whether classical or anti-classical; though when his story, or the effect desired, lent itself to the unities, in *The Tempest,* he adopted them, and when it lent itself to a fatal interposition and the relegating of the horrors to the background, in *Macbeth,* he was classical before that. And considering his material and his audience, not his present or future reputation, he varied his dramatic method and his poetic style or diction, from play to play, continually; but by the instinct to rouse or please, of his tactfulness only half aware. He seems not ever to have said, as he did it, I will try a new game:—for once observe the unities (having, indeed, tried my hand at them in *Othello*); plunge into action in the initial scene, in *King Lear;* put the "crisis-deed" not, as usual, in the middle, but at the end, in *Hamlet;* pile up situations and sensations in the denouement, in *Cymbeline;* let the action proceed from the character, without either fate or villain behind it, in *Coriolanus;* write now like Ben Jonson, in *The Merry Wives,* now like Beaumont and Fletcher, in the "dramatic romances." Painters both do so and say so—this time no middle distance, this other time, perhaps, no horizon—; and to judge from either their product or their prefaces or *discours,* French dramatists too have followed a deliberate purpose of technical variation or innovation.

Whether this defense applies to the miscellany now before him, the reader will, of course, judge for himself. But since this is likely to be my last volume of criticism he may perhaps be willing to hear, at the same time, still another word of defense, though in retrospect rather than in prospect. By one reviewer of my *Art and Artifice in Shakespeare* (1933) I was charged with sensationalism. Not unnaturally, to be sure, for I had found high tragedy rooted in melodrama, high comedy in farce. But the opinion was, I think, supported by the examples of Shakespeare and the ancients in the one case; of the ancients, Ben Jonson, and Molière, in the other. And study or enlightenment, how much there is or should be in us of either as we are attending to the highest forms of drama and other poetry, it is, of course, difficult to determine. Critics like Aristotle and Longinus have dwelt instead upon imaginative and emotional excitement, enlargement and purification; and in my own approaches to the subject, as particularly in my *Shakespeare and Other Masters,* pp. 81–84, and in this book, *passim,* I have leaned heavily upon them and upon those critics who are also poets,—Arnold, Abercrombie, and Yeats. They all are of one accord in thinking that the reader or spectator has, in the words of the last-named, "added to his being, not his knowledge." So Yeats has been quoted by Lennox Robinson since as saying "passion and not thought makes tragedy." And if the critics of Shakespeare, Milton, and Joyce had been such as these I should have had little or no occasion to take up the pen.

For my writing has been and still is rather argumentative or controversial; one of my persistent opinions, which I have not yet mentioned, being that the main hindrance to the understanding, and sympathetic appreciation, of the great national literary figures, Shakespeare, Dante, and Milton, discussed and interpreted through the centuries, is the criticism itself. This, all too often, has not judged with the same spirit that the author writ; and in the process Shakespeare has become Maurice Morgann, or Coleridge, or Dowden, or Bradley, or some nearer contemporary still farther remote. And it is especially in this matter of the knowledge—the philosophy, or psychology, or other doctrine—that Shakespeare or Milton has become, to suit the ingenious critic and then his studious reader, another man, a different, difficult artist, and often less of one, or a more incredible one, than he is.

Out of controversy, indeed (but not barren contradiction, I hope), came this miscellany—and the others. For to tell the truth, all my books have, in greater or lesser measure, been miscellanies. No treatises have I written, but essays and articles; and as occasion or provocation arose, that is, as the truth (or else a deceptive semblance of it) was borne in upon me. What I say of this volume, therefore, applies, if not so much, to the others; and here, in the preface, written last, I find myself controversial or argumentative to the end.

Sixteen of the twenty-one studies have appeared before: chapters I and X in the Publications of the Modern Language Association; chapters II, III, VII–IX in *Modern Language Notes;* chapter V in *Life and Letters* (London); VI and XXI in the *University of Toronto Quarterly;* XI and XX in the *Journal of English and Germanic Philology;* XV, XVI, and XIX in the *Review of English Studies* (Oxford); XVII in the *Modern Language Quarterly.* All of these, however, have been much revised and most of them considerably extended.

To these editors I wish to express my thanks; but even more to those critics, and to those few learned bodies, who have taken the trouble to show signs of that understanding without which, as with any other communication, one can hardly continue it. Only the deaf and blind go on talking to those who do not hear or heed. Shakespeare, I have long insisted, wrote, like the greatest musical composers, careless of posterity; scholars, though by no means so indifferent to print, cannot rely upon it, for more reasons than one; and in the present volume are laid bare some of the unhappy consequences nowadays as ingenious men (or women) of letters, "alone with English," fancy they can.

E. E. S.

Contents

FROM SHAKESPEARE TO JOYCE

CHAPTER I

Literature and Life Again

and though a lad,
Had seen the world—which is a curious sight,
And very much unlike what people write . . .
BYRON.

IN MY previous discussion[1] I said that it is not justifiable
to treat literary or dramatic art as a document, a record or
relic of the time, on the one hand, or of the author's life, on
the other; that, rather, art reflects the taste of the time, and
the taste of the author; and that while much of the life of the
period may be reflected, and of the author, too, it is only
with the greatest difficulty and uncertainty that this can be
isolated and defined. Imaginative literature (or painting,
sculpture, music) is not only not history or unconscious auto-
biography but not even raw material for it; big allowances
must be made both for the limitations and conventions of
the art and also for the character and talents of the artists.
Some of these, to be sure, are realists, intent on the external
object; some also are egoists, concerned, directly or indirectly, with their own nature and experience; but good
art—the greatest—is not limited or determined either by
the artist's person or his day. Rather similar are the opinions of the critics Mm. Rémy de Gourmont, Paul Valéry,
and Henri Bremond; and of recent notable novelists such

[1] *Shakespeare Studies* (1927), chap. ii.

as Proust and Gide.[2] Like writers of their nation and of England whom I have cited, they are of one accord against the biographical or historical attitude as unfruitful and irrelevant; and nearly all have much to say of Racine as one who did not recognizably reflect his time or his own life within it, and is, because of that, all the more significant as a poet.

The warrant and countenance of these and other great names suffice. Names, indeed, cannot insure me against error—I notice that one of our "humanist" editors avows that he thinks little of M. Valéry, which makes me tremble a little, if not for M. Valéry, for myself—but in such a matter it is the artists themselves that are most at home. And I shall not much venture upon philosophical questions concerning the nature of art; which, as Proust says, transforms, transposes the raw material, is not strictly comparable or commensurable with it—*en littérature, le vrai n'est pas concevable*,[3] says M. Valéry, like Poe before him—and is not limited to the artist's experience. All I wish here to do is, apart from quoting further authority, to point out some additional examples of the divergence upon which I am insisting, more especially as it may be recognized at the present day; and then endeavor, in some fashion, to indicate how far life and art may be considered to coincide.

Among the English who share this opinion is a writer in the London *Times Literary Supplement*, July 17, 1930, who ventures again upon that central battling-ground, the Restoration drama. Reviewing Mr. Stonehill's edition of the Works of Farquhar, he distinguishes between the type of society to be found in Congreve and another type of society

[2]Gourmont, as cited (above) in my *Shakespeare Studies*, and *Promenades* (1912), iv, 189; Valéry, *Variété*, i, *Au Sujet d'Adonis;* ii, pp. 84, 112; Bremond, *Nouvelles littéraires*, "Racine et la Poésie Pure," Sept. 14, 1929, et seq.; Proust, *À l'Ombre*, i, pp. 176f; ii, pp. 137, 175; Gide *Faux-monnayeurs* (1930), pp. 236–38.

[3]This is, of course, a rough statement only—"literature is no transcript." M. Valéry is speaking of self-revelation; and of the necessity of selection,—of lighting, coloring, and making-up to suit the needs of the *théâtre mental.*

in Farquhar, both licentious, but the one ordered and polite, the other a mixture of crude license and suppressed
protest against inhibitions and restraints. Rascally, rakehelly
fellows make a noise about their gaming, their drinking,
and their seductions, and carry them on with a vigor that
never would have been allowed in the polite world of Congreve's plays. And yet these two worlds are separated by
only seven years, and neither the interval in time nor the
disparity between Congreve's and Farquhar's social posi-
tions is enough to account for the difference. "In fact," he
continues, "the difference between civilization and its opposite seems to depend entirely on the mind which views it."
This is an opinion quite opposed to that of Professor L. A.
Strauss, who thinks Comedy of Manners (and Restoration
comedy is what he has in mind) "is necessarily immoral;
it is so because it faithfully reflects a mode of life that is
itself immoral"—a point of view in which are confused not
only art and reality but art and morality.[4] And (to turn
to the biographical aspect of the problem) another recent
writer in the *Times,* discussing Mrs. Carswell's *Burns,* remarks: "Poetry has its own language and its own laws. To
look beyond the poetry to find the man, is, usually, to lose
both. It is safer to assume that the poetry interprets the
man; not the man his poems." Mr. John Bailey, as we shall
see below, has lately expressed himself to similar effect concerning Shakespeare. And Professor Tinker, in his book *The
Good Estate of Poetry,* dwells on the fallacy of the historians and the biographers, among these especially the
psychoanalysts, in cases such as Shelley's, Byron's, and Poe's.
Certain poems of Shelley's and Byron's quite transform or
contradict the poet's known experience; and the results of
the psychoanalysis applied to Poe, in themselves quite dubious, contradict the poetry. Here is another instance of the
truth insisted upon by Gourmont as he criticized Taine,
who (without the light of psychoanalysis) continually re-
read *Le Rouge et le Noir* in his endeavor to discover the
soul of Stendhal: *Il n'y a que des rapports incertains entre*

[4]Farquhar (Belles-Lettres Series), p. xvi.

*la vie d'un homme et son œuvre, entre sa conduite et celle
qu'il impose à ses personnages.*[5]

In such cases, however, and still more in remoter ones,
like that of the dramatists of the Restoration, argument is
on either side rather fruitless. The facts, social or biographical, are too little known. After such a lapse of time incidents
and contemporaries cannot be identified, the conditions in
society cannot be reconstituted, the motives and intellectual
and emotional adventures of the writer cannot be traced.
It is attempted, to be sure, abundantly; and while we may
hold that the burden of proof rests on those who do this,
they have prejudice in their favor, and we cannot effectively
say them nay. But the present we more nearly know, and
can, in the contemporary art, more certainly recognize or
disavow.

2

The social aspect we will take up before the personal;
and if we have been asked to consider Restoration drama
a fairly faithful picture of Restoration society, or the Elizabethan drama of the Elizabethan, then the equivalent subject of consideration is the drama of today. Presumably
modern art is realistic; and modern literary drama is on the
whole much more realistic than the Elizabethan, or, I
should say, than that of the Restoration. And of those
plays which can pretend to dramatic excellence O'Neill's

[5]Since writing this, I have read Mr. I. A. Richards' sane and illuminating *Principles of Criticism* (1928), Harcourt Brace, N. Y. And
to profit by the prestige of his name I have added here and below
some excerpts from his book as footnotes. . . . "Even if we knew far
more than we do about how the mind works, the attempt to display
the inner working of the artist's mind by the evidence of his work
alone must be subject to the gravest dangers. And to judge by the
published work of Freud upon Leonardo or of Jung upon Goethe,
psychoanalysts tend to be peculiarly inept as critics" (pp. 29–30).
Poetic dreams are here in question; and Mr. Tinker quotes Mr.
Lowes (*Xanadu,* p. 400) to the effect that for *Kubla Khan,* after
the lapse of one hundred and twenty-seven years, the intimate,
deep-lying, personal facts on which alone such an analysis must rest
are no longer discoverable. What, then, of psychoanalysis applied
to Milton?

are as realistic and American as any. They deal, or ordinarily seem to deal, with the American local color: our
speech, types, and scenes. In a high degree this is true of
Desire Under the Elms. Here there is nothing fantastic, or
symbolical, or expressionistic, as in the later plays. And yet
who of us that know anything of the New England of the
fifties, or even of 1924, when it was written, but would
shudder from over the other side of Jordan if, a hundred
years from now, a literary historian should, as he may, take
this for a picture of that society? What a christening party,
of the family and their neighbors, as is found in Pt. III, sc.
I, with all its open and jesting allusion, by married and unmarried, male and female, old and young alike, to the un-
acknowledged fact that the newborn is not really the
father's offspring but his son's! That is not only not New
England, not history, as we know it; it is not the world, nor
human life. Surely not even in late-Roman or Byzantine
days was, in so mixed a company, adultery—and such an
adultery—a matter for general merriment at the expense
of the host. Such nasty nakedness and hideous obscenity,
such general contempt for the laws of society and also of
hospitality among one's neighbors and friends, could not, I
suppose, be found in any country, and not in any Restoration comedy that I remember, however loose. A far truer
picture of New England society is in Owen Davis' *Ice-
Bound*, an inferior play; and, indeed, it is ordinarily in
mediocre art that such faithful verisimilitude is to be ascer-
tained. Great art "is exaggeration," as in Shakespeare, and
in the painter Turner; or is abstraction, as in Racine, and
in the painter Ingres; and while O'Neill has none of these
great artists' balance and harmony, the exaggeration he
certainly has.

Or take another of his plays, the *Strange Interlude*. Such
a sexual and psychical chaos cannot be a real picture
of New York State since the Great War. Are apparently
good, sane, and simple farmers' wives, like Mrs. Evans, now
generally so convinced of the inexorableness of the law of
heredity (though the son has already escaped it) as to urge
a daughter-in-law to kill his child, while still in the womb,

and then provide him with another in its stead by secretly but promptly turning her attentions elsewhere? Good, sane, simple, and ungrammatical, she is, in her sexual notions, a Hedda Gabler or (of drama I am still speaking!) a Rebecca West. And does a so-called refined and charming daughter-in-law, like Nina Leeds, out of pure love for the unborn and devotion to her husband, then proceed to do all this, and yet manifestly belie these motives in the process, and yet (again) despite her fears for his sanity, because of the newborn passion in her bosom, undertake, in the sequel, to inform her husband of her eugenic adventure and also of the illegitimacy of the child? Her husband has done nothing that would warrant her, if she has any goodness or refinement in her nature. There is, of course, a great deal in the psychological analysis and the presentation to make this situation less unplausible in the play, but nothing which can convince us that it is representative of the time.

And if the mediocre drama be often truer, the positively low-class drama is so wildly romantic or so grossly melodramatic, so near, in short, to the level of the cinema, that it, too, though in the opposite direction, is representative of nothing but the taste of the time, among the lower classes. Or, not stopping to ask whether the art be mediocre, or low, or high, we might for a moment consider some of the great Broadway successes of recent days, no matter whether the reception be owing to the play's verisimilitude or not. The only one that I saw immediately before leaving the country a year and a half ago was the *Shanghai Gesture;* the only one since returning was *Strictly Dishonorable.* In neither, of course, can the matter of verisimilitude be much in question; but does the immense popularity of the product serve to indicate whether our public is morally superior to that (as depicted by Macaulay and literary historians since) which flocked to Wycherley's *Country Wife* and to Congreve's *Love for Love? Strictly Dishonorable,* a thoroughgoing comedy, dealing with life in our metropolis, lends itself better than the other favorite to the purposes of comparison. The indecency is as reckless as in either Restoration play. But the indecency or lasciviousness is not as in these great writers and in Aristophanes purged or (as it were) dehumanized by mirth. The wit is weak and poor, but even if it were far more vigorous and opulent it would not prevail against certain revulsions of our moral sense. We are invited to laugh, but cannot, when at the end of the first act we see an unsophisticated and appealing young woman fall, before our eyes, into the clutches of a young Lothario, with the connivance of an honorable judge. In truly great Comedy of Manners such considerations do not thrust themselves upon us: the characters have left their hearts and souls like troublesome luggage behind them. They are figures, almost marionettes, and they trip and dance about in an imitation world—"having got out of Christendom," as Charles Lamb says, "into the land—what shall I call it?—of Cuckoldry, the Utopia of gallantry." And though in the following acts this heroine turns out to be more aware of the situation than we had thought, and also by the generosity of the Lothario her honor is at the ultimate moment spared, the varied and lively situations are treated with comic intention, indeed, but immoral effect. After such a play Wycherley is, on the whole, a relief. And yet it has in one year been witnessed by many fold the number that saw the *Country Wife,* and by ladies not masked, and by young girls, who were not, as in Paris they would have been, duly warned away. All of which would tend to show, if anything, that the morality of this country (and of Ireland, too, as we shall see) is inferior to that of England (or of the fast set in London) at the infamous Restoration.

That is a conclusion from which one recoils. Yet remember not only our Broadway successes but our leading dramatist, and also the movies, which by their very titles, such as *Free Love,* and *The Call of the Flesh,* plainly and shamelessly indicate their nature; not to mention our current high-class novels, and stories in the magazines, which simply cannot be, as they used to be, read in the family circle aloud. The Restoration had nothing much in the way of prose narrative; but (dramatic and non-dramatic together) its literature could not vie in nastiness and pruriency, as well as abundance, with ours, Mr. James Joyce heading the Van-

guard. What, then, is to become of us and the Irish? As Mr.
William Archer said of the Restoration, "Had the theater
fairly represented its age, the British nation could never
have emerged from such a morass of levity, cynicism, corruption, and disease." If the theater and novel fairly
represent us, how then shall our nation and the Free State
emerge? But is it not mainly a matter of taste again, which
changes (and also of our philosophy and psychology, which
change too), not of fact? The scene of the one Broadway
success was a bawdyhouse, that of the other was a speak-
easy and bawdyhouse combined. These are, still, exceptional
places, and the people who frequent the theater are, for
the moment, exceptional people. When the play is over life
for most of them goes on as before. So with novel-reading—
after it, too, life goes on as before. And in O'Neill, and
Joyce, and lesser dramatists and novelists—there we have
the new psychology, which scents something carnal or
sexual behind or under almost everything in our mental and
moral activity.

Not only lascivious and prurient, the life presented in
our literature is, as Mr. Krutch says, mean and sordid, weak
and ignoble. Now Mr. Krutch, so far as I have read him,
does not roundly maintain that this is owing to the fact that
the observable life of the time, compared to the Elizabethan
or the Greek, is mean and sordid—the people, weak and
ignoble—but, rather, that our philosophy requires that it
should be presented as such. Our materialism and deter-
minism, our psychology and psychoanalysis, have brought
us to this point of view. For him, then, drama is the reflection of our philosophy. But since "thinking makes it so"
many people (and now and then Mr. Krutch seems to
be with them) would say that amounts to a reflection of
life itself. Yet we are not different simply because some of
us have a different notion of ourselves. In so far as the
philosophy or the psychology is firmly founded on reality,
that reality which it only now lays bare has been about us,
or beneath us, fairly since the beginnings of civilization.
What we now see here, or think we see, was then and there.
Nina Leeds's vagaries, as they spring from a powerful but

thwarted sexual impulse, are not limited to our day or land. The suppressions and inhibitions, complexes and fixations, of our dramatists and novelists are, if they exist at all, no more recent than the green flesh, blue shadows, and roseate haystacks of the impressionists. In so far as they are, they always were. And this vast body of aside and soliloquy in every role of the play—young Gordon and his sweetheart as well as Nina and her followers, of various mental caliber —all this represents our contemporary interest in psychology and psychoanalysis, not necessarily a more highly developed and complicated psychical condition in the people themselves.

And there is the further, artistic rather than philosophic, consideration on which I have elsewhere insisted, that seeing more clearly than they of old time, a man's fate or at least the seed of his fatal passion within him, we demand that we shall see it there in the play. The ancients, even Shakespeare, could present heroes, because the struggle wherein they were involved was more external—against fate or villain. The moderns cannot present heroes—their leading characters are fey within from the outset. But it is a matter more technical, less philosophic still. Conflict and contrast are indispensable to drama, and, fate and villain being devices outworn and exploded, where else than within could they well be placed? Hence, in large part, the enormous development in O'Neill of the aside. It is like his revival, in different form, of another exploded device, that of disguise or feigning, as in the *Great God Brown,* advantageous for contrast in a necessarily brief and compact type of literature such as the drama. Not merely for the psychology and characterization, but for the contrast, the right "duplicity" of effect, and even for dramatic movement and propulsion, are all these quite literal *arrière-pensées,* egoistic and carnal, thus directly brought to light.

3

Taste and technique appear still more clearly when we consider other aspects of modern drama as well as plastic art. I mean the open interest in sex and the predilection for the primitive. The mere choice is a matter of taste rather than of truth to life, for we are nowadays anything but primitive, and our artistic absorption in sex may in part be due to our own limitations and inhibitions. In both matters there may be an illustration of the truth expressed by Mr. Binyon: "The Spirit of Art is against the Spirit of the Age . . . we express our own age by resisting it, by creating something which will outlast its fears and disillusions." We seek to escape from it, or to secure amends. And this is particularly the impulse of the individual artist, as (in this very matter of heeding the call of the wild) of Stevenson and Henley, in the last generation, and Scott and Byron, likewise hampered by ill health or deformity, generations ago. *Tout écrivain se récompense comme il peut de quelque injure du sort,* says M. Valéry. *Comme tous les artistes, Byron et Shelley ne créaient que pour se consoler de ne pouvoir vivre,* says M. Maurois.[6]

However it be in the case before us, there are certainly technical considerations not to be ignored. Deprived of villain and fate, the dramatist is not to be deprived of his effects. In primitive characters and primitive societies the dramatist seeking a conflict and contrast finds abundance of both, without any distressing and undramatic morbidity and inactivity, as in the Caribbean Islands or in China, within the bosoms of Negroes and halfbreeds, sailors, stokers, and prostitutes. The thoughts and passions are naturally more abrupt and incongruous, and more naturally break into deeds. And in the sexual passion itself, as I have of late shown elsewhere,[7] there is provided material of contrast and contradiction, irony and paradox, more abundantly than in any other in the human bosom. *Odi et amo*—"His honor rooted in dishonor stood." This sort of situation is more frequent in literature today, but is not entirely novel:

> *Huc est mens deducta tua, mea Lesbia, culpa,*
> *atque ita se officio perdidit ipsa suo,*

[6]*Ariel* (1923), p. 308.
[7]*Poets and Playwrights* (1930), pp. 95–96.

ut iam nec bene velle queat tibi, si optima fias,
nec desistere amare, omnia si facias.

It is even somewhat the attitude of Helen to Paris, in the
third book of the *Iliad*. In ideal form it furnishes the tragic
fabric of Racine:

J'aime assez mon amant pour renoncer à lui.

And for more or less similar esthetic reasons this preference of the primitive and sensuous, as well as the ugly and
unideal, appears also in our plastic arts. The sculptors
Rodin, Bourdelle, and Epstein, the painters Cézanne and
Matisse, Gauguin and Van Gogh, have attained to forms
and colors, attitudes and gestures, in no sense representative
of our own; to a bold and sharp simplification of effect, a
height of exaggeration and an intensity of contrast, imitated
in some measure from primitive art, but more pronounced
than in any art before. The attitudes and gestures, the forms
and colors, are a product of the subtle modern imagination,
are not the image of our life. To be sure, this delight in rude
force and this disdain of beauty may be interpreted as the
expression of our present-day vigor, or as the feverish and
frenzied efforts of our weakness, or as both the one and the
other, side by side. But thus we make rather small progress
towards a conception of our age. That it should change is of
the essence of art, of style, while the people themselves remain the same. If art does not change, it becomes dull and
meaningless. The particular ideal beauty, sought in the
painting and sculpture, some generations ago, of the Barbizon School and the Impressionists, is a dream now gone
forever; but another ideal beauty will come in turn, and
then, perhaps, still another beauty, veiled, like ours, in ugliness; yet all the while the people as a whole and even the
artists and their public will present little appreciable difference to the eye of the judicious contemporary historian.
And the present questionable or debatable beauty has taken
something of the form of the primitive partly because of our
extraordinary present-day acquaintance not only with early

life but with early art. We have, to some purpose, studied both anthropology and archaeology.

Here lies still another explanation for the meanness and sordidness of the characters in our literature. Literary art, also, must continually change, must explore and discover. In serious vein, the world of the heroic and ideal had been presented from the time of the Greeks and the Renaissance. Even the world of the humble and simple had, since the eighteenth century, been exploited. And for our day the mean, sordid, and ignoble was the only novelty left. Not that the old fields had been worked out, like a mine: they never can be, except for intervals; but our time is one of these. Even in the Romantic Age and the Elizabethan, the Medieval and the Classical, there were periods of the cult of ugliness, and we certainly are in one of them now. But whether it is ugliness unrelieved depends on the artist, not the age. There may nevertheless be beauty of the sort most desired—strange and new. "It's a great rest I'll have now," says Maurya, the old woman in Synge's *Riders to the Sea,* after the drowning of the last of her sons,—"it's a great rest I'll have now, and it's time surely. I won't care what way the sea is when the other women will be keening." That is not ideal; it is, as Mr. Montague says, "the ideal thing somehow gone wrong, and missing its high notes, yet charged, through this very bathos, with fresh and rending tragic values of its own." It is a cry of nature there.

4

Turning now to the artist's own life or personality, there again I find no reason to modify the views I have previously expressed. Shakespeare is still the great and burning question. Thousands of Ph.D.'s, young and old, from Moscow to Seattle, from Helsingfors to Cape Town, continually dig and burrow in the plays themselves or in the contemporary literature and records, or apply to the author the fluoroscope of the new psychology, in order to discover the lineaments of his own inner person or that of his friends. Mere allusions, casual and incidental, topical or personal, would *à priori* be more credible; but those surmised are generally hazy and indefinite—for so concrete a poet![8] And the quest of the poet's personality and of his friends' can only seem to me to be hopelessly off the track. In such matters (as I have said before) we should be guided not by the learned but the imaginatively gifted, by men of letters and by poets. Coleridge was not an Elizabethan scholar, and in analyzing Hamlet as if he were a character of Goethe's or Schiller's was, I think, wrong; but when he speaks from introspection, of the ways of the imagination, he is right. And he notes as a sign of genius that Shakespeare chose even in his early poems "subjects very remote from the private interests and circumstances of the writer himself."[9]

Let me add to the opinions on this subject which I have previously[10] cited some of the present hour. Mr. John Bailey, also a man of letters, has, in his recent fine book on Shakespeare (1929), explicitly taken the same point of view. He approaches in novel fashion a time-worn theme:

. . . It is not merely contemporary practice in the matter of sonnets which tells us not to expect to find a Life of Shakespeare in the Sonnets. It is the nature of poetry itself. Poetry is imagination, not fact; the universal, not the particular, or, if the particular, then seen, not by itself alone, but in the light of the universal. And this has perhaps been especially true of the poetry of love. From the days of Petrarch, even from those of Dante, and earlier still, it had been a fashion to write poetry which, under the form of passionate affection for an individual, gave the poet an opportunity of pouring out his dissatisfaction with life as it is, and his aspirations after another life as it might be. With the Renaissance Platonism came into all this, and we see Shakespeare himself identifying his friend with the arche-typal Idea of Beauty of

[8]Cf. Mr. Bailey in note 11, below. There are more incredible ones than he mentions: cf. the seventy volumes of the *Jahrbuch!*—and, with no right to speak, I am skeptical concerning such discoveries also in Corneille and Racine.

[9]*Biographia Literaria* (N. Y., 1884), p. 376. This opinion coincides with that of Coquelin *aîné*, as regards both author and actor. Cf. my article, "Molière and Shakespeare," *Romanic Review*, February 1944.

[10]*Shakespeare Studies*, pp. 78–88.

which all other beauties are shadows. Is not this enough by itself to show the absurdity of any literalist interpretation of the Sonnets? The loves of the poets, from Dante and Beatrice to Waller and Sacharissa, have in fact always occupied a much larger space in their poetry than in their lives. The loves that have been great events in their lives sometimes hardly appear in their poetry; those which do so appear have been made part of the universal and have left the particular facts, if there actually were any, far behind them, forgetting history to become a greater thing, to become poetry. We may see this among poets centuries later than Shakespeare.

And the critic cites the cases of Shelley and Wordsworth. In the poetry of the former there is little about Harriet or Mary; much about Jane, and most of all, and the warmest, about Emilia Viviani, whom he knew little and very ill. "Of Annette Wordsworth wrote nothing and of his wife very little"; of Lucy Mr. Bailey says we do not even know that she ever existed, indeed it is now thought that she never did.[11] And Shakespeare's characters, Mr. Bailey insists, were not, as the critics like Brandes, Harris, and many others still living would have them, Shakespeare himself. They are not wise, he says, "who look behind the tragedies to find dark ladies or other private unhappinesses of the poet's life":[12]

. . . the characters on whom he most lavished his imagination, Hamlet and Brutus, Lear and Othello and Cleopatra, were, apparently, exceptionally unlike his own. What a man's imagination most powerfully and even sympathetically enters into as done or suffered by others is not what his will or his conscience or his judgment leads him to do or suffer himself (p. 15).

[11] Cf. *Times Literary Supplement*, August, 1935, p. 530. So it is with the "unfortunate Lady" on whom Pope wrote the "Elegy."

[12] By permission of Longmans, Green & Co., N. Y., pp. 204–5. Here Mr. Bailey also declares "no critical road more treacherous than that which attempts to cross the gulf between imaginative work and biography or history. To find France or Spain, Mary Queen of Scots or Henry of Navarre, in the dramas is to find what no one seems to have found at the time, and what is not at all likely to be there."—To the same effect cf. J. W. Mackail, in his *Approach to Shakespeare* (1930), as (pp. 5, 85) he touches on "the raging curiosity of the critics."

Paradoxical as it may seem, the late Sir Walter Raleigh, as cited by Professor Herford, is (if the apparent condescension may be permitted) nearer the truth than the critics whom Mr. Bailey is attacking. In reply to the question whether Shakespeare is Hamlet or any other of his creatures:

. . . He is visible in all, and answerable for them all. "No dramatist can create live characters save by bequeathing the best of himself to the children of his art, scattering among them a largess of his own qualities, giving it may be to one his wit, to another his philosophic doubt, to another his love of action, to another his simplicity and constancy that he finds deep in his own nature. There is no thrill of feeling communicated from the printed page but has first been alive in the mind of the author; . . .[13]

But Professor Herford properly subjoins the demurrer that here "the step from emotion imagined and described to emotion experienced is too lightly taken."

Shelley is a similar case. Mr. Bailey, as we noticed, touches on the matter of *Epipsychidion* and Emilia Viviani. To the same purpose Professor Tinker did so shortly before him.

It is when the character delineated by the imagination still bears a resemblance to the actual one as it entered the poet's experience, that the reader is likely to be most completely bewildered; for he inevitably tries to co-ordinate the two. . . . The few readers of this ethereal poem are likely to approach it with some knowledge of the actual Emilia. No preparation could be more inappropriate. . . . The illusion was speedily dispelled, and the Seraph of Heaven proved to be a designing and rather commonplace young person. . . . Emilia was important, but only as a point of departure.[14]

And in dealing, as we have been doing, with the biographical fallacy in the interpretation of Shakespeare, Professor W. W. Lawrence has recently reminded us of Shelley's own words about his tragedy: "In writing *The*

[13]C. H. Herford, *A Sketch of Recent Shakespearean Investigation,* pp. 37–38.

[14]*Op. cit.,* Little, Brown & Co., Boston, pp. 76–77.

Cenci my object was to see how I could succeed in describing passions I have never felt, and to tell the most dreadful story in pure and refined language. . . . *The Cenci* is a work of art; it is not colored by my feelings."[15] That is, Shelley himself was nothing of a Cenci; though the Cenci, father and daughter alike, were his. They are not himself, but are his imaginations. In writing the play he was like us when we read it. Neither Shelley nor Mr. Lawrence, either, I suppose, would adhere to the doctrine of *naturalisme* and the *roman expérimental*. They would not hold with Zola, who *ne s'est pas douté que ce n'est qu'en soi qu'on connaît les autres.*[16]

Of foreign literature I have no right to speak; and certainly satirists such as Molière and (especially) Voltaire took, like Pope and Dryden, many a shot at actual personages of the day. Yet in imaginative literature this is recognizable for the most part but incidentally; and I (naturally)[17] think that the always clever Mr. John Palmer is right in discountenancing attempts to identify characters like Tartuffe; and still more those to discover the dramatist himself and his wife in *George Dandin, l'École des Femmes, l'École des Maris,* or *le Misanthrope.* The great comic creations, however suggested by real persons, are, by virtue of their very greatness, not to be identified; and, great or small, they are, in that hard-hearted day still more than in this, unlikely to have been modeled upon the features of the author or his spouse. If Armande was frail and fickle, that, so early in their pilgrimage, was only the way to make her more so, on the part of the supreme personification of good sense. And how unlikely that the husband who exposes

[15] *Problem Comedies of Shakespeare* (1931), p. 228.

[16] Lanson, *Histoire* (1912), p. 1080.

[17] Cf. *Shakespeare Studies,* pp. 79–80, 307–8, 312, etc. This strange notion that Molière was thus consciously or unconsciously exposing his domestic life hangs together with another (which I there touch upon) almost as strange, that what apparently is comic is really tragic or pathetic.—Palmer's *Molière* (1930). Cf. also similar opinions on the biographical interpretation of Molière, as well as Racine and Shakespeare in F. Baldensperger's *Littérature* (1913) pp. 45–47.

Dandin, Arnolphe, and Sganarelle to the jeers of the court of the Grand Monarch, should really have been thinking of himself! A Rousseau gifted with a *vis comica* might have been. And nearer to our own time, when the facts are more easily ascertainable, the discrepancy between fiction and experience becomes clear and glaring, as with Lamartine. For a long time the world was fooled (or fooled itself) with his literary confessions. No dubious word or suggestion stains the pages of stories like *Raphael* and *Graziella*—I myself have confidently, and properly too, given them as presents to young ladies. But it seems that all the long memoir of these chaste, ethereal, and faithful loves is, as history, highly fallacious. Elvire, Graziella, Lucy, Julie,—though fine and faithful enough, they were regrettably complaisant, and though the romancer loved them for a time, he left them. What Lamartine was not in reality, he contrived to be in print; and here is Proust's transposing and transforming with a vengeance. But if, as Mr. Desmond MacCarthy insists, your writer's chief incentive be vanity, it is rather natural that his own experience, when used, shall be greatly embellished.

Both the social and the personal aspects of the problem are well illustrated by the case of Ibsen. He is, however inexactly, numbered among the realists; he is self-centered and self-conscious; and intentionally or unintentionally he has left behind him a mass of information about his experiences and artistic purposes and processes, rare in any author. We know (or are supposed to know) of certain incidents that suggested situations, of certain acquaintances or personages that suggested characters, and of social and political principles or criticisms that animated the dramatist as a member of Norwegian and European society. But he was a dramatist first and foremost, and in his best work all this raw material is transmuted in the alembic of his imagination. He himself is not Rosmer, Solness, nor, as he himself declared, even Stockmann, the Enemy of the People, though there is something of him in them, particularly in the last. And the fundamental incidents or persons, how little or barely recognizable are they in the play! The Swedish nobleman who left his wife because she was intellectually "unsympathetic to him," and took up with a female relative of his wife's—as Mr. Archer says of the story, used in *Rosmersholm,* "Not one of the traits that constitute the originality and greatness of the play is to be found in the actual circumstances." Dr. Brandes is the authority for the connection: here, as in his Shakespeare criticism, he shows his pronounced biographical bent. And to him often applies what Mr. Archer then says of the identification of Rebecca with Maria Stieglitz, who committed suicide in the vain hope of stimulating the intellectual activity of her husband, a minor poet,—"on rather inadequate grounds, it seems to me."[18] In so far as they are certain, such data are interesting psychologically, not esthetically or historically; in so far as dubious, they have little or no interest at all. Ibsen himself complained of philosophical or satirical meanings attributed to him; and of how much greater significance than these connections with single people or occurrences or with issues of the day, even when discernible, are those with the Scandinavian character, which has not changed for ages, with their customs, traditions, and superstitions, with the drama of the dramatist's predecessors and the currents in thought and literature in contemporary Europe!

Art cannot, then, be relied upon as a record of society, an abstract and brief chronicle of the time; often it is in revolt against the time—now behind it, now ahead; and it is not even a record of the individual. Art is not a function of society, nor even of the artist. The style is the man, but very often not the man as he is known, even not wholly as he is. Thought is not the secretion of the brain. It is free and irresponsible; it makes amends for our limitations; it flies off like a meteor from the rounded orbit. There are wide divergences between thought and conduct, between feeling and reality, for which we must duly allow; and this truth we are, in one respect, continually compelled to recognize. Knowing, or thinking that we know, the morals of an age or an author, we are moved to reject their art when the

[18]Introduction to *Rosmersholm.* It would be more natural to identify Maria with Beata.

morals are faulty. But if the immorality of the author con-
taminated his art what great art should we have? We have
all read Plato a little and his *Symposium,* and we know that
the Greeks of the greatest period were stained by the abom-
ination of pederasty as well as other serious vices. They were
venal, they were cruel. And yet as a whole there is no art
so glorious as the Greek. None but that of the Italian
Renaissance, which was Greece newborn. Sodomy was widespread in Italy, too; one of the greatest of all artists, Leonardo, was put in prison for it; and some other great artists
of the time were and still are under grave suspicion. In our
own day we have had Wilde, and Verlaine, and others
nearly as important, now living, whom we cannot mention;
but their art is noble, and many of us, if it came to a choice,
would rather give up almost any other recent French poet
than Verlaine. Even in English literature some of the most
uncorrupted art has come from hands which, if they were
offered us today, we might, forgetting ourselves, decline to
clasp. Robert Greene, Christopher Marlowe, Francis Bacon,
two of them among our greatest—do we number such men
among our friends? How little is their style (or thought)
the man as in the page of history we know him! Some of
our chief romantic writers were addicted to drugs—Crabbe,
Coleridge, and De Quincey, Rossetti and Francis Thompson
—and we need not undertake to read the long roll of those
given to pecuniary irregularity, drunkenness, and lechery.
"Longfellow," says Mr. Aldous Huxley, "was a bad *poet,*
while Beethoven's relations with his publishers were frankly
dishonorable." And if even a man's morals can be so remote
from his art, how much more remote can be his actual experience from the imaginative![19]

5

What, then, in art can we count on for historical or
biographical material, or how far is art by historical or biographical material to be explained? For that is a question

[19]I am in this paragraph indebted to Mr. Tinker, *op. cit.,* pp. 32–
33, 49–50.

which I must raise, and (though it is not to be disposed of in a page or so) endeavor to answer. Generalization is difficult and dangerous. Not only is it the very nature of art (as we have seen) to be varied and continually novel; its abundance is also such that of most of it even the widest reader and greatest writer must be ignorant. But my previous discussions have been negative and destructive, and experience has taught me that with many minds mere negation or destruction fails of effect—in intention it is thought to be total.

Before undertaking an answer we must for a moment fairly face the inner nature of art, at which we have been only glancing: *Le théâtre,* says Sarcey, *n'est pas la représentation de la vie humaine, mais un ensemble de conventions destiné à faire illusion aux spectateurs.*[20] And this is true, not only of drama itself but even of acting and producing. Like other art the dramatic is not a copy but an imitation. It is intent upon effect; and that, as Coleridge rightly says, is illusion, not delusion. The actor speaks, and moves, and looks, with far greater force, variety, and wariness than in life. His tones, glances, and gestures he skillfully chooses. His art is selective, and also (either traditionally or originally) conventional, like the dramatist's, and like (for that matter) the sculptor's and the painter's. Now conventions require more than a pair of eyes or of ears; and art cannot convey anything, as a photograph cannot, but a phonograph can, to infants, idiots, and beasts. Hence it is not only unplausible but empty praise of the painter to say that the birds would fly down to peck at his grapes, or of the dramatist (as has, practically, more than once been said of Shakespeare) that his characters "have been copied with so little alteration from the population of the world." Either artist, in a way, works on a flat surface to give effects of volume and perspective. In order to keep his values true a painter must pitch the key lower than in nature; for the sake of his illusion the writer must make mere description or representation give place to various methods of suggestion. And either artist is—and properly—intent less upon

[20] *Quarante ans* (1900), i, p. 151.

things as they are than as they appear to him. Art is a state of the soul, communicated. Moreover, it is now too late (though in particular cases we continually judge as if it weren't) to declare that, being like this, art is ascertainably but a product of *race, milieu,* and *moment.* Taine's theory explains too much, too little. Ultimately, to be sure, in the last analysis, in the great devious deterministic scheme, all may be thus explained; but it is by a curve which is beyond the reach of our calculus, which includes the seemingly erratic and fortuitous course of genius. Yet *race, milieu,* and *moment* are there. Within the conventional and arbitrary frame and pattern, there are necessarily the colors and figures of reality.

What, now, of this can be recognized as belonging to the particular time and place? Little of it when standing by itself. The evidence in art and literature is only corroborative, and can be used only when there is external evidence of the same tenor already. To pass from the art of the time to the time itself, says Wilde, is the error which all historians commit; yet it is not necessarily an error to pass, with due precautions, from the time to its art. Knowing the age of the periwig, we can confidently recognize traces of it in Addison or Pope, as, not knowing it, we could not infer them. And knowing the life of Burns or Byron, we can safely recognize traces of it in their verse, as not knowing it we could not infer them. Or, from art itself and especially from literature we can gain some idea of the life of a period when much of the evidence is of one accord. Even without much study of history, we could surely put together a pretty shrewd notion of the democratic upheaval and humanitarian reform of the nineteenth century from a wide reading of the novels, particularly the mediocre ones. But the novel is not drama—it is ampler, looser, less conventional in structure, has ordinarily undergone far less of the process of imaginative transformation and transposition, is much more nearly a transcript of life; and the mutinies and rebellions which are so common a means of denouement in Jacobean and Restoration romantic tragedy were not taken from the life of the day. In reading drama the need of compact structure, striking situation, swift movement, besides the importance of tradition and convention as means of expression, must, to correct our inferences, be constantly in our minds. The complication or the conclusion in Restoration comedy is frequently a marriage with the wrong person, or a marriage that turns out to have been no marriage at all. No doubt this sort of thing could have happened in England more frequently in the seventeenth century than today because of the comparative laxity or informality of the law; but it certainly was not common. And when it did happen, as I endeavor to demonstrate in chapter IV, it was more plausible.

Indeed, it is not in the main situations or the chief characters that the contemporary conditions and customs for the most part appear. They crop out in allusions or passing remarks, upon which nothing of artistic importance depends. The local color is more likely to be truly local if it be not laid on with a purpose. It is the language of the static scenes or those of lower tension that is more particularly of the time. The reflection is less exaggerated, distorted.

Even with the novel we have to be wary, particularly (as in the drama) with the lower and the higher forms of the art. The lower is extravagantly unreal, in its romance or melodrama. The higher has undergone more of the transformation and transposition of thought. We ordinarily think of the Russian novel as a slice of life, if any be. What in art could be more real than Tolstoy, before religious doctrine and enthusiasm warped him? But what of Dostoevski? So far as wealth of material is concerned, and the reality and the freshness of it, too, he is fairly Tolstoy's equal. Yet how strangely the material is put together! His characters often seem exceptional and queer. They act illogically and *à contresens,* hysterically and violently, hating because they love, loving because they hate. They lacerate themselves, doing what they do not want to do and not doing what they want to do, ruining their lives for no reason that anyone can easily conjecture and reveling in it, talking of murder (and even committing it) as if it were an everyday matter, and of simple everyday matters as if they were a spectacle for heaven and earth. Some are creatures of impulse and instinct; some, heroes and martyrs; some are silly, some sublime; some, now the one thing, now the other. And the young women in love? They slap their lovers' or their nurses' faces, bang doors and snap people up, lie and listen, leave the accepted lover at the church door (as in a ballad) and take flight with another, propose like Aglaia, laughing as they do it, and run out of the room and enter again in tears.

But that is Russia, we say. It is not Russia as we know it —far better, I think—in Tolstoy and Turgenev. Russia, though often to us queer and crazy, is not so queer as all that. It is more like the Russia that we see, darkly, in the dramatic mirror of Chekhov. In short, it is character not pictured but dramatized. It is a matter of conflict and contrast, again, but mainly for the sake of mystery and suspense; and these give structure and life to the novel. Matters of central fact and motive are withheld and the reader is kept guessing and conjecturing, somewhat as in Ibsen, but at the cost of greater exaggeration and distortion. In the end, of course, we see clearly, and the reflection, as in a doorknob, flattens out, as in a mirror—the character now appears human, vivid, true; but it remains highly exceptional, Russian yet not at all typically Russian.

And if such is the case with novel and drama, what of poetry? There, indeed, we scarcely expect a reflection of life, but (as I have freely admitted) the prevailing temper and taste. There we hear the voice of the time, do not behold its image. Yet even so it is not clear and unequivocal. If we did not know the Victorian Age, to whom, in poetry, amid all the conflicting tendencies, should we turn? Knowing it, however, we may find the prevailing temper and taste in Tennyson, Patmore, and some of the minor singers; in the Brownings, half-heartedly; but in Rossetti and Swinburne, Meredith, Morris, and FitzGerald, scarcely at all. These were in revolt. And yet all of these, together with their illustrious predecessors, are essentially romantic

—in the great industrial and commercial century! The spirit of their art is against the spirit of their age—they express their age by resisting it.

6

On the whole, we are safer if we simply shift ground. Truth to life we all crave and it is also by great art granted; but it is less of time than of place, less of a locality than of a country, less of a country than of humanity taken together. And this verisimilitude requires no history, or biography, or even comment, to be recognized; it is a matter for the imagination or intuition, and for the reader's or spectator's, as for the author's in the making. It is in Rossetti's *My Sister's Sleep* and *The Portrait,* which seem to be autobiographical if any poems be, though at that age, his brother declares, the poet had certainly lost no sister and in all probability no sweetheart. It is equally in the verses of his sister, Christina, who is far less dramatic, much more personal; and yet, if we did not know her story, she might, in poem after poem like *Isidora* and the *Convent Threshold,* seem to have been married, or else to have "sinned a pleasant sin" and then turned away in remorse, though still in love, to monastic seclusion. In these poets and in others it is recognized instinctively, instantaneously, if at all. It lies in the tone or accent, the color or drawing. With Shakespeare it is English, is human; with Racine it is French, and is again human; with Velásquez it is Spanish and human too. The country or its story we need not know. What is ordinarily imparted in the classroom we need not know. *Die Welt bleibt immer dieselbe,* said Goethe—for the essential purposes of art it does. The work as a whole, of course, can by the ordinary mind be thoroughly grasped only after study. The right and just conception of the work as a whole—which is the author's—can be attained only through a knowledge of the conventions and traditions of the author's art, belonging to the author's time; and if we are to have an exact and perfect knowledge of his art it must not be read or viewed as if it were contemporary.

Here, certainly, and by all means, the time plays a part—that is, again, the taste of the time. But the life of the time, the history of the period, is of secondary and often quite dubious or inascertainable importance.

Even in a work of art nearly or quite contemporary, the reflection of life is troubled or veiled, if not by tradition, by convention, by the artist's method, by his purpose or the resulting effect. Indeed, for all our realism it is in some respects less recognizable—we need no help with the history or the milieu, but we need much help with the technique. A painting of Rembrandt's or a play like *Hamlet* is a picture or a drama for everybody; but a nocturne of Whistler's or a symbolist play of Maeterlinck's can be a picture or a drama only to those who will consider it from a particular point of view. And since Whistler and Maeterlinck, how this gulf between universal art and the esoteric has widened! Portraits and landscapes are, without the hierophant's aid, no longer recognizable as portraits or landscapes, nor plays as plays, novels as novels. As for the latter, witness, in their last developments, Strindberg and Mr. James Joyce. I have touched on this subject elsewhere,[21] but from what I have said already the reader might expect me wholly (though humbly) to approve Mr. Chesterton's strictures and to share his misgivings. Yet even Rembrandt and Shakespeare did not deal with bare fact, or a round unvarnished tale deliver. They considered not fact but effect—it is the business of the historian of art to show exactly how. The color of rocks and flowers, of the skin of man or beast, changes, indeed, from day to day, from hour to hour; but not as it does when we turn from Rembrandt's canvas to Renoir's, from Raphael's to Rembrandt's. These men of genius all are true to life, and untrue. The difference between them and the tyro is that the untruth does not offend, is not that of incongruity, does not imply ignorance, or clumsiness, or a trick. Shakespeare, unconsciously following Aristotle, presents, again and again, but more or less probably, an impossibility; and even in so simple a matter as references to time and place he is, for one who reads and studies the play, irrecon-

[21]See my *Poets and Playwrights*, pp. 156–57.

cilably contradictory. But writing only for those who were to see it, he thinks, as Mr. Granville-Barker rightly says, of both time and place "in terms of effect."[22] By "short time" he gives to the action the effect of rapidity; by "long time," that of plausibility.[23] Likewise, on a stage where there was no setting, before an audience which did not in imagination relentlessly supply it, he is free, according to his purpose, to describe it or not, and, without distracting the attention, to shift the action frequently from one place to another. And when (to speak of lyric poetry and of lesser spirits) Christina Rossetti, in her last poem, murmurs,

> *Under the purple thyme and the purple clover,*
> *Sleeping at last,*

this does not mean, though *crimson* or some other epithet would fit the thyme more accurately, that she does not know this fact herself. She is not color-blind. Nor is she merely sparing words, either, for this one she repeats. But she has recourse to the noble artifice of simplification—is intent upon effects, not of accuracy and distinction, but of monotony and uniformity, and contemplates the all-leveling track of death, the all-obliterating course of nature. Thyme and clover are one color now, and sweep uninterrupted to the horizon. For in art, not science, is the strict relativity; and truth gives place to truth, or depends upon it, not capable, like a fact, of standing, in its own right, by itself alone.[24]

7

And who is it that thinks otherwise? The public, certainly, which is naïve, and their publishers, also, who are

[22]*Prefaces,* Second Series, p. 70.

[23]*Poets and Playwrights,* pp. 97–98.

[24]See Richards, *op. cit., passim,* for similar opinions, especially chaps. xxxiv and xxxv. Mr. Richards no more thinks than I do that art is quite aloof from life, or is for its own sake alone; but he does not take it for a document, a transcript. "It is evident that the bulk of poetry consists of statements which only the very foolish would think of attempting to verify. . . . There is a suppressed conditional clause implicit in all poetry" (pp. 272–76).

not—the one inclined to look upon art even as if it were
reality itself, like the Citizen and his Wife in the *Knight of
the Burning Pestle;* the others, as if it were so much merchandise, new or old. Racine, even in his own day, was old,
and was not "true," was no "life story." And two professions
take this point of view, without going so far as that—in-
structors in history and in literature. The material is so
tempting. History, particularly in the remoter period, is
deficient in records of customs and manners, entertainments
and diversions, and all the daily round. Letters and memoirs
are often dull and uncolored, and the contemporary biographers omit that upon which ours would dwell. How
irresistible, then, is the pictured page of Dekker or Ben
Jonson, Molière or Regnard, Etherege or Vanbrugh! And
is it not somewhat the same with the history of literature?
Teachers (like their students) take eagerly to the error of
passing from literature to life. And what is more exhilarat-
ing or satisfactory in the way of research? We are then in
the world, it seems, of facts, the facts of history and biography, and prettier and more alluring ones than these generally are. Taine's history is, as many a one isn't, entertaining; and modern language papers are so to their writers.
To others, even scholars, they seem—scholarly. And everybody (who is not writing it) now reads biography, even that
of Jesse James or Al Capone, self-made men; and (after the
brigands and Don Juans) more especially, strange to say,
the biography (instead of the writings) of the poets and
prophets—Maurois, for instance, instead of Byron or Shelley, Papini or Ludwig instead of Jesus, and, strangest and
oftenest of all, as with Jesus and Shakespeare, when there
really is no biography to read. We all ask for stories, and,
like Mopsa, prefer true ones; but the facts we take to most
are fancies in disguise. Indeed, without biography (or what
passes for such) in some way commingled with it, a good
discussion of a poet's, novelist's, or dramatist's art can (as
some of us to our sorrow remember) scarcely reach the
light of day. For external and compelling reasons, consequently, we, who call ourselves scholars, are this way much
inclined. Some of us, perhaps, have, in popular work,

already fallen, and have a stake in the issue. We have already, less entertainingly than a Frenchman but (in one sense) as profitably, treated literature as the mirror of the age or of the author. But is it not, as scholars, our chief business and privilege to distinguish fact from illusion?

1932

CHAPTER II

Belial as an Example

BELIAL AROSE: "the great seraphic lords in close recess and secret conclave sat." Satan had proposed the question, and his proud imaginations had displayed; Moloch had followed him,—"My sentence is for open war." And now, after this abrupt and hammering eloquence, the voice of Belial stole upon the deliberating fallen angels like music, which, indeed, it is:

> *I should be much for open war, O peers,*
> *As not behind in hate . . .*

The passion here sinks into a subordinate clause. For the speaker is too well bred to rage, too disillusioned to aspire, too consummate an artist to press his points. He emphasizes by contrast, not by added force; like the actor who at a great moment lowers his voice instead of raising it, or the contemporary actress who sets her feather boa in order as she faces the firing squad. And his thought is discreet and devious, his rhetoric supple and insinuating, his rhythm flowing, his emphasis hovering, his cadence a dying fall. I too should be for war, he confesses, if the reasons urged in

favor of it were not—against it; if he who counseled it did
not ground his courage—on despair,

> *And utter dissolution as the scope*
> *Of all his aim, after some dire revenge.*

There again the subordination; and on their own showing,
these heaven-storming counsels are deftly reduced to absurdity:

> *And that must end us, that must be our cure,*
> *To be no more; sad cure; for who would lose,*
> *Though full of pain, this intellectual being,*
> *Those thoughts that wander through eternity,*
> *To perish rather, swallow'd up and lost*
> *In the wide womb of uncreated night,*
> *Devoid of sense and motion?*

"After some dire revenge"—"sad cure," he sneers, faintly
and demurely, but with a languor that is only apparent. He
is not indifferent or blasé. He thrusts as he retreats; and
frankly lays bare before the embittered assembly his own
delight in life—in thought and imagination—and his horror of nonentity. Though a son of Epicurus, he is of no
lax or tenuous fiber, but makes light of the present disaster
before the thousand demigods on golden seats, Satan above
them. He loves company, discourse, the camp. "What can
we suffer worse?" he echoes—

> *Is this, then, worst,*
> *Thus sitting, thus consulting, thus in arms?*

Yet he is not unmindful of the dread hours of combat and
defeat—"*that* sure was worse"; anticipates disaster direr
still, within the compass of the Almighty's power—"*this*
would be worse"; and appreciates the folly and vanity of
any resistance in view of greater torments—"better these
than *worse*, by my advice." If then we really were brave
and clever, we were from the first prepared for such an
outcome:

I laugh when those who at the spear are bold
And vent'rous, if that fail them, shrink and fear,
What yet they know must follow, to endure
Exile, or ignominy, or bonds, or pain,
The sentence of their conqueror.

He can take his medicine, short of the hemlock; and, like your true Epicurean, is, in necessity, a Stoic, though with a grace, a smile. He can laugh—where the stern and stalwart Satan and Beelzebub can only scoff and jeer—in Hell. Things are bad, but might be worse, may be better—

Besides what hope the never-ending flight
Of future days may bring, what chance, what change;
Worth waiting, since our present lot appears
For happy though but ill, for ill not worst,
If we procure not to ourselves more woe.

Again the subordination, again the dying fall, which is really the curl and upturn of irony; and he seems to bow, and decline upon his throne, as he utters the final languid yet pointed words.

What an example of a poet's original and plastic power! Belial is not Milton, just as Lovelace is not Richardson[1]— out of the book and on the street creator and creature would have had little in common. "Specious" and "timorous," "slothful" and "counseling ignoble ease" (we remember the similarly disparaging epithets in Richardson's footnotes and table of contents)—such a one would never have been understood by the man (rather than poet) who appears in these comments and is considerably more at home with the rebel and recusant Prince of Hell. That uncompromising spirit, long afterwards, in the epic sequel, disdains Belial's counsel—to tempt the Saviour with women—as he disdains it now, then (as at present) "bringing a mind never to be changed by place or time." Really he contrasts with

[1]Leslie Stephen (*Hours in a Library,* 1899, p. 86) says that judicious critics thought the novelist "must have been himself a man of vicious life . . . which is little better than silly."

Belial more effectively than the bullheaded Moloch, is an
earlier Childe Roland—

> *And yet*
> *Dauntless the slughorn to my lips I set,*
> *And blew . . .*

"And yet"—for now, even as at the beginning, he sees and
confronts it all. To Belial such derring-do would be folly
likewise; but not to Milton, man or poet.

And plastic—in the form and movement of the speech
is the life of the character, as with Shakespeare. And (as
when applied to Shakespeare also) a paraphrase or a
résumé is nothing; an analysis, even in the pages of the best
of critics, except as it echoes the poet's wording, is nearly
nothing too. These are merely the framework, without soul
or expression. The soul—the expression—lies in the cast of
the phrase and the turn of the line, the personal accent and
individual tone. Ordinarily, Milton himself is supposed
always to be speaking. God, Satan, and Adam, Abdiel,
Raphael, and Gabriel, are really the downright, eloquent
Puritan; and Eve is but his ideal of a woman, or his experience of a wife. Somewhat too often, indeed, that is true.
But what is best about all these personages, as well as Belial
and Beelzebub, is—beyond the reach of Puritanism or "hu-
manism" either—the work of an imagination. It is an act,
not of self-expression, but of invention or discovery; not of
imitation, but of origination and projection. Though the
poet is still speaking, it is as a poet. And what startles us
into delight is not his accents, coming through the mask,
but another's—and as the mask changes, another's still—
though the voice itself is ever his own. Such is nearly always
the case when he puts on Belial, or Eve, or the Son (in
Paradise Lost, if not in the later epic), or (despite his
Miltonic rebelliousness) Satan. And it is Adam, not the
poet, that cries to fallen Eve,

> *How can I live without thee?*

And it is God the Father that charges Michael,

> *So send them forth, though sorrowing, yet in peace.*

For Milton as an epic poet is, like Homer and Dante, a dramatist, though in less measure, to a less degree. Paris is not cowardly or contemptible, though Hector and Helen sometimes call him so; and Farinata and many another tortured spirit there are too good for Hell. Poet and dramatist are not one and the same.

And that fact appears most clearly in one respect in which, like Richardson again, Milton is superior not only to those epic poets but even to Shakespeare,—the matter of giving a character a point of view of his own. Far inferior in plastic power, in the gift for differentiating speech —vocabulary, figure, and rhythm—to fit and distinguish the individual, the epic poet and the novelist have a clearer consciousness of the relativity of moral judgments. Morals are ordinarily supposed to trouble art, but when they are at their highest potency they too may be a manifestation of mental and emotional intensity; Dante and Milton, Bunyan, Defoe, and Richardson have the plastic power nonetheless; and Milton and Richardson are pre-eminent among dramatic casuists, or relativists. In the lines of the sterner poet the man in the wrong does not admit it, but puts others in the wrong instead; and what is good or noble to others is not made good or noble to him. Satan dwells on his own "injured merit," and the brute force and tyranny of God, whom he calls "the Thunderer"; as Belial calls him "the Enemy," and Eve, yielding to temptation, "our Great Forbidder, safe with all his spies about him." Also, despite his Puritanism, the poet knows—and makes it appear at the fall of the angels and of man—that temptations are, to the tempted, not ugly but beautiful; sin, to the sinner, not bitter but sweet; and remorse and misery not necessarily or immediately attendant upon them. To Shakespeare, though he was generally more flexible, and had seen more of life, these truths were, not improbably, less clear; and if so, his practice was in keeping. His villains, in general, avow their own wickedness, and acknowledge the goodness of their enemies; and if they do not repent, they undergo, except Aaron and Iago, at least some sort of internal torment. In this respect he is, in our sense of the word, less dramatic.

(But not as he conceived of drama, or as the ancients.)[2]

For imagination transcends experience,—may transcend the poet's character. Anyone—and how much more the poet!—sees farther than he can go, dreams of more than he can do, depicts both what he would and he would not be. In imagination he can think and feel what he cannot in reality. Even the lyrist is in a sense a dramatist; and "sincerity" is a word with a different meaning in the world of art. The greatest elegies in the English tongue—*Lycidas, Adonais, Thyrsis,* and *Ave atque Vale*—were not written upon the poets' dearest friends, if friends at all. *Thyrsis,* and *not* Arnold's *Rugby Chapel,* upon his father! Yet the great poems are not insincere, if the sincere one is not great. They are works of the imagination; and in art the only insincerity is want of imagination. There is moreover something in a sense dramatic, or histrionic, in the elegiac or lyric art, as in any. A painter is not necessarily in love with the woman he glorifies on his canvas, or religious because his madonnas breathe the spirit of devotion. Critics like Ruskin blame the artistic deficiencies of the Renaissance on a want of faith, true religious art welling, as in a state of enthusiasm or mania, "up from the burning core below." As M. Marsan says, it has long been the fashion to praise a writer, provided there was any discoverable warrant, for his sincerity, however ill he wrote. *La sincérité devenait l'alpha et l'oméga. Et non seulement de l'art mais de toute morale. Quels alibis!"* And the critic thinks this is owing to the nineteenth-century *romantisme moral.* At all events, the facts would show that it is as faith somewhat relaxes its hold upon painter or poet that he can be a great painter or poet; faith of itself, without imagination, produces pious but commonplace or silly hymns and images; and the beginnings of the Renaissance are clear and unmistakable in both Dante and Giotto, as are those of rationalism and romanticism in Milton. The more we know of a great poet's

[2]Cf. my *Shakespeare and Other Masters,* pp. 27–28, 260–61. Relativity in moral judgments is not for ordinary audiences even today.

experience, the wider generally is the cleft between it and his poetry; and we should not be so naïvely taken in by the grammatical first person he employs. In novels we are not, and Jim Hawkins and David Copperfield do not pass for Stevenson or Dickens himself. But in songs, sonnets, and elegies the passions and griefs, the sighs and tears seem necessarily to be the singer's. And especially when they are addressed to known individuals, such as "Mary," "Jane," or "Emily," "Edward King" or "Charles Baudelaire." But the striking thing is that the more we learn about these, often the more unrecognizable are they, or the poets' actual relations to them, in the poems; and, as Mr. Bailey has noticed, in some of the best lyrics, like Wordsworth's to Lucy and Shakespeare's Sonnets, the persons are unknown or undiscoverable. The Sonnets are certainly no mere poetical exercise, but they are in some measure, apparently, another dramatic achievement; and Shakespeare is sincere somewhat as Shelley is in *Epipsychidion,* or Lamartine in *Raphaël* and *Graziella,*[3] or Burns in his Farewell to Nancy, whom really he was then seeking to get rid of,[4] each depicting characters and relations different from the actual ones, or assuming emotions different from his own. What a difference, generally, between the letters and the lyrics of the poets, their poetry and their lives! Poetry is not a confession, true or false—it is false or true only as poetry. Shakespeare's Sonnets, indeed, are not so much dramatic and impersonal as conventional,—in substance and general attitude are those of his Petrarchian predecessors. But not in style, and it is his imagination that makes them his own. And just so Milton is not insincere when he sympathetically and vividly presents the fallen angels and Eve as having done or doing that which is half right in their own eyes, however severe and unindulgent he was with such people round about him.

Yet art is of many sorts. There are dramatists like Dekker and O'Neill (and even Shakespeare when dealing with low

[3]See above, chap. i, pp. 14–17.

[4]Richards' *Principles of Criticism,* p. 271: "Similar instances could be multiplied indefinitely."

life), and novelists like Dickens, George Eliot, and Hardy, all of whom depend for their success more upon their experience and observation; and there are lyrists like Christina Rossetti and Elizabeth Browning. Women, in both lyric and novel, are personal; and often you can be fairly sure who is speaking, and to whom. Nowadays, indeed, amid the popular craving for actuality, the woman's life with her husbands or lovers, a little colored or embellished, suffices. If irregular enough, she needs only to be herself in print, as on stage or screen. And George Eliot is not only not at home but not at her ease in Italy, as in *Romola*.

In the novel, to be sure, the ordinary novel at least, which depends for its interest and success more upon actuality and (as it were) ocular rather than imaginative illusion, and upon the creation of a milieu and background, the writer keeps almost perforce to the country or region that he knows. But the figures which he has simply transferred from the landscape before him to his canvas, or those which are replicas of himself, are not his greatest work. This is rather to be found in those which, suggested by his observation of himself or another, are enlarged and enriched by the observation and experience of others like them, but, far more, by the activity of his imagination; and with such result that the original is often lost to the view of the writer, and is ordinarily irrecoverable by a critic. If a portrait painter, the good novelist is like him approved by Aristotle; and makes the sitter handsomer, or (for our present-day taste) uglier, in any case more interesting, than he is. The characters that can with certainty be identified are generally not worth the identification—by art so little changed.

And in great drama or epic, where necessarily the milieu is less important, and for the belief that the thing happened is substituted "the heightened sense of its happening,"[5] the imagination has still wider sway. The characters of Æschylus and Sophocles, of Shakespeare and Molière, are Greek, English, or French, indeed, for the writers are. They speak the language. They dwell in their own country, and, liter-

[5] Max Eastman, *The Literary Mind* (Scribner, 1931), p. 226.

ally or figuratively, allude to the local customs, flora, and
fauna. But the finest drawn are not persons with whom the
writer was ever acquainted, including himself. They are not
his friends, neither are they (so sympathetically presented)
his enemies; they are even, like Satan and Belial, personages
of whom he could scarcely have had a glimpse. Prometheus
and Oedipus, Electra and Clytemnestra, Hamlet, Lear,
Othello,—for their portraits they never sat. They are not
myths, yet they are creations, and arose from the deep.
They are the product of the mind, working, in the colors
of human feeling and experience, and on the forms of
human thought and speech, to frame beings, of the world
but not in it, larger, fairer, yet esthetically "more real" than
copies of "living man." They represent, not fact, but as
Pater says, the poet's sense of fact.

Also Belial has much of that whereof a work of art, whatever the subject, must have at least a little; and that is,
beauty. "A fairer person lost not Heaven." And his tongue
drops manna; his thoughts wander through eternity; and
though "specious" and "timorous," "slothful" and "ignoble," he has a lofty charm. So it is, though in a different
way, with Iago and Mephisto, and (to a less degree) Richard III, and Lovelace, and Browning's Guido, wicked as
they are. As in life people so brutal and cruel could scarcely
be, they are witty and humorous, gay and fanciful, and are
exalted by poetry. How well Homer makes Paris talk, and
even the most ignoble of the Achaeans, Thersites! And as
the villains are not villains, the bores, like Shallow and Dogberry, are not bores. They are not tedious, on stage or page.
Folly and silliness, vanity and affectation, lust, greed, and
bad temper—when we meet them incorporated in the flesh,
and thereupon in the pages of Molière, Congreve, or
Thackeray, they are, like Belial as speaking and as described by Milton's disparaging epithets, though recognizable, not the same. Of Nora in the *Doll's House* it has been
said that "her talk is often silly and puerile"; but such
words apply only because of the poverty of our vocabulary,
and in so far as to noble art they can. And coquette and

scold, vampire and schemer, poser, cheat, and liar—do we (uncomfortably) recognize these in Shakespeare's Cleopatra? Put her, as one critic says, into the prose of the daily paper—yes, put her there if you can! Even her sensual indulgences and seductions appear, not directly and nakedly, but in her calling for mandragora and music and her feeding "on most delicious poison," in the provocation or enchantment of her changes and artifices, in the vivacity or luxuriousness of her rhythms. Her voluptuousness is like the profanity of Shakespeare's rogues and villains and (to couple the big and the little) the pirates in *Treasure Island,* or, indeed, like the dialect of Shakespeare, Burns, and Synge, all of which is dealt with only in terms of dramatic, verbal, and rhythmic effect. (What a dead deluge of billingsgate such people pour down upon us from the stage today!) So (however it has been of late) Praxiteles and Donatello did not put real hair on the heads of statues; nor would Haydn or Beethoven have inserted a phonograph record of the nightingale into an oratorio or a symphony. So, too, theatrical managers in those days did not, as in ours, require a real Negro to play Othello, a Sandow (as a generation ago) to play Charles the wrestler in *As You Like It,* or a genuine fallen woman for that role, as, recently, in *Rain.* And thieves, cheats, liars, and cowards like Falstaff and Autolycus are so blessed with wit and good humor that the literal-minded have taken the former at least to be only pretending or feigning. It is the poet who is "feigning" (as the word was then used), and not the iniquities merely but the man as a whole; it is the illusion of poetry again. One and all, these beings—these vices—so vivid and engaging, are not quite true or real, as art is not. In that the truth is never total, nor well-nigh. For charm or excitement of some sort, in form or matter, is its indispensable effect. Truth itself is bare and bitter, mean and dull. Art is the world created anew;—not always nearer to the heart's desire, but in such fashion that, by both its likeness and its unlikeness to the world as we know it,—both its simplicity and its mystery,—we are forced to think and feel. Art is

no flat, faithful mirror, to look at, but (as it were) the
magical glass of legend, to look into, with

> *composiciouns*
> *Of angles and of slye reflexiouns,*

and a light in it not of earth or heaven.

1933

CHAPTER III

The Beau Monde *at the Restoration*

Since my other discussions of the subject I have come upon Miss Kathleen Lynch's *Social Mode of Restoration Comedy* (1926), one of the most discriminating dissertations I remember to have read. Miss Lynch does not much undertake to discover sources or trace influences, matters too often undiscernible or unascertainable, but explores the less dubious or illusory course of tradition and development. And this she does, I think successfully, with the Restoration Comedy of Manners, or of the beau monde. It takes its rise not out of French comedy, though somewhat affected by it, but the late Jacobean and Early Caroline, and flows from Fletcher, Shirley, and Brome through Suckling and Davenant, Killigrew and Cowley, down to Dryden, Etherege, Wycherley, and the rest.

As she pursues the subject, however, Miss Lynch is in her forbearance less discreet. She does not much consider whether this comedy, containing so many traditional and conventional elements, is to be accounted a fairly faithful reflection of Restoration high society; but she strangely (as I think) inclines to do so. She "turns gratefully" to Mr. John Palmer as a critic of the Restoration comedy, and that is his thesis. She seems to take a change in English society itself to be the cause or occasion for the change in comedy; and is of the opinion that the Restoration dramatists accepted the heritage from Shirley and Suckling because of its fitness for the representation of contemporary life. Now expression framed before the object itself came into being can scarcely be very fit; and what Miss Lynch means may be something such as I have suggested, a drama only colored, so to speak, not drawn, from the life at hand. At any rate Miss Lynch's investigations seem to support such an opinion.

The writer defines the Restoration Comedy of Manners with greater technical exactitude than has been done hitherto. It is a gay satire on social relations, involving a contrast between the true beau monde and the false—between young ladies and gentlemen, on the one hand, and parvenus or affected folk on the other, between the pseudo-wit and the true-wit (male or female), the jealous man and the wittol, the prude and the libertine, as well as the larger matters of country and of town. But in Restoration comedy, as not in Molière, there is a double scope. The members of the beau monde are themselves the objects of satire, in so far as they are social more than human beings, beaux more than gentlemen, coquettes more than ladies. And to this end certain typical situations or bits of comic machinery continually recur: wit combats, whether between the professionals on the one hand or between lovers on the other, with lavish use (in battledore and shuttlecock repartee) of "similitudes" and fanciful ingenuities on the part of either set; and matrimonial bargains, with "provisos" for their individual liberty, like Mirabell's and Millamant's, on the part of the latter.[1] Wit, indeed, abounds, and much of it is discharged in rebellion against the conventional morality, and (it would seem) in the celebration of another, the beau monde's own.

Now the striking thing about this art form is its develop-

[1]The similitudes in repartee are to be found, for example, in Congreve's *Way of the World* II, ii; the provisos, in IV, i, a celebrated case.

ment. In its elements, in typical situation and animating spirit, it arose, as we have seen, a generation before the Restoration society—the "golden moment" of Mr. Palmer, which it is supposed to mirror, "when precept and practice were so clearly connected"—came into being; it was perfected, in Congreve, only after that age had fairly passed away; it came to an end, in Vanbrugh and Farquhar, after the reign of William and Mary, several years after the accession of Anne. It realized itself slowly and gradually: piecemeal the central idea of high society and "good form" eliminated the extraneous elements of the broader and humaner Elizabethan comedy, its "random adventure and farcical intrigue," and (in some measure) leavened the whole. Thus the development is similar to that of other art forms; as, to speak of things far more momentous, Gothic architecture. How long it took for the *cage à jour*—a system of thrusts and counterthrusts, with piers and buttresses (not walls) for structure, sustaining a fabric of stone high in air— to be born out of the Romanesque four inert walls and wooden roof! In drama things move, indeed, less slowly; but how long it took for the Elizabethan comedy of humours, out of the decay of which the Comedy of Manners itself sprang, to develop out of the native interlude and the Latin comic intrigue! There is more of imitation and representation in drama than in architecture, and a closer connection with contemporary life; but in all these cases the artistic evolution and realization, once under way, proceeded rather out of a germinal principle, from an inner necessity. The minds of the artists found no repose or respite until the possibilities of the structure had been explored and exploited, until the artistic conception which haunted them had been fully expressed.

So it was, it seems to me, with the Restoration Comedy of Manners, which, so far as realism is concerned, might better be called Early Caroline. In its beginnings, under Henrietta Maria, its connections with the life of the time seem considerably closer. And it may well be (though on drama I would not rely to prove it) that a beau monde was now for the first time arising, which comedy must take account of. It may well be that class distinctions, resting on birth and wealth, were breaking down, and those resting on refinement of manners were replacing them.[2] But I think it far more likely that even in Elizabeth's time there was, of its sort, a beau monde, too; and that now comedy began to deal more with manners and fashions because, under the growing Puritanical disapproval, it was depending more upon the small fashionable world for support and favor. And I think it likelier still that now comedy began to develop into high comedy, of social satire and raillery,—because this it had not done before. The possibilities, mentioned above, were now opening up—the field worked by the great Elizabethans and Jacobeans was, for the time, exhausted. The dramatists, in order to get a hearing, in order even to have something quite of their own to say, must turn in this or some other direction; and this direction, apparently, was that most attractive and of least resistance. The comedy of Jonson had been, as Miss Lynch says, one of morals and common sense; this of "good form" and "bad form" remained. And with these younger dramatists in relation to the older the situation is somewhat as with those pairs of contemporaries continually reappearing in the history of culture—Wordsworth and Coleridge, Byron and Shelley, Browning and Tennyson, Dickens and Thackeray, Meredith and Hardy, Ibsen and Björnson, Michelangelo and Raphael, Æschylus and Sophocles, Shakespeare and Jonson, Wycherley and Congreve themselves,—in subject and style how, even in their likeness, they always differ and must! There is no chance for them unless they do. *That,* for the most part, is the outcome of the "influence" of one upon the other.

The spirit of innovation prompted the rise of the Comedy of Manners: the spirit of conservatism, equally important, preserved it, until, in turn, its possibilities were exhausted. This is true generally of popular art, unlike the highbrow art of the present. Within the established medium the artist reaches his public more readily, so long as within it novelty or variety remains possible. Blank verse held the

[2]Miss Lynch, p. 28, and chap. iii.

Elizabethan stage until there was no new and beautiful way
of writing it and it was scarcely distinguishable from prose;
then perforce came prose or rime. And the heroic couplet,
which succeeded blank verse in both drama and epic, prevailed until it "reached in Pope's hand the final plenitude of
its nature—its ultimate significance—its supreme consummation."[3] Something similar may be said of both the form
and the substance of the sonnet and the popular ballad
at the same time; and of medieval epic and architecture.
Gothic was built till there was no new and beautiful way
left to build it. So the loose or licentious Comedy of Manners ran its course, through the respectable reign of William
and Mary, even into the moral reign of Anne. At its best
it "reflected" an age that had passed away.

As for the "new ethics," the anti-morality which, like
Mr. Palmer, Miss Lynch finds in the Comedy of Manners,
I do not, as I have said before,[4] see how it can be considered
to be the "code" observed in that day, even by the gallants.
These are not problem plays, but comedies; and the immoral sentiments uttered are meant to be startling, to be
witty. Partly because they are startling are they witty and
comic. "Constancy at my years?" cries young Dorimant in
Etherege's *Man of Mode,* " 'tis not a virtue in season. You
might as well expect the Fruit the Autumn ripens in the
Spring." "Monstrous principle," cries Loveit in reply, and
morality looms up in the background, not forgotten. Not
that the dramatist is on her side, either; for this is a comedy.
But it is because it is comedy, not tragedy, that he is more
on the gallant's side than Beaumont and Fletcher are on
that of Evadne when she cries, "A maidenhead, Amintor,
at my years?" to her husband in their bridal chamber.
As in literature generally, there is indulgence for a young
rake's audacity, if merry enough. Sometimes, indeed, in
their epigrammatic exaggeration, the sentiments contain
at bottom some real criticism of the hard-and-fast morality
of the day; but oftener they are the ribald defiance of a
reckless gallant. With him it is no anti-morality, no new

[3]Lytton Strachey, *Characters and Commentaries* (1933), p. 270.
[4]*Shakespeare Studies* (1927), chap. ii.

code of his own or his set; but the contumacy of one who knows or acknowledges the old. The effect of his speeches is owing to the contrast. In neither case is there what can be called any serious and considered presentation of the morals (or manners) of gallantry, like that of the morals of chivalry at the courts of love.

Nor are the sex duels and proviso scenes, as betwixt Mirabell and Millamant, penned in the style, for all their wit, of the colloquies on sexual privilege and enfranchisement in Shaw and Granville-Barker. They are not deficient in sense or wholly wanting in seriousness; but they are prompted by no principle and arrive at no conclusion. The dramatists generally have some notions of liberty and enlightenment, but they do not make these pervade the play. In the proviso scenes the dramatic and sentimental interests prevail; the wit combats are love combats; and the frailties and follies of the lovers so outweigh their virtues and principles that we wonder whether, and how, they can agree. Mirabell and Millamant are wooing as they thrust and parry; she is tempting him, in feminine fashion, as she retreats.

If the "new ethics" were at all serious, were, as Mr. Palmer says, "an actual and definite code of morality," surely jealousy, the chief vice or folly under the old proprietary system, would have been consistently exposed, as indeed Mr. Palmer thinks it is.[5] Really, it is treated pretty much as in other comedy before and after; only rakes and flirts are free of it, and these not altogether; and though the sensible and virtuous but not delicate Alithea in the *Country Wife* would have no jealous husband, it is because she would not put up with the annoyance and interference. She feels justified in deserting her fiancé Sparkish only when he betrays this weakness; but that she seizes upon as an excuse, for she was disgusted with him (even because, with provocation, he had not sense enough to be jealous) before that. Sparkish's jealousy, failing or asserting itself, is simply a dramatic device to point the contrast between Alithea

[5]Cf. *Comedy of Manners,* pp. 129–30; and my *Shakespeare Studies,* pp. 48–50. Cf. below, pp. 57, 226.

and her brother. Pinchwife, in his jealousy, is made ridiculous and a butt; but he would have been both the one and the other, in comedy or in life, whether before or since the days of the Merry Monarch.

For ideas, or principles, we must not look too obstinately in our early drama, whether for the dramatist's own or those of his age. Even the simple central one, that of a contrast between the true beau monde and the false, is far from all-pervading. These are comedies mainly of intrigue and amour; and how much space in them is given to what by no conceivable extension of the term can be considered a beau monde, false or true! The grossness and vulgarity (and not only of the supposedly fashionable but also of the obviously sordid and disreputable world) that there is in plays such as Etherege's *She Would if She Could,* Wycherley's *Country Wife* and *Plain Dealer,* and even, too often, in Congreve! The impudence and scurrility, the outrageous pranks and impostures, the continual marrying of objectionable men to prostitutes or objectionable women to fools, simply because such things were funny! Meredith declares the manners in the Comedy of Manners are those of South-Sea Islanders under city veneer. If there is any comedy that approaches a picture of the Restoration beau monde it is the *Way of the World.* Millamant, however, alone will do. Mirabell comes as near, perhaps, to being a gentleman as any hero in the Restoration comic drama; but could he (if indeed Millimant could have had such an aunt, or have been living with her) have done anything so outrageous or senseless as to pretend to make love to her himself, in the first place, and get her entangled with his valet as "Sir Rowland," in the second, and both alike in order that he might bring her to the point of permitting their marriage? But if Mirabell's conduct had been more proper and probable we should not have had such striking situations in the process and the discovery, nor had Lady Wishfort either delighting in endearments or writhing in a tantrum. What we are given here and elsewhere is not the image of the beau monde but an entertainment to its taste,—a taste, in this instance, moreover, for something in drama farther removed from its own image than that demanded by the taste of the contemporary beau monde, hard by the Louvre. For the morals and manners of Whitehall and Westminster are not—cannot be—to the morals and manners of the Louvre and Versailles, as are those in Wycherley and Congreve to those in Molière and Regnard.

"Life creates its traditions, and literature creates its traditions," says Professor Lascelles Abercrombie; "they are profoundly and subtly related; but they are not the same tradition." Yet it is the chief business and pleasure of the critic, it sometimes seems, and more strangely still of the historian, to confuse them. Fiction, in its relations, is not enough for the one; nor truth, in its relations, for the other. M. Baldensperger,[6] however, out of the abundance and profundity of his knowledge, judges that literature is, though an expression of society, not a description of it; that it does not so much reflect it as refract it, and magnify it; and that even the expression of society it can be only when taken as a whole. We know that the Comedy of Manners was played in two small theaters and much of the time only in one; that the runs were brief and the attendance slim; and that the number of playbooks printed from 1660 to 1670 was not more than two per centum of the publishers' output. Moreover, as M. Baldensperger also observes, with both Brunetière and Lemaître[7] to support him, the contemporary opinion of a literary work or of the genre must be reckoned in, which, to the most striking achievement, even so unadventurous a sort as Corneille's and Molière's, is in some measure inhospitable; and to the Comedy of Manners it was highly so. In their own day Sterne and Wordsworth, the Pre-Raphaelites and the Yellow Book, Synge's comedies and above all those of the Restoration were considered fantastic or crazy, morbid, immoral, or decadent, and since then have been accounted representative of that day. But, I remember, it is a matter, except for

[6] *Littérature* (1913), especially livre III, chap. i.

[7] *Nous connaissons les mœurs d'une époque beaucoup moins par les œuvres mêmes que par les jugements que les contemporains ont portés sur ces œuvres.*

those who think loosely and speak carelessly, of the beau monde. And this the Comedy of Manners does reflect—so far as that or any other mode of life can be mirrored truly in what is not a hybrid drama but a comedy, and a satire, and first and foremost not a document but a highly amusing entertainment, with fantastic and improbable situations, and with social and moral arrangements and principles, though near enough to the actual to be recognizable, pretty much upside down. It refracts instead of reflecting, so far as it reproduces at all.

1934

CHAPTER IV

Literature and Life Once More: Some Vagaries of History and Criticism

Unfortunately, words can convey facts; unfortunately, people in general have an insatiable appetite for facts. Now music cannot convey facts at all; painting or sculpture can only convey fact through a medium which necessarily transforms it. But literature is tied by that which gives it wings. It can do, in a measure, all that can be done by the other arts, and it can speak where they can but make beautiful and expressive gestures. But its paint, or clay, or crotchets and quavers, may be taken for the colour, or form, or sound, and not as the ministrants of these things.

SYMONS, *Studies in Prose and Verse.*

So far as literature imitates at all, it imitates not life but speech: not the facts of human destiny but the emphasis and the suppressions with which the human actor tells of them. . . . The novel, which is a work of art, exists, not by its resemblances to life, which are forced and material, as a shoe must still consist of leather, but by its immeasurable dif-

> *ferences from life, what is designed and significant,
> and is both the method and the meaning of the
> work.*
>
> STEVENSON, *A Humble Remonstrance.*

THOUGH MY SUBJECT is endless as life and literature themselves, my discussion of it must not be; but I have again been reading in the Restoration Comedy of Manners. That, as I have already intimated, is the crucial case, both the most widely accepted and the most sharply contested instance of the faithful reflection of life in our literature; in itself it provokes thought, the comments on it demand discussion, and with this the consideration of other periods is necessarily involved.

Without rehearsing what I have said previously, I will briefly summarize it. Though all art implies an element of "imitation," without which it cannot interest or touch us, it is never quite a copy or transcript; and that which most nearly approaches faithful imitation is mediocre and dull. Art can be counted on to reflect the life and character of a people in general rather than at a particular period; and more faithfully the taste of that people in the art in question, which often is at odds with their experience, than the experience itself. This same people, or part of it, is also the artist's public, which, in some way, must be pleased; the artist must at the same time please and (perhaps) express himself; the limitations of the craft must be observed and its requirements fulfilled; and with imitation all these concernments may interfere. Literature is supposedly the most pliable and adjustable medium—indeed it is, except as it is shaped anew, no medium but the thing represented, words, not mere sound, and not like paint or stone—; yet even in the novel, and, above all, in tragedy and comedy, it requires, for strong and fine effect, a special treatment, not to say a transformation, of the raw material: condensation and contrast; emphasis or exaggeration here, slurring or understatement there; and the observance of certain traditions and conventions. Tragedy must be tragic, comedy comic, with (at the Renaissance) death at the end of the one, marriage at the end of the other; both, to be interesting, must present a surcharged situation, or conflict, which almost unavoidably implies something contrived or improbable, though the good artist endeavors to conceal it; and in the long run realism is often merely incidental and a matter of detail. For the essential and vital material of art is not actual experience, but (whether of the artist or of his public) an imaginative one, from the actual often remote.

2

Now all this applies, I have previously argued, to the Restoration Comedy of Manners; that prose comedy of wit and (in large part) of the beau monde, initiated by Dryden, Etherege, and Sedley, and, in various ways, developed by Wycherley, Congreve, Vanbrugh, and Farquhar. It is not so much a reflection of the time as of the taste of the time, and the taste belonging to that small part, not of England but of London, which frequented the theater. "However pious we may appear to be at home," says the playgoer quoted by Farquhar in the preface to the *Twin Rivals,* "we never go to that end of the town but with an intention to be lewd." But is not then the Comedy of Manners a reflection of the life of the playgoers, of the fast and fashionable set? This, indeed, is all that some few of the critics now insist upon; for it has been borne in upon them that in England (or London) from 1660 to 1700 there were, at any given moment, no more than two theaters and for twelve years but one,[1] in contrast with the dozen (more or less) in Shakespeare's day; that often these were but slimly attended and almost continually were under Puritan fire; and that by long odds the larger output of the press in the period was of sage and serious works, not playbooks. Mr. Krutch, who thinks that the dramatists "were merely holding the mirror up to nature, or rather to that part of nature which was best known to their fashionable auditors," nevertheless recognizes that this part was not the greater, and quotes Arber, in his preface to the *Term Catalogues:* "We must

[1] Nicoll, *Restoration Drama* (1923), pp. 5–6.

largely reverse our ideas as to the general character of English literature during the Restoration Age—the general tone of its books was deeply religious; mingled with much philosophical inquiry." And he adds himself: "Far from from being debauched, the middle and lower class was permeated with a spirit of somewhat crude and narrow piety."[2] Professor G. M. Trevelyan, however, is both more explicit and more positive as he protests: "The society of Restoration Comedy was a real society and not as Charles Lamb argued, invented by the dramatists. That the society so represented was only a small part of all England I am well aware." And yet, again: "A faithful picture of contemporary fashionable life."[3]

Let, then, the Comedy of Manners be taken for the mirror (so far as it is a mirror) only of the fashionable, who under Charles II were, of course, merry and licentious; and let me, thereupon, ignorant as I am of letters and diaries, memoirs and state papers, undertake to show whether the reflection there, apart from the mere matter of gaiety and license, can be trusted. In this instance, if ever, ignorance is not a handicap: by my hypothesis, at any rate, it is not, —that life and art are of different jurisdictions. For I shall endeavor to judge of the matter simply by the evidence in the plays themselves, in the light of common sense.

What (meanwhile) of the drama at about the same time, under Louis XIV,—likewise written for the upper classes, first at two theaters and then at three,—that of Corneille and Racine, Molière and Regnard? I have elsewhere[4] made the contrast, and, ironically, inquired whether we are to draw the appropriate opposite conclusions concerning the morality of the two peoples. But what of the

[2] *Comedy and Conscience after the Restoration* (1924), pp. 35-37.

[3] See the controversy in the *Times Literary Supplement,* January 5, March 1, 8, 15, 1928, on "artificial comedy," engaged in by Mr. Trevelyan, Mr. T. A. Lacey, and the present writer. Also, Lascelles Abercrombie, *Year's Work in English* (1924), pp. 13-14, and *Progress in Literature* (1929), p. 23.

[4] *Shakespeare Studies,* pp. 54-55, and in the letter to the *Times,* cited above.

courts? Outwardly and openly those of Charles I and of
James II were probably more licentious (though by no
means those of William and Mary and of Anne, under
whose reign most of the so-called Comedies of Manners
were written) ; but were they in reality? And that the difference in drama—comedy and tragedy both—was also
mainly a difference in taste, between what Englishmen and
Frenchmen. expected and were offered (as at court) at the
theater, becomes more apparent when we remember the
very similar changes in the drama, and then the causes of
these. The dignity and the decency of French tragedy and
comedy under the Grand Monarch, though these may also
reflect the entire life of his court, as the Comedy of Manners could not that of William and Anne, were chiefly
owing to the classical revival, consummated just before his
reign, under Richelieu and the Academy; and an essentially
similar though less thorough-going reform was presently
to come about in England, in 1698, when Jeremy Collier
blew his blast, as a moralist indeed, but also as a classicist,
and only as the culmination of a movement in which both
Rymer and Dryden, though antagonists, shared. The moral
but elegant age of Anne, which ensues, is the age of Louis
XIV on English soil, in slighter and less symmetrical dimensions; in both countries the change in drama was the result
of prolonged discussion and agitation in criticism. And since
then, in the late-nineteenth and twentieth centuries the
parts have changed; and though both dramas deal much
more freely with sex matters than in the eighteenth, the
French is franker or more licentious than the English.
According to a scholarly investigation of 152 of the best
French plays from 1877 to 1914, more than 90 per cent
have to do, as the principal issue, with adultery or irregular
sex practices. "A social historian," says the London *Times*
reviewer, "judging French and English society in 1890 from
popular plays, might infer that every French wife was unfaithful, and that an English wife, though coming very
near, could never bring herself to be so."[5] Nations, cer-

---

[5]*Times Literary Supplement,* May 14, 1931, pp. 373-74, reviewing Professor C. H. Bissell.

tainly, do not change about like that, though taste and fashions do.

Even of the fast set the Restoration drama cannot be taken to be a presentation of a faithful picture. The colors are fairly natural, but not the proportions or the perspective, the light and shade; the materials and much of the detail are sufficiently depicted, but not in their true relations to one another. On the face of it, this is not a society, a moral or political organism, such as we ever heard of or (in the world as we know it) could easily conceive. What strangely assorted people mingle freely and familiarly together,—gentlemen with rogues and rowdies, ladies with bawds and prostitutes, whether occasionally in the street, or continually under one roof. Congreve was a gentleman if ever there was one; indeed, he insisted on passing for such, not an author, when Voltaire, as an author, waited upon him in England. But in his comedy, as certainly not in the life he led or knew, people are not to be judged, it seems, or even understood, by the company they keep. In his comedy the beau monde, or high life, denies its very nature, is not exclusive, is not high. And Congreve was a scholar and a classicist. But in his comedy the immemorial critical principle of *decorum,* which, in so far as it means the observance of social distinctions and propriety, has certainly some basis in experience, is pretty much ignored.

There is his exquisite and witty Angelica, in *Love for Love,* dwelling with her uncle, the illiterate and vulgar, half-mad Foresight, in company with Mrs. Frail, "A Woman of the Town," with his second Mrs. Foresight, this woman's sister, equally frail, and with Miss Prue, Mrs. Foresight's stepdaughter, an affectionate but silly bitch; wooed, moreover, both by the rakish though elegant Valentine, who, for the purpose, feigns to be mad, and also by his brutal and barbarous father. And yet by all this Angelica is not shocked, or disgusted, or bewildered, but, when she takes any notice of it, only—as in a comedy, again— amused.

There is Millamant, adorable Millamant, in *The Way of the World,* living with her ridiculous vixen aunt, Lady

Wishfort, and consorting with the foolish or freakish Witwoud, Petulant, and Sir Wilfull. She is not disgusted, either. And Cynthia, daughter of Sir Paul Plyant, limited to the conversation of the Plyants, the Froths, the strangely and arbitrarily mated Touchwoods, and the pseudo-wit Brisk— where, in such a world, did this and Congreve's other fine and graceful maidens at the outset ever get, or afterwards manage to keep, their wit and spirits, their character and manners?

It is the same question that is to be asked concerning Richardson's Clarissa and Fielding's Sophia, delicate daughters at the mercy of barbarous fathers; and the answer, apparently, is the same. Families here—witness the Touchwoods and Valentine and his sire—are sociologically incomprehensible. Or if some of these relationships and associations be not beyond the pale of probability because not wholly a matter of choice, what of others that unquestionably are? How did the elegant coquettes in Vanbrugh's *Relapse* and *Confederacy* and Farquhar's *Beaux' Stratagem* come to be mated with Sir John Brute, Squire Sullen, and the two vulgar curmudgeons of the second-named play? The marriages were, perhaps, "arranged"; but as Mr. Cabell notices, the situation is, in Restoration comedy, a favorite one; and in English middle-class life arrangement was not common then or since, and least of all, as here, so completely in disregard of social and personal distinctions. Marriages of the sort cannot have been representative—still less than they are (where they are little enough) in the novels of the succeeding age.

And, before matrimony or without it, the relations of the sexes in general are as bizarre and incongruous. They are less the English than a motley mixture of the early Spanish and the present-day theatrical or coeducational American. In a good many plays there is the institution of the duenna, who, in the person of an amorous virago of an aunt, like the Lady Wishfort above mentioned, flourishes in English comedy and novel as late at least as Mrs. Malaprop, and like her, is, for a purpose, ostensibly wooed by the hero instead of the fair one. In very un-English fashion, the young woman is then cooped up[6] (as in French, Italian, and Spanish comedies, but there considerably less than in those countries themselves) far from sight of a man—except, strange to remark, a good-looking young dancing-master or music master, or a pretended suitor to the dragon herself. Yet often, in the same play as well as in most of those where there is no duenna, respectable young women seem ordinarily to enjoy the greatest liberty with young men, consorting freely with both them and their companions, male or female, whatever their reputation at no cost to their own, by day or by night, in their parents' or guardians' houses or those of friends or even strangers, and on the Mall or in the Park. Under the duenna they now and then chafe, but ordinarily they are not troubled with a chaperon; and of the relations, in the seventeenth century, of young unmarried ladies, fashionable or unfashionable, to the other sex this can be no faithful picture at all. In such company, under so little control or restraint, they cannot well keep with us (if taken seriously, as a bit of life) the reputation that they enjoy in the play. And still less could they if so taken by the Restoration audience, for in that time, if not in ours, the unmarried daughters even of fast ladies and gentlemen did not run freely about.

Though for practical purposes still more unnecessary, there is another means of approach, which entails still greater improbabilities and further disregard of moral or social distinctions. I mean the go-between, or bawd, another Spanish-narrative institution of the early-sixteenth century and after, yet not infrequently employed in Elizabethan plays, as (without the moral taint) in the character, and dramatic function, of the Mrs. Quickly of *The Merry Wives*. More obviously corrupt and disreputable than the duenna, she is on a somewhat similarly incredible good footing with respectable and unrespectable alike. In Farquhar's *Twin Rivals* Mrs. Mandrake, a midwife, but also a

---

[6]In *The Way of the World* there is no such confinement; but there is in Wycherley's *Dancing-Master*, Shadwell's *Squire of Alsatia*, Crowne's *Sir Courtly Nice*, Vanbrugh's *Relapse*, et cetera.

bawd, a brothel keeper, and the two villains' ally and cat's-paw, has the entrée of the best houses and enjoys the confidence not only of the bad young gentlemen but of the good young ladies. In life it would have been only the approachable, questionable ladies; but here it is, as with Quickly and the subtler Spanish Celestina before her, for the sake of a much more interesting, though less probable, character and situation. How, except only for this artificial narrative purpose (and one not too well manipulated, either), can Amelia and Constance be imagined as having anything to do with her; or Aurelia, as accepting an invitation to her house, where presently she is assaulted? (Though virtuous, none of these young women is ignorant and naïve; in any case, a woman knows a bad and particularly a vulgar woman, if not such a man, at sight.) Much the same may be said of Araminta in Vanbrugh's *Journey to London* (who, though not so innocent, is a lady, and would fain appear to be such) so readily receiving Mrs. Motherly, on a social as well as a professional basis; and (though here it is the less conspicuous matter of the merely natural, immemorial restrictions) it may likewise be said of the above-mentioned Aurelia and Constance, and also of Araminta and Belinda in Congreve's *Old Bachelor,* so unhesitatingly familiar with Clelia and Silvia, whom they know to be already seduced. Mr. John Palmer, to be sure, would explain it all as "a golden moment" of sexual enlightenment and enfranchisement, evidence for which at the Restoration he finds—in these comedies! But, as I have shown before,[7] Etherege and Congreve are not serious but witty, not veracious but comical, and much of their wit or comic effect lies in being (to the audience at least) cleverly startling and shocking; while they keep not only the suspicious husband and the jealous, but also the cuckold and the wittol, still as ridiculous, and the disreputable female, still as undesirable, as ever they were. The *mores* are not undermined, though morals are made light of; the old order is a little shaken,

[7] My *Shakespeare Studies,* pp. 47–54, and above, p. 44f, and below p. 226.

but a new one is not thought of; and in general the spirit is festive and Saturnalian, not satirical or rebellious. It is a social chaos, not a new social order. It is comedy.

Without, of course, the writer's thinking of that. The disregard for the unlikelihood of such social relations is only such as appears, though less glaringly, in the much later novels, even in Scott and Dickens and (for that matter) in the French. In real life the go-between Dame Ursula Suddlechop, familiar not only with rakes but robbers, would not have had access to Margaret Ramsay as counselor and consoler, nor would Moniplies, the valet, have come to the wedding, with the usurer's daughter on his arm, into the presence of the king, as in the *Fortunes of Nigel.* The improbability here, as in the examples from the Comedy of Manners cited above, is, of course, less conspicuous in point of moral or sexual liberty or license than the quite outwardly social; which the impercipient world more readily recognizes and more instinctively abhors. High life is not kept apart from low life—does not itself keep apart as in reality it is above all other things careful to do; and except for the highborn rakes, who wanted to startle, more numerous now than usual, was careful enough to do under the Restoration.

In the *Twin Rivals* generally there is small likeness to a society, either in this or in a wider sense of the word; and of law and order still less. In the absence of the legal heir, his brother, Benjamin Would-be, takes possession of his defunct father's house and property, and when the heir himself arrives, lodges him, with a credible eagerness but a quite incredible facility, in jail; he, in turn, almost as easily escapes and ousts the upstart; and all this, simply by intrigue and *force majeure,* with the assistance of constables, to be sure, but not of the law. Such readiness of constables or bailiffs to arrest or let loose, with or without reason, but without either literal or metaphorical warrant, is one of the strikingly unplausible characteristics of this and many another comedy of the time. It reminds us of eighteenth-century novels, as when the lady Clarissa is incarcerated at the instance of Mother Sinclair and her crew. It does not much remind us of any quite civilized, law-abiding country, still less of England, even in the day of the scourers and the Mohawks. In the comedy of the seventeenth century the security and (as we shall see) the privacy of person and property are as little regarded as in the novel of the eighteenth, a time when in reality they were more so.

3

In the matter of marriages, too, in which Mr. Trevelyan is specially interested, there is but slight *vraisemblance*. There are mock marriages, which do not hold, as in Wycherley's *Country Wife* and Shadwell's *True Widow;* and fraudulent marriages to disreputable or otherwise ineligible females, which hold all too firmly, in play after play, from Etherege's *Love in a Tub,* Dryden's *Wild Gallant,* and Sedley's *Mulberry Garden* down, and three of them in two comedies of Congreve's. Mr. Cabell, before me, has commented on the absurdity of people marrying without licenses, or, indeed, without noticing very particularly whom they are marrying; but not long since[8] historians, of a different opinion, spoke up and pronounced banns and licenses to have been in those days unnecessary, or even any ceremony, if the union should be by the consent of the parties concerned. They pointed, moreover, to the actual fact that the Earl of Oxford once engaged in such a mock marriage (how could it have been such if the above formalities were unnecessary?) in order to get momentary possession of a virtuous young beauty; and that Beau Feilding was once tricked into real marriage with a prostitute.[8a] Does all this prove Mr. Trevelyan's thesis "that the society of Restoration comedy was a real society, not invented by the dramatist," the comedy "a faithful picture of fashionable life"? It proves that such an incident was not like that invented by Ariosto, of Astolfo's journey to the moon. What is a single incident or two, apart from the circumstances? Every day in the newspapers extraordinary occurrences are recorded that match anything in melodrama or movie. Yet

[8]See above, note 3. Cabell, *Beyond Life* (1921), p. 33f.
[8a]"Might have occurred at any time," says Abercrombie.

these last we, with reason, call improbable, not true to life. In themselves extremely exceptional, they are not made probable by circumstances or motives; which are ignored also in the newspaper but, for the effect of reality, are not to be in art. Just so in the Comedy of Manners. Generally either sort of tricky marriage is but a special form of an expedient still more common there,—concealment of identity or sex. Of this as effectual for a little season there are authenticated cases in the seventeenth century, no doubt, as in the Renaissance and the Middle Ages, and as (again) now and then today. Does that prove the society, in this respect, a real one in medieval and Elizabethan or the contemporary Continental drama and romances, where such disguise is remarkably frequent, and immediately and completely effectual for long stretches of time, between parents and children, brothers and sisters, masters and servants? Because of the abundance and unanimity of the "evidence," some good scholars have been of that opinion; as they might well have been if literature really were evidence, if fiction were "a record."

The tricky marriage is only a part of that all-pervading deception or imposture—false witness, slander, forgery, disguise, impersonation,—and of that unnatural lack of acquaintance with the features, gait, and voice of friends and relatives, which have, from the earliest beginnings, been warp to the woof not only of dramatic but of narrative fabric; and like much of that artifice, this is neither the faithful image of life nor made to seem such. If "the British nation could never have emerged from such a morass of levity, cynicism, corruption, and disease,"—of the morass of fraud and deception Mr. Archer might have said the same.[9] The imposture of some is outdone only by the gullibility or unconcern of others; and on such terms—under such conditions—a society cannot endure. In fiction mere disguise and impersonation enjoy a long-established status. But what warrant is there for the boisterous though gentlemanly Wildair's repeatedly taking Angelica for a harlot and her house for a bawdyhouse, in Farquhar's *Constant Couple;*

[9] See above, p. 8.

or Sir Francis and his family's taking a bawdyhouse for an inn, and, still worse, his worthy uncle's leaving him in the dark about it, in *A Journey to London?* The tricky marriages, really, are of the same order.

What, now, is a mock marriage, according to the historians? On and off the stage, it seems, they are not alike. The cases cited, Oxford's and Feilding's, are not in point. If by law and in fact a ceremony was unnecessary, on the stage, certainly, it was not. There (however untrue to life or law!) there is always a ceremony, and the tricky marriage holds or fails to hold only according as the parson turns out to be a real one or a fraud. Of such marital liberty and legal laxity as the historians know of, the dramatist and his creatures seem never to have heard; and, indeed, the historians have exaggerated it. In default of the formalities, it appears, there must have been a contract; a marriage without ceremony, moreover, was not reputable and (without a contract, of which, on the stage, we hear nothing) could not be reassuring; on the stage, therefore, more picturesquely and theatrically, and certainly in keeping with popular opinion and expectation then and even now (true not to life but to taste again) the ceremony is all-important.[10] And there *other* fraud, strange to say, as when one of the parties palms himself or herself off for another, does not count (though in life, as Sir Walter Scott, the lawyer, acknowledges, it certainly would), once the vows are spoken! Indeed, marriage law on the stage is like stage law generally, until our more exacting and critical times; in England and in London itself, it is, like that in *The Merchant of Venice,* and that in Massinger and Webster (where also the scene is *in partibus infidelium*), a fiction for theatrical purposes; and the parson, true or false, stands ready, like the constable, true or false, in the closet or at the door. Here, then, the appeal to historical fact, even on its own ground, simply does not apply.

[10]For my full rejoinder to Professor Trevelyan and Mr. Lacey, with a consideration of the law, so far as it applies, including Scott's remarks on marriages in plays and novels, *St. Ronan's Well,* chap. 26, see my article in *Modern Language Notes,* March, 1943.

The chief, and I think unanswerable, objection, however, is that, as not in life, these hymeneal pretenses are so apparently such: the marriages to the undesirable, if these more than questionable persons be already known to the groom, are generally, as with the three in Congreve,[11] performed in masks. Now a man (or a woman, either) not out of his or her senses, might, with a person in a mask, venture to tread a measure or two; but, however eager or frantic for a partner, not take his earthly journey, in a day when divorce was difficult and fraud (apparently!) so common. That is more improbable than the rendezvous, in the dark and in silence, of Boccaccio and Bandello, of Shakespeare and the other dramatists down to Otway. Here still less than above does history apply.

4

Another travesty of English law and order is the defenselessness of these people in their own dwellings. An Englishman's house (unless on the other hand the plot demanded that, as with Sir Tunbelly Clumsey's, in *The Relapse*) is here very far from being his castle. It has neither locks nor doors (even like the stage representation of it in those days and long after, till the box set was invented), to keep enemies or visitors out. Such is the case even so late as the *School for Scandal;* and Sir Peter, helplessly expecting to be jeered at for coming upon his lady, instead of the little milliner, behind the screen, is fain to make the best of it as the scandalmongers swoop down upon him, one after another, under his own roof. Sheridan himself—artistically—makes the best of it, by both localizing the scene and raising the

[11]Really there are four such marriages, three in the *Old Bachelor* and one in *Love for Love;* but one in the *Old Bachelor,* of Heartwell to Silvia, unmasked, is later made known to him as a fraud, to his relief, after her character has been made known. That in *Love for Love,* of Tattle to Mrs. Frail, is by means of disguise for both parties, each thinking to overreach the other. The marriage to a disreputable woman masked or disguised is found elsewhere, as in Crowne's *Sir Courtly Nice,* et cetera; and on the stage at least as early as Middleton's *Trick to Catch the Old One* (1606).

question of escape as little as possible: in Restoration comedy, on the other hand, there is generally a porter or a
maid at the entry to put up some show of resistance. So it
is now and then in Elizabethan comedy, such as Chapman's
Monsieur d'Olive, where the gentleman Vandome forces
his way with drawn rapier into the house of the Lady
Marcellina, vowed to seclusion. But freedom to intrude,
incongruously, does not mean freedom to escape. If the
house be a lady's, there is a man in her chamber, or if a
gentleman's, a woman in his; and then there is sure to be
no other entrance or staircase than that actually in use. No
doors to shut, in one scene, and only one to open, in the
next, and, in gentlemen's houses, no backstairs! These clever
and witty people before the footlights show no more foresight or readiness in framing their own contrivances than
in meeting the contrivances of others—when a situation is
at stake.

5

Evidently this that I have, so far, presented is not "a real
society," not a faithful picture even of the "fashionable
life"; evidently it is not England, even "under the Stuarts,"
whether since or before the Revolution or the Great Rebellion. To see that, historical erudition is not necessary: it
is (as so often!) a hindrance. What we have before us is
mostly a matter of playmaking (as with Richardson and
Fielding, Scott and Dickens, or Dumas and Hugo, it is of
novel-making)—effective, but more arbitrary and contrived, more regardless of probability and careless of motivation, than in our day, and in some respects even more
than in the Elizabethan. His famous essay Lamb entitled
"On the *Artificial* Comedy of the Last Century," illogically,
but instinctively, taking the matter for granted. All this
legal and social, marital and domestic defenselessness and
disorder serve the purposes of situation, of a speedy complicating or extricating,—the marriage to a prostitute is a
recognized form of comic poetic justice, as in *Measure for
Measure,* upon a rogue or a bore—; and the social and
moral incongruity or impropriety of intercourse serves the

ends not only of situation but of contrast and variety, if not indeed, of specifically comic effect.

So they do in Elizabethan comedy, and in the seventeenth-century French, Spanish, and Italian, as in the ancient; and I would not be understood to say that Restoration comedy is much less a faithful picture of the contemporary life but—as little. In the Continental, too, as any student of it knows, there is not only a tissue of trickery and deception but also much arbitrary manipulation of social fact and circumstance.

Particularly in the relation of masters and servants, which I have touched on before.[12] How does it come that the middle-class people in Molière and Regnard keep such malapert valets and plain-spoken maids, who with impunity intrude upon family business and thwart their masters' undertakings? And why is there the same improbable relation between master or mistress, on one hand, and man or maid, on the other, in the comedy of the two peninsulas and even in Terence and Plautus? Because this is comedy —is life turned end for end or upside down, the servant vexing and saucing master or mistress, and these impotently fuming. Perhaps the most improbable but most comical effect is on the stage of Spain, land of strictest formality and etiquette; where the cowardly servant, or *criado,* accompanies the master, as inappropriately as Falstaff and Panurge do theirs, on military expeditions, and advises him, rallies him, complains of his conduct and that of his friends, without scruple or reserve. And yet by the historical-minded this too has been taken to be "to some extent a correct picture of contemporary manners."[13] Indeed, from such questionable evidence have been drawn serious historical con-

---

[12] *Shakespeare Studies,* pp. 58–60.

[13] Norman MacColl, *Select Plays of Calderón* (1888), p. 380. Mr. MacColl recognizes both that "such conduct was wildly improbable in days when distinctions of rank were clearly marked and no one dreamed of the possibility of their being ignored," and also that "a good deal of this is conventional . . . and merely intended to make the audience laugh." I wonder, then, at his thinking the picture of manners correct; unless merely in detail and in mannerism, as I am here contending.

clusions (or literary justifications) ; such as that of an abrupt
change in Elizabethan society, a contrast between the defi-
niteness and fixity of distinction in Jacobean plays and the
"social democracy" in Shakespeare.[14] In the drama itself,
to be sure, there *is* such a difference; but that is owing
mainly to Jonson's rigorous regard for *decorum* (or the
preservation of social distinctions in both doctrine and practice), and is merely partial and temporary. What Professor
Gayley says of verisimilitude in Fletcher's comedy of manners and intrigue, Jacobean also, but the remote forerunner
of that of the Restoration, here applies, though he is speaking rather of moral distinctions and barriers than of those
of rank. *The Wild-Goose Chase*—then *Monsieur Thomas*—
is in question:

The manners themselves, though purporting to be those of the
day, are factitious or, at the truest, of a fashion-loving, theater-
haunting coterie utterly unrepresentative of the law-abiding and
normal European of that or any other day.[15]

In Restoration comedy the servants are not so much med-
dlesome and impertinent as unduly knowing and witty, en-
terprising and managing, like Jeremy in *Love for Love* and
Flippanta in *The Confederacy*. It is only people to servants
unused, as these (apparently) are not, that thus take them
into their confidence and hand over to them their vital
affairs; and for so doing they even today are ridiculous. In
themselves, moreover, the servants are improbable. The remark of Richardson's widely read Lovelace, in one of his
many lucubrations and digressions, is to the point:

We have not in any of our dramatic poets that I can call to
mind one character of a servant of either sex that is justly hit off.
So absurdly wise some, and so sottishly foolish others; and both
sometimes in the same person.

But as the great wit strangely fails to realize, a delicious

[14]Discussed in my *Shakespeare Studies,* pp. 56–57.

[15]C. M. Gayley, *Representative English Comedies* (1914), iii,
pp. lxiv, lxv.

absurdity is desired; and as he fails to remember, frequently secured.

6

What gives the impression of reality to the English plays is mainly that native quality of English and Teutonic art which we have touched upon above, the concreteness and vividness of detail. In Restoration comedy situations recur, character types (besides those mentioned) recur,—the graceful rake and clever libertine for hero, with a bird of his feather for his friend; the clever and charming coquette for heroine; the true-wit and the pseudo-wit, male or female; the doting husband, the unfaithful wife, and the cast-off, vindictive paramour; the avaricious or usurious hypocrite, the false ingénue, the sophisticated or the clownish servant. And this recurrence may indicate that they are either representative or—conventional. So far as essentials are concerned (though the concreteness conceals it) the characters and situations are almost as stereotyped as in Continental comedy, and might as properly as these keep their names from play to play—Sganarelle, Scapin, Harlequin, Géronte, Pantaloon, Elisa, Isabella. Many of the situations or incidents, indeed, as, for example, the oft-repeated bargaining before matrimony (like that between Millamant and Mirabell), and sometimes the greater part of a whole plot, are borrowed from that comedy or from the French romances.[16] Nevertheless, by speech and manner, rank, business, and diversion, time, place, and circumstance, the characters are made superficially more definite, individual, and various. They talk and, in part, act more like persons we know or recognize, if they are not more like them within. And the fast set, especially, have much of their own individual way of doing and talking—their wit and impudence, their ruffling and racketing, their delight in town life and

[16]The "proviso scenes," as in Dryden's *Wild Gallant* (1663), supposedly the first Restoration "Comedy of Manners"; *His Secret Love* (1667); and probably indebted to late Jacobean comedy and L'Astrée of D'Urfé, as shown by Miss Kathleen Lynch, *Philological Quarterly*, 1925, pp. 302–8. Cf. also her *Social Mode of Restoration Comedy*, pp. 145, 147, 199, 201, 202; and chap. III, above.

scorn of the country, their playgoing, gaming, and horse-racing; above all their gallantry and coquetry, life itself being a game of trickery and intrigue, and (as such, towards the end) of matrimony. *Decorum* of this sort—an appropriate social mannerism—is often admirably kept.

Yet I cannot but find better represented than these transient types or roles the English character and human nature in general. Shadwell, who is rather of the Jonsonian Comedy of Humours, is ordinarily considered best at the "manners" of the time, the most faithful realist; but the speech of First Bully in Act IV, "What Play do they play? Some confounded Play or other," justly admired by Saintsbury, is neither of high class nor of low, neither of the Merry Monarch's time nor of Victoria's, but of any. And the dramatists who give the most recognizable image of reality, such as not only Shadwell but also Vanbrugh and Farquhar—inferior as writers to Congreve, as playwrights to Wycherley, and as masters of the art of consistent comic illusion, to both—are happiest when dealing with their minor characters and the lower orders, which are less wrenched or strained by the exigencies of the situation. It is as in Shakespeare, the Nurse and Mercutio being taken more directly from life than Romeo and Juliet; and M. Mauriac notes the same sort of difference generally in the novel.[17] "No, my reputation's as good as the best of them," cries Mrs. Amlet to her son Dick: "and tho' I am old, I'm chaste, you rascal, you!" To appreciate that, as indeed almost anything else of value in Restoration comedy—or in any literature, for that matter—no reading of memoirs or diaries is required.

7

The ideas, interests, and movements of an age are easier to recognize than (if we already know them!) its peculiar-

[17]Cf. my *Shakespeare's Young Lovers* (1937), p. 33, and Edmond Jaloux, reviewing Mauriac's *Le Romancier, Nouvelles littéraires,* October 21, 1933, and quoting him: "Moins un personnage a d'importance, plus il a de chances d'avoir été pris à la réalité." Cf. Lanson on Corneille, *Histoire* I, 328.

ities of morals, mood, or manner. They appear more immediately; and there is no mistaking a connection, for instance,
between English Romanticism and the French Revolution.
The references to it, the echoes from it, are too definite and
numerous. But is the connection deeper, organic?

The usual explanation of the great outbursts of romantic literature [says Mr. Palmer] is that they are expressions of the vitality
and creative power which result from great historic contests and
achievement. M. Lenormand finds for them a precisely contrary
explanation . . . not in the achievements themselves, but in the
effort and suffering,—so soon forgotten or neglected by the historians—by which these achievements were won. The romantic
literature that follows such a period is not an expression of hope
or vitality, but an instinctive recoil from realities too hard of
acceptance.[18]

The theory, then, cuts both ways; and, either way, explains too little. M. Brunetière, on the contrary, declares
that such moments of national achievement accompany or
precede the flourishing of drama, which in the time of
Pericles or Louis XIV, certainly, was not Romantic. And
if Spenser, Marlowe, and Shakespeare were fired by the
enthusiasm in the days of the Armada, and Blake, Wordsworth, and Coleridge by that at the fall of the Bastille, what
then of Tirso, Lope, and Calderón, or of the French Ro-
manticists, who followed in the wake of defeat or failure?
The English Romantic Movement and the French Revolution, moreover, were somewhat remote, were not the expression of the same vitality and creative power; and here
it is a matter of thought rather than of contact and partici-
pation. Yet the ensuing sobriety and conservatism of Wordsworth and his peers, on the one hand, and the melancholy
or pessimism of the younger poets Byron and Shelley, on
the other, are attributed to the Terror and to the Napole-
onic and Royalist reaction. "It is well," says Dowden, "in

[18]*Studies in Contemporary Theatre*, Secker, London, (1927),
p. 83. Cf. Mr. T. S. Eliot's comment on Shelley's words about poetry
as the herald, companion, and follower of the awakening of a great
people, *The Use of Poetry* (1933), p. 85. He is skeptical.

considering each important writer to note the date at which he reached early manhood." But like your poet himself, an optimist or a pessimist is born, not made. Why did not Wordsworth, Coleridge, and Southey, after the collapse of their high expectations, become pessimists like the later Romantics at the outset? Would these last, indeed, have become such if they had been of the elder poets' fiber, or if the elder poets had not, for the time being, worked that vein out? And who that knows the preceding eighteenth-century poetry, English, French and German, can doubt that there was to be a Romantic revival in all three countries, whether Paris razed the Bastille and overthrew the King or not? With English lyric verse these matters had not much more to do than (despite the commonplaces and clichés of literary history) the Armada had with English drama.

So far as French literature is concerned the Revolution seems to have had little fruitful effect upon it. As M. Baldensperger notices,[19] although Madame de Staël in 1799 expected great things of it—of this *ordre dans la liberté,* of this *morale et indépendance républicaines sagement et politiquement combinées*—really the new spirit in literature manifested itself in the writings of nostalgic nobles and *émigrés*—Chateaubriand, Sénancour, and Nodier—whereas the revolutionists themselves, Joseph Chénier, Ginguené, and Legouvé kept pretty much to the traditional forms; and the high tide of Romanticism, with all its extravagances and excesses, came a generation afterwards under the Citizen King, in an age of middle-class conservatism and sobriety. *Si les lettres étaient l'expression de la société, écrivait Salvandy en 1836, il faudrait désespérer de la France.*[20] Political changes have little immediate effect in art, as M. Baldensperger observes also of the revolutionary movements in Italy from 1789–1815, that in America in 1783, as well as the awakening of national consciousness and assertion of national power in Germany after 1870. In 1894 Litzmann wrote of the great expectations of a golden age of poetry,

[19]*Littérature* (1913), pp. 84–85.
[20]*Ibid.*, p. 189.

such as that under the Hohenstaufens, which had not been realized.[21]

We are nearer the truth when we keep more to the surface, and trust our senses and wits rather than our deductive or inductive powers. There is, perhaps, on the whole, no mistaking a Catholic country, a monarchical one, a martial, romantic, and (despite the servants' sallies and the romantic young ladies' escapades) a rigidly feudal and decorous one, in the drama of Spain. Likewise, for all the cynicism and indifference of the Restoration drama, there is no mistaking in that, as in the Elizabethan and Jacobean, a Protestant spirit and, at the same time (especially since otherwise we know of this!), a reaction against Puritanism. And in the Jacobean, particularly in Beaumont and Fletcher, we readily recognize something of the *jure divino* royalist spirit, just as we do, though far more clearly, the spirit of democracy and of socialism in much of our drama at present. But to nature the mirror is held up rather than to the time. It is easier to recognize the ideas and interests of a people than of a period; or rather, their traits and idiosyncrasies—their prejudices or prepossessions. In what here is certain and unmistakable time scarcely counts. In Homer there is the same readiness to propitiate the gods and to look for signs and omens on every occasion as, so long after, in the record of Herodotus and Thucydides; also the same thriftiness—how presents are delighted in and the waste of Telemachus' patrimony bewailed!—and the same cunning at a bargain—how chivalrously Ajax and Diomed exchange arms with their foes, but to their own enormous advantage and the poet's satisfaction!—as in the record to this day. In the Levant it is still nip and tuck between this and two other redoubtable commercial peoples; and who that knows them can fail to recognize the national vice of the French and the Italians in Plautus and the *Commedia dell' Arte,* in the pages of Molière, Balzac, and Maupassant? So in Restoration drama, for all the license of the age, there is, generally, something of the English sense of propriety in sexual matters that has prevailed since

[21]*Ibid.,* p. 88.

the earliest writing, in contrast with the Continent before it came under the domination of neoclassicism; the difference, that is, between Chaucer and Boccaccio, Spenser and Ariosto; and there is little of the dirt and filth of the Germans or of the gaulois Rabelais. In Restoration drama there is something of the reticence and cleanliness that, even in this decade of Joyce and O'Neill (both Irishmen, however), are to be found in the English translation of *Jüd Süss* as compared to the original. There is also little of that comic pleasure in the physical suffering of man or beast[22] which is to be found in Latin and Celtic literature. And there is, on the other hand, the English indifference to human beauty except the female (contrast Greco-Latin literature, from Homer and Virgil to Stendhal!), their delight in "a character," their predominant interest in the matter-of-fact and concrete. Of ideas, to be sure, there are, on the whole, not many abroad in Restoration comedy. It is comedy, and therefore topsy-turvy; it is a literature of Saturnalian rebellion, as that of Molière and Regnard is not (indeed, the gallants' scorn of country life and home life and contempt for law and order only betray the more the native predilection); and besides, the characters are not discursive, and keep pretty much to the affair of gallantry or trickery in hand.

8

The Elizabethans, on the contrary, expatiate, particularly in tragedy, and more fully reflect the thought, if not the life, of the time. And recent American scholarship is right in tracing further than Dowden did the direct influence of the contemporary—still medieval—psychology (or physiology) and ethics upon the text. There are ideas and sentiments and fairly technical terms and phrases embedded in

[22]This is counterbalanced by the bloodshed on the English tragic stage, lacking on the Continental; but as I have indicated in chap. I, the safer path to tread is not from literature to life, but from life to literature, and knowing the Island and the Continent as we do, we may, possibly, attribute the bloodshed on the English tragic stage to the taste for presentation rather than narration. In the Continental drama the blood is shed, but behind the scenes.

it which need nowadays some explanation, but did not then. Verbal or incidental vestiges are, however, a different thing from an Elizabethan psychologist's framework, upon which the character is modeled, or a Schoolman's scheme of a virtue, upon which the plot is modeled, both of these undiscernible until our all-scrutinizing, all-penetrating day. It is a mistaken conception of art whereby one would discover in the characters or the story anything less than a work of imagination, instead of the intellect; anything less, in short, than a creation human and poetic, immediately intelligible and effective, instead of scientific or didactic. And when, in psychologizing, Shakespeare goes farther, as when he lets Ophelia report Hamlet's appearing, like a madman, in her chamber, or Hamlet himself describe his distempered state of mind to Rosencrantz and Guildenstern, he makes either matter—one as a case of feigned erotomania, the other, of Elizabethan melancholy—almost as plain to the uninstructed but open-minded reader nowadays, who has attended to his dramatic method,[23] as to the Elizabethan playgoer. Shakespeare is no scholar, expecting scholarship in his audience; and scholars must not so conceive of either as they labor in their vocation. Ben Jonson himself, for all his learning and his preoccupation with the humors, touches us directly, imaginatively, too, and requires no such exegesis; the same may be said today even of James and Proust in the novel, both deeply imbued with psychology, though of a sort somewhat less inhuman; and how much more, of the light-armed, swift-footed Shakespeare, on the stage, who does not (except in comedy, and then but momentarily, as with Ford in *The Merry Wives*) frame his characters in such formal fashion at all. To him might be adapted Lanson's remark in 1895 about all French literature: *la psychologie dont notre littérature est pleine n' a rien de com-*

---

[23]The characteristic symptoms are noted elsewhere in Shakespeare, as in Rosalind's account of lovesickness in *As You Like It*, III, ii, 397–400; and cf. *Two Gentlemen of Verona*, II, 3, 79–83. The point lies in Polonius and Ophelia's diagnosis, which fits in perfectly with Hamlet's previous expression of an intention to play a part.

mun avec la science.[24] A great role is played in the above discussions by the seven deadly sins, by sloth in Hamlet, by wrath in Lear—but scarcely a tragic or esthetic one: to demonstrate their working the dramatic structure is turned upside down, and we are made to hearken unto the words of Goneril and Regan and Edmund against their fathers, and of Laertes and the King and Queen (though these last are really consoling, not reproaching, him) against the Prince. But on this subject of mistaken antiquarianism I have touched before this, and shall do so again.[25]

Poetry deals not with the technical or scientific but with the "familiar," as Wordsworth says, and as say also poets so different as Pope and Rossetti. To this "knowledge which all men carry about with them," says Wordsworth, "and to [the] sympathies in which without any other discipline than that of our daily life, we are fitted to take delight, the Poet principally directs his attention." The whole of that preface, upon the theme of Milton's phrase "simple, sensuous, and passionate," together with Coleridge to the same effect in the *Biographia Literaria,* ought to be imprinted upon the memory of all literary investigators—and even of authors. Donne, for whom I have much reverence, and his disciples today, for whom I have not so much, are, in so far as in their own day they require footnotes and interpreters, not poets, and minister not to the imagination but to the intellect. And dramatists of this description—great, popular dramatists—why, there simply are none. Even in after times they need footnotes only for the jokes' sake, in comedy.

Such criticism as I see it, is, though it deals with ideas, not facts, essentially the same as that which identifies characters and incidents in the contemporary history or in the author's own life. It is prompted by the same literalism, the same implicit notion that a great story, as a whole or in part, is a record, or pamphlet, or document (which can scarcely be artistic); or else a satire or burlesque (which can be artistic only in a comparatively minor way). And it

[24]*Hommes et livres* (1895), p. 355.

[25]*Shakespeare-Jahrbuch* (1938), pp. 77–80; and chaps. VII and XIV below.

is lured by the same historical fallacy,—that what belongs to the life or thought of the period must find some reflection in the art of the period. Both the one sort of criticism and the other illustrate the literature-and-life tenet in its most dogged and downright form; they discover the original, and detect the hidden *in*artistic intention; and neither proves the point, which is bad, though to prove it would be worse. The chief difference between them is that the criticism which identifies facts and persons follows the path of least resistance, and of less destruction: this, intent upon erudition, the textbooks or the milieu, blazes a trail as a pioneer. Yet in both alike is that propensity of the human understanding, which Bacon deprecates, to suppose the existence of more order and regularity in the world than it finds; to draw, when once it has adopted an opinion, all things else to support and agree with it; and to be more moved and excited by affirmatives than by negatives. One mind, full of the sociology of the period—the vendetta, the point of honor, and the cuckold's shame—cannot rest content until it has established a connection, and conceiving Iago to be actually honest or honorable, and, according to the professional standards of the time, pretty much justified in his diabolical revenge upon Othello (though not one in the story shares those opinions at the end, nor Iago himself from the beginning), turns the most unmistakable of tragedies into a "problem play"—which in the critic's hands it indeed becomes.[26] Others, still more rigidly literal, full of the historical facts of the period, also cannot rest content until they have established a connection, and bring the Gunpowder Plot and St. Bartholomew's Eve, the murders of Rizzio, Darnley, and Coligny, Essex's Rebellion and the Scottish Succession (how, pray, could they have been passed over?) all into *Hamlet, Macbeth,* and *King Lear.* For James (though he is given parts in still other plays!), like Hamlet on one occasion, took notes; the great bell of St. Germain l'Auxerrois was the signal, like the lady's hand-bell "when

[26]See *Publications of Modern Language Association,* 1931, pp. 724ff, "Honest Iago." The writer has a citation or reference to justify him in every error he makes.

my drink is ready"; there was a knock—like Macduff's—
at Coligny's door and at Darnley's, though these before the
murder, not after; and, like Lear, the Admiral had white
hair, and if he could not boast of such a retinue himself,
was descended from a house of which one of the privileges
was that of "a hundred knights." And other—soberer—
minds, full of the psychology of the period, cannot rest content (for is there not also psychology in Shakespeare?)
merely with the humble, but serviceable, explaining of a
few terms or phrases.

9

It is, apparently, the natural way to study literature,
though by no means to read it; nay, it is the scholarly way,
for by the formula in question a good deal of our learned
criticism is, implicitly, guided. It must be a business of affirmatives, or of negatives for others' affirmatives, or else for
scholarship what place is there left? The less sophisticated
connect poetry with the data of history and biography, if
they don't even derive these from it; the more sophisticated,
with those of the contemporary psychology or philosophy;
neither set remembering that poetry and knowledge belong
to different orders, and that knowledge (as has been said)
has to do with facts or ideas, poetry with relations or values.
Either set is bent upon "discoveries"—unknown or hitherto
unconsidered contemporary facts or ideas—and upon their
application to poetry. Neither set realizes that nothing quite
relevant to art can be discovered except in the work of art
itself; which, though not independent (for it is a work of
imitation, also), is self-contained, the parts, as Coleridge
says, mutually supporting and explaining each other. (Sarcey is right in saying Taine is wrong in thinking that the
young prince in Racine's *Athalie,* talks, anachronistically,
like the proper children of the French court replying to
their teachers, and in saying that the poet, as he made Joas
so primly respectful, was but conforming to the logic of
the situation, which requires the aspirant to the throne,
groomed by a priestly politician such as Joad, should be

only a tool in his hands.) Neither set realizes that the essential preliminary labor of criticism is, as Mr. Eliot says, mainly a matter of analysis and of comparison, whether in the single work of art or others of the species. Before that, of course, with a work of literature, comes the reading: we must understand the language and allusions. Shakespeare now needs footnotes, but in his own day he needed none, nor provided any, and still less introductions or prefaces. The immortal novel of his contemporary, Cervantes, according to the great Menéndez y Pelayo, needs none even now.[27] And Shakespeare himself would not now need them so much if, as I have elsewhere endeavored to show, he hadn't had so many.

Indeed, Mr. C. S. Lewis as against Mr. Tillyard, and Professor Spitzer as against Professor Lovejoy[28] (though they are taking account of nothing so serious as the positive damage done to Shakespeare), are, I think, justified in their contention that scholarship, biographical or cultural, as applied to literature, is, even when sound, often not only not illuminating, but distracting and misleading in its effects. Fielding, as Stevenson says, was a gentleman and Richardson wasn't, and yet Richardson could make a gentleman and Fielding couldn't;[29] and M. Valéry dwells on and recurs to the point that *les prétendus enseignements de l'histoire littéraire ne touchent presque pas à l'arcane de la génération des poèmes. Ce qu'il y a de plus important,— l'acte même des Muses,—est indépendant des aventures, du genre de vie, des incidents, et de tout ce qui peut figurer*

[27] *No necesita interpretaciones—Interpretacion del D.Q.*, p. 17.

[28] "History of Ideas," *Southern Review* (winter, 1940), pp. 584ff. Cf. T. S. Eliot, *Selected Essays* (1932), p. 199; one of Mr. Clutton Brock's last essays, *Art and Science* (p. 29): "This [historical investigation] is often blindly pursued in the belief that *any fact about a great artist* must have some undefined value; or that his art can be fully explained in terms of its origins and material conditions . . . the proper aim of the historic method, as applied to Shakespeare for instance, is *to remove obstacles to the experience of his plays.* However, cf. Geoffrey Tillotson *Essays* (1942), pp. xxv–xxvi, on the Lewis and Tillyard controversy (*Personal Heresy*, 1939).

[29] "Some Gentlemen," South Seas Ed., XXVII, p. 84.

dans une biographie.[30] And he uses Racine as an example, whose observable life, he says, had much in common with ten thousand other Frenchmen. Certainly Professor Spitzer is right in maintaining that knowledge of Lamb's life and of the circumstances attendant upon the composition of *The Old Familiar Faces* (though true enough, while much so applied is not true) lessens rather than heightens the comprehension and enjoyment of the poem. Also he is right in thinking that Professor Lovejoy misunderstands "self-contained," which means not "uncommunicative" but "containing in itself all that is necessary to its meaning" (or as Coleridge has it, containing "within itself the reason why it is itself and not otherwise"); and that the really great works of art, like Dante's Comedy, Sophocles' Antigone, and almost any one of Calderón's tragedies upon the point of honor, are palmary examples of this. The widely different ethical ideas and the alien cultural background become clear to the reader or spectator as the story moves on. Such authors, and the still greater Homer and Shakespeare, have been acknowledged by critics who are also men of letters— Grillparzer, Arnold, Croce, Yeats, Quiller-Couch, Drinkwater, and Maugham,[31] to be "universal" even in the sense of appealing, and (in the main) of being comprehensible, to all men. And it is not through history or the history of ideas or culture, either, that critics have come to a finer understanding (after criticism!) of Shakespeare's or Sophocles' own intention in a play, but through analysis of it and comparison of it with others by him and by other poets.

10

The psychology of the time is a different matter from the philosophy; a doctrine or science implied, from that directly expressed. The psychology involved in a wholly successful

[30]*Variété* (1928), p. 69. Cf. pp. 207-8.

[31]For Maugham see below, chap. XI; for Croce, *Ariosto & Shakespeare*, p. 183: *uno dei poeti più chiari, più evidenti, più comprensibili anche ad uomini di scarsa ed elementare cultura.* The others I have quoted elsewhere.

dramatic performance can never be that of the textbooks or the schools, but only that of our common human nature, immediately appreciated, emotionally responded to. And of psychology presented directly there is next to nothing in good verse or (for that matter) prose. But the contemporary, or not yet outdated, philosophy has been, now and then, happily presented in the epic, in meditative poetry, and reflected even in the lyric when not meant to be sung. Lucretius, Dante, Spenser, Donne, Milton, Goethe, Wordsworth, and Shelley are examples. The ideas of the age, as we have already noticed, are more recognizable in poetry than the character and doings of the people then. But they too are transmuted. It is an imaginative re-creation and simplification of pantheism that Goethe, Shelley, or Wordsworth has left us, not any adequate transcript. "The poet who thinks," says Mr. T. S. Eliot, "is merely the poet who can express the emotional equivalent of thought. . . . Dante had behind him the system of St. Thomas . . . Shakespeare, [that of] Seneca, or Montaigne, or Machiavelli. . . . I can see no reason for believing that either Dante or Shakespeare did any thinking on his own."[32]

II

And still less of a bearing has our historical or (even) biographical lore. Of what artistic relevance are, for the most part, the facts of Burns's and Wordsworth's, Byron's, Shelley's, and Coleridge's lives and loves, continually accumulated and presented anew (and when prettily, read, as the poets themselves are not); or the latest notable discovery concerning Shakespeare, this Justice Shallow in Southwark, who, correctly or incorrectly reported to us, has in either case so little resemblance to the fiction that a connection seems inconceivable—what, often, but to demonstrate anew the truth in question? They are relevant if at all mainly in their irrelevance; are important, not ar-

[32]"Shakespeare and the Stoicism of Seneca," *Selected Essays* (by permission of Harcourt, Brace, N. Y., 1932), p. 116. Cf. Wilson, *Axel's Castle* (1931), pp. 118–20.

tistically, but biographically, historically; and it is in this interest, principally, that they should be discovered and recorded. For biography, however, so great is the craving on the part of both critic and public that in poets like Shakespeare, whose "life story" is meager, it is not so much connected with the poetry as forcibly derived from it. The old favorites Essex, Southampton, and Rutland are continually called up again upon the stage. Raleigh, their enemy, is Don Armado. Portia, in the mercy speech, is appealing to the better nature of the anti-Semitic Essex, who in *Troilus and Cressida* is Achilles, but (more deeply considered) is Hamlet, though (previously) exhorted to be a Henry V, while Burleigh, another of his enemies, is Polonius. Shakespeare himself is Prospero (once again); though before that he has been as melancholy as Hamlet, as jealous as Othello, as cynical as Iago, as disillusioned as Macbeth, coming to the verge of madness with Lear and Timon, and breaking down in health because of them, but, before *The Tempest,* restored in both body and spirit, "perhaps by the ministrations of his daughter."

Thus William Shakespeare, with no external evidence, is turned into a sort of George Sand or Sinclair Lewis or, we might say, an American professor- or student-novelist, whose every fairly plausible character has its recognizable model in the neighborhood. Of the Frenchwoman, Gourmont, who like most good French critics thinks little of her, declares that she continually made copy out of her loves and her lovers—*quel cimetière que cette littérature de Sand, que d'ossements, que de suaires!*[33] To appreciate *her* work, we must certainly know her life and environment. Not so, that of a great imaginative writer.

. . . the more perfect the artist, [says Mr. Eliot, in harmony with Coleridge] the more completely separate in him will be the man who suffers and the mind which creates; the more perfectly will the mind digest and transmute the passions which are its material . . .[34]

[33]*Promenades littéraires* (1913), ii, pp. 141–42.

[34]*Selected Essays* (1932), pp. 7–10, 93; Scott-James, *Making of Literature,* pp. 235–36.

In fact, his art is more often a reaction, a refuge. To the list I have drawn up elsewhere of those who are different as men, let me add Cervantes, Molière, Mozart, Beethoven, Chekhov, and Dickens. In the novel, Professor Spitzer says, "Cervantes shows nothing of the jail (if really he wrote *Don Quixote* in it), nor anything of the dirty affairs in which, according to the nineteenth-century biographers, he was involved."[35] And the same scholar rightly rejects the notion that Molière exposed his matrimonial troubles on the stage.[36] (Even in print and in the day of Rousseau and after, it is doubtful if any Frenchman would thus give himself away.) Of Dandin and Arnolphe he makes sport. To be sure (though, so far as I know, it has not been suggested) that may have been to throw dust into people's eyes; but, more probably, it was because he knew how welcome the sport was. The delicate, ineffable Mozart was personally, Ernest Newman gathers, "as hard as steel and as corrosive as acid," besides being coarse and vulgar in his speech. Beethoven was plunged in gloom and despair when he wrote the gay and cheerful Second Symphony. The same is to be said of Tschaikovsky and his Fourth. "When I think of any great poetical writer of the past," says Yeats, "I comprehend, if I know the lineaments of his life, that the work is the man's flight from his entire horoscope, his blind struggle in the network of the stars." And he cites the cases of William Morris and Landor, irascible in action, pensive or lofty in writing. Keats and Dante are his further illustrations, the one poor, dreaming of luxury, the other celebrating purity and justice "because he had to struggle with his unjust anger and his lust."[37] "Such tides of drink in his novels," says Chesterton of Dickens, "and yet Dickens himself drank little." And of Chekhov Mr. Maugham observes that "he seems to have been of a cheerful and practical disposition but as a writer he was of a depressed and melancholic nature that made him turn away with distaste from violent action or exuberance."

[35]*Southern Review* (1940–41), p. 589.

[36]Cf. above, pp. 16–17.

[37]*Essays* (Macmillan, N. Y., 1924), pp. 489–92.

"Literature of escape" for the writer, whether from himself or the age, and whether for the reader or not! Professor Spitzer, again, says the like of Villon, and his serenity in the ballade of dead ladies: "the whole book of Huizinga, which analyzes the ghastly fear of death obtaining in the fifteenth century, is contradicted by this one poem." And so with the drama, and even in Greece. "In Athena's city," says Mr. F. L. Lucas,

"where women were kept in almost Oriental suppression as odalisques or drudges, the stage produced figures like Clytemnestra and Cassandra, Atossa and Antigone, Phaedra and Medea, and all the other heroines who dominate play after play of the misogynist Euripides,"[38]

and the critic dwells upon the same predominance in Racine and Ibsen. That "remains a strange and almost inexplicable fact," says Mr. Lucas. "It might," as he thinks, "have been explained on the theory that as plays have been written by men, mainly for men, the romantic instinct did the rest. Only in Greece, of course, woman was not an object of romance." But is not the "fact" in harmony with all we have been finding? And in myth (or at least in Ovid) there is the romance in abundance; one maiden after another like Medea, Scylla (the daughter of Nisus), Ariadne, and Hypsipyle, falling in love and taking the initiative as they repeatedly do in medieval and Renaissance story and in Shakespearean and other Elizabethan drama. Even in Greek drama and major epic woman was an object of romance, as when Euripides' Andromeda speaks to Perseus like Miranda to Ferdinand:

> *Sir, take me with you, whether as your servant,*
> *Or wife, or handmaid;*[39]

and when Homer's Nausicaä speaks of Ulysses like Desdemona to Othello, wishing that Heaven "had made her [the case is dative] such a man!" (*Od.*, VI, 244.)

[38]*Tragedy* (Hogarth Press, 1935), pp. 114–15.
[39]See below, p. 159f; and for Andromeda, Lewis Campbell, *Greek Tragedy* (1891), p. 254.

And is English literature a literature of escape in general? "It is a curious fact about our literature," says Mr. Lytton Strachey, "that such a small proportion of it reflects the dominant characteristics of our race. Its greatest achievements are poetical; and we are a nation of shopkeepers. Nor is our poetry of the sober and solid kind," but it is remarkable for "high fantasy, as in Shelley . . . intellectual subtlety, as in Donne . . . or for pure artistry, as in Milton and Keats"; qualities "the ordinary Englishman notoriously lacks."[40] Whereupon Mr. Strachey expresses the opinion that either this notion of the English national character is wrong or else that the average English reader is in an alien world. But to that is he too not escaping?

12

In comedy generally, the best critics such as Yeats and Stevenson acknowledge, there is a greater approximation to reality than in tragedy. "It is a humorous criticism of life," says Mr. W. L. Courtney in *Old Saws and Modern Instances* (1918):

There is no lack of humor in Shakespeare, but there is no criticism of life. You cannot have a criticism of life, and therefore no criticism of contemporary manners, if you insist on putting your characters into a purely ideal scene . . .

such as Belmont, Messina, Illyria, and the Forest of Arden are. There is study of character, but

a comedy of character—character as educed out of the clash of real living personalities and vital incidents—cannot be found in the Shakespearean comedies. . . . They are artificial in the sense that they are purely fantastic, whereas characters of true comedy

[40]*Characters and Commentaries* (Harcourt, Brace, N. Y., 1933), p. 158. Cf. Hazlitt, *Principles of Human Action* (*Works,* VII, p. 409), who contrasts English and French in poetry; the French, "a lively people, fond of shew and striking images," with a drama "which abounds in nothing but general maxims and vague declamations and which would appear quite tedious to an English audience, who are generally considered as a dry, dull, plodding people, much more likely to be satisfied with formal description and grave reflection."

are artificial because they are abstracted as types from the actual circumstances of the real world. . . .—(P. 139.)

13

The novel has more of actuality and local color about it than the lyric or the drama. Yet who needs to have been in France, or Germany, or Russia in order to appreciate Proust, Mann, or any of the great Muscovites, or to have perused their biographies? That you do not need to is one of the chief signs of their artistic value. Mr. Sinclair Lewis, to be sure, is rated high in Sweden. But in art documentation—sociology—does not count. We know a character (if ever we do) when we see him, or hear him, though we never met one like him in the world. Mostly we know him by the way his thoughts and words hang together. The more we learn of life and nature, of course, whether our own or that of the age and country in question, the better, in the end, even for our knowledge of poetry; but in the application this is of no avail except when, as with the author himself, it is subdued to an artistic purpose. The character is a work of art, to which in vain, as M. Hankiss says, we shall seek a living parallel;—*dont la vérité consiste dans sa solidité*. Here and there in the story the author may copy for a bit, as a painter, in an ideal scene, may insert a little portrait; here and there he may express his own or the contemporary opinion for a moment, and in an epic he may do this at length, through the mouth of his Raphael or his Virgil; and when this happens, and the writer ceases to write for the ages, we should be ready for him and note it.

But a transcript or a doctrine must not be expected of him and allowances must be made (again) for the prevailing style or taste, without rushing to social conclusions. Fainting or swooning for both women and men, both knights and paladins, as a means of story-making in the Chansons de Geste and the medieval romances, I took up in my first discussion;[41] and of the misunderstanding of it in Jane Austen's early novel Mr. Chesterton complains:

[41]*Shakespeare Studies* (1927), pp. 40–41.

"Beware of fainting fits, etc." Such were the words of the ex-
piring Sophia to the afflicted Laura; and there are modern critics
capable of adducing them as a proof that all society was in a
swoon in the first decade of the 19th century. But in truth it is
the whole point of this little skit that the swoon of sensibility was
not satirised because it was a fact . . . but because it was a fiction. . . . Those ingenious moderns . . . have swallowed all the
solemnities of the *Mysteries of Udolpho* and never seen the joke
of *Northanger Abbey*. (Preface to *Love and Friendship*, 1923.)

And Mr. Chesterton is right—Jane in person, it is said,
fainted but once—though he insufficiently allows for the
effect of literature on life itself. There was more swooning
among real women then than now because there was or
had been so much in the novels, just as before that, in
the days of Sentimentalism, there had been weeping; and
now there were morbid and melodramatic practices, like
building ruins and planting dead trees, public swaggering
or moping, drinking from skulls and cultivating the passions
and the amorous vices, brooding over vestiges of death or
actively embracing it, all imitated from romantic or decadent prose and poetry, in England, and later but more
extravagantly and abundantly, in France. For the imitation of Art by Life, which Wilde insists upon in his "Decay
of Lying," there is abundant evidence quite apart from his
hyperboles and paradoxes. as furnished, for instance, by
Mario Praz, in the *Romantic Agony* (1933).[42] That is a
subject upon which I must not here embark, except to say
that Signor Praz is, I think, right in considering the so-
called "decadent" literature not necessarily a reflection of
social decay. Many of the French writers, as well as their
more susceptible readers, practiced the sexual excesses and
perversions, the sadism and the masochism, which they depicted, but not a large element of the population; and the
fashion of giving unrestrained expression to lofty individual
feeling which came in with Romanticism furnished a sort
of warrant for the expression of feelings which otherwise

[42]Pp. 121, 139, and *passim*. Also, F. L. Lucas, *Decline and Fall
of the Romantic Ideal* (The Macmillan Co., N. Y., 1937), chap. ii.

"would have remained latent and repressed."[43] Moreover, the principle touched upon in chapter III here applies, particularly in a country like France, where, in art and in politics, ideas are carried out to the limit. A successful artistic movement tends to proceed until the possibilities are exhausted; and unrestrained expression of healthy emotion would naturally be followed by the unrestrained expression of the unhealthy.

With Dostoevski in his novels and Chekhov in his plays, as I said in the first chapter, it is more a matter of the author's individual technique. The suspense is centered in the character; the motives are mixed and mysterious; the conduct is extravagant and full of contrasts, apparently contradictory. Undoubtedly such extravagance and unreasonableness are Russian; nor would such characterization, with an appropriately different local color and concrete detail, do for an action laid in France or even Germany. But we see that not all of this is Russian, nor all which is Russian is here, when we remember Tolstoy or Turgenev.

Indeed, Dostoevski is like the Byronic Hugo.[44] There is in some of the characters a similar mixture of motives, a similar paradoxical and extravagant conduct and combination of hero and villain in one. The combination is less logical, less rigidly antithetical or geometrical, more human and various, decidedly less French. Still, in Hugo himself the life is wildly exaggerated and distorted, and for the same purpose as in Dostoevski. It is no more France in the one than Russia in the other. Both novelists are dramatists, as intent upon emotional effect as Aeschylus or Shakespeare with their external fate or villain, attaining, by their similar improbabilities, to extremities of tenderness and terror that in probable situations would be impossible.

The quieter, less manipulated high-class novel, on the other hand, because of its amplitude and detail, its prose and comparatively everyday doings, is especially liable to being taken for something of a document—an actual experience. It is so real, the ordinary reader says again; and

[43]*Praz*, p. 381.   [44]See below, chap. xvi.

he naïvely concludes or, often, remembers,—that the writer
had been in that place, seen such people and doings. Conrad had been in the tropic seas. But, as Mr. Desmond Mac-
Carthy says, it was not that, or his having been in the
forests, either, which made him a novelist; and

his Soho was as much part of this world as the Amazon. Meredith, Henry James, and Hardy have done the same; they, too,
have blown great comprehensive, iridescent bubbles, in which the
human beings they describe, though they have of course a recognizable resemblance to real people, only attain in that world their
full reality. (*Portraits*, 1931, p. 75.)

And of James he says that the "reality," again, is simply
a matter of successful art, that the independence of the
world we know

. . . becomes clear the moment we imagine a character moved
from one imaginary world into another. If Pecksniff were transplanted into *The Golden Bowl,* he would become extinct . . .

So it is with the slices of life inserted:

either they kill the book or the book kills them. The unforgivable
artistic fault in a novelist is failure to maintain consistency of
tone. (*Ibid.,* p. 156.)

Or as Wilde extravagantly puts it, "Truth is entirely and
absolutely a matter of style." And of himself and his own
world of imagination Mr. Sherwood Anderson (to cite the
case of a minor figure) says about the same.[45] It was from
the opposite point of view that the older critics used to
insist that Shakespeare had been in Italy because of the
incomparable Italian atmosphere in *The Merchant of
Venice;* must have navigated because of *The Tempest;*
and so on. But as Gourmont would have it, this is our *manie
de la documentation,* which makes us think that you must
know a country before venturing to lay there the scene of
a drama . . . Hugo was never in the Orient, nor even in
Italy, and of Spain had seen only what is taken in by the
eyes of a child.[46] So with Rossetti, never in Italy. And in

[45] *American Spectator*, April, 1934.

[46] *Promenades* (1913), v, pp. 187–89.

the preface to *The Old Wives' Tale* Arnold Bennett says that, according to Frank Harris and others, unless he had actually been present at a public execution he could not have written the chapter about Sophia at the Auxerre solemnity. Harris then gave his own description, "A brief but terribly convincing bit of writing."

. . . I wrote to Mr. Frank Harris, regretting that his description had not been printed before I wrote mine, as I should assuredly have utilized it, and, of course, I admitted that I had never witnessed an execution. He simply replied: "Neither have I."

Most people who thus sit in judgment on the author are in Harris's position, without his talents.

14

History and biography, psychology and philosophy, are not so important to the right documentation of literature as the other arts. The pictorial, plastic, musical, and architectural likewise reflect the taste of the time (though still more that of the country and race); and it is the less imitative, the more "abstract and ideal" arts, music and painting, that, as Wilde says, better "reveal to us the temper" of the age. "What do the drunken boors and brawling peasants tell us of the great soul of Holland? . . . Surely you don't imagine that the people of the Middle Ages bore any resemblance at all to the figures in medieval stained glass or in medieval stone and wood carving," and so on. But reflecting the taste of the time, the arts have interplay and do somewhat reflect each other. And so long as the student remembers the necessary differences in medium and technique, the special differences in tradition and changing style, he may discover much that is akin. Discretion—illumination—taste of his own—is his guide. The firm and logical structure, the economical, symmetrical, and rhythmical structure of French drama, both classical and modern, is to be found also in French architecture, modern, classical, and medieval, as not in English drama and architecture or the German. There we find instead greater variety of

material and treatment, greater richness of detail and
bolder emphasis of contrast. And in one and the same
period the likeness may be still more conspicuous; as in the
age of Louis XIV, not only in the arts above mentioned,
but also in the structure of verse and prose, in painting,
sculpture, even landscape-gardening and furniture. Everywhere there are rules and limits, frames and outlines, order,
parallelism, and rhythm, decorum, propriety, uniformity;—
a chair or a plate of Louis XIV, XV, or XVI can be told
at a glance;—and what a difference, in range of variation,
between the Alexandrine, with its fixed and prescribed
caesura and final pause, allotted number of syllables and
accents, unfailing alternation of masculine and feminine
rimes, on the one hand, and on the other, the blank verse in
its development from Marlowe to Shirley, even from *Titus
Andronicus* to *The Tempest!* It is (roughly, very roughly)
the difference between the façades of streets in Paris and
in London or New York. Corneille, Racine, and Molière,
Perrault, Mansard, and Le Nôtre, alike cherished and followed the classical or pseudo-classical ideal. For this the
criticism of the time—another certain connection, as we
have seen—prepared the way. Also, at various periods in
the same country, as in France once more, there may be
something of the same artistic device, continually recurring:
like the repeated *motif,* from *laisse* to *laisse,* or stanza to
stanza, and from speech to speech, approaching a musical
effect, in the medieval epics such as the *Roland,* in the
farces and the *chansons populaires,* in the comedy of
Molière and Regnard and, at the present day, by way of
prose, not only on stage and screen, but in leading articles,
the comic papers, and the very clown's tricks at the circus:
whereas in England, outside the lyric, it has appeared
sparely, and, for comic effect, mostly in Jonson and at the
Restoration, under French or other Continental influence.[47]
At the same period, moreover, in different countries, who
can fail now and then to notice a similarity in the various
arts not necessarily or easily attributable to influence? Mr.
Mencken has somewhere spoken of the Haydnesque rhythms

[47]Cf. my *Shakespeare Studies,* chap. iv.

of Addison; and indeed, though Addison's are in prose and
Haydn's in music, they are alike simple and tuneful, balanced and symmetrical, rounded and defined. Others than
Mr. Mencken must, in reading Addison, have thought of
eighteenth-century music. How different from the rhythms
of both are (in the various countries) those of the Romantic age, these themselves not being all alike! How much
have Romantic music and painting, prose and poetry, in
common with one another,—directness of approach and
immediacy of transition, range and irregularity of expression, richness of coloring and vagueness of outline—more
discernible and ascertainable than anything that they have
in common with the life of the time! Was it not Romantic
poetry and drama and Romantic delight in Shakespeare,
the medieval and the Gothic, the grotesque or tragi-comic,
that prompted composers to supplant the minuet in the
symphony with the scherzo?

The larger the territory, in fact, and the wider the stretch
of time considered, the greater the similarity to be detected
in the arts of one period as contrasted with those of another.
There is a national flavor to Italian, Spanish, or German
painting, music, or drama much more ascertainable and
discernible than the relation of any of these to the moods
or manners, doings or experiences of that country. More
ascertainable still is the relation of these modern arts to the
Greek. For all the audacity and arbitrariness of Spengler's
syntheses, there is point to the community that he discovers
among the arts of either period and to the difference that
he discovers between the periods themselves. Gothic architecture, perspective painting, contrapuntal music, with their
depths and distances, their focuses of multiple contending
forces, their play of light and shade—these all belong to one
world, widely different from the Greek. There is very little
point, on the other hand, to Spengler's notion that by the
Renaissance—anti-Gothic and Hellenistic, with a Grecian
want of feeling for space and time, of historic sense and
forward-looking resolution—Florence was incapacitated or
frustrated politically; and that "only that city where sculpture gained *no* foothold, where the Southern music was at

home, where Gothic and Baroque joined hands in Giovanni Bellini and the Renaissance remained an affair of occasional dilettantism, had an art of portraiture and therewith a subtle diplomacy and a will to political duration—Venice."[48]

15

The arts of a period, if it is big enough, keep fairly together in spirit; but in the past, at least, they have followed in the rear of the thought, the philosophy of the period. The arts, to have effect, cannot be far in advance of the common public, which absorbs ideas but slowly. There are repeated examples of this in the course of the development traced by Professor Lovejoy in his *Great Chain of Being* (1936). In the late-seventeenth and the early-eighteenth centuries

La nature est partout la même was the premise from which, explicitly or implicitly, the neo-classic theorists had deduced the consequence that art should be the same among all people and at all times; but the writers on the Chain of Being—who were in many cases the same writers—had endlessly reiterated the contrary of this premise: that "Nature diversifies its art in as many ways as possible." (p. 294.)

Another example of this aloofness confronts us in Elizabethan times. There is on the one hand a certain connection between the widespread poetic and dramatic activity of the age and the enormous interest and delight in language and rhetoric which preceded and accompanied it. That is only natural: as at other great periods, such as the Periclean, it prepared the way. In fact it prepared the way in single instances, namely Chaucer (as Professor Manly has shown) and Shakespeare himself.[49] It is the youthful lover of words and fancier of style that is likely to turn out a poet. It is on the other hand a different matter to discover a connection in Elizabethan times between the prevailing "conception of logical argument as the effective instrument

[48] *Decline of the West* (1926), chap. i, p. 273.
[49] *Review* in *Southern Review*, autumn, 1938, p. 403.

for truth's discovery" and the flourishing of the drama.
Then truth was suspended, says the reviewer, "not between
hypothesis and verification but between the affirmative and
the negative in debate," and "drama itself is debate and the
issues it loves to treat are debatable issues." "It is no wonder that drama flourished," Professor Matthiessen continues, who considers this generalization "one of the rare feats
of the intellectual historian, an illuminating connection between the habits of thought of the time and its principal
art form." But, as is generally and rightly recognized, English drama is not a debate, neither a logical nor even an
emotional one; and the "connection" might be more plausible if discovered, or posited, between "the English habits
of thought" and the drama (a little later) of the French.
The examples of dramatic debate produced from the
Honest Whore, Parts I and II, between Hippolito and
Bellafront, on the subject of chastity, make, in their wooden
—their schoolroom—fashion, some of the poorest drama in
either Dekker or his contemporaries; and there is nothing
like them in Shakespeare. There is also nothing that I
should call a debate of any kind "between Richard and
Bolingbroke, Brutus and Caesar." Indeed, the political
principles of any of them, particularly the latter pair, supposed to have some, are not ascertainable. And is the degeneration of drama nowadays owing to our own "suspen-
sion between hypothesis and verification"? Certainly, if the
discovery of truth plays any considerable part in drama
(which, I think, it does not) it would, of necessity, fall back
on the old way of affirmative and negative (though, it is to
be hoped, not after Dekker's fashion), and simply because
in drama there is no other.

In the eagerness of the critic to match the art or poetry
with the period he is often liable to being taken in by his
own words. Like Professor Matthiessen's "debate" is Professor Theodore Spencer's "conflict." The latter scholar,
finding in Shakespeare's time (as he would in most times,
to be sure) both faith and doubt, optimism and pessimism, a school of poetry that reflects the joy of living and
also one that, like Marston's and Webster's, reflects gloom

and cynicism, declares that "when Shakespeare's development as a craftsman reached its climax, this conflict also reached its climax"; and thereupon adds, "we shall soon attempt to discover how Shakespeare, practicing the type of writing which relies on conflict, was able to use it."[50] "The time was ripe for tragedy"; but how does Professor Spencer, at this late day, know so much about the chronology? Both Professor R. W. Chambers and Professor Sisson, as appears in chapter XIII below, dispute, with cogent evidence, the accuracy of the almost identical assertions by Professor J. D. Wilson and his school; and are not these scholars all taking liberties with history in order to match it with the experience of one poet, as they have previously conceived of this? The climax of gloom and cynicism in Shakespeare's tragic period (what tragedy is wanting in gloom and cynicism?) miraculously coincides, at the death of Elizabeth and accession of James, with the climax of gloom and cynicism in England, if then really there was much of any! And the reflection of this in the drama? Where is to be discovered the "conflict" between the opposite philosophies, supposed to be then raging in the world outside? In Shakespeare, as in most Elizabethan drama and the best of it, in most drama for that matter and the best of ours, the conflict is between persons or groups of persons. At all events, the conflict outside is pretty much only the difference in faith or opinion, in poetic spirit or attitude, to be found in any age, which does not necessarily lead to tragedy or drama of any sort. In poetic spirit and content, indeed, it is not so marked as later, in the time of the cavaliers and the metaphysicals, or as in the eighteenth century or the nineteenth; and critics like Sir Walter Raleigh have, on the contrary, insisted upon the prevailing unity and harmony of temper at this time, such as England was not to see again.

It is in somewhat the same spirit of audacious hypothesis that the rise of the "metaphysical school" itself has repeatedly been explained by the "collapse of the medieval

[50]*Shakespeare and the Nature of Man* (1942), p. 45.

conception of the world beneath the reiterated blows of newly acquired knowledge." Professor Praz (*Romantic Agony*, p. xi) rightly objects to it as explaining too little. "Metaphysical" is here, of course, really a misnomer; and this ingenious and contorted style has little to do with philosophy or religion, either, except as drawing from them novel material for figures of speech. And as for the gloom and pessimism, ordinarily this collapse, which actually took place much earlier, has been considered an enfranchisement, and made to explain, on the other hand, the Renaissance high spirits.

Not that the critics are the only thinkers to be taken in by their own words, as appears if we consider the purely historical generalizations which are now being daily produced. Why this other collapse (or else outburst) of the Germans into barbarism? One Czech scholar, with the high approval of his reviewer, explains it as owing to the fact that the Germans were not conquered by the Romans, nor converted by the Christians. Both statements are true enough; and an unconquered, unconverted nation, too much for the Romans and the Christians, certainly sounds dangerous. But what nation ever was converted, or effectively turned from its instinctive ways of doing by a new religion? It was as Christianity became paganized that Europe became Christianized. And the conquering of the Germans in 1918 seems only to have made them more savage and pitiless since 1939. In such matters, as so often, not why but how—how much and how variously—is the scientific question. Recognizing the German temperament, one should endeavor to see how by the mere unifying and centripetal tendency in a nation its special and more prominent characteristics become accentuated and exaggerated, and by warfare, of course, still more. In German science, in German philosophy, in German military theory itself, with its "total war" and indiscriminate destruction, there has, for generations, been the same refusal to shrink from the uttermost consequences that may be drawn from the premises; and by the shrinking of their enemies, on the other hand, together with their enemies' blindness to what they themselves intended, this spirit was only encouraged.

16

And the arts of today? They (unfortunately!) are not so far aloof or behind. It is the age of history, of archaeology, and of no one style, but many; yet that itself is a note and character of the age, in the arts. Scarcely an innovation or revival in one but is in some fashion imitated in the others. The trend or tendency in all is commonly said to be realistic. The favorite highbrow material, indeed, the harsh or brutal, the ugly or humdrum, even the fleshly and fecal, as well as anything else that can be seen, heard, touched, or smelled, is often registered with an ingenuity and audacity or effrontery never known before. Yet we see (and depict) mostly but what we have been taught to see or feel, these subtle nuances—or startling clashes—in form and color, in thought and conduct. Science has taught us, and art itself, too, in its progress; but it has not taught the public. It is they that are behind. In the supposedly higher forms of art, moreover, the real is not even the artist's objective, but the effect of the real—not by a copy, but by some device of simplification or concentration, projection or suggestion. This is, of course, most manifest in the more obviously representative arts, such as painting and sculpture. But even the *plein-air* school, who forsook the studio to paint with the eye on the object, and to paint sunlight itself—did not do this. How they exaggerated their impressions, and recklessly took to subterfuges! Nowadays even the effect of the real is often abandoned; the super-real and abstract or symbolical is striven for instead; and here most clearly of all is apparent the interplay among the arts, or among the arts and philosophy. Relativity—subjectivism —has taken possession of our minds—that is, those of artists and coteries—not only in metaphysics and ethics, but also in all forms of expression, to the point that expression is no longer true to its name. In verse and prose, in painting and sculpture we have sound or image, form or color, with rhythm, perhaps, but without content, logic, or sense. So far indeed has this artificiality gone that not every school but almost every individual genius demands a special interpreter, not for after ages, but even for this. *Thus* our arts reflect our age!

17

In fact, so well do the various arts of any one epoch agree that for most of us they *are* the period; and our thought, as often it does, unconsciously moves in a circle. The material of actual history being so manifold and heterogeneous that it does not lend itself to forming a concept or mental image, to arriving at the unity after which our simple minds aspire, the age of Louis XIV becomes for us that of the dramas and romances, the palaces of Perrault and the churches of Mansard, the paintings of Claude and the Poussins; everywhere there is classical logic, refinement, and harmony; and the age of Charles and James, in turn, is that of heroic rimed tragedy and the Comedy of Manners! Thereupon, having thus constructed our notion of the epoch, we are delighted to see how well each art reflects it. And where are we then but where we were before?[51]

Here is the fallacy on the grand scale, much affected in our histories of literature and civilization today, where fact and fiction intertwine. In the instances just given half of the evidence is ignored—the moral and pious literature in England, the popular realism in France. But the more serious and insidious matter is the breaking down of the boundaries between life and art, the merging or confusing of the two sets of traditions, which, as Mr. Abercrombie observes in the passage cited above, page 47, are related but not the same. These literary histories are Taine brought up to date; but Taine was begotten by Michelet, and Michelet by Vico; with which last, it seems, arose that perilous notion of a people as an organism, possessed of a soul. There are books nowadays such as *The Soul of Spain—of Italy—*and the

---

[51]In this paragraph I am making free with an idea expressed by a foreign critic in a letter from which, without his permission, I do not presume to quote.

figurative phrase has indeed its advantages. The biological analogy serves an expository purpose. Moreover, Taine and his predecessors did a great work in enlarging the scope of history, breaking down the artificial barriers of knowledge, and laying bare hitherto-unperceived relations of a nation's activity. Of some of these we have taken notice above. But manifestly a people is not an organism, has not a mind or soul; and with our present knowledge, at any rate, there is no means of integrating a people's achievements in industry and commerce, social discipline and government, science and philosophy, language, literature, and art. Those who have attempted to do this have at the best made literature, not history or criticism. The valuable things they have said are incidental,—vivid appreciations of national traits or of literary qualities. When, speaking of the Renaissance, Taine says that then, in their exuberance, men "made a holiday of life, a splendid show, so like a picture that it fostered painting in Italy, so like a piece of acting that it produced the drama in England," he furnishes the reader with a convenient summary, no more. The reasoning will not bear inspection. Renaissance Italy, with its endless strife and turmoil, its factions and intrigues, lent itself to drama, if anything, more than the life in England did; even present-day Italy, with its gestures and outcries, is more dramatic than present-day England on the streets; and if the Dutch, with a national temper and a climate (which also Taine considers) much the same as the English, could have a school of painting, why could not the English too? The immediate reason for drama in England and for painting in Italy at the Renaissance is that there was a continuous popular dramatic tradition in England, and a pictorial one in Italy, down from the Middle Ages; for great art, of any sort, arises only when the art has been long and widely practiced and favored; but the ultimate reason why, in either country, it should happen to have been a tradition in drama or painting and not the other or still another art, is simply undiscoverable. And as for Taine's Renaissance Englishmen, upon whom he dilates, a prey to brutal impulse and to gloomy fantasy, they are derived from *Tamburlaine* and

Hamlet. In French tragedy there were horrors, too, as in the Greek, but behind the scenes. How long that myth of the flesh-and-blood Englishman brooding over a skull has lasted in France (though in the time of Hugo and George Sand it was really a Frenchman)! And myths are dangerous. At two notable and momentous junctures such popular misconceptions, disseminated by the press, have played a part in leading whole nations to disaster. With much reason M. Baldensperger[52] judges that in 1870 the French, depending on what they had heard or read of the Germans and their literature or upon what Frenchmen had written about them, went to war with the Germans thinking them sentimental dreamers. That he wrote in 1913. In 1914 the eminent French critic may have had at least the savage satisfaction of seeing that his rule worked both ways, when the Germans, similarly misled, went to war with the French as with frivolous degenerates. In 1939 they were in some respects better informed, alas! and so in 1941 were the Japanese.

(But not concerning themselves, and history and biology together have lately been playing havoc. Both the fascist and also the communist dictators have, in their violence, internal and external, been fulfilling an "historical mission." It used to be *Dieu* [or *Allah*] *le veut:* destiny it is still, but disguised and embellished. Crudely and arbitrarily conceived, history furnishes the general and plenary justification; and as men of destiny Hitler and Mussolini proclaim themselves, like Napoleon. To their cry, moreover, their peoples duly respond; the more ignorant, through mass-contagion, the instinct to follow a Leader, or the crusading religious fervor that in them lingers on, but the more cultivated find it easier to join in because history has become the form or pattern of their thought. They feel as well as think in terms of rise and fall, development and decay, evolution and revolution, physical life and death. The myth-making biological analogy is directly and literally·applied to movements political and social, even religious and artistic. A nation has not only a soul but even a body—is "young" or

[52]*Littérature,* p. 201.

"old," is "healthy" or "degenerate," and therefore is called either to rule or serve. Survival of the fittest! Just so, any organization is an organism; and art is only a "function" of the people, reflecting the state of health, the vigor or decadence, but, in the changes, has a life and death of its own. Long after writing this chapter I have come upon Mr. Lionel Abel's discussion, "History, Snobbery, and Criticism," in which he shows how contemporary critics have taken up this point of view. "When attacking a belief, tradition, or ideal, instead of setting forth their reasons for disliking it, they simply declare it is dead." The "times" are against it, and particularly if it does not make for revolution.

"Seen from a perspective of years the process is as logical as the growth of a tree: one might say that the Dada movement and its ending were both foreshadowed in the letters of Gustave Flaubert." According to this interpretation of the literary events of the last eighty years, the will to create works of art for the disinterested joy of so doing is dead and done with. By what technique of discovery has Mr. Cowley arrived at this important bit of news? (The *Nation,* April 25, 1934.)

Hegel said there was no philosophy but the history of philosophy. Is there no art, then, but the history of art, it, too, predestined, the art being a history itself? If so, we are caught in a web. No longer is literature an "escape"; no longer is it a consolation, whether for one writing or reading, *de ne pouvoir vivre.*)

And if the Gallic, the German, the English mind is so unascertainable, what shall be said of the American, which may be presumed to be still in the making? But much has been said, for all that. I have not read it, but if Mr. De Voto, in an article "How Not to Write History," in *Harper's* magazine, 1933, is fair to the writers, they now confuse literature with history far more unhappily than ever did Taine. They introduce the new psychological, sociological and economic notions, with the purpose, indeed, of simplifying the problem—they too have "a hunger for unity"—but with the result of complicating or muddling it. One writer finds occupational rhythms in American speech and writing; and would have it that in his Gettysburg Address Lincoln fell unconsciously into the stride of a man walking a woodland path with an ax on his shoulder. And presently the writer finds there a very different thing, even the rhythm of the rail-splitting, the upswing and the downward stroke, sadly misquoting in order to make it out. Another "reduces the complex and inharmonious class and sectional interests of three centuries to a Marxian Class Struggle"; and has much to say of a "bourgeois ideology" which, in America, where according to Mr. De Voto there has been no bourgeoisie, or if any, not one but fifty of them, can have no meaning. Still others pursue other "phantasms," such as the Puritan, the frontiersman, the individualist, instead of the already much-belabored bourgeois, and explain the common course of history and literature by one or more of these. Concerning one writer, who makes out frontier society to be infantile in its homicidal impulses, its mental development, its humor, its tastes, interests, and preferences, Mr. De Voto exclaims, "Observe with what assured ease the 'critic' reduces to unity the greatest confusion of cultures, nationalities, and races in modern history, diffused over one of the largest national areas and most diversified geographies in the world, subject to change and circumstance through three centuries!" Elsewhere the same "critic" speaks of the frontier as inhabited by a race of "obstinate individualists." And this logical irresponsibility Mr. De Voto blames upon the assumption of the role of historian by the literary critic, "to whom impreciseness of idea is a virtue and a generalized sentiment is much better than a fact," and "success is attainable by sustained thinking." The slur is not undeserved, though, as we have seen above, the historians share the blame. The difference between these writers and Taine, apparently, lies chiefly in the nature of the mind that does the thinking.

18

It is loose thinking, in any case. To this we are rather accustomed, in our profession; yet the main trouble is not with the reason but the imagination. As historians, manifestly, but as critics—readers and spectators—still more, we literary scholars are simply not what we ought to be. Lamb, though, as I have shown elsewhere, he in isolating Restoration comedy went too far, is, in his strictures, just and sound (the belletristic trifler of his caliber is more likely to be than scholars are):

We have no such middle emotions as dramatic interests left. We see a stage libertine playing his loose pranks of two hours' duration, and of no after consequence, with the severe eyes which inspect real vices with their bearings upon two worlds. We are spectators to a plot or intrigue (not reducible in life to the point of strict morality) and take it all for truth. We substitute a real for a dramatic person, and judge him accordingly. . . . What is *there* transacting, by no modification is made to affect us in any other manner than the same events or characters would do in our relationships of life. We carry our fireside concerns to the theater with us. We do not go thither, like our ancestors, to escape from the pressure of reality, so much as to confirm our experience of it; to make assurance double, and take a bond of fate.

What Elia is contending with more particularly is Victorian morality (for that came in long before the Queen), shortly to find its definitive expression, in connection with the seventeenth-century Comedy of Manners, on the lips of Macaulay; and, also, nineteenth-century sympathy, which would stifle the immemorial marble-hearted laughter of the comic stage. And if neither the one nor the other troubles much the learned or the exquisite critic today, especially when confronted with our earlier literature, still he is open to Elia's fundamental reproach. Though he can laugh at the cheating of the miserly or usurious and the cuckolding of the jealous or the fatuous, or in response to the audacious witticisms of the gallant or coquette; still he is not free, not truly critical. He reads the text as he does (and these too not quite truly) comedies of Shaw or Granville-Barker, of Becque or Philip Barry. He takes it for a criticism of life, a study. Thus, despite his enlightenment, he commits not only one but both of the fundamental errors of criticism:—the failure to enter into the spirit of the author and respect his purpose; and the failure to distinguish between illusion and delusion, fiction and a copy of fact. Nay, has not Lamb himself touched on them both, in passing? "But when you read it," (and I leave, somewhat after Elia's own fashion, the conclusion in abeyance)—"but when you read it in the spirit with which such playful selections and specious combinations rather than strict *metaphrases* of nature should be taken. . . ."[53]

Nor is the trouble confined to comedy, though, to be sure, I can only hint at the matter here.[54] Such literalism has disturbed the equilibrium—has broken the illusion—of tragedy as well, particularly Shakespeare's. If a "strict metaphrase of nature," Emilia, in not suspecting Iago, must be taken to be stupid, as she is by Bradley; or, in not betraying him, to be disloyal to her mistress, as she is by Schlegel. Either conclusion is contrary to the dramatist's manifest intention, though the latter is more so. But if stupid she be, then Othello, Cassio, and Desdemona are stupid too, and even if she sees through the villain, still they are stupid in comparison; and thereupon, in either case, what is perhaps the greatest of tragedies becomes another (though horrible) comedy of *All Fools*. Not before the last scene is the shrewd but stoutly devoted waiting-woman, as she gasps out, "My husband!" three times over, permitted to "tumble"; and this is in order that the fiction of the impenetrableness of his mask of villainy may be preserved, and that the most poignantly passionate (though not the least improbable) of situations—a noble soul made jealous without the base inclination or a good reason, either,—may be secured. Here, again, are "selections and specious combinations," though far from "playful" in purpose or effect. Here, again, is not life as we know it, but simplified and concentrated, composed and projected; and this, to move us more powerfully to terror and pity, as in *The Country Wife* or *The Way of the World* to laughter, than life itself can do.

It is a structural matter. If Emilia suspected Iago or any-

[53]The essay preceding "On Some of the Old Actors," with regard to a passage in Congreve.

[54]I discuss it at length in *Art and Artifice in Shakespeare*, chap. ii.

one else did, or if anyone besides his cat's-paw Roderigo knew that he had a grievance, there would be an end to our wholehearted sympathy and admiration for Othello, Desdemona, and Cassio, and a collapse for the play. Here we have Aristotle's "impossibility," which is "to serve the ends of poetry itself . . . to make the effect of the work more striking"; Dryden's "reason [which] suffers itself to be so hoodwinked that it may better enjoy the pleasures of the fiction"; Thomas Hardy's Art, which is "the secret of how to produce by a false thing the effect of a true."[55]

The effect is produced, he says, by "disproportioning realities, to show more clearly the features that matter in those realities." With the result that years after he had written his last novel he declared that at the beginning of every new one, were he still writing them, he would have placed the legend: "Understand that however true this book may be in essence, in fact it is utterly untrue." He disclaimed fidelity to Wessex, and insisted that Casterbridge was not Dorchester but "a dream-place that never was outside an irresponsible book." Minterne, likewise, is not Little Hintock—"I myself do not know where Little Hintock is . . . It has features which were to be found fifty years ago in the hamlets of Hermitage, etc. . . . The topographers you mention are merely guessers and are wrong."[56]

So with the situations and the characters. Life, as M. Mauriac, another great novelist, says, furnishes the occasion, "a point of departure, which permits the novelist to venture in a different direction."[57] And "for the characters," says M. Duhamel, another prominent member of the craft, writing of the vain efforts to identify the originals, "the true novelist has not one, but twenty—but a hundred —models. He himself is his most perceptible model, even if he is making ghosts, and even if he is making monsters.

[55]Florence Hardy, *Early Life of Thomas Hardy* (1928), p. 284.

[56]The material of this paragraph is taken from Miss Gladys Watson's *Thomas Hardy: the Reflections of a Novelist,* a master's thesis at the University of Minnesota.

[57]Edmond Jaloux, as cited above.

. . . The work, in fine, is so far from the models that it is truly free of them. The models are necessary, and always thrown into the shade."[58] And I wonder whether he is not echoing Molière in the *Impromptu de Versailles,* where he says, in the words which Coquelin *aîné* does not, like the literary researchers, discredit or ignore:

. . . que son dessein [Molière's own] *est de peindre les moeurs sans vouloir toucher aux personnes, et que tous les personnages qu'il représente sont des personnages en l'air, et des fantômes proprement, qu'il habille à sa fantaisie, pour réjouir les spectateurs; qu'il seroit bien fâché d'y avoir jamais marqué qui que ce soit; et que, si quelque chose étoit capable de le dégoûter de faire des comédies, c'étoient les ressemblances qu'on y vouloit toujours trouver. . . . Et, en effet, je trouve qu'il a raison; car pourquoi vouloir, je vous prie, appliquer tous ses gestes et toutes ses paroles, et chercher à lui faire des affaires en disant hautement: il joue un tel, lorsque ce sont des choses qui peuvent convenir à cent personnes! Comme l'affaire de la comédie est de représenter en général tous les défauts des hommes, et principalement des hommes de notre siècle, il est impossible à Molière de faire aucun caractère qui ne rencontre quelqu'un dans le monde. (sc. iii.)*

Now these unrealities are given reality, the novelists agree, by an individual tone or accent. So the character is one—so it holds together. But it generally has no separate life of its own. It holds together along with the other characters of the story, in the world of that story and not another. There may be no poised, reciprocating and self-supporting structure of impossibilities as in *Othello;* but there is an animating spirit or atmosphere, a system, a congruity and harmony, of ideas and sentiments, in which the character belongs and from which, like a branch, it cannot without damage be cut. "If Pecksniff were transplanted into *The Golden Bowl* he would become extinct," says Mr.

---

[58]Cf. Mr. Eliot on Wordsworth's emotion recollected in tranquillity (*Selected Essays,* Harcourt, Brace, 1932, p. 10): "It is a concentration, and a new thing resulting from the concentration, of a very great number of experiences which to the practical and active person would not seem to be experiences at all."

MacCarthy as quoted above, "and how incredible would 'the Dove' be in the pages of *Martin Chuzzlewit*." And if one character is not substantive enough to be removed from one book into another how much less can he be brought for the purposes of identification into the strange and variable air that we and all other men have breathed!

1942

CHAPTER V

Kent and Gloster

THE TWO gray-bearded noblemen Kent and Gloster, who are grouped together as friends themselves and faithful followers of their ruined king, admirably illustrate Shakespeare's methods of characterization. If with the critic, as I think, the ear, not the reason, should be the judge, it is because it was so with the dramatist before him. He must, like Dickens, have, in imagination, heard every syllable each of his persons utters. There is little or nothing of what could be called psychology. There are, instead, Shakespeare's opportunism and impressionism, his conventionalism and plastic poetic power. At the beginning, for the situation, Kent is still more tactless and uncompliant than Cordelia; and later, as to accompany and serve his master he puts on disguise, he must needs cloak his character too. For a while, like Hamlet, he must play a part, and in a measure be a different man. And at the beginning, for the situation, Gloster hearkens to his illegitimate and landless son, whom, because of long absence, he cannot much know or love, to the detriment of Edgar, whom he both loves and knows; and he likewise must, so far, be a different man. Yet (though not internally—in point of motive—or even ex-

ternally—in point of conduct) they are consistent characters. They are, except at the above moments, alive and
appealing: they have life by virtue of the dramatist's immediate imaginative power, as revealed in trait and speech.

Both noblemen illustrate a virtue and a passion now
fairly extinct among us: that of feudal loyalty and devotion
to the sovereign, not only as a great person but as the State.
Kent is both the finer exemplification of these qualities
and the greater artistic success. With him the situation does
not so much trouble the impression of the character. Even
at the beginning he is not his real self as he interferes so
emphatically and insistently when the King turns against
Cordelia, but he is attractive and as much his real self as
he can well be. It is like him to speak up to save the King
from his own undertaking and to save from his wrath Cordelia; but it is not like him to beard his King, or talk back
to him:

> LEAR. Now, by Apollo,—
> KENT.   Now, by Apollo, king,
> Thou swear'st thy gods in vain.

Yet it is like him enough to begin with "Good my liege,"
and thus to continue:

> Royal Lear,
> Whom I have ever honour'd as my king,
> Lov'd as my father, as my master follow'd,
> As my great patron thought on in my prayers,—
> LEAR. The bow is bent and drawn, make from the shaft.
> KENT. Let it fall rather, though the fork invade
> The region of my heart . . .

In him, as in Cordelia, consistency goes as far as the requirements of an extreme situation permit.

Disguised as Caius, he serves his master (for the purposes
of the situation, again) no better, tripping up Oswald at
Goneril's house, and beating him at Gloster's, and thus, in
loyalty to Lear, only giving provocation to his enemies. But
soliloquizing in the stocks, and above all bestirring himself
on the heath, where, amid Lear's distractions and distresses,

he, though still incognito, can lay aside his borrowed character, he is himself altogether, the finer nature partly made known to us in Scene 1. Mostly it appears in matter-of-fact doings and sayings. How his importunate concern and devotion find expression in the mere repetition and rhythm as he beseeches the storm-beaten King:

> Here is the place, my lord; good my lord, enter.
> The tyranny of the open night's too rough
> For nature to endure.

LEAR.   Let me alone.

KENT. Good my lord, enter here.

LEAR.   Wilt break, my heart?

KENT. I had rather break my own. Good my lord, enter.

There must be a comma, as Professor Francis Child thought, after "wilt break"; Kent misinterprets him intentionally, or unintentionally; and not only his reply but the cadence in "For nature to endure" shows how much his own heart is in the matter. "Though the fork invade the region of my heart," he said at the beginning. And it is the same person (still by the ear and the imagination, not by reason and analysis, do we know him, like the poet himself before us) that in a moment, as the Fool runs out, crying:

> Come not in here, nuncle; here's a spirit.
> Help me, help me!

simply says to him,

> Give me thy hand. Who's there?

He comforts and quiets him as if he were a child. And so we know him when, as the King, raving on about the cause of Edgar's calamity, bursts out:

> Now all the plagues that in the pendulous air
> Hang fated o'er men's faults, light on thy daughters!

the Earl at last interposes, in reverent condescension and anxious reassurance:

> He hath no daughters, sir.

That, I think, is Kent's finest speech. It is conversational simplicity and objectivity itself, such as the modern dramatist seeks for but seldom achieves. It is tenderness and reticence mingled, as in Cordelia.

All through the experience on the heath, in the hovel, and in the house, Kent is solicitous for the King's welfare and comfort. But his feelings appear almost wholly in his ministrations and in his mere remarking of the changes in the King, as when he says, at intervals, to Gloster:

> Importune him once more to go, my lord;
> His wits begin to unsettle. . . .

All the power of his wits have given way to his impatience.

The gods reward your kindness!

Here, sir; but trouble him not, his wits are gone.

Yet along with the King the faithful Fool is in his thoughts as, warned by Gloster, he gets them under way towards Dover:

> Come, help to bear thy master;
> Thou must not stay behind.

It is here as if he took his hand again. For they have been comrades together, both in fealty and in folly, as several times before this the Fool himself has intimated:

> KENT. Where learned you this, Fool?
> FOOL. Not i' the stocks, fool.

And, like the other, *this* "fool will stay, and let the wise man fly"!

Afterwards we see him only in talk with the Gentleman, about Lear and Cordelia, and at their recognition, and at the end. In all these situations he is unmistakable, but in the last two he is finer. Here he is still more reticent than the lady—with instinctive propriety he steps into the background. "Kind and dear princess," he murmurs, as if in benediction, after her first appeal to her father, before he wakes. And when the bewildered King inquires, "Am I in

France?" again, as in the hovel, and in words that are
almost an echo, he reassures him:

> In your own kingdom, sir.

That, while the King and Cordelia are on the stage, is all.

The ties of affection and gratitude binding Kent, Cordelia, the Fool, and Gloster together in their common devotion to the King, are among the most delicate touches in the play. And it is appropriate that Kent should meet again his *other* comrade in folly, though only after Gloster's death, and then only in report upon the stage. But the account of it is unsatisfactory, as Edgar tells how, before the combat, while he was lamenting his father's death, Kent broke in upon him:

> He fasten'd on my neck, and bellow'd out
> As he'd burst heaven; threw him on my father;
> Told the most piteous tale of Lear and him
> That ever ear received. . . .

Unsatisfactory, for I cannot but think this a case of Shakespeare's not knowing, as Dryden says, when to stop. It is well that the scene is not presented—but then it would have been a different scene! It is a remarkable fact that such instances of bad taste, like the Gentleman's account to Kent of Cordelia's grief at hearing of her father's distresses:

> those happy smilets
> That play'd on her ripe lip seem'd not to know
> What guests were in her eyes; which parted thence,
> As pearls from diamonds dropp'd;

or Octavius' account (in apostrophe) of Antony's hardihood:

> thou didst drink
> The stale of horses, and the gilded puddle
> Which beasts did cough at . . .
>   on the Alps
> It is reported thou didst eat strange flesh,
> Which some did die to look on . . .

that these, I say, are descriptive, incidental to the action, and beyond its magic circle, the poet endeavoring to hold the attention by extremity and extravagance. Certainly Kent did not bellow, despite the fact that one great critic has even declared the phrase felicitous.

It is not with such a voice, but with his own, that, as near the end he next enters, he speaks the words:

> I am come
> To bid my king and master aye good night;
> Is he not here?

Or as, the King coming in with Cordelia, dead, in his arms, he gasps out:

> Is this the promis'd end? [The *dies irae*]

Or as, recognizing that the King's hopes and efforts to revive his daughter are in vain, and kneeling before him, he offers consolation and does homage:

> O my good master!

The stage direction is Theobald's, one of his inspired emendations: it is thus that by speech and gesture the pent-up feelings of his long, self-effacing service would find utterance. But he is too late for more than partial recognition; and with infinite propriety, as the change comes over the King, it is Kent, not another, that pronounces farewell:

> Break, heart; I prithee, break. . . .

The words bring memories.

2

Gloster says much more, but has less to say. He is of a looser grain, a coarser fiber, not, like Kent, fine, firm, and reticent. His gross way of speaking to the Earl of Edmund's birth in his presence grates upon us; and his harkening later to the slander is, in comparison with Othello's, so little prepared for that he can scarcely escape the charge of a willing credulity. But through it all we see that, though not a noble or lofty character, he is a kindly and true-hearted one; though not a hero, is the stuff that heroes may be made of.

He does not mean to wound Edmund; and not recognizing that he has done so, he turns to him like the good father (as well as true friend) that he evidently is:

> Do you know this noble gentleman, Edmund?
> ED. No, my lord.
> GLOS. My lord of Kent. Remember him hereafter as my honourable friend.

Not clear-sighted, he has no suspicion of a motive for the slander when it comes. And Shakespeare makes his acceptance of it more plausible by his old age and his superstition, his fumbling intelligence and his concern about the "late eclipses in the sun and moon." These phenomena, he thinks, explain Edgar's conduct as well as the trouble between the King and his daughters. What wins us, however, is his manifest affection for Edgar, his grief at the treason, and his friendly old-fellow's manner of talk:

> My son Edgar! Had he a hand to write this? A heart and brain to breed it in? . . . He cannot be such a monster to his father, that so tenderly and entirely loves him.

> O! Madam, my old heart is crack'd, it's crack'd!

> O! lady, lady, shame would have it hid.

> I know not, madam; 'tis too bad, too bad.

There we have him in his upset condition, his grief and his affectionateness, with the senile repetitions to express them. He is much given to "alack!" the old man's mournful, deprecating ejaculation:

> Alack, Alack! Edmund, I like not this unnatural dealing,

as he says to him later. Lear and Kent too are old; yet his repetitions are not like those of Lear, insistent and vehement, nor of Kent, heartfelt and importunate; but are those of decrepitude, as if he were wagging his head. And his thoughts move somewhat like those of a Chekhov character, in eddies. In the second scene he enters ruminating:

> Kent banish'd thus! And France in choler parted!
> And the king gone tonight! Subscrib'd his power!
> Confin'd to exhibition! All this done
> Upon the gad!

Yet he goes off the stage, after the terrible slanderous disclosure, with the apparently, superficially, irrelevant remark:

> And the noble and true-hearted Kent banish'd! his offence, honesty! 'Tis strange!

He contrasts, as we have intimated, with both Kent and Lear. Though suffering like his sovereign from ingratitude, he pours out no such torrent of grief or rage. His heart and mind are of smaller dimensions; his thoughts and feelings have no such profundity or variety. The experience is bitter, and he does not forget it; he is constantly reminded of it in his concern for the King and amid his sufferings in consequence; but it does not bring about an upheaval in his whole nature.

And in the method and manner of his service to the King he contrasts as strikingly with his friend. He is not alert and resolute, direct yet reticent; that is, not reticent as Kent is after the first scene. Unlike the other, he is undiscerning, and fails to detect the iniquity of Cornwall, Regan, and her sister, along with that of Edmund. He is only deprecatory, conciliatory. He beseeches Cornwall not to put the disguised Kent in the stocks:

> His fault is much, and the good king, his master,
> Will check him for't;

and he fears "the king must take it ill." Left alone with the man, he then says, quite sincerely:

> I am sorry for thee, friend; 'tis the duke's pleasure,
> Whose disposition, all the world well knows,
> Will not be rubb'd nor stopp'd; I'll entreat for thee.

And, as he goes out, he mutters, with characteristic reiteration and headshaking:

> The duke's to blame in this; 'twill be ill taken.

When the King appears he says much the same:

> My dear lord,
> You know the fiery quality of the duke;

and that not appeasing the King, at the words "bid him come forth and hear me" he mumbles goodheartedly, as he obeys,

> I would have all well betwixt you.

That is his note, not Kent's. During the great quarrel which ensues he says nothing—Kent does not either, but as a servant, just freed from the stocks, he has no right or occasion—yet Gloster too follows the King out in his rage, as titular host or as of his party, and on his return deplores the situation:

> Alack! the night comes on, and the high winds
> Do sorely ruffle; for many miles about
> There's scarce a bush.

It is in the same mood and tone and gesture that he reappears three scenes later:

> Alack! alack! Edmund, I like not this unnatural dealing,

and he complains. Lover of peace that he is, he does not hesitate thereupon to side with the King and succor him; yet there is something not only of the wiseacre but of the worldly-wise man in his directions and injunctions to his son:

> Go to; say you nothing. There is division between the
> dukes, and a worse matter than that. . . . These injuries
> the king now bears will be reveng'd home; there's part
> of a power already footed; we must incline to the king.
> I will seek him and privily relieve him; go you and
> maintain talk with the duke that my charity be not of

> him perceived. If he ask for me, I am ill and gone to bed.

Nevertheless he manfully and truthfully adds:

> If I die for it, as no less is threaten'd me, the king, my old master, must be relieved. There is strange things toward, Edmund; pray you, be careful.

How this exit resembles those cited above, in its recurrent rumination and misgiving; and this expression of his devotion to the King, those of his affection for Edgar! They are alike in prose, and that looser rhythm is in keeping with his vein of sentiment, less fine and vibrant than Kent's

> I'd rather break my own. Good my lord, enter.

> He hath no daughters, sir.

The difference in the ring is in the metal. Gloster, indeed, keeps his word, and has to pay the penalty for it as Kent does not; but now he is not expecting to do so, and his utterance is simple and appealing rather than gallant and heroic. You feel like patting the old fellow on the back—till afterwards.

For he rises to the occasion, and steadfastly holds the perilous course that he has chosen. As he busies himself to save the King, he steadily comes nearer to being an heroic and tragic figure—a companion figure, not only by his devotion in the face of danger but also by his own experience of filial ingratitude:

> Our flesh and blood, my lord, is grown so vile
> That it doth hate what gets it.

And the parallels and contrasts between him and both the King and Kent stand out clearer as he confides in the latter, still not knowing him:

> Ah, that good Kent;
> He said it would be thus, poor banish'd man!
> Thou say'st the king grows mad; I'll tell thee, friend,
> I am almost mad myself. I had a son. . . .

The speech is needed not only to bring out their comradeship in desperate devotion but, like Gloster's previous expressions of affection and concern for Kent (or Caius), to deepen our regard for him and also preserve his identity.

So far, however, does this tragic change and transfiguration proceed within him that I confess to some difficulty in recognizing the homely old fellow we knew, particularly after the blinding. Him I cannot believe capable of the speech:

> As flies to wanton boys are we to the gods;
> They kill us for their sport.

The image is matter-of-fact enough for him; but the sentiment is worthy of Prometheus, the rhythm worthy of Hamlet. Nor does he seem capable of this other speech:

> There is a cliff, whose high and bending head
> Looks fearfully in the confinèd deep.
> Bring me but to the very brim of it. . . .

That high, anthropomorphic imagination, with its metrical realization of the dizzy leap, is worthy of Lear or Othello. The maundering graybeard, with his rambling prose, has vanished. Yet, even in heroics, Shakespeare contrives to keep something of him, his "alack," his "the king my master," his senile repetition and homely ways. "Take up thy master," he cries, before this, in his anxiety as he comes in on his last errand: "Take up, take up . . . Come, come away." Here, as before this, his manner is less refined and more familiar than Kent's. Even at the blinding he is like himself, as he says of Lear:

> Yet, poor old heart, he holp the heavens to rain,

a bit of kindly familiarity to which the other earl would not have presumed. As Professor Bradley notices, the latter never addresses the madman without the old terms of respect, "your grace," "my lord," "sir"; and the reader himself will have noticed above the difference between his and Gloster's use of the same phrase concerning his sovereign. It is "the *good* king my master," and "the king my *old* master," fairly forgetting the distance between them. And Kent disguised as an attendant he always addresses as "friend," like the friendly, homely fellow that he is. Perhaps he is his superstitious self of the second scene now as he accepts Edgar's tale of the demon, with eyes like two moons and a thousand noses, that had tempted him to take the leap. Certainly he is himself in the pathetic simplicity of a devoted vassal as he meets the King in the field, decked with flowers. That scene is an "obligatory" one. Tragedy requires that Gloster, who has lost his eyes to save him, should meet the King in this condition; that the King should only half know him, as at the last he does Kent, without realizing what either has done for him; and the effect of all this is heightened as Gloster never thinks of regretting the price that he has paid. This is like him; and so, at the end of the scene, is his breaking out, irrelevantly to what Edgar has meanwhile been doing and saying: "The king is mad." That is the outcome, that is what sticks in his mind—and he himself is not.

How different, though, this irrelevance from those instances cited above, in particular, his exit in the second scene. There we have the helpless, garrulous recoil of the mind upon its preoccupation; here Gloster, after the King's disappearance and Edgar's fight with Oswald, utters what has in his mind all along been uppermost. There Gloster is something of a "character" part; here a tragic one. There his rumination comes to nothing; here it points the tragic parallel and contrast. This is not in the price which he has vainly paid but in the fact that he is not mad himself:

> how stiff is my vile sense,
> That I stand up, and have ingenious feeling
> Of my huge sorrows!

Such a change in a role from a lower level to a higher, from something verging on the comic to the tragic, is not without counterpart in Shakespeare. It is to be found in Cleopatra as well; but in her, as I have elsewhere shown, with happier effect. There is no reason why a character should not, with cause sufficient, rise above himself to higher things. The only question is whether he is still the same person. Cleopatra, fired by Antony's example, and on her mettle against Caesar, is.[1] She keeps her vanity and amorousness, her spirit of intrigue and cunning, her tricks of speech and her humor, to the end. Gloster, as we have seen, keeps all his good points but almost none of his faults, a few external mannerisms but not the deeper-seated ones; in his suffering and his simple human relations he fairly seems himself, but in his utterances concerning life and fate he seems to pass a little beyond his range.

This, however, is a minor matter. In both role and method of presentation the two earls are alike; and such pairs in drama are seldom distinguishable. This pair is. Yet the two men are alike in age and rank, in kindliness and devotion, in the nature of the service that they render to the King and in their friendliness to each other. Moreover, the impression of the character is somewhat troubled and disturbed (except as we allow for these) by the requirements of the situation; the characters are not presented by analysis, or what may be called a psychology. What makes the two men distinct and unmistakable is the contrasting individuality of their traits and speech. Each for himself has the semblance and the accents of a man.

1934

[1]Cf. my essay on Cleopatra, *Poets and Playwrights* (1930).

CHAPTER VI

Shakespeare's Jew

SHYLOCK AGAIN? But I shall endeavor to forget what I have written about him, and others have written about him, and be for the time the simple auditor and spectator whom Shakespeare sought to interest and move. I cannot turn into a London citizen at the Globe or the Curtain; but I can rely upon my eyes and ears and everyday wits, as he did and Shakespeare expected him to do, instead of examining my own consciousness or bowing to that of my predecessors.

> SHY. Three thousand ducats; well.
> BASS. Ay, sir, for three months.
> SHY. For three months; well.
> BASS. For the which, as I told you, Antonio shall be bound.
> SHY. Antonio shall become bound; well.
> BASS. May you stead me? Will you pleasure me? Shall I know your answer?
> SHY. Three thousand ducats for three months, and Antonio bound.
> BASS. Your answer to that.
> SHY. Antonio is a góod màn.

There has been no preliminary remark except Antonio's word to Bassanio in scene 1,

Therefore go forth,
Try what my credit can in Venice do;

in scene 2 we have been in Belmont; and the Jew's first
four words arouse us. It is a fine instance of an abrupt
beginning that on second thoughts is not so abrupt; and
what does the moneylender mean by his echoing responses,
and especially by the final speech, not echoing or echoed, or
apparently relevant?

That he is a Jew we see by his beard and gaberdine, probably also by his high hat, red hair, big nose, and foreign
accent. Is he, then, doubtful of the security, or intent upon
a bargain, or now that for once he has the whip hand, tan-
talizing his suitor? But in a moment our curiosity shifts a
bit and focuses upon Antonio. "Good," spoken cautiously,
not admiringly, is a professional word, we either perceive
or presently learn. Antonio is "good" in the sense that a
"risk" is so pronounced by an insurance agent, a book (another risk) by a publisher; but the import of this Bassanio
is not businesslike enough, or disinterested enough, to discover. (Though it is not wholly to be explained by character and situation, we shall see.)

BASS. Have you heard any imputation to the contrary?
SHY. Ho, no, no, no, no. My meaning in saying he is
a good man is to have you understand me that he is
sufficient. Yet his means are in supposition: he hath an
argosy bound to Tripolis, another to the Indies; I understand, moreover, upon the Rialto, he hath a third at
Mexico, a fourth for England, and other ventures he
hath, squand'red abroad. But ships are but boards,
sailors but men; there be land-rats and water-rats, water-
thieves and land-thieves, I mean pirates, and then there
is the peril of waters, winds, and rocks. The man is,
notwithstanding, sufficient. Three thousand ducats; I
think I may take his bond.

Concerned for the security, he yet thinks he may take the
bond: he has in mind, then, something else. Interest, any
sort of which was at that time "usury"? He keeps his counsel, and asks for none. "Be assured you may"—"I will be
assured I may; and that I may be assured, I will bethink

me." No ordinary bargain this, and he enjoys it as perhaps
never before. "May I speak with Antonio?" Bassanio invites
him to "dine with us," but at that the old man rears his
head: "I will buy with you, sell with you, talk with you,
walk with you, and so following; but I will not eat with
you, drink with you, nor pray with you. What news on the
Rialto?" He is precision and decision itself, in matters not
now of importance; and he pointedly changes the subject.

In comes Antonio; and thereupon Shylock has an aside
in which he lets the audience get a glimpse of his hand,
his heart. "If I can catch him once upon the hip!" Such is
his purpose—though we see not the whole of it, and nothing of his plan. Even this much one of our present-day
dramatists would not have disclosed, nor have vouchsafed
him a soliloquy. He would have kept the audience guessing
to the end of the scene, after the proposal of the "merry
bond": he would have forced his audience to think rather
than to feel. Shakespeare chooses the middle course—makes
them think first, then feel, but upon feeling he is more intent. He does not expect too much of them, and insures his
effects: he throws a light both backwards and before. So
we begin to attribute a deeper import to the Jew's interest
in Antonio's ventures, perceiving that the interests of lender
and borrower are not, as they are ordinarily supposed and
are now pretended to be, identical. Less puzzled, we are
more concerned.

Had the lender's further purpose remained longer or
more completely a mystery, it is doubtful if the full impression of the tone and manner of his speech could have been
produced. By his repetitions the Oriental wraps and muffles
his purpose up, keeping the Christians, though not the audience, in the dark. But what does he mean by his hurried
"Ho, no, no, no, no"? It is an effusive disavowal of anything like an imputation; as he presently protests, with an
insinuating inflection and an insidious rhythm, to Antonio
himself when he appears, "I would be friends with you, and
have your love." To Bassanio now he has only given the
merchant's "commercial rating." Good he has not really
called him—"my meaning in saying he is a good man is

to have you understand me that he is sufficient." By his quick reiterated interjections the stately gravity of his demeanor has been broken; and now upon them comes this devious, specious reassurance. But after that sly rising inflection, the rhythm takes a fillip—"Yet his means are in supposition"—and we prick up our ears. The whole sentence breathes uncertainty and expectancy, with perhaps a financier's contempt for a merchant's "venture," a Hebrew's scorn for a Christian's prodigal folly, in the retarded movement of "squand'red abroad." For him the accursèd traffic! Immediately thereupon the pace of his thought is resumed and accelerated, and he runs from one concrete anticipation to another, the metaphors being not of the prettiest! In the midst he pauses to explain one of them—"I mean pirates"; but only to run on again—"and then there is the peril of waters, winds, and rocks." With that he reins himself in; and pursing his lips, pulling at his beard, lifting his eyebrows, duly weighing his syllables, he surprisingly, but not too positively, comes back to the opinion from which he started: "The man is, notwithstanding, sufficient. Three thousand ducats; I think I may take his bond." These are strange ways for business, meant, evidently, to be the crafty and devious ones of them that wear the gaberdine, moneychangers of the Temple.

2

In the subsequent long aside or soliloquy, mentioned above, Shylock gives his reasons for hating Antonio—his being a Christian, his bringing down the rate of interest by lending gratis, his "hatred of our sacred nation, his railing on me, my bargains, and my well-won thrift, which *he* calls interest." All of which reflect upon Shylock, not Antonio, particularly in Shakespeare's and earlier days. Thrift is a word to which the usurer is addicted, and on his lips it has a special meaning. "And thrift is blessing," he presently avers, "if men steal it not"—keep within the law. Interrupted in his ruminations, he replies:

> I am debating of my present store,
> And, by the near guess of my memory,

> I cannot instantly raise up the gross
> Of full three thousand ducats. What of that?
> Tubal, a wealthy Hebrew of my tribe,
> Will furnish me. But soft! how many months
> Do you desire? [*To Ant.*] Rest you fair, good signior;
> Your worship was the last man in our mouths.

A faithful account of his meditations he could hardly be expected to render; but is he any more sincere in saying that he hasn't the money at hand, or that he has forgotten the number of months, than he is in his pretense of not having noticed Antonio before, or in his sentiments of politeness? His memory really is excellent, as appears next moment and frequently afterwards. "Is he yet possess'd how much ye would?" asks Antonio, and before the lender knows it he is himself giving answer:

> Ay, ay, three thousand ducats.
> ANT. And for three months.
> SHY. I had forgot; three months; you told me so.
>   Well then, your bond; and let me see;—but hear you;
>   Methought you said you neither lend nor borrow
>   Upon advantage.

Evidently he is beating about the bush. He has been cogitating upon something else than an ordinary humdrum Rialto bargain; and also, if he has enjoyed his new-found importance with Bassanio, he enjoys it still better with Antonio. For once he has the floor, and he will keep it. "I do never use it," Antonio simply replies to the question about interest, but for Shylock the words contain a reproach:

> When Jacob graz'd his uncle Laban's sheep—

and as he starts the story he raises his hand and rises to his full stature, with a preacher's or a rabbi's zeal, pride, irrelevance, and want of humor. For once the Gentiles cannot choose but hear. Antonio, in the interval, has contrasted with Shylock, as, though a suitor, he has pretended to no politeness: "Shylock," he said coolly, in response to the cringing salaam of "Rest you fair, good signior"; and now he does no more. "Did he take interest?" he inquires; and the usurer falters and stumbles, then stiffens and perseveres:

> No, not take interest, not, as you would say,
> Directly interest. Mark what Jacob did. . . .

There off he goes again, and, in self-justification, complacently repeats the sacred story of patriarchal perfidy. He has interest "on the brain," though this time, for once, he will not take it. He is determined to make his point, though here it has no connection. He has all of a Hebrew's relish for argument. Antonio picks flaws in the precedent, especially on the principle, accepted among the honest and respectable in Shakespeare's day and earlier, that gold and silver, "barren metal," should *not* be made to "breed" like ewes and rams. Thus Shylock's analogy collapses; but after this unsuccessful sortie he has his impregnable practical advantage to fall back upon. As if merely ruminating and deliberating, he covers his retreat by again taking up the tune—

> Three thousand ducats; 'tis a góod roùnd súm.
> Three months from twelve; then, let me see: the rate. . . .

In " 'tis a good round sum" he feels and weighs the bag in his hand.

"Well, Shylock," interrupts Antonio, "shall we be beholding to you?" But not so fast! And now, without more ado, comes a broadside, the explosion of his long-pent-up resentment:

> Signior Antonio, many a time and oft
> In the Rialto you have rated me. . . .

So the Jew recalls his grievances, which he has borne with a patient shrug but which, if only by requiring a hearing, he will make the Christian pay for now;

> Hath a dog money? Is it possible
> A cur can lend three thousand ducats? Or
> Shall I bend low and in a bondman's key,
> With bated breath and whispering humbleness,
> Say this:

> "Fair sir, you spat on me on Wednesday last;
> You spurn'd me such a day; another time
> You call'd me dog; and for these courtesies
> I'll lend you thus much moneys?"

But Antonio, strong and stout in his medieval and Elizabethan virtue of contempt for both usury and usurers, has
nothing to retract. He is likely to call him so again, to treat
him so again; and for his straightforwardness he meets with
the straightforward spectators' approval. He does not
"storm," though Shylock says so as he now takes pains to
smooth things over:

> Why, look you how you storm!
> I would be friends with you, and have your love,
> Forget the shames that you have stain'd me with,
> Supply your present wants, and take no doit
> Of usance for my moneys, and you'll not hear me.
> This is kind I offer.

"No doit of usance," of itself, arouses misgivings in the
spectators, and the words "your fair flesh" in the terms
of the contract, presently proposed, do so still more. Bassanio demurs, but up the Hebrew lifts his hands in depre-
cation:

> O father Abram, what these Christians are
> Whose own hard dealing teaches them suspect
> The thoughts of others!

And again he proceeds to argue:

> A pound of man's flesh taken from a man
> Is not so estimable, profitable neither,
> As flesh of muttons, beefs, or goats.

He is as literal-minded as when he explained the figure
water-thieves; he has no sense of humor, or (what comes
to the same thing) does not stop to consider whether Bassanio and Antonio have any. Of tenderness and delicacy
he has still less—"taken from a man"!—and there he gives
himself away, as also he does when, in the excitement of

closing the bargain, he forgets what he had said of borrowing from Tubal—

And I will go and purse the ducats straight.

Tubal was a blind, afterwards not unknown to Little Moses, Isaac of York, and Fagin.

In this latter part of the scene the Jew's hypocrisy is more obvious, his friendliness more fulsome. Bassanio, therefore, must needs have misgivings in order to preserve his reputation for intelligence and affectionateness; and only by Antonio's confidence in the arrival of his ships is he justified in permitting the bargain to be closed. But Shylock in the first place is made so egregious and unctuous on the same principle as Tartuffe, for the sake of the audience. Like him, he is, in the words of Dumas the Younger, "modeled in high relief"; for though off the stage successful hypocrisy must not be perceptible, on the stage it must be. How he cringes and fawns, and as he appeals to the patriarch plays the innocent! Yet through all his changes, from hypocrisy to caustic bitterness and bloodthirsty villainy, the method of expression is remarkably identical—harsh but harmonious, and, on the surface, grave, stately, and proud. His homely full-syllabled Anglo-Saxon vocabulary is charged with biblical reminiscences; and, as Brandes has noticed, is frequently cast in the mould of a question (with or without an answer) instead of a statement, a thing not uncommon in the Hebrew Scriptures. "What of that?"—"Hath a dog money?"—"Hath not a Jew eyes?" In the Old Testament this rhetorical method is prominent. "But what! is thy servant a dog?" asks Hazael of the prophet. "Why have ye conspired against me, thou and the son of Jesse?" cries Saul. "Then Abimelech answered the king and said, 'And who is so faithful among all thy servants as David, which is the king's son-in-law . . . ?' " Jehoram, Rabshakeh, Naaman—"Are not Abana and Pharphar, rivers of Damascus . . . ?"—have the same way of answering, and so has many another. Often the sacred writer himself thus comes to a conclusion: "Now the rest of the acts of So-and-So are they not written in the book of the chronicles of the Kings of Israel—of Judah?" Hebraic, too, are Shylock's sarcasms, his caustic, sardonic wit instead of humor. "I will be assured I may," he retorted early in the scene; and now he puts the pointed question, "Is it possible a *cur* can lend three thousand ducats?" There is sting after sting in the harsh melody and taunting rhythm of the passage ending

> and for these courtesies
> I'll lend you thus much moneys?

How he sneers, and jeers, and "rubs it in" as he hisses out his ironical inquiry, bowing and looking sidelong up!

3

He does not appear again till Act II, scene 5. When last on the stage he was on the way to his house, "left in the fearful guard of an unthrifty knave"; but in the interval we have made the knave's acquaintance. A victim of thrift, he is as eager to leave the house as Jessica herself, who finds it "hell"; and if anything were lacking to Shylock's humorlessness it is now provided in his first speech as, nettled by his servant's want of appreciation, he pursues the subject incidentally, while he calls his daughter:

> Well, thou shalt see, thy eyes shall be thy judge,
> The difference of old Shylock and Bassanio.—
> What, Jessica!—Thou shalt not gormandise
> As thou hast done with me,—What, Jessica!—
> And sleep and snore, and rend apparel out;—
> Why, Jessica, I say—

In this matter Launcelot's eyes are the judge already! And in keeping with the old skinflint's humorlessness are his sobriety and his pride in that. He is a Puritan; and the Puritans of Shakespeare's time (or on his stage), who gave their offspring Hebrew names and much preferred the Old Testament to the New, were Pharisees. He has their hatred of innocent mirth:

> What, are there masques? Hear you me, Jessica,
> Lock up my doors; and when you hear the drum

> And the vile squeaking of the wry-neck'd fife,
> Clamber not you up to the casements then, . . .
> But stop my house's ears, I mean my casements.
> Let not the sound of shallow foppery enter
> My sober house.

Again he translates his metaphor—were not the Puritans "precisians"?—"I mean my casements." Launcelot, as he runs away on Shylock's errand, bids Jessica look out, nevertheless, for Lorenzo.

> SHY. What says that fool of Hagar's offspring, ha?
> JES. His words were "Farewell, mistress!" nothing else.
> SHY. The patch is kind enough, but a huge feeder,
>   Snail-slow in profit, and he sleeps by day
>   More than the wild-cat. Drones hive not with me.

Nor do they care to! There is a momentary relenting in "the patch is kind enough"; but tenderness and humanity are immediately swallowed up in the abysmal afterthought. For an instant Launcelot is to him a human being; the next he is an animal again, the sort of horse or dog that the canny owner takes pains betimes to get rid of. In the two long syllables of "huge feeder" the groan of parsimony reaches our ears; then the grave and harsh melody of his speech is resumed. "Drones hive not with me"—in itself the sentiment is not ignoble, nor profane. "Go to the ant, thou sluggard!"

4

The next scene in which he appears is the first in Act III, where Salanio and Salarino are discussing reports of Antonio's losses. In a previous one they have chuckled over Shylock's passion, "so strange, outrageous, and so variable," as he bewailed his daughter, his jewels and ducats; in this we are to enjoy the spectacle for ourselves. He comes in brooding, and on espying these young blades, reproaches them as parties to the conspiracy against him, with characteristic repetition, but now more agitated and less controlled: "You knew, none so well, none so well as you, of my daughter's flight." And here his literal-mindedness appears again: "My own flesh and blood to rebel!"

> SALANIO. Out upon it, old carrion! Rebels it at these years?
> SHY. I say, my *daughter* is my flesh and blood.

Either he thinks Salanio has misunderstood him, or he has misunderstood Salanio. Yet, though he misses the impudent jest, he keeps his own wit in trim. "Why," Salarino interposes, "thou wilt not take his flesh. What's that good for?" And Shylock: "To bait fish withal. If it will feed nothing else it will feed my revenge."

Then follows the famous speech—"Hath not a Jew eyes?"—full of rhetorical questions and answers, but too long and too familiar to quote. As it begins with revenge, so it finishes; and the point is not that because your Jew is like your Christian, the Christian should spare him, but that for this reason the Christian should expect like treatment from him, only more of it—"it shall go hard but I will better the instruction." In such a spirit he engages in the delectable colloquy with Tubal. To the question, "Hast thou found my daughter?" his compatriot replies, "I often came where I did hear of her but cannot find her"; and not really irrelevant is the rejoinder:

Why there, there, there, there. A *diamond* gone, cost me two thousand ducats in Frankfort. The curse never fell upon our nation till now. I never felt it till now. Two thousand ducats in that; and other precious, precious jewels. I would my daughter were dead at my foot—and the jewels in her ear. Would she were hears'd at my foot—and the ducats in her coffin! No news of them? Why so? And I know not what's spent in the search. . . . Why, thou loss upon loss! the thief gone with so much, and so much to find the thief. . . .

With that he falls into an Oriental wailing. Except in Germany, where there is small prejudice against it, I have never witnessed the scene upon the stage: as it must needs be acted, it would not harmonize with the pathetic or prophetic Shylock that with us precedes and follows it. But it harmonizes with the Shylock before and after it in Shake-

speare. The avarice in him is now more vociferous; but now
it is the avarice in him that is touched—"When you prick
us, do we not bleed?" Before and after, the motive is the
less sordid one of revenge, this being somewhat elevated by
racial and religious sentiments. It still appears, but—"the
curse never fell upon our nation till *now!*"—in its more
comic aspects. A diamond gone—"two thousand ducats"—
and other precious, precious jewels, each of which he remembers with a pang,—it is these, not the daughter, but
"the thief gone with so much, and so much to find the
thief," that are the subject of his heartfelt lamentation. He
wishes her "dead at his foot"—"hears'd at his foot," for
better so than mated with a Christian; but what would be
the good of wishing her there without the jewels and ducats
upon her?

The great thing, however, is the expression. It is prose
now, not verse, for the passion is more extravagant, the
vein comic, not tragic. The cloak of dignity is flung from
him but many of the mannerisms, exaggerated, remain. The
repetitions are insistent, like those in the first scene, when
he feared the borrower might escape him—"Ho, no, no,
no, no"; but this excitement is of a different and heightened
sort. It is frantic. Cries of rage and shrieks of joy alternate
and accumulate as Tubal tells him of Shylock's own misfortune and then, for comfort, of Antonio's:

> TUB. Yes, other men have ill luck too. Antonio, as I heard
> in Genoa—
> SHY. What, what, what? Ill luck, ill luck?
> TUB. Hath an argosy cast away, coming from Tripolis.
> SHY. I thank God, I thank God. Is't true, is't true?
> TUB. I spoke with some of the sailors that escap'd the wreck.
> SHY. I thank thee, good Tubal; good news, good news! Ha,
> ha! Here in Genoa!
> TUB. Your daughter spent in Genoa, as I heard, in one
> night fourscore ducats.
> SHY. Thou stick'st a dagger in me. I shall never see my gold
> again. Fourscore ducats at a sitting! Fourscore ducats!
> TUB. There came divers of Antonio's creditors . . .
> SHY. I am very glad of it. I'll plague him; I'll torture him. I
> am glad of it.

Fourscore ducats—'tis a good round sum. It is not at seeing his daughter no more that he is grieving. At every word he has of her he is angered; and for a miserable monkey she has given a ring, he remembers which: "Out upon her! Thou torturest me, Tubal. It was my turquoise; I had it of Leah when I was a bachelor. I would not have given it for a wilderness of monkeys." At that we do not, like some modern readers, drop a tear; we have more sense of humor than Shylock himself, less tenderness than the critics. But "Antonio is certainly undone," croaks Tubal, to console him.

Nay, that's true, that's very true. Go, Tubal, fee me an officer, bespeak him a fortnight before. I will have the heart of him if he forfeit: for, were he out of Venice, I can make what merchandise I will. Go, go, Tubal, and meet me at our synagogue; go, good Tubal; at our synagogue, Tubal.

Wherefore? why away to the synagogue? the honest Elizabethan wonders, and suspects. These writhing repetitions suggest all sorts of sanctimonious deviltry, and demand of the actors an Oriental winking and leering, wagging of heads and waving of hands. This can be no honest business, the usurer's and good Tubal's, "at our synagogue." "For, were he out of Venice". . .

Not that this is his only motive, though it is more urgent than the loss of his daughter. He seeks revenge for injuries past and present, not only for bargains "thwarted"—"he hath hindered me half a million"—but for contemptuous usage. And in refusing Bassanio's offer he even goes the length of losing more ducats still. It costs him no visible struggle; he hesitates not an instant. *Il faut voir,* says Joseph Baretti, in 1777, *avec quelle rage le maudit Fils d'Israël sacrifie son avarice à la soif du sang de son ennemi.* That is as it would have been in Molière, after the French fashion of a contention of motives. In Géronte's bosom, however, it is an alternation between two agonies, his son or the ransom; in Shylock's it is between agony and delight, his losses and Antonio's own. His avarice he sacrifices unflinchingly, for it is but as, later, the flesh escapes him that he

snatches at his pelf. And yet in the long run as he sees it
—"make what merchandise I will"—is he sacrificing much?

5

It is in keeping not only with the situation but with Shylock's mind and temper that he should insist on law to the
last jot and tittle. It is also in keeping with the Jewish mind
and temper as we know them both in the Scriptures and in
present-day intercourse, and as the report of it has descended to us with all the prejudice of tradition. A stiff-
necked people who worshiped the law, when they were not
breaking it, who kept it on the whole and profited by it,
and they have been the greatest arguers, lawyers, and liti-
gants to this day. And so, with no tenderness or indulgence,
Shylock is presented here. In the scene with Salanio and
Salarino he harped on the theme "let him look to his
bond"; and now, in the next, with Antonio and the gaoler,
he cries, "I'll have my bond—" "I'll have my bond—" "I
will have my bond," and stops his ears. He has sworn an
oath, he insists, that he will take no less.

In this spirit he appears in court. He has resumed some
of his gravity, but underneath it the fires are burning. "I
stand here for law"—"I crave the law"—"My deeds upon
my head," he cries at intervals—like his forefathers before
the Roman. Again and again he declares he will have nothing but "the penalty and forfeit." Early in the hearing he
refers to his oath, in relentless accents:

> And by our holy Sabbath have I sworn
> To have the due and forfeit of my bond.

Later he is offered thrice the principal:

> An oath, an oath, I have an oath in heaven!
> Shall I lay perjury upon my soul?
> No, not for Venice.

The latter is, perhaps, his most picturesque and concentrated utterance. In the first line he bursts out in pas-

sionately pious reassertion, in the second he bows in cunning and sarcastic inquiry, in the third he pulls himself up again in the pride of refusal. But, however picturesque and prophetic, he is a perjurer; for later, when he finds that he cannot have the flesh without "the penalty," he is eager to take three times the principal, or even the principal alone—without thought of his oath. "Shall I not have barely my principal?" The oath may be only a pretext, like his having to borrow of Tubal, but in effect it is the same as if it weren't. And his literal-mindedness and insistence upon the letter of the law are now given their finest illustration as to Portia's recommendation of mercy and charity he rejoins,

> On whát compúlsion must I, téll me thát. . . .
>
> Is it so nominated in the bond? . . .
>
> I cannot find it; 'tis not in the bond. . . .

And therefore it is not binding! When it is a question of mercy or charity, with him it is one of compulsion, and he cons the wording of a document! Of the New Dispensation he has heard but knows it not; and he argues shrewdly before this, within the rigid limits of his logic. It is "a losing suit"—on that specious, pitiful bit of idealism he plumes himself, in the spirit of what he has said about the marketable value of man's flesh in comparison to beef or mutton —but he nevertheless would win it. And still he wags his bitter tongue. "Can no prayers pierce thee?" cries Gratiano.

> No, none that thou hast wit enough to make.

But even so he shows again no humor, which is a living and generous sense of the complications and limitations of human nature. When Bassanio and Gratiano frantically vow to Antonio that they would sacrifice everything, even their own wives, to save him, he snarls to himself:

> These be the Christian husbands. I have a daughter;
> Would any of the stock of Barrabas
> Had been her husband rather than a Christian.

So, in his argument to the court before this, he gives himself
away as he insists that if he can produce no other reason
for his suit than "his humour"—his fancy—he is only like
a man who does not love a gaping pig, or is mad if he
beholds a cat, or cannot contain his urine when the bagpipe
sings i' the nose; and as he insists that if, the pound of flesh
being dearly bought, and therefore his, he "will have it,"
he is only like those who, purchasing slaves, use them as
they will because the "slaves are ours." Even in the manage-
ment of it the argument is like him—clear-cut and incisive,
with question and reply. It is all ordered, pointed, punctu-
ated. "Is it answer'd?"—"What, are you answer'd yet?"—
"Now, for your answer"—"Tell me that." He has the con-
tentious and hortatory, didactic and dialectical, quibbling
and sophistical genius of his race.

Above all it is the same style of utterance—question and
repetition, apostrophe and exclamation—the same grave
and relentless bearing until his tenderest spots are touched,
and thereupon frantic and explosive. Towards the end, however, not only his combative but his stately manner collapses; the spirit has gone out of him; and it is thus, in
aftertimes, that he has moved men to compassion:

> Nay, take my life and all; pardon not that.
>
> I pray you, give me leave to go from hence.
> I am not well.

But there is no compassion on the stage. Everybody there
and in the audience has seen how with what measure he
meted it had been measured to him again; and his not
feeling "well" probably got him only a laugh or a jeer. In
the courtroom it has not been "healthy for him," as the
schoolboys say; and it is old-fashioned, schoolboy justice
that here prevails. Not a soul considers how, if the Jew is
cruel and revengeful, he has in the long run been made so.
And indeed these last words of his are not noble. Money
gone, all is gone.

> You take my life
> When you do take the means whereby I live.

Not a word is there of his daughter: she has little more place in his heart than he in hers. And this is the first scene of the fourth act, with his exit from which he drops out of the play, forgotten.

6

Of what would the figure of Shylock remind the audience? Of Jews at first hand they may have known little. There were Jews in England, but illegally and by connivance. As I have suggested, he would rather remind them of the precisians and Pharisees in their midst, who "put on gravity," were keen on money and, more than other Christians, addicted to usury. They, too, were given to biblical phrasing and scriptural allusions, preferably of the Old Dispensation. They Hebraized, in short. Shylock would not be taken for a Puritan with a capital letter, and was not meant to be. Yet the Elizabethans could hardly help thinking of the Rabbi Zeal-of-the-Lands, the Ananiases and Tribulations round about them, if not as yet upon the stage; and it is not unlikely that such picturesque customers as these offered suggestions to Shakespeare's imagination.

The thoughtful, however, would be reminded still more of the Hebrews in the Scriptures; and it must have been mainly these that, in the dim distance, sat as Shakespeare's models. A great dramatist has not one model but many, and depends on none; he picks up a hint here and another there —or rather in the past he has done so—and makes a new creation. And Shylock is highly individual, not a type, by no means the Jew in general. Yet this grim gravity, this prophetic manner, these proud memories, this cursing, railing, and wailing, this stubbornness, relentlessness, and fanatical cruelty, this trickery and cunning—such striking features, which, in combination, Shakespeare may have had little chance to paint from life, he could easily have found in the Old Testament. The duplicity of Abraham, of Rebekah and her favorite in dealing with his father and his brother, of Jacob (again) in bargaining with his father-in-law and of Rachel in absconding with the teraphim, and their descendants' wholesale murderous treachery practiced upon the Shechemites! The vindictive Hebrew Deity himself can for the most part afford to dispense with deceit, but he stoops to it when he makes use of "a lying spirit" (like Zeus on one occasion in the *Iliad*) to lead Ahab to destruction. So with the humorlessness and the sardonic wit. There is, for example, Elijah, who "mocks" at the priests of Baal before he slays them by the brook, four hundred and fifty together: "Peradventure he sleepeth." Of the rhetorical and disputatious, picturesque and exalted style we have spoken already. Something of that is to be found in the utterance of the Jew today when not too much in converse with the Gentiles; and some of Shylock's intonations are more like those of the Jew of the Ghetto or the Judengasse than anything I recognize in the Bible:

> Shall I lay perjury upon my soul?

> Shall I not have barely my principal?

There, particularly in the second line, is, if my ear does not mislead me, the very undulation of pitch that would accompany his wheedling, reproachful utterance. The upper note would be struck at the first syllable of "barely" and at the first and the last of "principal," as certainly as his palms would be uplifted and outspread. The imagery, however, drawn from nature—the dog, the cat, the pig, the snail, the wildcat, the drone, the rams and ewes—seems, in homeliness and raciness, and the ugliness and offensiveness of some of the particulars, to be biblical in cast. There is in the Bible noble and beautiful imagery; but its imagery is often more forcible than beautiful, like that of the dog and his vomit. And the gestures! Is not Shylock of these who grasp each other's beards and kiss, bow to the ground, fall on their knees or their faces, take to their beds, turn their faces to the wall, tear their hair, rend their garments, beat their breasts, throw ashes on their heads or else sit down among them? And to mingle with the dramatist's biblical lore came the inherited and accumulated prejudice of more than a thousand years against a strange and peculiar people, with different manners and *mores* (and therefore suspected), different ethics and religion (and therefore detested), but also charged with crucifying children, poisoning wells, periodically cursing Christ, and continually hatching plots, against church or state or individuals, in their synagogues. It is remarkable that, with all these temptations to caricature, the Elizabethan has succeeded in giving us so human and interesting a figure.

7

In prejudice he was created, like Dickens' Jew; for like every popular artist, especially a dramatist, Shakespeare shared the opinions and morals, the sympathies and antipathies of his public, but from a higher level. Like everybody else he believed in omens, ghosts, and witches, and yet he was not what then or now would be called superstitious. He was enlightened and tolerant, without, apparently, the principles of enlightenment or tolerance. In his own day he is not conceivable as engaging in persecution, or as approving it either, and still less—at the moment had I better say, "not even"?—in this. Hear him joining in the totalitarian hue and cry, hear him transcendentally defending it! Not long before he wrote the play a Jewish physician had been executed on the charge of attempting—after an impossible fashion—to poison the Queen; but there is not the slightest echo of the incident. And in the last act the Jew is forgotten; and before that he has been made more laughable than hateful, more human than villainous. Even as such, he is of course not a fair or faithful presentation of the Jewish type: in his "heavy" role he could not be. Besides, Shakespeare is still more indifferent to the psychology of races than of individuals; he treats character poetically, with due regard to reality but in no subservience to it; he creates it. The important thing to him and to us is not that the creature should stand the test of racial realism, or of a merely human psychological consistency, but that simply as we see and hear it on the stage it should hold together—act and above all speak like a man, the sort of man it is intended to be—and move or amuse us. And both Shylock certainly does![1]

1939

[1]In the *Shakespeare-Jahrbuch* (1938) I took up the subject of Shylock because of Professor Charlton's treatment; but I forgot there to cite Mr. Middleton Murry's able reply (*Shakespeare* N.Y., 1936, pp. 164–73) to the New Cambridge editors' interpretation of the play, which Mr. Charlton's resembles.

CHAPTER VII

Jaques, and the Antiquaries

THE INTRUSION, recently, of antiquarian learning into the interpretation of Shakespeare's characters seems to me a serious matter. It is not, however, a serious matter whether Shakespeare's Jaques and Marston's Malevole (the leading character in the *Malcontent*) are similar enough to be, as I think, in some way connected, or, as Professor O. J. Campbell thinks, not sufficiently so.[1] The play was published in 1604 but possibly written as early as 1600;[2] and in one paragraph of seventeen lines, which Mr. Campbell quotes on p. 72, I indicated a few (not all) of the numerous points of external resemblance. Some of these, I may say in passing, Mr. Campbell thinks "may be questioned" but he doesn't really question any of them, insisting only on matters which, as I thought, I had taken account of—that Malevole is feigning while Jaques is not and Malevole in reality is a "blacker cynic." The fundamental objection which Mr. Campbell raises is not the want of resemblance but (and that is my fundamental objection against Mr.

[1]*Huntington Library Bulletin,* October, 1935. My article referred to is "Shakespeare, Marston and the Malcontent Type," *Modern Philology,* III (1905–6), pp. 281–303.

[2]*Review of English Studies* (January, 1935) "The Date of the Malcontent."

Campbell) the fact that there is no medical diagnosis furnished. By the dramatist, that is to say; and the point would seem to be that to all appearances Jaques is like Malevole but at bottom isn't. Externals here will not do (though in a drama you would think they might). "Jaques would much more easily be recognized as a type by an Elizabethan audience if he were presented as suffering from one of the carefully differentiated forms of melancholy described in the medical treatises of the age." For this, following the lead of Miss Lily Campbell, to whom he acknowledges great indebtedness, the critic provides. You would think the dramatist himself would have made it easier for his audience. No blame, however, is fastened on him, and yet in view of "the convincing evidence that Miss Lily B. Campbell[3] has presented to prove that Hamlet is an accurately conceived type of the sanguine adust temperament," Shakespeare by 1600 must have been "familiar with the standard analysis of melancholy. Hence it should not prove wasted labor to discover whether Jaques is a figure drawn closely upon a scientifically accurate model."

Distinguishing, then, melancholy "natural" and "unnatural," Mr. Campbell after consideration of the symptoms—sluggishness, terrors, hallucinations—determines that Jaques is not suffering from any form of the "natural." Of the "unnatural" not so much can be said. This sort is produced by "adustion," and Jaques suffers from "melancholy formed by adustion," or burning. The symptoms are: emotional instability, lively wit, figurative and sententious utterance, solitariness, madness at the worst. Also, because of his interest in water—weeping by "the brook that brawls along this wood"—Jaques is "a phlegmatic person of some sort. . . . A character who was introduced to an Elizabethan audience poring over a brook and there weeping and meditating, would write himself down at once as a phlegmatic person who had been rendered melancholy." To cut the matter short (as for fear of blundering or boring I am eager to do) Jaques's case is "the unnatural melancholy produced

[3]*Shakespeare's Tragic Heroes: Slaves of Passion* (1930).

[though some authorities, quite naturally, doubted the possibility of this sort of burning!] by adustion of phlegm."

After that I wonder that the critic does not proceed to prove Malevole also of "the sanguine adust," or something as remote, and so settle the business between him and me for good and all. But the Malcontent he has forgotten, and me as well, and almost Jaques too as a human or a tragic figure. He does make sensible remarks about identifications, and, happily, will not hear of Jaques as Jonson or Marston or Sir John Harington. He also appreciates him rightly and aptly as a comic but not a ridiculous figure, and yet bears in mind that he is treated not quite sympathetically, either, but is a disillusioned "libertine." With that, however, the antiquarian in the critic again gets uppermost, and the Duke's (and Shakespeare's) way of putting it is not sufficiently "scientific." "This cynicism of an exhausted roué . . . has been the agent of the adustion of his phlegmatic nature, the cause of his psychosis" (p. 93). As one himself half Scotch, remembering the qualities of Burns and Barrie and ignoring Lamb's opinion to the contrary, I am disinclined to think that Mr. Campbell is wanting in a sense of humor. Here he is in the throes of research or the first flush of discovery, that is all.

It isn't, however, the language merely, but the ideas, their disturbing intrusion! Why should spectator or reader, or Shakespeare either, be burdened with such lumber when all three understand a played-out "libertine" "chiding sin" perfectly well without it? It is possible that for some quite learned Elizabethan spectators a character poring over a brook, and there weeping and meditating, should "at once" write himself down as a *phlegmatic* person who had been rendered melancholy; but for an audience it is not possible that he should. So some similar few in the house today might "at once" analyze him in the jargon of Freud or Jung. But neither is or was the effect desired by dramatist or poet. He would be as much disconcerted as Heine was when on his giving a young lady a wild flower and on her mother's asking for its name their hitherto silent companion counted the stamens and declared, *ganz trocken,* "It belongs to the eighth class." "As the phlegmatic partie dreameth commonly of rivers of water, and the cholerike of flaming fire," quoth Mr. Campbell's Elizabethan Laurentius—in poetry or in reality, either, were Elizabethans and Jacobeans who pensively gazed at the brook or, of evenings, into the grate, at once written down for either phlegmatic or choleric because of it? The superfluous psychologizing and physiologizing of poetry and drama cast a blight upon both.

Not that much damage is done in the article before us. Mr. Campbell fails, indeed, to realize that while in life it is well to remember "Things are seldom what they seem," it is not so well for the spectator or critic at the theater; and that only with appearances drama or other art has to do unless (and until) those appearances are penetrated in the work of art itself. His detective activity is, however, so much in the background that it does not upset the story or distort the features of the dreamy cynic. It is otherwise when a great hero like Hamlet, who fills the play, is in question, and the key to his character and the story is carelessly left in a book, not considerately put into the spectator's hand. Miss Campbell is not only a detective but a reformer. She goes farther than Miss O'Sullivan in 1926 with Hamlet,[4] and farther than her clansman with Jaques, expecting of Shakespeare's audience, without any of the guidance furnished by Jonson's or Marston's *raisonneurs,* that they should then and there, out of the abundance of their own knowledge, recognize and distinguish not only "natural" humors but the "unnatural," not only the simple but the "compound." The Prince is "naturally sanguine" but "unnaturally melancholy," and "his melancholy is inevitably the sanguine adust" (p. 113). The audience must look sharp, therefore, and perpend. Playgoing, those days on the Bankside, was, it seems, no idle pleasure. The Globe was a school, if not a *Seminar.* With no helpful reference or allusion to Timothy Bright, whose book it was, Hamlet's particular and formidable variety of the disease is plainly and "inevitably" the cause of his aversion to action. The

[4] Cf. my *Shakespeare Studies* (1927), p. 146.

very center and pivot of the plot, the core of the character, is not in the play. Even had Shakespeare himself read and pondered the book would he have left the explanation out? It is not merely that this method is difficult and exacting. It is not dramatic or poetic; it is not imaginative or emotional, as drama and poetry should be. The passions, indeed, Miss Campbell frowns upon. Her Shakespearean heroes—even in her title they are "passion's slaves." "Excessive grief," from the beginning, has brought Hamlet to this dire pass of the "sanguine adust"; and it "renders him dull [alas, poor *Hamlet!* I knew him, Herr Kollege!] and makes him guilty of the sin of sloth" (p. 115). (A slothful character would do in a satirical comedy, but even there, without some added means of acceleration, hardly in the leading part.) "It is that wicked grief which refuses to be consoled" (p. 132)—what of Orestes and Electra, then, what of tragedy?—and the guilty king and queen in their counsels to the hero on their first appearance after their unholy marriage, it is these that have the correct ethical position. But they say the same thing to him, in almost the same situation, that is said to Sophocles' Electra by her adulterous, murderous mother: "Impious and hateful girl, hast thou alone lost a father, and is there no other mourner in the world?" (ll. 288–90).

In Shakespeare and other Elizabethan drama there are, to be sure, ideas and sentiments, slightly technical terms and phrases which ordinarily needed no explanation then though they somewhat need it now. There are the terms "humours," "spirits," and "complexion," "dry brain" or "hot liver," "blood-consuming sighs" or "the precious square of sense." Or there are phrases like Lady Macbeth's "That I may pour my spirits in thine ear," which conveyed a sufficient meaning into the ear of the groundling then as it does today, though not the full meaning of a "transfusion of soul." But such momentary verbal or phrasal matters, perfectly intelligible or not, are a different thing from an Elizabethan physiologist-psychologist's framework, upon which the character is "accurately modelled"; or from a scholastic scheme of a virtue, upon which the plot is modeled. Not only is Lear not an habitually angry man, as Miss Campbell would have him (so, like Hamlet he would be robbed of our respect and sympathy); his story itself also is not a demonstration of the Elizabethan or ancient technical definition of justice, in all the prescribed or accepted seven subdivisions, as another investigator of the school would have it. In so far as the story really is such, the Elizabethan textbook definition squares with the human and universal conception, which does not require statement. Lear is not a criminal offender, either, or again he would be robbed of our respect and sympathy. And when in *Hamlet* the dramatist is actually psychologizing a little after the Elizabethan technical fashion—as in Ophelia's report of Hamlet's visit or in the hero's own account of his condition on their arrival to Rosencrantz and Guildenstern—he makes the matter almost as plain and acceptable to an open-minded reader who has observed his dramatic method here and elsewhere as to the seasoned playgoer at the Globe.

To Miss Campbell and Mr. Campbell all this may betray a "blindness to ideal values," which is Mr. Campbell's phrase elsewhere. But if the moral values are meant, why, is it not a blindness to the noble and illustrious qualities of Romeo and Hamlet, Lear and Othello, this turning of the heroes into "slaves" and their passions into "deadly sins"? So the *critic* becomes a malcontent, a "blacker cynic" than Malevole. Or if the higher esthetic values are meant, is it not a blindness to poetry, this making more of the humors than the dramatist himself does and reducing a character or a plot to the proportions and vitality of a textbook scheme?

The Campbells, thus standing or hanging together, are, alas! by no means alone. Others than her fellow clansman have praised the lady, and emulated her, and that's the reason I have had to say so much of her. Her influence upon American students is unmistakable—of her vogue she cannot be unaware and much of it indeed she merits. But in the very conception of the nature of tragedy, I think, she is in error, or else the study of tragedy might well be abandoned; and she is equally so in her method of applying antiquarian lore, whether her initial conception is right or wrong.[5] Yet who of us scholars (if we deserve the name) has not in one way or another been so too? All we like sheep —after their leader—have gone astray, often with far less of learning and acumen than the redoubtable Caledonian pair to justify us. In Elizabethan drama it used to be recent or contemporary philosophy and psychology: now it is the Elizabethan. Or it is topical or personal allusions, or else sources or influences, or else a kind of historical sociology, or else (worst of all) it is a notion that the play (not merely a character) is by no means what it appears to be and must be made over into what it is. Most criticism is of little value —and less pleasure—to any but the writer himself, and that is truer in the field of Elizabethan drama (Shakespeare, of course, above all) than in any other. "Much learning hath" —no, not *that* has brought us to the above-mentioned extremest consequence of "unnatural melancholy, adust," for who, even though a scholar, ever really had too much? But we have failed to keep it in its place. We have failed to remember that criticism is not history or science but an art; and not that of detecting or "reconditioning," either, but the simple though seldom successful art of reading and responding, both analyzing and judging as we do it.

Too simple and humble for a fair number, at least among the learned. Not only writers but some sturdy and resolute readers prefer to the analytic and impressionistic criticism this that is, however wrongly, called the historical. This is scholarship, no belletristic trifling, and they grit their teeth. They like its solidity, they say; they are impressed by the paraphernalia and maneuvers of research; they are imposed upon by the signature of sophistication. Taking their fiction in the guise of biography, as in *Ariel,* they are ready to take their criticism in the guise of history. It is natural to like what is true, or even what pretends to be. Or if detective stories are their choice, detection and history or biography can easily be combined. How much better or more edifying

[5]This subject of antiquarian criticism I have touched upon in an article on "Recent Shakespeare Criticism," *Shakespeare-Jahrbuch,* 1938, and more fully in *Shakespeare and Other Masters.*

a mystery in one or all of the thirty-seven glorious plays than in the Rue Morgue or Halstead Street! Especially for the detective himself, who, without being quite aware, has both cleared it up and created it!

The two scholars whom I have been discussing, of course, are above that sort of legerdemain. (They are quite above, of course, the mare's-nesting after Bacon, Rutland, Derby, Oxford, and now, of late, Sir Edward Dyer.) But there is a good deal of it in historical criticism (particularly that of Shakespeare), whether it cares to pass under that name or not; and the criticism of the two shares the historical glamour and prestige.

1939

CHAPTER VIII

Shakespeare Forbears

IN MOST FIELDS of thought there is progress, or something like it: the novelty or heresy of one age becomes the commonplace or dogma of the next. Of criticism, practiced now for over two thousand years, that can scarcely be said. How little here can be taken for granted! In all forms of communication, even a play or story, there should be some common ground, something familiar as a starting-point; and in criticism there ought, by this time, to be certain accepted premises from which to proceed, certain established fundamental principles upon which to build. But the critic knows scarcely where to begin or where to end, when (or rather, when not) to turn aside for the purpose of guarding against opposition or misconception. If he is an adherent of pure impressionism, indeed, he and his reader may seem to have no common ground at all, and you would think there would be no beginning. But however little he believes in esthetic truth generally, he does and would have you believe in his own; actually, though furtively and inconsistently, something or other he takes for granted. The "rules" of the eighteenth century are no more, but something of the sort is indispensable. Feeling of itself will not carry him far, in a reader's company. For practical purposes he must refer to a standard. That may be the conscious or unconscious intention of the author, or the work of art as a reflection of the author's experience, or of the time and place, or of any time and place. In short, he is biographical, historical, psychological, or philosophical, or all of these together. He cannot, however, count on his reader's being so. The result is that criticism is as bewildering as it is bewildered, and so is pretty thoroughly discredited; no one wants to read it, still less buy it, unless he receives a trustworthy guarantee; and the most generally acceptable one is the name on the title page not of a critic but of another author. Then the criticism is not so much itself as literature, but thus it may at least be illumined and safeguarded by a knowledge of the ways of authorship.

All I have said applies pre-eminently—that much I myself now take for granted!—to Shakespeare. Of him anybody writes anything, not only of the man himself but his creation, as of God and his; and to judge from the variety of the readings Shakespeare's page, which is said to be Nature's, is quite as mysterious and undecipherable as Nature itself. If any criticism is bewildered it is this; and that, surely, I may take for granted. Even here, however, we can, with a little patience, make distinctions, and perceive some traces of order—of progress. Certain living figures dominate, certain weighty opinions are beginning to prevail. Mackail and Elton, MacCarthy and Eliot, Murry and Abercrombie, John Palmer and Granville-Barker will not warrant abuses that used to be readily or helplessly permitted, or at least will not warrant them when practiced by others. Such are: the confusion of art and life in the form of speculations upon the hero's experience before the play begins or (in comedy) after it is over; the identification of characters with the dramatist himself or his contemporaries; the influence of heredity and environment upon the hero; the intrusion of nineteenth-century philosophy or Kulturgeschichte, psychology or psychoanalysis, into the characters or the action.

These are negative rather than positive principles, but

the former are nearly as important; and I wonder whether another taboo for which I am now pleading might not be included among them. This is only a special application of two above mentioned—those on the confusion of art and life and the intrusion of psychology. It is one on the intrusion of sex matters, which have now overrun all our thinking and writing.

A reputable scholar has of late taken the position that Iago really suspected Othello of corrupting his wife, Emilia, and with good reason for it. To argue either point, I think, is needless. Before expressing the opinion, the villain has both betrayed and avowed his own unscrupulous duplicity; in expressing it he admits that he knows not if it be true and yet "for mere suspicion in that kind will do as if for surety"; and presently he invokes the power of hell and night as the devil-in-the-flesh which the most enlightened critics from Schiller, Coleridge, and Lamb to J. J. Chapman, Lytton Strachey, and John Palmer have taken him to be. Of the same offense he in turn suspects Cassio too, and manifestly that is his way and bent. Even those who, like Bradley, endeavor to humanize and psychologize him do not generally think he believed Othello guilty, still less that he had reason to do so.

What concerns me here is not the particular interpretation but the critical attitude; only for that purpose do I touch upon the evidence. "There is nothing in the play," says the scholar, "to contradict it or make it impossible." The man is a soldier, a creature of flesh and blood; middle-aged and, prior to the opening of the play, unmarried. There is no reason to think him physically incapable.

Now all this raises questions not raised by the dramatist and takes us outside the tragedy, or, so to speak, behind the scenes. Iago indeed has raised the question of a fact (not of an *a priori* probability), but by his own admissions and self-betrayals has sufficiently answered it. Had it, however, been part of the tragedy—really touched the character— it would, according to Shakespeare's dramatic method, have been answered, one way or the other, in no uncertain terms. The only important questions in his plays left open, except through hastiness and carelessness, are those put by the critics themselves.

"Nothing in the play to contradict it"? The whole tenor of it does. Othello is a high-romantic warrior and lover, and such hard-headed realistic considerations occur not to the spectator but to the present-day reader. That is because he does not surrender to the romantic spell, or follow the dramatic movement, but pauses and looks up from the page; or because he reads it as if a modern novel, where a character is planted in sociologically appropriate environment; or as if either a modern novel or play, where the sexual experience or background omitted would be missed. Or else because of all this together, on the basis of the notion, now rife among the knowing, that a middle-aged celibate, in a monastery or out of it, is either "irregular" or "abnormal." But a generation ago, whether in reality or in fiction, a middle-aged bachelor could still hold up his head; and of a great and manly American preacher it used to be reported, while yet there was no fear of Freud and Oedipus was but a prey to fate and mistaken identity, that according to his own words he had not married because he never met a woman like his mother. The story would not have the same effect upon an audience today. Had Shakespeare himself, to be sure, at the Mermaid, been asked whether in real life a stalwart veteran would have preserved his chastity, he might, without the scholar's up-to-date psychology and physiology to support him, have likewise shaken his head. But he wouldn't have thought ill of the veteran if he had; and what is more important, as dramatist he here says not a word about it. In any case, Othello, Desdemona's lover, in this high-romantic Venice and Cyprus, entangled with Emilia, his subaltern's wife, in whom, however, he shows no interest, of whom he has no memories,—that would have made a very different and incoherent play.

A great difference between Shakespearean drama and the modern lies, so far as the subject matter is concerned, in its not ordinarily involving the characters' sex record; and so far as the technique, in its not being suggestive in procedure. The young lovers like Romeo, Orlando, and Florizel, though not Galahads, have evidently had no compromising relations with women; and the same may be said of older ones like Orsino and (though the Freudian would sniff and prick up his ears at his inquisitorial and reforming spirit) the Duke in *Measure for Measure*. By "suggestive" I do not mean anything prurient or corrupting. Of that to be sure there is little or nothing in Shakespeare. The insidiously or lingeringly erotic or voluptuous?—as with most Elizabethans, impropriety takes the direct, momentary, unprovocative form of jokes. What I do mean is that there is little suggestion whether of sexual or any other matters by merely the connections or implications of the play.

Shakespeare's dramatic fabric, said Maeterlinck years ago, is "wide and loose"; and a case in point is Hamlet in his relations with Ophelia. Almost everything conceivable has been said about him; but so far as I am aware no important critic has yet dared to say he had seduced her, though two reputable German men of letters, Tieck and Boerne, did. Why not, though? Here, really, "there is nothing in the play to contradict it," and much, it might seem, to confirm it. Early in the action both her brother and her father warn her, and not so much against losing her heart to him as her virtue. He, in turn, playing mad, warns the wiseacre himself not to let her walk in the sun, in allusion to its traditional impregnating power; asks her whether she is "honest" (or virtuous), then bids her get her to a nunnery, avowing that he loved her once but only to disavow it; and jests intimately and indecently with her at the theatrical performance. She, heartbroken after her father's death, and mad in reality, sings songs about true loves, Saint Valentine's Day, and opening the chamber door. Little is lacking but the hero's remorse, yet for the psychologists that would be a trifle; and if, just as it is (inconceivable!), the play were in French or German, whether of 1603 or any date since, Ophelia would be another Gretchen. Goethe, though imitating Ophelia, was writing in the spirit of his time and country, which were Tieck's and Boerne's; and what saves Ophelia for us from that is mainly the stage tradition, less interrupted through the three centuries in its effect upon *Hamlet* than upon *Othello*. On the boards, in the spirit of early criticism and despite that of the later, Hamlet is to us, as to our playgoing fathers and grandfathers, a romantic, not a realistic, hero, and Ophelia a delicately romantic heroine; both, moreover, not of the "courtly" order, like Lancelot and Guinevere, Tristram and Isolt, but of the Elizabethan, like Romeo and Juliet, Orlando and Rosalind, the lovers in Greene and Lyly. Ophelia's ditties are not her own, but snatches of folk song, familiar to the audience; and her memory is merely that of the crazy, for what they have never repeated before. That trait of insanity Shakespeare knew of, as we all do, without any psychology of the subconscious; and the only inner significance here is in her thoughts running upon "young men," with one of whom she has, manifestly, been in love. The other apparent indications of a seduction only serve the purposes of the main story: the warnings of father and brother lead to her repulsing Hamlet, which thereupon gives him a pretext for playing mad for love of her, which last then in the succeeding scenes he continues to do. The details hang together so far as the revenge affair is concerned but not the love affair. This, incidentally, is a remarkable example of Aristotle's principle, which by most critics Shakespeare is supposed to contradict, that plot comes first and tragedy is primarily an imitation not of character but action. Not that in characterization the dramatist restricts himself to the requirements of the action; Hamlet's discursiveness, his interest in the life about him, his love and admiration for his friends, his anxiety for the welfare of his mother and his sweetheart, prove the contrary; but not everything in the action contributes, as in Ibsen, to the characterization, and in particular, there is no dependence, for that purpose, upon the connections or implications of it.[1] Even apart from the sexual, this is true; and Banquo, in a tragedy played before the newly enthroned king, his descendant, is, despite his silence, not the assassin's accomplice.

[1] Cf. my *Shakespeare and Other Masters,* pp. 16–24.

If, then, where by modern standards a sexual relation seems suggested it really isn't, what of *Othello,* where the suggestion is lacking? More than suggestion, indeed, would have been needed to make one of Shakespeare's romantic heroes appear to the Elizabethan audience to have betrayed the heroine or to have had a vulgar adulterous liaison. More still would have been needed to make it acceptable.

Macbeth in his relations to his Lady is another case in point. A man and a woman desperately conspiring together, to win a crown by a murder—what an opportunity thrown away! In Shakespeare it might almost as well (but not quite, as we shall see) have been a sister. The Lady shames her husband, dominates him, moves him to admiration and emulation; but she does not fascinate him, lure him, or set the murder as the price of her favor. She brings no amorous enticements to bear upon him beforehand and showers no amorous distractions upon him afterward. She has little of Browning's Ottima in her or even of Milton's Eve. As the woman sinner contrasted with the man, she is like them both. She too has less of reason and imagination, less of conscience or of regard for law or honor. She too is more personal and practical, reckless and defiant. But unlike them, she does not now love the man more because of the crime or exult in it as proof of his love for her. And Duncan in his blood she does not hate as Ottima does Luca and as Eve, in her disobedience, fairly does God and the angels. By their exhilaration or resentment they smother some of their sense of guilt: the Lady, like her husband, feels the pangs. But that is not the way the French actress played her. In the much later sleep-walking scene "to bed, to bed, to bed" was given what was for the actress the natural meaning but for Shakespeare would have been all-too-natural.

This enrichment is not in the Elizabethan's vein. A modern dramatist would have made them lovers or, as in Browning, paramours. They are but man and wife, the relation which, as Hazlitt said of Milton's Adam and Eve's, is "the least interesting of all others." And yet even with that load to carry Milton comes closer to our art, if not to

us. Shakespeare is (however surprisingly) more austere. The
only reminders of the marital relation are the Lady's words:

> From this time
> Such I account thy love

and

> I have given suck, and know
> How tender 'tis to love the babe that milks me,

as she drives him on, and

> My husband!

as she acclaims him entering with blood on his hands. That
he is still, as well as the traitor and assassin which she has
made of him! He and she are now doubly bound together,
and by her homely outcry all that they have been in the
past is flung into contrast with what they are at this moment. The situation here, and in "to bed, to bed, to bed"
as in somnambulistic retrospect she hears the knocking, is
simpler than it would have been made by the moderns, but
is complicated enough. It is more steeply tragical. It is
murder, murder, and their love is swallowed up in the
horror of it.

> These deeds must not be thought
> After these ways; so, it will make us mad,

she now cries out in alarm at the effect upon him: waking
or sleeping afterwards, she thinks it all over to the point of
madness herself. Eve and Ottima have another thing or two
to think about and feel.

In this conception of drama Shakespeare (but not of
course because of any "influence") is like the ancients. His
"romantic" art is like the classical in its simplicity, its intensity. Still less than with Aeschylus and Sophocles, are
his tragic heroines in the foreground; often the heroes, such
as Macbeth, Lear, Timon, Brutus, and Coriolanus, are not
lovers; and none of the heroes or heroines, either, except
Antony and Cleopatra, has clearly had a "love life," as now
it is called. The change comes with Shakespeare's succes-

sors, Beaumont and Fletcher, Ford and Webster, as with Euripides; and in the Restoration dramatists there is suggestion besides. In Shakespearean tragedy love is seldom an issue. The dramatist might have let Ophelia stand between the Danish Prince and his revenge—love against duty or honor, as in Corneille and Racine; but though she serves to shed a light upon his character she is only a pawn in his game against Claudius and Polonius, Rosencrantz and Guildenstern. Not for want of interest in the subject as, in some measure, with the ancients. Shakespeare is what Mr. Murry calls him, the laureate of love. His sonnets, his comedies, and still more his tragedies are the proof. But because of his own taste and that of his public he is shy of studying the passion or analyzing it, of dramatizing it or making it the center and pivot of either tragedy or comedy. For love his Macbeth does not murder and seize the crown, nor his Antony wage war. In his plays at least it suffers from few doubts or questionings, few internal struggles or vicissitudes, and (except through others' troublemaking) still fewer treasons or defeats. He is romantic, fairly simple and reverential in his attitude. He sings of love, and gives love its own individual voice to sing. In his comedies, in *Othello* and *Romeo and Juliet,* there is the finest love-making in the world; but generally from a distance, whether in fact or in thought—by way of narrative such as the Moor's story, through disguises and impersonations, such as Rosalind and Orlando's, or as one on the balcony and the other in the garden, with seldom a suggestion of a caress, kiss, or sensuous imagination between them. And "a past," as in Victorian parlors it was gingerly called, which is now allowed for in all our novels, that is as seldom to be met with in Shakespearean high society as it was in those parlors themselves. Falstaff and Shallow are the sort that have it, with their memories of Jane Nightwork and Saint George's field.[2]

The matter under discussion is, then, partly one of structure, partly one of romantic integrity. The taboo, in the first place, was, whether consciously or unconsciously, observed

[2]The subject of this paragraph is discussed more fully in my *Shakespeare's Young Lovers* (1937), chaps. 1 and 2.

by Shakespeare himself, as well as the other early Elizabethans and the ancients; and there lies the reason—in
criticism are reasons often so good and simple?—why in
dealing with them it should be observed by the critic in turn.

1939

CHAPTER IX

Modesty in the Audience

Mr. MAURICE EVANS, in a "mass interview" at his theater with 1,600 students as reported in the *Herald Tribune* of December 2, told them that "very young children get profoundly embarrassed by love scenes." He did not say whether it was so at Shakespeare performances. Certainly there is far more occasion for embarrassment at modern plays, and if children are put out by Shakespeare's love scenes it is because of the way they are acted now. Physical familiarity or intimacy is seldom suggested in the text, and the reason (which I have touched on before[1]) is, I think, now more than ever apparent. The Elizabethan spectators were like the children (the words "very young" seeming to me superfluous), and would have been embarrassed.

Not that (any more than our children) they were innocent, "sweet-minded," pure in heart. The Elizabethan audience delighted in smutty jokes, and most vigorous youngsters who have not been well guarded and educated do so too. The point is that ordinary healthy human beings, whether children in fact or the children of nature only that

[1]*Shakespeare's Young Lovers* (1937), pp. 52–58, and chap. VIII above.

the Elizabethans were, do not relish amorous demonstrations in public. They are unwilling to look at what they may be willing enough to read of or think about. On the stage or off it, in parks or in cars by the roadside, it brings blushes or laughter, if not a jeer. It is received, if at all, though less comfortably, like the smutty joke. And deliberately or instinctively the Elizabethan dramatists wrote to suit. What a difference between Shakespeare's love scenes and his Venus with Adonis; between Marlowe's Tamburlaine with Zenocrate or Faustus with Helen, on the one hand, and his Hero with Leander, on the other! *Venus and Adonis* and *Hero and Leander* were, we know, widely read; but put on the stage—or on our stage, either, for that matter—would have been insufferable—too much simply to jeer at.

The public sense of decorum even in our shameless and lawless days is far more exacting than the private, and in Elizabethan times was still more so. In my highly respectful and amicable disagreement with Mr. Granville-Barker I endeavored to show that this was not owing to the fact that women's parts were played by boys. The Elizabethan audience, accustomed (like their fathers and forefathers and all the rest of the world) to no other players for the parts, would have been in danger of laughing or jeering only at the embraces or caresses, not at the actual boy who received them. It is a curious fact that on the French stage until a generation or two ago the kissing of men and women was only suggested; and the reason that it has not been infrequent on the English stage is simply that in Elizabethan life it was a matter of courtesy, Cassio and Emilia kissing, as lovers don't. And on the late Jacobean stage, as the moral tone degenerated, and on the Restoration stage, as the tone degenerated still further and the boys were replaced by women, how little evidence there is of kissing or fondling in the text! There are scarcely any caresses and little imagining of them, either, such as there are in the lyrics then or since. The voluptuousness is still by way of the joking, though now the witticisms on the lips of the high-class characters are less gross, indeed, but more ingenious and insidious. The audience hear improprieties enough but wit-

ness none; and the improprieties are of course, even as in
Elizabethan times, less exciting or corrupting because the
effect is dissolved in merriment. Wit mitigates the indecency; laughter palliates the shame. The theater, so far
as the spectators themselves are concerned, is the place for
laughter or tears, for exultation or terror, not for blushes;
we must be able to look our companions or neighbors comfortably in the eye. And it is disconcerting for them and so
for us (and then for the actors in turn) to laugh when they
are wincing—whether at sheer indecency in speech or at
an amorous intimacy proper enough if in solitude.

The laughter, whether wholehearted or mingled with
sentiment and tears, should be unanimous and by the
players expected. In love-making, even when truly romantic
and wholly irreproachable, merriment, either as actually on
the stage or only as duly expected in the house, is generally
welcome. It is for want of this today that children and some
few adults are embarrassed, as well as because of the inde-
corum of the players. The bright accompaniment to the
tender tune is provided in Shakespeare from *Love's La-
bour's Lost* even to *The Winter's Tale* and *The Tempest,*
though there is more of wit and humor at the beginning
and of naïveté and fantasy towards the end. This is not
exact and faithful realism. Lovers don't joke much—to
either one the other's intentions then would not seem sufficiently "serious"—nor do they talk much, for that matter.

And yet how in Fletcher and in the Restoration dramatists, just as in Shakespeare, though differently and less
charmingly, the romantic lovers keep their distance and let
their tongues run on! The wooing is a wit combat or, as between Congreve's Mirabell and Millamant, a "proviso"
scene.[2] Even in some contemporary plays, like Maugham's
Circle, it is still voluble, still witty and merry. And why so?
Partly because these plays are comedies and must live up
to expectations. (But *Romeo and Juliet* is not a comedy.)
Partly (and much more) because the medium of all plays,
unlike that of novels, is dialogue and action. Now the

[2] See above, p. 41f.

natural action is here, as we have seen already, avoided. And as for dialogue, the Shakespearean medium is also poetry; the lovers are not poets, any more than Hamlet or Lear or Macbeth, though by one critic lately taken for such —any more than Mozart's Don Giovanni or the ladies are musicians—and though flesh-and-blood lovers may meditate the muse, they do it painfully, in solitude, and mostly to painful effect. Shakespeare's, particularly his maidens, are not even aware that they are poetical, nor are they so with lyrical license and abandon. For caresses by word of mouth, however poetical, are not much more acceptable on the stage than those by the touch. A lyric of Swinburne or Rossetti, even the corresponding chapter in Meredith or Hardy, cannot well be enacted. But love scenes on the stage must be acceptable or else be forborne. By some dramatists, Molière for instance, they are. By others, like Corneille or Racine, they have been dramatized, the passion pitted against duty or honor. By still others the passion has been thrown under the shadow of death. By Shakespeare, among them; and there would, of course, have been no temptation to laugh or jeer as Cleopatra receives Antony in the monument. But Shakespeare and most of the English after him have preferred to present love in the sunlight, for its own sake, apart from tragic complications; and yet that they must in some way make dramatic too. By wit and humor they have given liveliness to their scenes, something else than "love, and love, and love, my dear" to fill up the lines, and not only negatively—by the action improbably omitted —but positively—by the badinage improbably provided— have spared our blushes. Not a case of "imitation," it is (as often in art) one of substitution, and here (as also often in art) with the happiest results. Who even today would rather look at or listen to lovers just as they move and talk and are? There is still a sense of shame in the theater. There is still something else than realism on the stage. And *on admet en art,* says Lanson, *un art qui dépasse la nature en la respectant.*

These are not the only violations of realism in Shakespearean and Elizabethan love scenes, and some of these may seem to be in the other direction. The maidens often put on hose and doublet and in the wooing sometimes meet their lovers more than halfway. They even follow them up when they have departed. All this, too, I have elsewhere endeavored to show, was not, as it has been said to be, true to life. It is to be found not only in Elizabethan drama but in the novels before it, and not only there but also in the drama and novels and court epics of Italy and Spain, where women were still more carefully guarded; and there can, in this connection, be no question of realism at all. This sort of irregularity, or impropriety, however, would obviously cause no uneasiness in the audience and bring no blush to any healthy cheek. It produces no sensation as the caresses or embraces do. Propriety is overridden by the dramatist or poet only in the interest of romance; and then the boldness, if not of pure love, becomes at least a measure of the love—if with grace and charm, heightens the charm. Shakespeare's maidens in love, indeed, are still more unrealistic than those of the other Elizabethans or the Continental poets. They are wholehearted; they do not coquette. Yet they are the most delightful and at the same time the most convincing ever staged.

In all the arts there is substitution, manipulation, something of pretense or make-believe. Description, as any good writer knows, must conspire with narration. Not space but time is the literary element; not shape and color but movement, and in good description the verbs involve it. The mountain rises, instead of standing; the plain stretches, does not lie. Painting, in turn, does all in its power to reach beyond the limits of its two dimensions and the colors of the palette. It too deals with appearances, not facts. Perspective —foreshortening—is a falsification of the bare facts in the interests of a higher reality; and snow to seem like snow and have the effect of it harmoniously, in a picture, is not, as would be expected, painted white, still less (as it used to be in our naïver American painting) with diamond dust upon it.

Quite as much adjustment is required for the stage, and

in earlier times that was more boldly and frankly supplied. Improbable stories like those of Hamlet and Lear, Macbeth and Othello, Oedipus and Orestes, for otherwise unattainable enthralling situations—large elements of melodrama in order, as Mr. L. A. G. Strong has it, to "exhibit character at the highest pitch of intensity"—but on the subject of plot and fable we cannot here embark.[3]

Others than the lovers are unnaturally loquacious; Hotspur and Henry V, for instance, true Englishmen both, who protest that they are men not of words but deeds. For the leading roles deeds are not enough. And to those of us who psychologically peer and pry, many of the chief characters now seem still more self-conscious, but not to the Elizabethan or the Athenian audience. The grief-stricken, like Constance and King Lear, parade their grief or cherish it. Villains like Richard III and Iago, but unlike the criminals we know of, avow their villainy; cowards like Parolles and Falstaff, but unlike those we know of, betray or joke about their cowardice. Even the heroic are at times made aware of their heroism, the innocent of their innocence. And hypocrites like Richard and Iago, but unlike the hypocrites we know of, put on or off the white mask or cloak before our eyes. In France this treatment of hypocrisy by Molière, which (independently of course) is similar to that by Shakespeare, is recognized to be owing to the *optique du théâtre*. Though to meet other requirements or overcome prejudices of a different sort, the adjustments above mentioned are made for the perspective too.

"The transcript of his sense of fact," says Pater of the fine prose writer, "rather than the fact, as being preferable, pleasanter, more beautiful to the writer himself!" But drama is (if it is any) a far more popular art, a matter, not of beauty merely but, indeed, of power, and of the taste of the writer only in so far as this is at one with that of his audience. It is a matter also of immediate effect, and that highly charged. (Why go to the theater if the effect there is not to be more powerful than from what is read?) And to produce it, so as to be both pleasing and moving to every-

[3] Cf. *Shakespeare and Other Masters* (1940), p. 202, etc.

body, requires a double dose—a profounder sense of fact and (if need be) more of a change brought upon it. Shakespeare's love scenes, apparently among his closest approaches to realism, seem a case in point.

1940

CHAPTER X

Poetry and the Passions: An Aftermath

IN MY recent discussion of drama and the passions[1] I here and there cited Cicero and W. B. Yeats; and on further reading in them I find that I had more occasion than I suspected. In criticism, since there are no longer any rules or scarcely any generally accepted principles, argument from authority is almost the only argument acceptable; and the best authority is a genius, either a critic like Aristotle or Longinus, who has had a wide and lifelong experience,[2] or else an artist who takes to criticism for a change. Some of the most notable critics have been artists—Horace, Petronius, Sidney, Milton, Dryden and Pope, Wordsworth and Coleridge, Shelley and Keats, Goethe and Heine, Arnold and Swinburne, Molière and Sainte-Beuve, Gautier, Delacroix, Wagner, Berlioz.

Cicero was not primarily a poet; but oratory is treated by Longinus and Cicero himself—and here is my first point already—as if a species of poetry. The Greek holds up Demosthenes as an example of the sublime as well as

[1] In my *Shakespeare and Other Masters* (1940).

[2] Longinus, *On the Sublime*, VI, "a just judgment of style is the final fruit of long experience."

Homer. The Roman, in his oration for the poet Archias, declares at the outset, in words which nowadays ignominiously serve to justify the jumble of our present-day helter-skelter education, that *omnes artes habent quoddam commune vinculum.* He means by that (O tempora, O mores!) the fine arts, and at their finest. In their lower manifestations poetry, drama, and oratory, painting and music, are as remote as they appear. In the highest they are at one and together in arousing—through different senses to be sure—noble emotions.

I cited Hazlitt's account of Chatham as, other things being equal, a good description of a great dramatist:

he electrifies his hearers not by the novelty of his ideas but their force and intensity. He has the same ideas as other men, but he has them in a thousand times greater clearness and strength and vividness . . . not superior to the common interests, prejudices, and passions of mankind.

In short he does not philosophize or subtilize, does not, with only one eye on his audience, tax his hearers' wits. And that is what Cicero says of the orator again and again. The expression must not be high-flown or remote and difficult:

in dicendo autem vitium vel maximum sit a volgari genere orationis atque a consuetudine communis sensus abhorrere. (*De Oratore,* I, iii, 12.)
hoc enim est proprium oratoris, quod saepe iam dixi: oratio gravis et ornata et hominum sensibus ac mentibus accommodata. (*Ibid.,* I, xii, 54.)

The orator must be intelligible, not to the highbrow only but to the lowbrow, that he may move them all. For his purpose is like that of the poet, to rouse the passions or allay them, the poet or dramatist doing both the one and the other:

quod omnis vis ratioque dicendi in eorum qui audiunt mentibus aut sedandis aut excitandis expromenda est. (*Ibid.,* I, v, 17.)
neminem posse eorum mentes qui audirent aut inflammare dicendo aut inflammatas restinguere (cum eo maxime vis oratoris magnitudoque cernatur) nisi qui, etc. (*Ibid.,* I, li, 219.)

"For there the author's virtue and range are chiefly discerned":—And the great Roman goes farther. He himself claims not that oratory closely approaches poetry, but poetry oratory, and not only in expression but in subject, in the liberty of choice and range of treatment:

Est enim finitimus oratori poeta, numeris astrictior paulo, verborum autem licentia liberior . . . in hoc quidem certe prope idem, nullis ut terminis circumscribat aut definiat ius suum, quo minus ei liceat eadem illa facultate et copia vagari qua velit. (Ibid., I, xvi, 70.)

"One of the most important critical principles ever enunciated," says Churton Collins,[3] "we owe to Cicero. He was the first to demonstrate that the test of excellence in oratory lay in its appealing equally to the multitude and to the most fastidious of connoisseurs." Our mode of speaking is to be adapted to the ear of the multitude, according to the master of the art, to fascinate and excite their minds, and [like Chatham!] to weigh things not in your goldsmith's scale but, as it were, in the balance of popular opinion:[4]—

haec enim nostra oratio multitudinis est auribus accommodanda ad oblectandos animos, ad impellendos, ad ea probanda, quae non aurificis statera, sed populari quadam trutina examinantur. (De Oratore II, xxxviii, 159.)

And in his *Brutus* Cicero declares that he had rather his sentiments on the qualifications of an orator should please Brutus and Atticus to whom he is talking, than all the world besides; but his eloquence, he should wish this to please everyone. For he who speaks in such a manner as to please the people must inevitably receive the approbation of the learned—*eloquentiam autem meam populo probari velim. Etenim necesse est, qui ita dicat, ut a multitudine probetur, eundem doctis probari.* (xlix, 184.) Concerning the truth and propriety of what I hear, he continues, I am indeed to judge for myself . . . but the general merit of an

[3]*Ephemera Critica* (1902), pp. 278–79.

[4]Though taking some liberties, I have made use of the translations of J. S. Watson for the *De Oratore* and the *Brutus,* and of C. D. Yonge and Sir J. E. Sandys for the *Orator.*

orator must and will be decided by the effects which his eloquence produces. . . . By what qualities in the speaker they are produced or fail to be is an inquiry which none but an expert (*artifex*) can resolve; but whether an audience is really so affected . . . must be left to their own feelings and the decision of the public. The learned therefore and the people at large have never disagreed about who was a good orator [or actor or dramatist], who was not: *Itaque nunquam de bono oratore et non bono doctis hominibus cum populo dissensio fuit.* (*Ibid.*, 185.) Or, as the great critic and orator puts it a little later, when the audience is moved, you, who are possessed of a critical knowledge of the art, what more will you require? "The listening multitude is charmed and captivated by the force of the orator's eloquence and feels a force that is not to be resisted. What here can you find to censure? The whole audience is either flushed with joy or overwhelmed with grief . . . what necessity is there to await the sanction of a critic?"

Gaudet dolet, ridet plorat, favet odit, contemnit invidet [*the criticism itself is oratory, is poetry!*], *ad misericordiam inducitur, ad pudendum, ad pigendum; irascitur mitigatur, sperat timet; haec perinde accidunt, ut eorum qui adsunt mentes verbis et sententiis et actione tractantur. Quid est quod exspectetur docti alicujus sententia?* (*Ibid.*, 188.)

For, as I have elsewhere said, the critic is only the public or audience in finest form, at highest potency.

"What advantage, then, has the critic over the illiterate hearer?" Why, that of "analysis and comparison," says this T. S. Eliot, in the toga. "A great and very important advantage; if it is indeed a matter of any consequence to be able to discover by what means that which is the true and real end of speaking is either obtained or lost. He has likewise this additional superiority, that when two or more orators, as has frequently happened, have shared the applause of the public, he can judge, on a careful observation of the principal merits of each, what is the most perfect character of eloquence; since whatever does not meet the approbation of the people must be equally condemned by a more intelli-

gent hearer. For as from the sound of a harp the skill of
the player, so from the emotions of the audience"—

*Ut enim ex nervorum sono in fidibus, quam scienter ei pulsi sunt,
intellegi solet, sic ex animorum motu cernitur quid tractandis his
perficiat orator* (liv, 199).

What is as interesting, Cicero fully appreciates the reciprocal relation of orator and audience. He plays upon them
as upon an instrument, but if they do not respond he must
play no more. "If Demosthenes, deserted by the rest of the
audience, had even Plato left to hear him but no one else,
I will answer for it he could not have uttered another syllable." (191.) "The eloquence of orators," he affirms in
his third and final discussion, "has always found its standard
in the judgment of their audience"—

*semper oratorum eloquentiae moderatrix fuit auditorum pru-
dentia. Omnes ènim, qui probari volunt, voluntatem eorum qui
audiunt intuentur ad eamque et ad eorum arbitrium et nutum
totos se fingunt et adcommodant.* (*Orator,* viii, 24.)

Here are examples. My ears, says Cicero, delight in a
well-turned and properly finished period . . . why do I
say *my* ears? I have often seen a whole assembly raise a
shout—*Contiones saepe exclamare vidi cum apte verba
cecidissent.* (*Orator, l,* 168.) Again, turning to the theater
(for of the parallel the orator is himself aware), he says that
when verses are being repeated the whole assembly raises an
outcry if there is one syllable too few or too many.[5] (li, 173.)
"Not that the mob knows anything about feet or meter,"
but their ears are the judge. And (back to the Forum or
the Campus Martius) once when Caius Carbo, a tribune
of the people, addressed to them four clauses, the last two
each ending with a dichoreus—*persolutas, comprobavit*—
the second raised an outcry that was amazing. Was it not
the rhythm that caused it? the master asks. Not, of course,
without the greatness of the sentiment:—

[5]*Si fuit una syllaba aut brevior aut longior.* Possibly a false quan-
tity is meant.

O Marce Druse, patrem appello. Tu dicere solebas sacram esse rempublicam. Quicumque eam violavissent, ab omnibus esse ei poenas persolutas. Patris dictum sapiens, temeritas fili comprobavit (lxiii, 214).

But no outcry without the rhythm!

Now all this but completes the parallel between the orator and a dramatist such as Sophocles or Shakespeare, who told "tales that any lackey could understand," as Drinkwater and Grillparzer, dramatists both, declare, but "in terms of poetry that would storm Olympus." And the intimacy of relation, of action and reaction, is that of the ancient and the Elizabethan theater as I have recently endeavored to present it. Those were the great days—there are no others—of oratory, of drama. And they were the days when in either art there was one taste, for both artist and public. But this unanimity was a living, a changing one. Orator or dramatist and audience—dramatist, actor, and audience—had developed together, each learning of the other, from year to year, from decade to decade; *comprobavit* wouldn't have produced such an effect had Caius Carbo not followed in the line of Cato, the Scipios and the Gracchi, and his audience in the line of theirs; and the response in the Athenian theater and the Elizabethan must have been as quick and instinctively sympathetic or critical as in the Roman Forum. The like of it is scarcely to be found today except at the opera. By ear the audience there, especially in Germany and Italy, responds to the niceties of the art; by ear the audience through lifelong attendance responded to the niceties of the different art in the Forum and the Athenian and London theaters. The technique as such they did not understand; but the ideas, sentiments, and morals, the language and situations, were not above their heads, and to what they heard they were accustomed, attuned.[6]

[6]I wonder whether M. Herriot was really echoing Cicero when in 1936 he said, at Geneva: *"qu'est-ce que l'éloquence? C'est l'art d'exprimer les idées des autres. Nous n'applaudissons jamais que nous-mêmes . . ."*

Elsewhere, in the *De Finibus* (v, xxii, 63), Cicero alludes to occurrences in the theater the like of which I myself have never witnessed there. (The King of the Tauri is about to kill whichever of the captives is Orestes) :

think of the uneducated multitude,—what a tempest of applause [*qui clamores*] rings through the theater at the words:

> I am Orestes

and at the rejoinder:

> No, no, 'tis I, I say, I am Orestes.

And then, when each offers a solution to the king, in his confusion and perplexity:

> Then prithee slay us both; we'll die together:

as often as this scene is acted, does it ever fail to arouse the greatest enthusiasm?

When I have been at the theater the only response (except the hand-clapping at the end of a scene or after the expression of a patriotic or humanitarian sentiment, often without dramatic import or connection) has been to comic effects, by laughter. But here *qui clamores . . . excitantur!*—the passions crying out together as they should do, on the stage and in the house.

2

The late Mr. Yeats had as a critic the big and rare advantage of being a poet and a painter and of possessing a singularly impressionable and yet unprejudiced mind. He was a patriot but not a hater, an Irishman but not a Catholic, a Protestant but not an entrenched dissenter, a man strangely interested in magic and spirits, dreams and presentiments, but not one who could be called either superstitious or heathenish. That quality he clearly enough discerned in the Christianity round about him. And the

sensitiveness and open-mindedness he kept, where it is
hardest to keep, in criticism. He is nothing of a party man
there. He has the historical spirit in dealing with literature,
as with religion; he knows the literature of other countries
and of earlier times. But he instinctively feels that history
does not hold the key. He sees that what is alike in the arts,
at the same or different times and places, is more important
than what is unlike; that the reflection of reality in poetry
(whether that of the poet's own life or of his age) is not
important, for it is not to be depended on; and though himself a literary leader, he has no doctrine to preach, no program to carry through. His shortcomings are only on the
side of his sensitiveness. He does not always succeed in shaking off the estheticism of *fin de siècle* days or wholly
emerge from the Celtic twilight. And as in telling of Gogarty
and his vow of two swans to the icy Liffey if it saved him
(*Modern Verse,* p. xv), he does not always succeed in escaping the spell of Irish theatricalism. Gogarty's life was
saved but not, for the moment, his own or his critic's wit.
It is in another vein, however, that he says, before this:
"Then in 1900 everybody got down off his stilts; henceforth
nobody drank absinthe with his black coffee; nobody went
mad; nobody committed suicide; nobody joined the Catholic church; or if they did I have forgotten." (Pp. xi–xii.)

I have recently taken notice of the overriding of logic in
the Elizabethan and ancient treatment not only of time and
place but also of incident and of motive, for the sake of a
greater range or intensity of effect. "How galling and re-
pressive it is," says Galsworthy of the one and smaller matter, "to have to remember that our fancy man or woman
can only do this or that owing to the conditions of a time
and space which cannot be enlarged!" Shakespeare, as is
well known, like Aeschylus at the beginning of the *Aga-
memnon,* enlarges them. But Mr. Yeats even dislikes "the
clear and logical construction which seems necessary if one
is to succeed on the modern stage."[7] And as for outward
realism, it is all right with him that Richard's and Rich-

[7] *Essays* (1924) by W. B. Yeats, p. 265. By permission of The
Macmillan Co., publishers.

mond's tents should be side by side.[8] Here it is not merely
a matter of time and place but of two men's seeing at once
and together the same ghosts in a dream.

What of psychology, then, what even of character? I have
elsewhere dwelt on the fact that in the earlier and greater
drama imaginative and emotional effect came foremost,
and in this interest motivation was sometimes either omitted
(Iago as a rejected suitor) or made rather superficial (Iago
losing the lieutenancy). Tragedy Aristotle holds to be
"essentially an imitation not of persons but of action and
life, of happiness and misery": the happiness and misery
are heightened by Iago's being, with only a vestige of a
motive, little short of a demon, and Othello's being a noble
soul, not jealous or suspicious or vindictive by nature.
Neither in the practice nor in the early criticism of ancient
and Elizabethan drama does character play the clear and
prominent part that it plays in the modern. Mr. Yeats finds
that as we look back through "the great periods of drama
character grows less and sometimes disappears, and . . . its
place is taken by passions . . . one person being jealous, another full of love or remorse or pride or anger."[9] It is only
in comedy and the novel, he thinks, that character is continuously present. I wonder whether Mr. Yeats was here
remembering (all the better if he wasn't!) Longinus' ob-
servations upon the *Odyssey* and the decline in Homer: "I
wished to make you understand that great poets and prose
writers, after they have lost their power of depicting the
passions, turn naturally to the delineation of character.
Such, for instance, is the lifelike and characteristic picture
of the palace of Odysseus, which may be called a sort of
comedy of manners" (ix). It was the passions, at the Ionian
Father's prime! Or remembering Hugo, in the preface to
*Ruy Blas: Le drame tient de la tragédie par la peinture des
passions, et de la comédie par la peinture des caractères.*
Even in comedy character is not ever-present. There are
Jonson, Molière, and Aristophanes, who are often lyrical;
Volpone and *Tartuffe* are certainly not "passionless"; mirth
itself is an emotion, says Longinus in another connection,

[8]P. 346.   [9]Pp. 296–97.

"an emotion which has its root in pleasure";[10] and concerning the novel Yeats himself later asks the question "Did not even Balzac find it necessary to deny character to his great ladies and young lovers that he might give them passion?"[11] I wonder, too, whether Mr. Yeats was not here remembering Stevenson in his "Humble Remonstrance" as he celebrates the "dramatic novel," citing Balzac also and such as Meredith's *Rhoda Fleming,* in which

> passion is the be-all and the end-all, the plot and the solution, the protagonist and the deus ex machina in one. The characters . . . become transfigured and raised out of themselves by passion . . . nice portraiture is not required. A novel of this class may be even great and yet contain no individual figure; it may be great, because it displays the workings of the perturbed heart and the impersonal utterance of passion.[12]

In the novel and in comedy also character is, however, certainly more continuous, more distinct and prominent, than in poetry or drama.

In ancient tragedy and even in Shakespeare character is not only not always continuous but often not clearly differentiated. As a recent reviewer of Mr. T. B. L. Webster's *Introduction to Sophocles* has remarked: "Oedipus is a good king and Creon a bad king and that is about all" . . . But the passions are "set aflame." And something like that may be said of Shakespeare's more poetical figures. It has been said of his young women in love, mostly in comedy, whom Mr. Yeats does not discuss. They have the same smile, said Chateaubriand, the same look, the same tone of voice. That is, because they have similar ideas and opinions, similar mental processes and points of view, in which a Frenchman more particularly expects to find character—"what beautiful woman delights us by her look of character?" asks Mr. Yeats, which to some of us, however, sounds more French than English—and the expression, a matter of

[10]xxxviii, 5.

[11]*Dramatis Personae* (The Macmillan Co., N. Y., 1936), p. 128.

[12]South Seas Ed. (Scribner, N. Y., 1925), xiii, p. 155. Stevenson, in turn, may have been Henley's original as quoted in my volume (cited above, note 1), p. 53.

phrasing and rhythm, of tone or accent, where we readily discover the emotion, leaves the foreigner rather untouched. Mr. Yeats, having quoted Congreve as the latter denies humor (character, that is, as in the Elizabethan and Jacobean comedy) to women, "in whom the passions are too powerful to let humor have its course," later declares that "women dislike pure comedy . . . How few women like Molière!" English women he must mean or the Irish; but Chateaubriand, if more at home in the English language, verse, and dramatic method, would, as a poet, have perceived the emotional differentiation in Shakespeare's maidens and, provisionally at least, have taken up with Congreve and Yeats's opinion.

The matter is clearer when we turn to painting. The similarity between figure and figure there who can deny? How disappointed tourists are in early Italian pictures as they look for character in the faces; and what a difference there is in this respect (as we go back still farther) between the ancient marbles or bronzes and the modern! And yet in the great periods, ancient or modern either, it is mainly in the portraits that there is much individuality. The madonnas, the tourists say, are all alike; and far more alike are those of a single painter—a Botticelli, a Titian, a Leonardo, or a Raphael—as if they all were but one and the same, his Queen of Heaven continually reappearing to him, and differing, on his canvas, only in emotional quality, as he approaches or circles round her perfection. The ancient Aphrodites or Apollos, moreover, are, except as "early" or "late," to the ordinary eye nearly indistinguishable. Even modern painters like Rossetti, and in their very portraits, are ever re-creating one countenance,[13] hopefully—hopelessly—depicting anew an abiding invisible presence. *Ipsius in mente insidebat species pulchritudinis eximia quaedam,* says Cicero of Phidias, though he is here falling into the language of Platonism and abstraction. Individuality is not what the artists one and all were seeking but beauty, passionate beauty;

[13]Cf. *Dramatis Personae*, p. 127. The quoted phrases in the preceding paragraph are to be found on p. 128.

and the way of least resistance for both them and the spectators was, as in literature, that of tradition. And just so, even in their innovation, moderns like Rossetti or the Renaissance painters soon make a tradition for themselves and their public, profiting, in their successive efforts, by this "economy of attention" (to use Professor Matthews' phrase for another purpose), as they focus it upon the emotional expression alone. The path of least resistance is here also the nearest: they can begin where they left off instead of starting over again. So Shakespeare does with Imogen and Perdita, after Juliet and Viola, and (though the beauty of these is not in the subject) with his Fool in *Lear* after those in *Twelfth Night* and *As You Like It,* or with his villain in *Othello* after that in *Richard III.* If your novelist, as a Frenchman once said, spends his entire life writing one novel, and your painter his entire life painting one picture, something the same may be said of a poetical dramatist in relation to his comedy and tragedy and the various types of person he presents.

Modern drama, to be sure, thinks to present character both distinctly and continuously, deriving the action from it. But the psychology on which it plumes itself it does not introduce effectively. There may be discussion of motives, of subjective causes, but there is "no means of projecting them," as Mr. Barron has it, "in purely theatrical terms."[14] And objective behavior, on the other hand, modern drama cannot present so effectively as the Shakespearean. For it has limited itself, as the Elizabethan and the ancient did not, to the language of everyday speech or conversation. And of "the play of modern manners" Mr. Yeats, before Mr. Barron, says that it

has one mortal ailment. It cannot become impassioned, that is to say, vital, . . . Educated and well-bred people do not wear their hearts upon their sleeves, and they have no artistic and charming language except persiflage, and no powerful language at all. . . .[15]

It is the minor or less well-educated characters that are most convincing; and Mr. Yeats wonders why, meanwhile,

[14]*Harper's Magazine,* December, 1935, "The Dying Theatre."
[15]*Essays* (1924), p. 339.

"the man who is to bear the burden of fate is gushing and sentimental, and without ideas." But when the great scene comes he understands that the hero cannot be well-bred or self-possessed or intellectual, "for if he were he would draw a chair to the fire and there would be no duologue at the end of the third act." Ibsen, he says, "understood the difficulty and made all his characters a little provincial so that they might not put each other out of countenance, and invented a leading-article sort of poetry—phrases about vine leaves and harps in the air"—for their moments of excitement. The happiest writers nowadays are, however, those who keep to the surface, to argument and persiflage, or now and then, instead of the expression of passion, a stage picture. The novel, "having the power of psychological description," "can follow the thought of a man who is looking into the grate." But on the stage, like the common man, the critic prefers life "at high tide"; and "in fine literature," he says, "there is something of an old wives' tale."[16]

Mr. Yeats does not pause to make the applications, but they should be made. By "an old wives' tale" he means such a situation as Richard's and Richmond's dreams in concert, or as Hamlet's hearing and heeding the bloody mandate from another world, or as Lear's dividing up his kingdom according to his daughters' answers, or Othello's and Macbeth's hearkening to the devil's suggestions, in all of which the passions can be let loose as in merely probable ones they could not be. ("Life cannot be put into narrative exactly as it is,"[17] says Mr. Belgion, and in all narrative there is more or less of simplification and condensation; in Shakespeare's effectively more.) He means something the same as M. de Miomandre, who is impatient of local color and tolerant of anachronism, declaring that art *ne vit pas de scepticisme* but *de foi et d'illusions,* and must be *libre à l'égard de l'espace et du temps, et de tous les personnages, vrais ou légendaires et* [whether duly motived or not] *de toutes les situations psychologiques possibles.* He means in short, though he doesn't say so, tragedy enjoying the liberty of melodrama, like that of Shakespeare and the ancients,

[16]*Ibid.,* pp. 339–42.   [17]*Criterion,* October, 1930, p. 139.

to whom melodrama offered "the chance to exhibit character at its highest pitch of intensity."[18] And Shakespeare, like the other Elizabethans, could follow the thought of a man looking into the grate, for he has at his disposal the unrealistic soliloquy, only, like them, he ordinarily employs it for nothing so unexciting. Like them and the ancients, he too would have life at high tide.

Curiously enough, there is here, on different levels, a parallel; for the essential conditions and limitations of drama remain much the same. Like the moderns, Shakespeare makes the minor characters truer to life, the Nurse and Capulet truer than Romeo, Horatio than Hamlet, Kent and Gloster than Lear. And, though he has the soliloquy at his disposal, Shakespeare does not, of course, even venture upon psychology, upon subjective behavior. But as for the first point, his leading characters are not gushing, sentimental, or unintellectual, whether in themselves or in comparison to the minor ones, because they have at their command the language of the passions; that is, poetry, and are moved by passions that warrant its use. Exclamation and apostrophe, the lyrical murmur or outcry that ordinary life does not know or tolerate, are here unquestionably in place. And as for the second point, Shakespeare does not cope with subjective causes not only for the reasons mentioned— that like the moderns he cannot project them in purely theatrical terms—but sometimes for the more cogent reason that, his characters doing things extraordinary and improbable, such as playing the lunatic when a difficult and dangerous business is in hand, or giving heed like Lear and Gloster, Othello and Macbeth, to the bare words that people utter, no satisfactory motive for their own conduct is to be produced. Shakespeare too, though in another sense, keeps to the surface, that is, to superficial motives,[19] as I said above, and to a poetical treatment, by preparations and ad-

[18]L. A. G. Strong, *Common Sense about the Drama* (1937), p. 47. The ancients Mr. Strong does not include.

[19]Even here Mr. Yeats seems to have anticipated me: "an essential part of his method to give slight or obscure motives of many actions that our attention may dwell on what is of chief importance" (*ibid.*, p. 124).

justments, the parts mutually supporting and explaining each other. He lets Hamlet simply serve notice that he perchance hereafter shall think meet to put an antic disposition on; and he makes Iago's success in slander both credible and acceptable by such devices as his universal reputation for honesty and sagacity, as Othello's for nobility of spirit, and as an utterance and deportment for either that justifies his reputation. Like the ancients, less interested in anything that can be called a psychology, in motives or mental processes, and vastly more resourceful in expression, Shakespeare presents the character, minor or major, chiefly by the form and tone of the speech; but he does this more distinctly in the minor ones only because, even as with the moderns, the tenor of it is less interrupted there by the situation, by the requirements of emotion, though these lead to passionate outbursts, not sentimental gush. Ibsen and his followers, to be sure, more interested in subjective behavior, or the undercurrent of thought and feeling, have recourse to suggestion. "Expressing life directly," says Mr. Yeats, the modern drama "has been driven to make indirect its expression of the mind, which it leaves to be inferred from some commonplace sentence or gesture as we infer it in ordinary life."[20] Too indirect, he thinks, however, for the highest effect on the stage.

There is more to this parallel and contrast. Comment by other characters, though indirect, is a resource for Ibsen and Shakespeare alike; besides, the soliloquy has, since Mr. Yeats first wrote the above, in 1906, been revived, as in the *Strange Interlude,* though not for the purposes of story but only of character, not for what is said to the audience but to oneself. That, however, like the use of masks in *The Great God Brown,* is not a highly successful, not a purely theatrical "projection." It is unrealistic, in the midst of realism; it interrupts the dramatic current; it does not distinguish between what is partly conscious and what is not. In so far as the spoken but uncommunicated is meant to be partly hidden from the speaker himself, there is no way but suggestion and comment by others—no way indeed, that greatly

[20]*Ibid.,* p. 414. Cf. *Poets and Playwrights,* pp. 101–4.

differs from Shakespeare's own on the very few occasions
when he seems to deal with the like, as when Othello denies
that he is much "moved" and Iago insists that he is (III. iii.
224). Even when the mental processes are all in the open
there may be an advantage in Shakespeare's reticence. If
the situation is a striking one, that is, a rather improbable
one, the deriving of the action from the characters in modern drama is often either unconvincing or unappealing. It
is by the poetical treatment mentioned,—as in *Othello* when
the hero is led to hearken unto Iago, or as in the *Iliad* when
brave Hector (and no wonder!) takes to his heels, not by
any reasoning or psychology,—that the improbable can be
made probable or acceptable. In the suicide of the lovers
in *Rosmersholm* and the *Axel* of Villiers de l'Isle Adam
there is poetry enough but not this method of preparations
and adjustments, of mere story balanced and holding together. There are motives. With Romeo and Juliet, Antony
and Cleopatra, the bare situation is the same (though in
the two modern plays it is a situation more improbable because the lovers die together), yet the motives attributed to
them are not (as above) "superficial." But they are simple,
peremptory, unanalyzed: love and fate for the youthful
pair; love and pride for the queen. For the death of the
two modern pairs of lovers, on the other hand, the motives
are fully exhibited; yet leave us unsatisfied or incredulous,
troubled or shivering, not greatly touched or aroused. It is
not for love but to escape from life that the Norwegian's
and the Frenchman's lovers die; the one pair because of
loss of faith and the feeling of a need for retribution; the
other, because of disillusionment, distrust of experience, distaste for it besides. Their emotions go deep enough; but
ours, in response, do not. And it is not in this state that
Aristotle and Longinus, Cicero and Quintilian would have
us; or Mr. Yeats, who admires the passionate, poetical simplicity of the suicide in *Deirdre of the Sorrows*.

3

As a critic should be, Mr. Yeats was detached but not aloof. Though as a poet, dramatist, and theatrical producer he was the leader of a movement, as a critic he was not; and, in his Abbey Theatre, he was not so far as one would think from Cicero (or Chatham either) in the Forum or the Capitol. As critic or artist alike he was not for ingenuity,[21] and shared the opinion of Arthur Hallam in the Essay on Tennyson, which he admired: "Undoubtedly the true poet addresses himself, in all his conceptions, to the common nature of us all." As the orator does, that is to say, and as Shakespeare and the ancients did. And Mr. Yeats complains of present-day performances that actors move the audiences through their eyes rather than their ears; that they have forgotten "the noble art of oratory and given all their thought to the poor art of acting";[22] that they and their audiences together (tradition again!) have lost the arts of speaking and listening.[23] The opportunity for that, of course, is not given by the dramatists (all three collaborators should go hand in hand), for they have kept to the level of conversation. And though in poetry he had been a leader or follower of the movement that was for taking eloquence and wringing its neck, with Verlaine, and in drama had been of the movement which demanded quiet and simplicity, with Maeterlinck, still Mr. Yeats was, especially toward the last, like Blake, like Longinus before him, and like the greatest tragic poets and above all others Shakespeare, a believer in excess. He repeatedly quotes Blake's disciple Samuel Palmer: "Excess is the essential vivifying spirit of the finest art and we must always seek to make excess more abundantly excessive."[24] For with him drama and poetry alike are mainly neither a mirror of reality nor a

[21]Yeats, *Essays,* p. 263.

[22]P. 207.   [23]Pp. 245, 263.

[24]Pp. 151, 227. Cf. Longinus, i, 4; xv, 2, 1–6. Also Keats, letter to John Taylor, February 27, 1818: "I think poetry should surprise by a fine excess and not by singularity." Cf. Flaubert on *exubérance.*

vehicle for a doctrine (whether a philosophy or a psychology) nor a criticism of life. "Art is a revelation and not a criticism."[25] That is, a transcript, as Pater says, not of fact but the artist's sense of fact. And like Pater, the critic-poet would have been amazed at the deductions of our historians, the political and social or the literary. He dwells on the difference between William Morris, Landor, Keats, and Dante, each as a man and as a poet.[26] As he says in his Essay on "Synge and the Ireland of his time," Dante, Keats, or Synge may represent Italian, Greek, or Irish life

so vividly that ever after I shall look at all with like eyes, and yet I know that Cino da Pistoia thought Dante unjust, that Keats knew no Greek, that those country men and women are neither so lovable nor so lawless as "mine author sung it me"; that I have added to my being, not my knowledge.[27]

And just so it is with us, I think, at a good performance or a right reading of *Hamlet* or *Othello*. We rouse and dilate, instead of learning, or of puzzling, which is worse.

4

To all this Tolstoy—a mixed company is ours!—would have said both yes and no. He too is for what is simple and intelligible and emotional, but not at all for old wives' tales, nor anything unmotived or illogical, excessive or exaggerated. And in Shakespeare he finds rather little to his satisfaction.

I have come back to his essay after thirty-three years, and in rereading his forgotten startling pages I have at moments wondered whether those years had been thrown away. But reduce almost any high tragedy, whether Shakespearean or Hellenic, to its lowest terms, from poetry to prose, and it becomes as *King Lear* does in Tolstoy's ruthless grip, sheer melodrama and bombast. Much the same thing happened to the *Oedipus Tyrannus* in the hands of

[25]*Op. cit.*, p. 243.   [26]Pp. 489–92.   [27]P. 421.

the youthful Voltaire, who however lived to regret it and make amends. Tolstoy, like Voltaire, is on the one hand that rarity, an honest, fearless critic, and on the other hand a critic who reads the text by no light but his own. Tradition he knows not, though of it he is of course not wholly free. He is shocked and disgusted at Lear and his followers' not recognizing Kent as Caius and at Gloster's not recognizing his son Edgar as Poor Tom, at Lear's not seeing through Goneril and Regan's hypocrisy or Cordelia's reticence and at Gloster's being taken in by Edmund's elaborate deception. He is a child at his first play, with Shakespeare's book in hand. He simply has not heard about or has forgotten the ancient conventions of disguise and slander. He observes that neither Lear nor Gloster knows Kent's voice and that Gloster does not know Edgar's while later in his blindness he does Lear's, ignoring the fact that in the two former cases and not the latter the audience has previously witnessed the characters taking on different clothes, bearing, and fashion of talk. And yet Tolstoy is not unfamiliar with early literature, in which conventions abound. He contrasts Shakespeare with Homer, greatly to the latter's advantage, particularly in the *Odyssey;* but he might well be troubled as much by the improbability of Odysseus' deception in Polyphemus' cave and of Penelope's being so much slower than his old dog and the servants to recognize the husband she has for so long been eagerly awaiting. In the same spirit he complains of the omission of motives for Iago's conduct and Othello's, found in the source, not perceiving the artistic advantage thus secured.

A genius, however, must, as I said, be listened to, particularly a critic so honest. For one thing, Tolstoy lays bare what most Shakespeare critics have not noticed, the fact that individuality of language is the chief means of portraying character.[28] Only, like Chateaubriand and for the same reason, he denies Shakespeare's command over language for that purpose, which the whole English-speaking world (Mr. Shaw being part of it), not to mention many

[28] *Essay on Shakespeare* (1907), p. 53.

foreigners, have always praised. For another thing, he admits Shakespeare's power over the passions:

However unnatural the situations may be in which he places his characters, however improper to them the language which he makes them speak, however featureless they are, the very play of emotion, its increase and alteration, and the combination of many contrary feelings, as expressed correctly and powerfully in some of Shakespeare's scenes . . . evokes even, if only for a time, sympathy with the persons represented.

The great novelist goes on to speak of exclamations, gestures, weeping, the repetition in moments of great agitation; but then he adds that "such clever methods of expressing the development of feeling, giving good actors the opportunity of demonstrating their powers, were and are often mistaken for the expression of character."[29] How clearly he sees, despite himself! That is about what Yeats would have said, but in a different spirit, with another intent. Tolstoy, independently, takes much the same position as Shaw. Both, of course, perceive the importance of the emotions, but demand character besides, the action duly proceeding from it. Both complain of the want of motivation in Shakespeare. Both look upon speech as an important means of characterization. But while Tolstoy insists that Shakespeare's people talk all alike, Mr. Shaw plainly and emphatically asserts the contrary. He can hear as well as see. For though Dublin was his birthplace, that is not Yasnaya Polyana.

Like most men of genius with a philosophy, Tolstoy as a critic is at his best (as we have gathered already) incidentally and by the way. He too notices that Shakespeare's minor characters are truer to life. And being himself a dramatist, he does not go in for puzzles. Laertes and Fortinbras are *not* manlier than Hamlet, and Falstaff is, in the face of danger, nothing short of a coward. Shakespeare's villains are too plain-spoken for life,[30] yet that does not mean they are so for drama. In short, Tolstoy sees clearly a lot of things that thorough-going Shakespeareans have

[29]*Ibid.*, pp. 75–76.   [30]*Ibid.*, p. 55.

not seen or else not reported. Like Voltaire, like Dr. Johnson, not an unbiassed critic, he is a weighty, formidable one.
All three are of the sort you delight to find backing you;
and when the contrary is the case you pause and question
yourself (I trust I have done so), you weigh and consider.

1940

CHAPTER XI

Poetry and the Passions Again

> Science is the response to the demand for informa-
> tion, and in it we ask for the whole truth and
> nothing but the truth. Art is the response to the de-
> mand for entertainment, for the stimulation of our
> senses and imagination, and truth enters into it
> only as it subserves these ends.
>
> SANTAYANA, *The Sense of Beauty* (1896).

I AM ATTRACTED to this subject again by what Mr. Maugham in his *Summing Up*[1] (1938) says of the ending
of Stendhal's *Le Rouge et le Noir;* and thereupon I have
occasion to consider again Sophocles' Oedipus, Masefield's
Nan, Hardy's Tess, and Browning's Pompilia, as well as
Dostoevski's Raskolnikoff.

Though here I must differ with the eminent critic, dramatist, and novelist, I have little or no reason to do so elsewhere. As is to be expected, his conception of a dramatist
in relation to his audience and to posterity is—a dramatist's.
Like Hazlitt and Cicero on the orator, like Longinus and
Wordsworth on the poet, Mr. Maugham says that the
appeal of artistic genius "is not to this type of man or to
that type but to all men." "To be great" is *not* (as for the
ethical philosopher) "to be misunderstood"; and the artist
does not keep one eye upon posterity. "The emotion of the
audience, its interest, its laughter, are part of the action

[1] *Op. cit.* (Doubleday, Doran & Co., N. Y.), p. 76. Cf. Brunetière,
Hugo (1902), ii, p. 107, on the *lieux communs* in the most poetical
passages; and Quiller-Couch, *Art of Writing* (N. Y., 1916), p. 13,
quoting Johnson, George Eliot, and Emerson.

of the play" (p. 127); and Hamlet, or Iago, or Falstaff does not anxiously await our own momentous emergence from the womb of time. The audience "is careless of probability if the situation excites its interest, a trait of which Shakespeare made extravagant use, but jibs at a lack of plausibility" (p. 128). "The only ideas that can affect [the spectators] when they are welded together in that unity which is an audience are those commonplace fundamental ideas that are almost feelings. These, the root ideas of poetry, are love, death, and the destiny of man . . . the great truths are too important to be new." (Pp. 131–32.) Plays containing original ideas, like Shaw's and Ibsen's, are because of them soon outmoded. "The disadvantage of ideas in the theater is that if they are acceptable, they are accepted, and so kill the play that helped to diffuse them." (P. 133.) The only plays that are not ephemeral are in verse, which "delivers a play from sober reality . . . and so makes it easier for the audience to attune themselves to that state of feeling in which they are most susceptible to the drama's specific appeal. . . . For the drama is make-believe. It does not deal with truth but with effect." (Pp. 134, 140–41.)

In the mouths of many critics "effect" is a word of reproach. But there are more ways than one of getting it, as also of being "theatrical"; and the dramatist indifferent to either matter is more than likely to be a failure. Surely Mr. Maugham would agree with what Mr. Strong has said of melodrama[2] as offering Shakespeare in tragedy "the chance to exhibit character at its highest pitch of intensity," for he says something parallel of farce. "It is the life-blood that makes the body of comedy viable" (p. 145). And in "sober reality" he refers of course to the hampering restrictions of faithful realism, not the philosophical or psychological "reality" of Freud, which his introvert genius flees from and returns to in the form of his daydreams, by the way of art. Like Mr. Roger Fry, Mr. Maugham would brush this sort of art aside, paying tribute only to that which

[2] *Common Sense About the Drama* (1937), p. 47.—Cf. my *Shakespeare and Other Masters* (1940), pp. 202, 219, 230, 243, 248.

creates its own world, the parts of which, as Coleridge says, mutually support and explain each other, or, as Mr. Fry says, are "in completest relationship."[3] Most of these principles Mr. Maugham himself applies explicitly to Shakespeare. "Only idolatry can refuse to see the great shortcomings in the conduct and sometimes in the characterization of Shakespeare's plays; and this is very comprehensible since, as we know, he sacrificed everything to effective situation." (P. 160.)

To all the above, as anyone who should have read my previous article or any of my other writings would expect, I readily subscribe; except in so far as the "shortcomings" are made out to be "great," for then with "the effect" they would interfere. The plays being written, as Mr. Maugham says, "in imperishable verse," and thus "delivered from reality," the liberties are taken even for the sake of the effect; and it is merely on the greatness of the shortcoming that I disagree with him about Stendhal, though here, of course, verse is not in question:

This is a very great novel, but it is generally acknowledged that the end is unsatisfactory. The reason is not hard to find. Stendhal got the idea for it from an incident that at the time made a great stir: a young seminarist killed his mistress, was tried and guillotined. But Stendhal put into Julien Sorel, his hero, not only a great deal of himself, but much more of what he would have liked to be and was miserably conscious that he was not; he created one of the most interesting personages of fiction and for fully three quarters of his book made him behave with coherence and probability; but then he found himself forced to return to the facts that had been his inspiration. He could only do this by causing his hero to act incongruously with his character and his intelligence. The shock is so great that you no longer believe, and when you do not believe in a novel you are no longer held. The moral is that you must have the courage to throw your facts overboard if they fail to comply with the logic of your character. (P. 211.)

Actually, in both the record and the novel, there was no killing; but the intent was the same, and most critics, both

[3] *Hogarth Essays* (1924), "The Artist and Psychoanalysis."

French and English, are—and rightly—of the opinion that the deed of horror is inadequately motived. Some fall back upon the original story, not, like Mr. Maugham, to blame the author but to excuse him, as has been done for Oedipus' blinding of himself, and for many of the improbabilities in Shakespeare. But from the historical account of M. Marsan, it appears that Stendhal was little troubled by fidelity to his "facts," refashioned both them and the characters for his purpose. What he does retain and preserve is precisely the shocking and (for a hero) improbable deed of horror to which Mr. Maugham and the others object: —the situation of the young seminarist of remarkable intelligence who shot his former mistress (whom he loved more than the later one), the wife of his employer, in church, during the celebration of mass, because, as he thought, she had thwarted him in his intrigue with the daughter of a later employer and in the brilliant career opening up before him. Thus what the author wanted—and what almost alone he took—is explained away as inseparably attached to what he took. It is as if a kidnaper went after not the baby but its clothes. On the contrary, it was, as I conceive it, by the murder of the beloved in the church that Stendhal was fascinated, much as Shakespeare was by Holinshed's three women in strange and wild apparel, bidding the victorious thane "All hail, Macbeth, that hereafter shalt be king of Scotland," which he then conspires to be; and by Cinthio's Ensign leading the deeply enamored Moor to murder; and by Kyd's Hamlet learning the secret of the murder from the Ghost and then taking to madness, which both betrays and hinders him in his revenge; and by the traditional Lear casting off his only loving daughter because she does not love him, to die of a broken heart because she dies.

Psychologically, to be sure, that will not do. As I have said before,

. . . there is no adequate motive for the tender and noble Madame de Rênal's sending the disparaging letter which (when he learns of it) provokes Sorel to rush off and shoot her, and none for his taking such vengeance or not suspecting that she was under undue influence or coercion. . . . The deed and the letter both are justified only by the situation that ensues—the ecstasies of penitence and devotion, self-renunciation and heroism, for which in more natural circumstances there would have been no occasion. Never had he known how much she loved him as now when, wounded, despite scandal, she visits him in prison; never had she had such a way of showing it.[4]

That is a meager and inadequate account; but for the improbability there is warrant, and it lies in the situation. It is in the intense concentration and summary (thus made available) of the whole previous story, whether through the visits of his friends and of his two mistresses, jealous of each other, or through his remorseful retrospect, and courageous and magnanimous bearing, under the shadow of death. Death brought upon him without his own guilt would not make a situation so deep or so sharply cut. It would not make drama, with no fate or villain at hand.

Thinking of his first mistress he says to himself, in the presence of the second, who in all good faith has been vowing suicide: *la personne à qui j'ai voulu ôter la vie sera la seule qui sincèrement pleurera ma mort.* (ii, chap. 42.)

Before that, because of the attitude of her family, he begs Mathilde to put her child, when it comes, to nurse at Verrières, under the supervision of Madame de Rênal; and then silently he says that "after fifteen years she will adore him and you will have forgotten him." (ii, chap. 39.)

And when Madame de Rênal herself, having somewhat recovered, comes imploring him to make the expected judicial appeal, and to her he promises what he has refused to Mathilde, in return for the promise to visit him in the interval every day, she gives, amid the rapture of his embrace, a little cry of pain, from the wound: *"À ton épaule,"* s'écria Julien, *"fondant en larmes."* (ii, chap. 43.)

Surely the above details make drama, and so do these:

—*Qui me l'eût dit, la dernière fois que je te vis, dans ta chambre, à Verrières?*
—*Qui m'eût dit alors que j'écrirais à M. de la Mole cette lettre infâme?*
—*Sache que je t'ai toujours aimée, que je n'ai aimé que toi.*

[4]*Shakespeare and Other Masters,* pp. 403–4.

—*Est-il bien possible! s'écria Madame de Rênal, ravie à son tour.
Elle s'appuya sur Julien, qui était à ses genoux, et longtemps
ils pleurèrent en silence (ibid.).*

And how far her passion goes appears from the fact that
despite her piety, which forced her at the dictate of her
confessor to write the letter, she can declare:

*Je crois sincèrement en Dieu; je crois également, et même cela
m'est prouvé, que le crime que je commets est affreux, et dès que
je te vois, même après que tu m'as tiré deux coups de pistolet.
. . . Dès que je te vois, tous les devoirs disparaissent, je ne suis
plus qu'amour pour toi . . . (Ibid.)*

Greater love hath no woman than this, that she brave together scandal and damnation.

But the situation, the soul-searching passions, are not all.
For the hero there is purification as well. This young low-
born ambitious egoist with a grudge against society, this
proud and dauntless soul to whom a desire is a duty and
any difficulty but a challenge, learns under the stress of solitude and under the pressure of introspection to know himself. When checked by the letter in the career that now
seemed assured, he has wreaked himself on the obstacle
or offender, as he had done or been on the point of doing
in the past, without thinking. Now he thinks. Shortly after
the crime he writes to Mathilde, *Je me suis vengé;* and a
little later he says to himself, *Je meurs après avoir soldé
mon compte envers l'humanité* (chap. 36). Only when he
hears that Madame de Rênal is not dead and is recovering,
does he begin to repent. Only then, as Mr. Green says, "does
the criminal visualize her as an individual." *"Grand Dieu!
Elle n'est pas morte"; et il tomba à genoux, pleurant à
chaudes larmes. Dans ce moment suprême, il était croyant
. . . "Ainsi elle vivra. . . . Elle vivra pour me pardon-
ner . . ."* (chap. 36). Thus he gradually comes to realize
as never before what was false and pretentious in his life;
and to deplore his egoism and ambition. His purification,
however, is more passionate than moral: what he calls his
repentance is a higher, finer devotion to Madame de
Rênal (chap. 39). His chief regret, as Mr. Green says,

"is that in those bygone days . . . he wasted the golden hours in futile, ambitious schemings." But even "this regret," as Mr. Green[5] also says, "is submerged in the immense happiness created by the knowledge that now, for the first time, he can talk to his mistress with complete sincerity."

It is for this greatly passionate situation, I think, and this purification or refinement of the hero, that the improbability is incurred. It is a considerable one, we must confess. It is not only that the hero should thus treat his former mistress as if she were the mere embodiment of high-class society, but also that she should, under whatsoever influence or compulsion, have penned such a letter and, still more, that he should not have suspected the compulsion (along with a little jealousy) there. Plausibility, however, Stendhal, like other novelists and dramatists, has provided for as best he could. Not, like Shakespeare with Othello and Iago, by traditional conventions or the creation of an independent world, the parts of which mutually support and explain each other; not by calumny credited, and the frank, initial assumption of the hero's trustfulness and his inexperience with Venetian women, of Iago's impenetrableness and his unquestionable reputation for sagacity and integrity; but by fairly realistic analysis and the repeated previous exhibition of the traits now brought to bear. The preparations are less poetic and external, more psychological and internal, as in a novel they must or can be. From the beginning Madame de Rênal has been under the sway of religious scruples, and frequently in that spirit resisted Julien's advances and suppressed her own response. And from the beginning Julien has been animated by pride and ambition and, in his ventures, impelled by unscrupulous daring or social resentment. Both of his amours were undertaken as much in the spirit of bravado and pique as in that of personal attraction; and though in the end he was in love with the woman, he continually revenged himself upon her, particularly upon Mathilde, who was as proud as he and higher than her rival in rank. And the outbreak, when

[5]F. C. Green, *Stendhal* (1939), pp. 233, 237.

he shot Madame de Rênal, even that is repeatedly prepared for. Nothing has ever baffled or daunted him. He has fought a duel. And Mathilde herself, though only a few days after she had surrendered her honor to him, he was at the point of stabbing because she was offish and had pricked his *amour propre*. (ii, 17.) Before the conquest:—*"Eh bien, elle est jolie!" continuait Julien avec des regards de tigre* (ii, chap. x); and after he has received from her a compromising letter but suspects a trap:—

Il faut en convenir, le regard de Julien était atroce, sa physionomie hideuse; elle respirait le crime sans alliage. C'était l'homme malheureux en guerre avec toute la société (ii, chap. 13).

Long before that, at Verrières, as the venture into Madame de Rênal's chamber impended, he said to himself:

Au moment précis où dix heures sonneront, j'exécuterai ce que, pendant toute la journée, je me suis promis de faire ce soir, ou je monterai chez moi brûler la cervelle. (i, chap. 9.)

An *homme terrible,* and theatrical too after the Renaissance French or Italian style; and to the North he seems also unbalanced, or unconvincing. He is certainly, despite his sympathy and tears for the poor and downtrodden and his generous admiration for what is fine and noble, a character considerably wanting in the solid attractiveness Anglo-Saxons demand of the leading figure in fiction. That is partly French taste (for in French fiction the heroes are often more interesting than amiable); partly the result of internal psychological preparations for the critical change. Psychology, as Mr. Abercrombie says of Hardy below, somewhat troubles the emotional effect; and a character is more real if either like Othello he enchants or like Iago he enthralls. And even after the crisis the psychological procedure is continued. Once he is lodged in prison, as during the brain storm before, the novel reads a little like Lombroso or Havelock Ellis, like Dostoievski, not Shakespeare:

Il se sentait la tête comme si elle eût été serrée avec violence. Il regarda pour voir si quelqu'un le tenait. Après quelques instants, il s'endormit profondément. (ii, chap. 36.)

So a few hours later, after writing to Mathilde and saying to himself that he has *soldé son compte envers l'humanité,* but before having word of Madame de Rênal:

> *Je n'ai plus rien à faire sur la terre . . . et il s'endormit profondément.* (chap. 36.)

A dreamless sleep, in reaction, and because the score is paid.

For Julien is a study, an emotional but not a poetic and imaginative creation like Othello. He is in prose there, is more the product of analysis than imagination. Yet, like Othello, improbable in his deed of horror, he is made plausible, though to a less degree. But it is in prison, by way of his improbable crime and unnecessary penalty, that he becomes less studied, more emotional and attractive. His courage itself is purified, ennobled. It has no longer anything of the unscrupulous gallant or housebreaker in it. He disdains to save his life, though by love implored. He disdains to accept the lawyer's plea of insanity or to countenance any other excuses. To do so would have blotted his scutcheon, bedimmed his new-found happiness. Nothing in life becomes him like his surrender of it. *Laissez-moi ma vie idéale,* he cries so pregnantly; *. . . On meurt comme on peut.* (ii, chap. 40.)

2

The *Oedipus Tyrannus,* like its author, is of a different order; and yet the ending of the tragedy, as indeed the tragedy (but not the novel) as a whole, has a similar justification—it presents the passions. From the beginning the situation is improbable; and though in a different way, the blinding of the hero by his own hands is so as well. For like most of the other greatest tragedies ancient or modern, the *Oedipus* is, in the finished product, sheer poetry, and in the raw material, sheer melodrama. It is but the supreme example of the principle pronounced by Corneille in his *Discours du poème tragique: Les grands sujets de la tragédie, qui remuent fortement les passions . . . doivent tou-*

jours aller au delà du vraisemblable. This is in order that, as his contemporary and rival Racine puts it in the preface to *Bérénice,* we may have the passions in "their violence"; or as Mr. L. A. G. Strong puts it, "character at its highest pitch of intensity." And in the *Oedipus,* as all the world knows, are attained the uttermost limits of pity and fear. But how the improbable is made probable—by the familiarity of the story which disarms incredulity, by the poetry which delivers the play from sober reality, by preparations and gradual development, by the operation of fate under the semblance of justice, by the superficial fitness of the hero for the role despite the essential contrast of his character with it, and by the engaging of our wholehearted admiration and sympathy for him—all that I cannot now consider again.[6]

What here concerns us is the catastrophe, which is shocking, not, like that of *Le Rouge,* with surprise (for it is part of the familiar story) yet, like that, with horror. And like that, again, though prepared for, it cannot be made wholly acceptable. Nowadays, to the reader, far from the stage and beyond the spell of poetry and the sway of the Greek *mores* and religion, it is acceptable in a still less degree. It is even more for the passions' sake, and psychology does not here apply. Oedipus is not a study. Neither Lombroso and Ellis, on the one hand, nor Freud, with his unfortunately named complex, on the other, has anything to do with the case.

Suicide, as with his wife (and mother) Jocasta, would, to our way of thinking, have been much preferable; but that would have been contrary to the familiar myth and would have disappointed the audience both by the innovation and the undiscriminating repetition. It would have spoiled the story. What is more, it would have offered less of a tragic opportunity. In the narrow compass of three hundred lines after his desperate exit, and of less than two hundred with him on the stage, is a situation not unlike that in the chapters after the murder in *Le Rouge.* As there, this hero, though incomparably nobler, appears in a new and better light. He has here no occasion like Julien's for

[6]See *op. cit.,* chap. 2, 6.

remorse, but he has it—and so have we—for realization of the horror of his fate, his own and his wife's and children's. In blindness he sees better than with his eyes. His pride is humbled. His generosity is awakened, his affections quickened. He thinks of his family now, not merely of the state. He pleads for his children to Creon, whom, as he recognizes, he had unjustly accused. And he begs to be cast out of the city that it might not be ceremonially polluted by his unholy presence. The great king, reader of riddles—on whose fortunes what citizen did not gaze with envy?—is, like no other mortal, now brought low, but not daunted or abased. Suicide would not have brought him so low nor have opened the way to such thoughts and emotions. And suicide would have interrupted the process of purification gloriously consummated in the sequel, the *Oedipus Coloneus.*

The deed of self-laceration is not, even so much as Julien's crime, to be interpreted psychologically, on the rebound. It is not morbid or abnormal, is not, however frenzied, an act of masochism. Julien's deed of horror can only in part, as we have seen, be psychologically interpreted; but that of Oedipus not at all. The very familiarity of the legendary story forbids us to inquire too curiously; the situation is epical rather than, in our modern sense, strictly dramatic. In the ancient sense, however, it is dramatic enough. It involves the notion of justice, of retribution, of nemesis, which the hero heroically brings down upon himself. This is his high desperate desire. Seeing, he has been blind—what is there now to see? How could he, a patricide, incestuous, "hated of heaven," "look with steady eyes" on his people, on his children, or—for the ghost was as the body—on his father, when he came to the place of the dead?[7] Still, matters of justice or of purification, either, as well as of psychology, are not the primary intention, but the emotions produced, the fullest possible realization of the hero's fate. As Mr. Lubbock has it, "the novelist's ingenuity is always the same; it is to give his subject the highest relief [not the closest verisimilitude] by which it is capable of

[7] Ll. 1334-35, 1370-85.

profiting;[8] and that is still truer of the tragic dramatist, who has poetry at his disposal.

For Aristotle rightly holds plot—structure and situation —not character, to be the first essential, and the life and soul, as it were, of tragedy; rightly he is preoccupied with its emotional effect—that of pity and fear—considering tragedy to be essentially an imitation not of persons but of action and life, of happiness and misery.[9] That is, not of character, not of life just as we know it, but as in the oracular Miltonic lines,

> Of fate and chance and change in human life,
> High actions and high passions best describing.

And this is in keeping with the practice of dramatists in the greatest days and even in ours, as dramatists, poets, and critics like Yeats, Henry Arthur Jones,[10] and Mr. Santayana have lately acknowledged. In the prose drama and the novel—both not delivered from reality—character necessarily plays a larger part; is more strictly the source of the action. But in the poetic drama, like *Der Arme Heinrich,* and in the earlier drama, which is mostly poetic, the action is not primarily so to be interpreted. Hamlet in speaking of the national vice of drunkenness as the one little defect that spoils the Danish people's reputation is not betraying a sizable defect that spoils his own character; his admiration for the active Fortinbras and his sympathy for the reckless Laertes are not intended to make us wish him appreciably more like either; and his meditating on death in the graveyard is not meant to seem an irrelevance or an act of procrastination. So Othello in hearkening to Iago is not stupid; and Iago himself when his hypocrisy is too transparent for successful deception in life (remember Tartuffe and the *optique du théâtre*) is not clumsily showing his hand.

[8]*The Craft of Fiction* (1921), p. 173.

[9]*Poetics,* chap. 6.

[10]*Strand Magazine,* vol. 34, p. 379. For Yeats see the preceding chapter and for Santayana, chap. XVII below.

And still more should we be wary of such interpretation in ancient tragedy. Still less should character there be interpreted on the rebound. Many years ago I observed in print that contemporary criticism of the classics has been corrupted by that of Shakespeare, making Orestes, for instance, a Bradleian irresolute Hamlet. Since then several classical scholars have endeavored to clear the atmosphere. One of these, Professor Owen of Toronto, has recently protested against Professor Goodell's principle:

> Given an old myth to be dramatized, Sophocles' primary question was, "Just what sort of people were they, must they have been, who naturally did and suffered what the tales say they did and suffered?" That was his method of analysis.[11]

Mr. Owen, rightly, does not think so. Jocasta's "skepticism about oracles is brought in not because in view of her experience she would naturally or probably be skeptical, but because it is dramatically valuable . . . deepens the emotional effect of the whole." That is, the oracle is "coming true through events that seem to disprove it." And the dramatic value of that lies not by any means so much in the naturalness of Jocasta's skepticism as, I think, in her skepticism in the teeth of fate, and in her naturally eager inclination to such skepticism in the circumstances. It lies in the irony, in her hybris. After her first utterances in this vein she re-enters with propitiatory offerings to the gods because of her misgivings. But hearing of the death of Polybus, Oedipus' putative father, she breaks out for all that—not so much because of the past as because of the present—in skepticism once more. How could she, in the circumstances, believe and live?—as speedily appears.

In ancient as in Shakespearean drama the subject of the hero's or heroine's past, of such matters as environment, heredity, and previous experience, is not to be entertained unless the dramatist directly touches upon it. It is, moreover, not likely to be touched upon; for as Goethe says, Sophocles *ging bei seinen Stücken keineswegs von einer*

[11]*University Toronto Quarterly*, October, 1940, p. 56.

Idee aus, but took a legend and made it effective on the stage. Such matters are like the *arrière-pensées* and undercurrents in the psychology. "In drama," says Mr. Lubbock,[12] like Burke and Wordsworth and William Archer before him, "the spectator must judge by appearances." Even in contemporary highbrow drama, "considerations which are not suggested to the audience," as Mr. Courtney has it, "are considerations which do not exist for them." And in tragedies such as the *Oedipus,* involving improbabilities so prodigious, since the past will not bear uncontrolled inspection we are to consider only what the dramatist himself recalls. Oedipus and Jocasta both are, like Othello and Hamlet, Lear and Macbeth, so far from being each the source of the action, the arbiter of his own destiny, that in large measure they are thrown into contrast with it. There mainly lies the tragedy—the hero doing, through external influence, what he is not inclined, but is bound, and abhors, to do. Jocasta is not cruel, though, in deference to the oracle, she had exposed her child. Neither she nor Oedipus is at all stupid, and yet not only before the tragedy opens but also during the course of it both have repeatedly failed to take the hint. Even that there may be a tragedy they must fail, but this improbability is subdued and obscured as much as may be. The truth—that he has killed his own father, married his own mother and cursed himself— is too horrible to be accepted: the truth itself is what is most improbable: and thus the improbability of the initial situation supports even that in the course of the inquiry. Moreover, the story is well maneuvered for the purpose. Continually Oedipus and Jocasta are led astray, are given straws to snatch at. Laius' death, for instance, is reported as at the hand of robbers, not of a solitary unoffending traveler. A report not unheeded!

While, however, Oedipus, like Hamlet and Othello and

[12]*Op. cit.,* p. 162; and for the others cf. my *Shakespeare and Other Masters,* p. 355, where their words are cited as bearing upon Falstaff, apparently a coward and one therefore actually. The Falstaff of criticism, as the wisest critics have insisted or admitted, would not become apparent on the stage.

in less measure Lear and Macbeth, is not essentially to blame for his dire misfortune, he like them somewhat contributes to it, for otherwise he would be less tragic; and this is some preparation, or artistic justification, for the blinding at the end. He is high-tempered and impetuous, dauntless and relentless. So it is that at the beginning he calls down a curse upon the slayer of Laius, who has brought the plague upon the city. So it is that he quarrels with Teiresias and Creon, who covertly bring the terrible charges or insinuations against him. And so it is that he presses forward over all obstacles and past all warnings in his way. This last, certainly, is not to be reckoned against him, though, indeed, it has been—"gross moral impropriety in the bias whereby he seeks for himself the solution of his own problematic existence"! It is to his credit, as Mr. Sargeaunt rightly thinks, "this passionate search for the truth and devotion to it though it kill him"; also it is a duty to his stricken people and his plighted word.[13] And thus, as he presses on to discover (even after he has more than a suspicion), the man whom he has blindly cursed, he, if any normal person ever could, was the one in that day, when a curse had a meaning, when purity was a matter hieratic and ceremonial —external as much as internal—and expiation was indispensable, to face the music and fulfill the curse himself. And in such fashion? That was justice in kind,[14] (which appealed to the ancient religious sense—Hebrew, Christian, or pagan), like old Cranmer's when he stretched his right hand, which had "offended," into the fire. And if to do so was not morbid or abnormal, it was certainly more terrible and religious than to die.

3

Of Masefield's Nan and Hardy's Tess I have recently said that they are:

... sweet and patient, brave and loving creatures, and the deed of horror is warranted by no motive such as self-defense or the de-

[13]Cf. my *Shakespeare and Other Masters*, p. 74.

[14]Cf. line 1273.

fense of another, but only by an accumulation of injury. In the flesh either woman would have turned her back on the man and faced life anew. But with that ending, of course, such passions could not be let loose in the story, nor such emotions of pity and fear in spectator or reader. What Tess has done and what she is to suffer are what makes the scene at Stonehenge so poignant. Her seducer's death and her own are the measure of the "happiness" which she her whole life long had missed, and now, after bloodshed, has for a moment attained. And this terror there must be, as the price of that pity which we unquestionably feel.[15]

In both the play and the novel the writer has not the advantage of poetry: of both is true what at the same time I said in defense of *Tess,* that if the critic's "preference of *Jude* is justifiable, this is only because *Tess* too is a novel, not a tragedy, in prose, not verse, and is in language and circumstance too little removed from reality to give the poetic conception full sway, or warrant the violence done to the psychology."[16] It is only since then that I have read Mr. Abercrombie (writing in 1912, however) and found him saying that though *Jude* has "a decidedly richer humanity [truth, in short, or realism] than *Tess of the D'Urbervilles;* for this very reason it has also perhaps a less tremendous mastery over the reader's emotions than that bare tragedy; for tragedy is somewhat mitigated when attention is curiously employed with psychology."[17]

While, however, not enjoying the full liberty of poetry, this novel and this play participate in some of its high privileges. In both, time and place are appropriate, season and circumstance: in *Nan* night, the tide coming in, and the coach horn; in *Tess* the forest, Salisbury Plain and the vast changing but unrelenting heavens. And in language the drama, especially, approaches the freedom of verse. The dialect of the impassioned Nan and the half-witted Gaffer rises to the level of Synge in the *Riders to the Sea;* it goes

[15]*Op. cit.,* p. 404.

[16]*Ibid.,* p. 406. Both novels, however, like Stendhal's, suffer from the unfamiliarity of the improbable situation as ancient or Shakespearean tragedy does not.

[17]*Thomas Hardy* (1912), p. 159.

over the bounds of realism. Besides, the passions themselves and the deeds of horror, though without adequate motive, have the poetical or narrative equivalent—adequate preparation. Tess once struck Alec on the mouth when he spoke insultingly of her husband; and now he has spoken of him worse, after being the cause of her losing him again. So Nan drew her knife on her aunt when she discovered that she had thrown her new gown into the pigwash. And both heroines have even a real motivation by a sort of unconscious self-deception. Like Othello, Nan stabs Dick, else he'll betray others; and Tess stabs Alec, not only because of his heaping insult upon injury, but also because she thinks Angel "would be sure to forgive me now I have done that." "And his horror at her impulse was mixed with amazement at the strength of her affection. . . ." In real life we expect people who do jealous or vindictive deeds to be prompted by jealous or vindictive emotions, or if there be a slanderer, to be apparently the persons to lend him an ear. But not necessarily on the stage or even in the novel. In real life self-deceptions and paltering with motives are frowned upon, but not so rigorously on the stage or even in the novel. A hero or heroine in fiction is not an ethical pattern: a play or novel is not a lesson for edification, nor a study in casuistry either. Here there are larger issues, wider, finer sympathies. The last-quoted sentence ends with the words "and at the strangeness of its quality, which had apparently extinguished her moral sense altogether." Then the author continues:

Unable to realize the gravity of her conduct she seemed at last content; and he looked at her as she lay upon his shoulder, weeping with happiness, and wondered what obscure strain in the D'Urberville blood had led to this aberration . . . he supposed that in the moment of mad grief of which she spoke her mind had lost its balance, and plunged her into this abyss (chap. 57).

A young English critic[18] seems to think the chief improbability lies in Tess's returning to Alec—as he conceives her she would not have done so "even to save her family from

[18]W. R. Rutland (Blackwell, Oxford, 1938, pp. 237–38).

starvation." Her devotion, however, a woman's, is not to ideals—to abstractions—but to persons. She returns to Alec, who seems to love her a little, because of her family, and because of her husband who seems now to love her not at all; and she breaks out wildly against Alec because he had (indirectly) brought about Angel's desertion, and just now his leaving her anew, and has spoken insultingly of him into the bargain. Who has not known of a fine and affectionate woman taking up with the man who wants her even because she cannot have the man she wants? Tess had the family on her mind, besides. And how, on the other hand, in the face of this killing, can Mr. Rutland then say, "This is the love that seeketh not her own, that is not easily provoked, that thinketh no evil"; though, indeed, "it never faileth"?[19] The novel (again) is not a lesson or a study. The character cannot be made perfectly consistent but the emotional impression is. "What the story does for Tess," says Mr. Abercrombie, "is to accept her with all the sympathy and understanding of love. A charity that is infinitely larger than forgiveness accompanies her, loving her weakness as well as her strength, exquisitely understanding how her beautiful nature is forced by agony into crime."[20] Or as another critic and man of letters, Gissing, says of another novelist, Dickens, "Abstract the sympathy, substitute cold observation, and we should have a truth, perhaps, but wholly uninteresting. It is only by the vehicle of emotion that life can be translated into art."[21] So it is with Tess. *Multum amavit.* And if her story is not strictly probable, partly because it is not is the greatness of her love so completely borne in upon us. "Half the sculptor's touches," says Ruskin, "are not to realize but to put power into the form."

[19]*Op. cit.*, p. 238. However, Mr. Rutland does object to the murder with the carvingknife; and he is the only critic I have noticed who finds fault with the extraordinary blood, which ran through a mattress and a ceiling. "Drip, drip, drip"—this is the great improbability, melodrama for which there is no tragic excuse.

[20]*Op. cit.*, p. 144.

[21]*Immortal Dickens* (1925), p. 214.

4

Pompilia, the last and by far the most faultless of the tender, patient, and affectionate young women whom we are considering, does herself no such violence. But neither does she create so big a situation as the others or thus awaken such emotion in reader or spectator. Her seizing Guido's sword to defend Caponsacchi is morally fine, is (in itself) artistically admirable. And Browning here is following his source, like Sophocles and Stendhal. Like Stendhal, however, but unlike Sophocles, he did not need faithfully and punctiliously to follow his source, for it was not, as the Greek's was, well known; yet like them both, and more completely than they did, he followed it from a storyteller's true inclination. It is a good and indispensable point in the story —the child heroine's striking at the enemy, as not for herself, for him who has braved so immeasurably much for her. Not to have done so would have been a failure to rise to the occasion, leaving a gap in the story. Still she is not, convincingly, the woman to do it. One so patient, tender and unresentful, who in her instinctive purity, finds evil an unreal thing, a nightmare, and who, unlike Caponsacchi when deeply regretting his failure to kill Guido at the time he had the chance, wishes him no evil, hopes for his salvation, and once out of his way, in the fullness of love and spiritual happiness has nothing to regret—of her it is difficult to think as using the sword against her husband or even drawing it on him. There is preparation for it, to be sure, in the legend she remembers, as she awaits Caponsacchi's first appearance (l. 1376), of the virgin who grasped the sword of lightning and brandished it against her enemies. And she was fearless and gallant enough in breaking away from Guido, but that was without bloodshed and for the child; while before that she was charity itself, which beareth all things, endureth all things. And how ill at ease Browning is with her at this moment appears from her speech. As Caponsacchi reports her, it is

    . . . "Die," cried she, "devil, in God's name";

and as she reports herself, it is

> I did spring up, attempt to thrust aside
> That ice-block 'twixt the sun and me, lay low
> The neutralizer of all good and truth.

Neither speech is like her, so marvelously identical in thought and utterance elsewhere. The first is melodrama unrelieved; the second—"neutralizer," on those heavenly, yet untutored lips!—is only Browning. A story, however, needs incident—with striking attitude and gesture—as well as appropriate utterance; needs passions in their intensity rather than in perfect consistency, even though, as here, the intensity thus attained is not at the highest pitch. In *In a Balcony*, certainly, the poet succeeds with the venturesome undertaking. In Pompilia's immortal monologue, the consistency—the psychology, as some would call it—at one point failing, the poetry there fails too. But with Sophocles and Shakespeare—even with Hardy in a sense—such a point, above all, is the opportunity for poetry, which does not fail.

5

Men naturally are less a prey to passion; and a more convincing modern example of the storyteller seizing upon a bold sharp contrast for a situation at the cost of probability, is Raskolnikoff in Dostoevski's *Crime and Punishment*, much praised for motivation and psychology both, but, as it seems to me in rereading, rightly only for the latter. The psychical mechanism and maneuvers are subtly presented and acceptable, but only after the motive for the murder is taken for granted quite as much as if it were the compelling influence of fate or of a ghost or of a clever villain. A cultivated youth of good family kills a woman pawnbroker and her sister, with no reason but his need of money and his "advanced" idea that the extraordinary people have a right to it and his victim is but vermin. Yet, both before and after the deed, he is indifferent to money and generous with it, making no use of the stolen, and considers the deed itself ignoble and odious; whereupon there is nothing left but the advanced idea, together with a distressed and morbid condition, and a craving for a show of power, to cover over the contradiction, and neutralize the sophism, in a good, tenderhearted, high-minded man's committing a cruel, treacherous, and sordid crime. And sympathy? Since the passions play so small a part, and influence, conventional or natural, none at all, sympathy, except in the subsequent developments—the punishment and purification—is almost wanting. Even for the situation, then, without much emotion, the improbability offers advantages.

1941

CHAPTER XII

Falstaff Again

> *They have introduced an almost insane individu-*
> *alism into that one form of intercourse which is*
> *specially and uproariously communal. They have*
> *made even levities into secrets. They have made*
> *laughter lonelier than tears.*
>
> CHESTERTON, on esoteric humorists.

FALSTAFF UND KEIN ENDE, for this is the third time[1] I have
tackled the subject. But the first of the Romantic and
philosophical re-creations dies hardest, though the case
against it is, I think, the plainest and strongest of all. Like
the literary (rather than the dramatic) Hamlet, Shylock,
and Iago, it was produced when Shakespeare was losing his
hold on the stage, partly in the critics' thought that he was
too good for it; and in the closet, the stage was no longer
remembered. Maurice Morgann, though actually not so distant from the theater as the Scotchmen William Richardson and Henry Mackenzie, upon whom his mantle immediately fell, was as much so in spirit; and in his essay of 1777
he not only fixed the features of the Falstaff of criticism

[1]*Shakespeare Studies* (1927), chap. viii; *Shakespeare and Other
Masters* (1940), chap. x.

but provided the doctrine for the new critical school. Bradley, Cazamian, and Charlton have merely finished the picture—elaborated the apologia—; and in the treatment of
Shakespearean characters as if "historic rather than dramatic beings," in the preference of "secret impressions" to
the "apparent" ones, subsequent criticism has, illegitimately,
delighted.

For on such tenets no criticism worthy of the name could
be securely founded. According to these, Falstaff's conduct
is cowardly; but his character, that subtler essence or entity,
is courageous; and he must have had the constitutional
instincts of courage although (before the play began, without, in the play itself, any hint of the calamity!) he had
lost the "principles" which ordinarily accompany them.
The play presents a problem, is a puzzle; and that, still less
than a tragedy—"to be followed with perfect comprehension and profoundest emotion," Matthew Arnold remarked
in one of his most inspired and (what in a poet is not always the same) most sensible utterances—can a successful
comedy do or be. Johnson, as quoted by Malone, in reply
to Morgann declared that "all he should say, was that if
Falstaff was not a coward Shakespeare knew nothing of his
art"; and Dryden, as well as all England up to that time,
stood behind him.[2] Here is, then, a puzzle—if this critic,
with his doctrines, is (as he has been) to be heeded. But
for laughter, still more than for tears and tremors, unanimity in the audience (there the critics do not matter!) is
indispensable; and at a comedy still more than at a tragedy
(though that Professor Kittredge did not say) "the audience is never to be perplexed."[3] Nor should a reader of a
closet drama be, either—of such a one as, by his criticism,
Morgann himself is really writing. That is, unless he reads it.

The like considerations, however, have been ignored;

[2] For Dryden, see below, and cf. *The Monthly Review*, LVII
(1777), 80, quoted by Professor R. W. Babcock: "In dramatic
writings, especially, the obvious meaning is most probably the true
one; and it is surely no great compliment to Shakespeare's admirable delineation of the character of Falstaff, to suppose that it had
hitherto been generally misunderstood." Such compliments are still
freely paid!   *Shakespeare* (1916), p. 19.

and the problem has been complicated as, later, in various
fashions and degrees, not only the fat man's cowardice but
his other vicious qualities have been either condoned or
explained away. This, for readers or students, seems to
make him more "intriguing," more appealing. For the same
reason they will have him no longer a butt as well as a wit.
The joke is never on him, they say (though on the stage it
sometimes inevitably and confessedly is,[4] which Addison,
in his time, even took for granted). This exemption makes
him less inconsistent, to be sure, but not funnier. Quite the
contrary, I think; and as for the vicious qualities—his cowardice and lying, thieving and swindling—by minimizing
them, taking them for sheer "merriment" and make-believe,
or raising him to a philosophic level above them, Morgann
and his school not only do violence to the text but, as was
clearly recognized in his own day and after, further reduce
the comic impact. They relieve the rascal of his predicaments—his evasions and excuses are then unreal as well as
his plight. That state of affairs, to a normal and natural
audience at any rate, cannot be hugely amusing. The contrast is lost. "And what could support Falstaff," Morgann
cries, "in such a situation [on the battlefield]? . . . What,
then, but a strong natural . . . constitutional courage,
which nothing could extinguish or dismay?"[5] Courage is
not amusing, but to one who vividly remembers the comic
scenes in question that sentence is. And, as I have elsewhere
said, his vices must be real vices or there is no comedy in his
virtuous pretenses; his predicaments must be real predicaments or there is no comedy in his escape.[6] That drama-

---

[4] "Ah, no more o' that, Hal, an thou lovest me," et cetera. Pt. I, II,
iv, 310; "No abuse, Hal; o' mine honour, no abuse," et cetera.
Pt. II, II, iv, 340.

[5] Morgann's *Essay* (1777), p. 97.

[6] *Shakespeare-Jahrbuch*, LXXIV (1938), 61. Tom Davies (*Dram.
Misc.*, 1785, I, 272–73: "the whole mirth in the admired scene of
his detected tergiversation, depends upon it" [cowardice]; Richard
Stack, my *Shakespeare Studies*, p. 445; *Shakespeare and Other
Masters*, p. 354. Davies, the actor friend of Johnson, thought, like
him and Stack and *The Monthly Review* as cited above, that
Morgann was endeavoring to display his ingenuity.

tist, moreover, who does not distinguish the real from the unreal, knows, as Johnson said, "nothing of his art."

In fact, by the intended merriment (not Morgann's), at Falstaff's expense, and by his again in retort, the vices are not extenuated but, as it were, disinfected or deprived of their sting. Professor Elton agrees with George Gissing in finding in Falstaff, as in Sairey Gamp (who also, in her swindling and other professional misdemeanors, is certainly not pretending), "the same perfect method of idealism put to use in converting to a source of pleasure things that in life repel or nauseate, and in both cases the sublimation . . . is effected by a humour which seems unsurpassable"; or, as Mr. Elton himself has it, this is "the triumph of an adroit idealism, by which their traits are not only selected and massed but purged of all that might simply affront or disgust, or above all weary, in the idiom of their far-off originals."[7] That is, there is no make-believe which takes us in; yet, while we laugh, we scarcely judge. Both eminent critics are like Dryden and Johnson in frankly acknowledging the vices—"cowardly, drunken, amorous, vain and lying"[8]—the latter of whom, after similarly enumerating them, also comes to a similar (though less intellectualized) conclusion: "Yet the man thus corrupt, thus despicable, makes himself necessary to the prince that despises him by the most pleasing of all qualities, perpetual gaiety, by an unfailing power of exciting laughter, which is the more freely indulged as his wit is not of the splendid or ambitious kind but consists in easy escapes and sallies of levity, which make sport but raise no envy. It must be observed that he is stained with no enormous or sanguinary crimes, so that his licentiousness is not so offensive but that it may be borne for his mirth."

For Morgann and his followers, to be sure, there is little or nothing to be "borne"; yet there is then not only less

[7]Gissing, *Charles Dickens* (New York, 1898. Reprinted by permission of the publishers, Dodd, Mead & Company, Inc.), pp. 223–24; cf. pp. 114–15; Elton, *Survey 1830–80* (1920) II, 206.

[8]*Dramatic Poesy* (Oxford, 1900, I, 84): Preface to *Troilus and Cressida* to the same effect.

point to the old rogue's mirth but also less contrast and complication to the situation. This, externally (that is to say, the only situation apparent to an audience), in being deepened has been narrowed; to the outer ear or eye his wit is blunted, his bulk reduced. Their Falstaff, in the process, has been not only disinfected but (so to speak) disemboweled, and become what might be called "the modern reader's" Falstaff. Not the spectator's, certainly, at any time. Not every man's, which he was certainly meant to be.

"To the prince that despises him" is of course too strong. "I could have better spared a better man," Hal mutters as he finds him on the battlefield, mistakenly, dead, and leaves him alone, though *not* "in his glory." More happily than the redoubtable arbiter Mr. John Bailey puts it as he speaks of the Prince's "mingled affection, amusement and contempt, in which the contempt is certainly not the least conspicuous of the three."[9] But Prince Hal liked Falstaff, as Pulci's Morgante liked Margutte, Folengo's Baldus liked Cingar, Pantagruel ("all his life long") Panurge, not for his humor only but even (a little) for his boasting and lying, his indecency and deviltry, or else despite them all. Our taste, for the most part, is not so medievally robust; but even as applied to genuinely "historic" figures, that earlier taste survives. A far cry from Falstaff to Oscar Wilde, and not merely from fiction to reality, either (though to the Morganns that would not matter!); but their saving grace (of a not quite holy sort!) was the same. As Frank Harris, remembering all his vices, declares that he would rather spend an evening with him than with Renan or Carlyle, or Verlaine or Dick Burton or Davidson (those "better" men!), he continues: "It may be that I prize humor and good humor, and eloquence of poetic speech, the artist

[9] *Shakespeare* (1929) p. 132. One great scholar, recently dead, clung to the notion that Falstaff was no coward because he was treated with too much respect for that. As I have said before, he is no ordinary, contemptible coward like Parolles, whom, nevertheless, he much resembles; as Tom Davies says, he has an "impudent dignity," and unlike other cowards he carries all before him by his wit, turns defeat to a sort of triumph, and so, no wonder, is not despised.

qualities, more than goodness or loyalty or manliness, and so overestimate things amiable. But the lovable and joyous things are to me the priceless things, and the most charming man I ever met was assuredly Oscar Wilde."[10] With all *his* vices not previously extenuated, explained away! And if still so acceptable, how quickly that slighter spirit would by the prince of companions have been thrown into the shade!

2

Morgann and his followers, however, do not so much like as love him, and so (vindictively, perversely, like a Dostoevskian or a Freudian character, and therefore quite unesthetically) they come near to hating Hal—the national hero. Indeed, in their frantic efforts to rescue Falstaff's good name they run down not only Hal but Poins and—particularly Professor Charlton—the unquestionably heroic and chivalrous Percy, as well as Sir John's various unoffending victims,—Quickly, his tailor, the Gloucester recruits, Shallow and the rest. All historic beings rather than dramatic! And thus the manifest intention of the author they ignore, and comfortably settle down to literary entertainment pretty much of their own making.

Mr. Charlton's misreading and mistreatment of Hotspur I have considered elsewhere,[11] but that of Prince Hal is not

[10]Quoted by Stuart Sherman, *Critical Woodcuts* (1926), pp. 190–91.

[11]*Jahrbuch*, LXXIV (1938), "Recent Shakespeare Criticism"; *Rylands Library Bulletin*, January, 1935. I have not compared this with the version in Mr. Charlton's subsequent volume. At some points the misreading appears unquestionable, as: p. 7, where Falstaff's impudent reply to Lancaster is called a "right rebuke"; pp. 34–35, where, in *The Merry Wives*, Falstaff's reference to his "transformation," which means his disguise as an old woman, is made to mean the change in his character from *Henry IV*, Parts I and II (which reminds one of "transfigured" in *Midsummer Night's Dream* interpreted metaphorically instead of literally, i.e., "metamorphosed by the magic juice," *Jahrbuch* article cited, p. 51); p. 33, where the critic finds "sorrow" in Doll's parting phrase "and whether I shall ever see thee again or no, there is nobody cares." (References to Charlton here and in the text are to a reprint, Manchester, 1935.)

less flagrant. *A priori,* at least, the evidence is all against the critic. With Percy's reputation Shakespeare might conceivably, though not probably—*sit Medea ferox!*—have taken some liberties, but by no manner of means with Henry the Fifth's renown. Yet Mr. Charlton quotes approvingly the pacifist Mr. Masefield as he calls the prince a "wildcat" (though the latter grants it to be "hardly thinkable that Shakespeare expected us to feel so bitterly"), and presently—even repeatedly—he himself uses language still more bitter and irresponsible. "Unthinkable inhumanity" he calls the Prince's conduct (pp. 7, 39).[12] "It was murder in Hal," he says of his rejection of the old rogue at the end; although, however jestingly, he says still worse of Shakespeare—"the crime [is] worse than parricide, the slaughter of one's own offspring." Mr. Charles Williams, on the other hand, but in a not dissimilar spirit, puts the blame on us. "It is we that have betrayed him because of our own respectability."[13]

That is what comes of taking the character for "historic," a practice to which Mr. Charlton himself is incorrigibly addicted. To the mere metaphor there can of course be no serious objection, as when a critic says of Shylock in his "Hath not a Jew eyes?", and so on, that for the moment Shylock has got out of hand, taking the bit between his teeth and running away with his author,—to such language, I say, there can be no objection, provided he does not run away with the critic too.[14] For Mr. Charlton Sir John is, practically, flesh and blood; but (what is almost as queer) the writer is now on the creature's side, now on the creator's. The moment before or after he speaks of Falstaff's degeneration as if the poet were not a "maker" but a spectator—of Sir John's "falling from Shakespeare's grace" and

[12] Also p. 12: "If indeed a greater falseness is within the scope of conjecture."

[13] *The English Poetic Mind* (1932), p. 40. And what can this writer mean by "the infinity of Falstaff's prose"? Will this sort of talk among sensitive critics never come to an end?

[14] See my *Shakespeare Studies* (1927), pp. 260–61.

of his "almost forcing his author, though reluctantly, to
face up to the situation"—of "his letting Shakespeare
down" (p. 37). And the moment before or after he speaks
of the author's "grief at seeing it" (p. 31), his "cynical
revenge" by way of *The Merry Wives* (p. 33) and his "bitter disillusionment" (pp. 33, 38, 45). Can this be the
language of criticism?

3

Hal himself, however, rather more conveniently bears the
brunt, though he too of course is Shakespeare's own. I
would gladly give ten-and-six (if that is still the price) to
see the partisan critic at the play, hissing the hero (and
along with him Hotspur) as once (more agreeably to the
author) the gallery did, I remember, the villain and the
villainess at *The Lights o' London*. Like Mr. Masefield,
Mr. Charlton has it in for the Prince, and not only for
turning off the thief and extortioner, swindler, deadbeat,
and whoremonger upon his accession, which even Morgann
approves of, but also for his excuses at the outset:

> I know you all and will awhile uphold
> The unyok'd humour of your idleness . . .

That is of course a highly artificial and rather clumsy way
of saving the face of the paladin of Agincourt; but the
more primitive the technique the less it should be interpreted in terms of psychology. Yet this, too, is taken for an
"offense against humanity" (p. 11). By my troth, Captain,
these are very bitter words—and queer!

"I know my friends are shaking their heads over me,"
so Mr. Bailey paraphrases the passage. "They see me playing the fool and think I am not capable of playing anything else. But they will one day find out their mistake. . . ."
What, Mr. Bailey then asks, is the harm of that? "And
Johnson," he continues, "who understood human nature
[and the nature, I would add, of an audience] so much
better than most of Shakespeare's critics, makes the right

comment on it. 'The speech,' he says, 'is very artfully introduced to keep the Prince from appearing vile in the opinion of the audience; it prepares them for his future reformation and, what is more valuable, exhibits a natural picture
of a great mind offering excuses to itself, and palliating
those follies that it can neither justify nor forsake.' "[15]

The unpleasant impression of self-consciousness Johnson
here ignores—partly, no doubt, because he is nearer in time
and spirit to the explicit early Elizabethan technique;[16]
but he is far truer than the moderns to Shakespeare's meaning. Hal, really, is the only one pretending—that is to say,
the only one playing robber for fun—; and if Falstaff were
another, he would not only have to act very, very differently but chime in with the Prince's cry, "Well, then, *once*
in my days I'll be a madcap," and on hearing of the repay-
ing of the money, *not,* as he does, see fit to grumble.

As for the Prince's heartlessness in joking, his teasing
of Francis the drawer, his getting a commission in the in-
fantry for Falstaff, to whom, afoot, "eight yards of uneven
ground is three-score and ten miles," Mr. Charlton is so
demoralized in his partisanship that he evidently finds more
of the milk of human kindness in the fat man's own joking
at the (quite literal as well as metaphorical) expense of his
tailor, of his landlady (not only for lodging, board, and
drink, but for the shirts to cover his precious old body), of
the helpless, pitiful recruits in Gloucestershire, and of the
friendly Justice Shallow, his host, whom, however foolish
or well to do, he has not the slightest good reason to skin.
In the way of practical merriment I myself considerably
prefer the Prince. Falstaff is not for my table, till he shakes
down his sleeves.

And the Prince's final repudiation, what else so clearly
indicates (if that is still important) Shakespeare's own
moral attitude? What so decisively discountenances the
notorious trickster's supposed philosophy or (in effect) so
discredits the "impressions" received by the Morgann
school? In Shakespeare's own eyes, as in the new King's,

[15]*Shakespeare,* pp. 131–32. [16]Cf. below, pp. 214, 229. The good,
like the bad or the funny, now and then lay themselves bare.

he, the funny man, does *not*, I trust, also make truth absurd, or honor, or law, or patriotism, or duty, or courage, or war, or religion, or [least of all!] the fear of death, thus lifting "us into the atmosphere of perfect freedom."[17] Yet this fact, when honestly perceived, would, with Morgann's followers (though not with him, we have seen) only aggravate the grievance against Hal or Shakespeare. And what comfort is there in Johnson, who "understood" so much better? "If it be considered that the fat knight has never uttered one sentiment of generosity, and with all his power of exciting mirth, has nothing in him that can be esteemed, no great pain will be suffered from the reflection that he is compelled to live honestly, and maintained by the King, with a promise of advancement when he shall deserve it."

The right complaint, as against the Prince's soliloquy near the beginning, is on the score not of morality or of humanity but only of art. The dramatist's hand is here too heavy, and the new King speaks unnaturally, not like himself but a preacher. The play is not, however, as Mr. Charlton calls it, a "comedy," but a "history," in which the Falstaff story is but a comic episode. Serious considerations, therefore, may now properly assert themselves. It is not, moreover, the King himself that orders Falstaff and his hangers-on off to the Fleet—poetic justice upon him, as Morgann, more sensible as well as ethical than his followers, acknowledges, for, at the news of the old King's death, had not the lawless (though timorous) rogue cried out "and woe to my Lord Chief-Justice"?[18] And that even-handed retribution is, on their unequivocally anti-social record, no more than their due.

4

In Falstaff's "degeneration" one sees better cause for complaint. But the case is like that of Harold Skimpole in *Bleak House*. He is another impostor, sponger, and deadbeat, who repays his creditors or benefactors not even in

[17]See Professor Bradley's rhapsody, *Oxford Lectures* (1914), pp. 262–63.

[18]*Essay* (1777), p. 179.

the coin of gratitude but of wit, not with goodness but good humor. He too degenerates, taking bribes from Vholes and from Bucket, and betraying the boy Toughey in his hiding-place, thus playing false with his own protector, Jarndyce. Also he defends himself like Falstaff with frivolous ingenui-ties and sophistries. Now though his record has not the advantage of a poet's pen, and though, on the other hand, it is by no means so dirty as Sir John's, yet as it darkens and sullies, the critics here too rebel. And that is somewhat because, like the Morganns, they have winked at the ras-cality or explained it away. Like them they have sentimen-talized it. This story is a Rake's Progress; yet so is Falstaff's; and Shakespeare, Hogarth, and Dickens are akin.

The earlier dramatists—Heywood, who formed the cow-ard Roughman, and Beaumont and Fletcher, who formed the coward Bessus, all three somewhat on Falstaff's model, and then Dryden, Rowe, Johnson, Cumberland—together with the dramatic critics still in close and vital contact with the stage, Tom Davies and Joseph Baretti—all these who (to turn Johnson's words round) did know something of Shakespeare's art and also of the actor's as well, are, in recognizing the cowardice, of one accord. (That stubborn, all-important fact, the judgment of the fellow craftsmen, at one with that of actors and audiences, which Morgann irrationally deplores, has never been squarely faced!) So, too, they are of one accord about the multiplicity (doubting not the reality) of the coward's vices. "A liar," says Dryden, "a coward, a glutton, and buffoon," in the preface to *Troilus and Cressida* (and he would, probably, still include the other traits in the previous statement in the *Dramatic Poesy,* "old, fat, merry, drunken, amorous, vain") "because all these qualities may agree in the same man." "A thief," says Nicholas Rowe, "lying, cowardly, vainglorious, and, in short, every way vicious." "A thief and a glutton," says Johnson, "a coward and a boaster, always ready to cheat the weak and prey upon the poor; to terrify the timorous and insult the defenseless. At once obsequious and malig-nant, he satirizes in their absence those whom he lives by flattering." *Menteur,* says Baretti, *gourmand, paillard, voleur, poltron, bravache, fanfaron, fatteur* [*sic*], *et médi-sant.*[19] And as such, more or less, the coward had, for comic purposes, been represented from the time of the ancients; and not infrequently, moreover, like Lyly's *Sir Tophas,* as big and fat, accompanied by a plucky little page, as Falstaff is. (If *he* is plucky too, what of the contrast?) As one present-day Shakespearean puts it, who in the overpower-ing presence has managed to keep both his senses and also his morals untroubled, Falstaff "resumes in himself all the familiar qualities of which, since before the dawn of re-corded things, farce has made its inexhaustible and unvary-ing sport. He is a sot, a lecher, a coward, a braggart, a hypocrite."[20] Now that this cowardly rogue should be and have been so readily recognizable, and should, as I have elsewhere shown, so evidently resemble other cowards on the boards in the multiplicity of his vices, as well as the likes o' them there or anywhere else in his running away, fall-ing flat, whimpering, evading and excusing, and yet, never-theless, without clear indication to the audience, be in all this only feigning, merely pretending, would be simply for the dramatist to defy comprehension—to fly straight in the face of tradition and the established customs of the stage, and those of life besides. Above all, pretending coward-ice, which is the kernel of the comedy,—after hacking his sword and bloodying his garments, like the poltroon Parol-les, in *All's Well* (IV, i). Established associations are for that too strong; indeed the mere fatness, bibulousness, and gluttony, on the one hand, and the bragging and lying, on the other, would of themselves lead the audience to expect the cowardice as boon companion. And in life itself what man in his senses would pretend to a vice like this, to which, un-like wenching, surely no man ever pretended without speed-ily and decisively clearing the matter up? Another associ-ated trait, noticed by Johnson and Baretti but ignored by others, is incidental evidence of importance—I mean the

[19]*Discours sur Shakespeare et M. Voltaire* (1777), p. 72.

[20]Sir Edmund Chambers, *Survey* (Sidgwick and Jackson, Lon-don, 1925), pp. 121, 125–26. The *Variorum* omits what he has to say of Falstaff's "dishonesty" and "utter anaideia."

médisance. Parolles is a conspicuous example, and there are others in France and Spain. "They fled from me as I appeared," says Calderón's Don Juan of those who had been slandering him:

> *me huyeron*
> *Luego: que es usado estilo*
> *Ser cobarde el maldiciente.* (À secreto Agravio, III.)

That, to be sure, is the converse—the slanderer is a coward—; but on two occasions Falstaff speaks ill of the Prince and Poins behind their backs, besides calling them cowards to their faces—till Poins, with just the monosyllable "stab," shuts him up.[21]

5

And what of the wit-and-butt-in-one, which still another humorist-and-moralist-in-one, Joseph Addison,[22] recognizes, like (no doubt) Dryden—"glutton *and buffoon*"—before him?[23] To save his reputation for cleverness and to secure greater psychological and moral consistency the Morgann critics would have him tell his tale of buckram and Kendal

[21]II, iv, 159–60. To one acquainted with the language of either the stage or life itself this should be enough—the braggart sidling off, "too proud to fight," as Poins threatens or, as in Part II, I, ii, 98, the Chief Justice's servant tells him he lies in his throat. Cf. my *Shakespeare Studies*, p. 421. Also cf. the same situation, *M. W. W.* I, i, 127–34, Slender backing down even before Bardolph; and *Every Man in His Humour*, I, ii, Stephen before Knowell. Now that pacifism is in less repute among us the literary critics may be better able to read our older drama as Sir Edmund, Mr. Bailey, and Mr. F. L. Lucas do (*Decline and Fall of the Romantic Ideal*, p. 194).

[22]*Spectator*, No. 47. Cf. Richardson's Lovelace, quoted above, though of this art he disapproves.

[23]Both Thomas Fuller and George Daniel (1647) apply the word "buffoon" as well as "coward" (see Allusion-Book). The late W. L. George is one contemporary akin to Addison, finding it essential that Falstaff should be "absurd as well as fat, coarse, salacious, superstitious, blustering, cowardly, and lying . . . a butt for pranks." (*A Novelist on Novelists*, 1918, p. 164.) In short, a comic figure, not merely what is logically congruous with perfect wit.

green from sheer high spirits and for entertainment, not expecting any credence; and (though here the inconsistency is
not so glaring) would make out his excuses for fraudulent
recruiting as he does it and his battlefield catechism of dishonor to be only financial and military freethinking (both
nowadays but too familiar), not unconscionable shuffling
and dodging, oh! not dishonor. But in drama, particularly
in comedy, it is more important that there should be point
to the situation than a sound motive for it—and probability
in the dialogue than in the psychology. What is the fun
in exposing a fellow who is not really (and extravagantly)
boasting or has not really run away? What is ingenious and
interesting, on the other hand, in his extricating himself
from predicaments if really there aren't any, in his evasions
and excuses if there is nothing much to evade or excuse?
And particularly in the theater. A strange practical joke,
this of Poins and the Prince, if it turns out a boomerang
upon them without their seeing it, and (in consequence)
without our seeing it, either? But if the spectators who
have laughed at Falstaff's conduct on Gadshill, his crying,
"Zounds, will they not rob *us?*" his running and roaring
and larding the lean earth, presently to make his entry at
the Boar's-head still sweating but crying out, "A plague
of all cowards," and boasting and lying on top of it, just
as had been predicted by Poins to the Prince and just as
the coward he has already shown himself to be would
naturally have done,—if after that, I say, the spectators
are now by his "I knew ye" and his "instinct" really and
completely convinced, why, they, as well as Poins and the
Prince, have had the tables turned on themselves and will
certainly be wary of laughing again. How little desirable,
for both company and dramatist! "The audience is never
to be perplexed," still less disconcerted, or in its own laughter left in the lurch.

The fundamental trouble is that Morgann and his followers in giving (contrary to Aristotle) first place to character, not situation, have upset the dramatic structure of
the Falstaff story and confused its effect. (In comedy they
have done somewhat the same as others since Morgann

have done, after a different fashion, in tragedy.) Keeping
the wit in him, they have thrown out the butt—have made
the Prince—"famous to the world alwaie"!—the butt instead. The clever Prince and the incisive Poins, who together have taken the audience into their confidence! And
into the simple and solid Elizabethan farce they have im-
ported something of the "romantic irony" or "transcendental farce" of an expressionistic drama, such as Andreyev's or O'Neill's. In *He Who Gets Slapped,* the hero is
apparently the butt but really the wit and ironist; and
those on the stage and in the Circus who slap him and
laugh at him are the butts instead. By M. Cazamian indeed
the doctrine of transvaluation of values has been openly
applied to the Falstaff story. But in Andreyev's esoteric
drama, however much else is left cloudy and mysterious,
the transvaluation is made plain as day. "He" laughs, as
Falstaff doesn't; and at the others, who are more or less
aware of the fact but not at all of the reason why. "He"
does not keep his own higher, ultimate, overwhelming and
devastating joke entirely to himself. Highbrow Andreyev
does not tax men's attention or baffle their wits as the popular Shakespeare at the Globe has, since Morgann, been
supposed to have done! For us psychologists (rather than
playgoers), to be sure, who fail to remember that the unity
of Falstaff lies only in his comic quality, his tone and manner, butt and wit together are perplexing; and the latest
editor is right enough, psychologically, as he declares that
the tale of the robbery, in the expectation of being believed,
is "inconceivable." (*Variorum,* 1936, p. 144.) But that
Falstaff's ignorance of the identity of the two "in buckram," now standing before him, is also "inconceivable"
(*ibid.*) is another matter. There is no way of his learning
their identity but by recognizing them on Gadshill; and
then he must, as indeed Lloyd, echoing Morgann, and also
quoted (p. 136) by Mr. Hemingway, conceives it, have
"run and roared to hold the good jest up, and not only
bragged outrageously because he was aware of the effect
he was producing, but hacked his sword and made his
companions stain their clothes with blood, on the certain

calculation that he would be betrayed." Yet why so "stick
his neck out," so exert himself? A studied, laborious, suddenly silent, masochistic wit! And all those "quick evasions"
and "easy escapes" (as Dryden and Johnson call them),
both before this occasion and after, "when" as Dryden says,
"you imagine him surprised,"—in them you, in so imagining him, are quite mistaken, are not plumbing his profundity any more than those two famous wits, who are not
on the stage, or than Hal and Poins, who are! What, however, by this interpretation Falstaff may gain in acuteness
he loses in common sense, and Shakespeare with him. Even
in his first scenes (which is important) Sir John is the mark
and target for the Prince. He is for giving over this life—
"I'll be damned for never a king's son in Christendom":

> PRINCE. Where shall we take a purse tomorrow, Jack?
> FAL. Zounds, where thou wilt, lad; I'll make one. An I do
>   not, call me villain, and baffle me.
> PRINCE. I see a good amendment of life in thee; from pray-
>   ing to purse-taking.
> FAL. Why, Hal, 'tis my vocation, Hal. 'Tis no sin for a man
>   to labour in his vocation.

But Lloyd (*Variorum*, p. 135) consistently enough, and
possibly with Mr. Hemingway's approval, even here takes
Falstaff to be artfully playing into the Prince's hands, instead of plumping into them and then artfully escaping.
And in his next scene, that of the robbery, when he cries
"Zounds, will they not rob *us?*" the Prince exclaiming,
"What, a coward, Sir John Paunch," and Falstaff coun-
tering, "Indeed I am not John of Gaunt, your grandfather;
but yet no coward, Hal,"—why, then, I suppose, the pre-
meditated self-effacing process is repeated. Here are no
"ripples" in the current of the dialogue such as we have
from time immemorial been given and been delighted with
in drama; no telltale outcry, no unexpected thrust and
counterthrust, no discomfiture, and then—not much of a
triumph, either! Still waters run deep but are not for
the stage.

In the interests of their psychology the Morganns have

blunted the point of the situation and complicated its simple purport. (In his inmost nature, so far as we know it, the funny man must be deceiving others, as Hamlet and Iago must be deceiving themselves!) At the end of Falstaff's first scene, the second of the play, the stage has by Poins (and by the dramatist!) openly been set for his discomfiture and exposure:[24]

The virtue of this jest will be the incomprehensible lies that this same fat rogue will tell us when we meet at supper; how thirty at least he fought with; what wards, what blows, what extremities he endured; and in the reproof [confutation] of this lies the jest.

Then, the rogue and his fellows having acted just and quite as faintheartedly as predicted, in the inn at Eastcheap the Prince and Poins await them, the former telling the latter that he will "play Percy"—be absent-minded and abstracted —thus letting the turn-tail braggart fairly hold the floor, expose himself. Our expectations in the interval have been not only aroused but also in part satisfied. Falstaff had been wailing, scolding, and cajoling in no formidable robberlike fashion. To his "but yet no coward, Hal," the Prince has retorted, "Well, we leave that to the proof." And when the Travelers appear and are robbed, it is he that does the shouting, then cries out upon the absent Prince and Poins as "two arrant cowards," and when they in disguise set upon him and his fellows, takes to his heels, "roaring" and "sweating to death."

What, now, after that, would be the effect on the audience of his entry, sweating still and thirsting, and bawling out,

A plague of all cowards, I say, and a vengeance too! Marry and Amen! Give me a cup of sack, boy.

Nothing short of a roar, in our day as in that of Aristophanes or Thespis, if the audience has any understanding of either life or story, or any appreciation of expectations duly and amply met; and the laughter, as certainly, would

[24]The simple dramatic method is the same as in *All's Well,* III, vi, *et seq.:* the cowardly lying, slandering, and betraying come exactly as expected.

not be directed at either the Prince or Poins. But the Prince gives him play or (to shift from the aquatic to the terrestrial) rope; and from this unwonted innocence the Swaggerer himself ought to take the hint. But if he were still cleverer —the wit unfailingly!—he wouldn't swagger, wouldn't after such misconduct have made such an entry in the first place, still less would he now undertake the preposterous tale of his derring-do, and consequently—there would not be the rollicking merriment we have been promised. "Incomprehensible lies" were predicted; and the commentators object to them, or misinterpret them, when they come, even because just such they are! For them, the comprehensible! Of course it is not psychology—who in the theater expected it?—nor anything like realism: it is extravaganza, farce (and not the transcendental variety, either), simply, in short, the traditional and ancient *motif* of reckless bragging after cowardly behavior, developed to the limit. This the Prince's sly comments and inquiries during the story make still more "inconceivable," yet more comical, breaking up the narrative and, point by point, bringing its absurdity home. And the "reproof"—the confutation—which the Morganns think a boomerang, how in the world is the audience to discover that it is not merely what was promised and what it so exactly appears to be? Time and again in Parts both I and II the Prince and Poins twit Falstaff, corner him,[25] momentarily embarrass him before his usual verbal triumph or embarrass him more seriously after it; but if everything else in his conduct now at Eastcheap could be shown to be pretense and make-believe, taking in the Prince and Poins (and certainly the audience as well), what could be made of his disconcerted coaxing after (to be "merry" and change the subject) he proposes a play extempore? "Content," cries the Prince, "and the argument shall be thy running away." "Ah, no more o' that, Hal, an thou lovest me!" Thus (instead of dropping the mask and crowing!) he throws himself on the Prince's mercy. (If he has no need of that, by acting as if he had he loses not in common sense alone but also in spunk and

[25] Pt. I, II, iv, 311; Pt. II, II, iv, 338–45.

grit.) [26] Still, four times afterwards ere the long scene is over, the Prince twits him about "instinct," thus demonstrating the old roysterer's philosophic sweetness and exaltation, perhaps, and betraying his own impenetrable thick-headedness, yet, if so, making no sense to any audience that outside of a school or a college could easily be got together. And even there, would they laugh? confidently and unanimously? at the Prince or Falstaff, then, or (quite desperately) at *both?*

Now such a compound of fool and wag Ward, Schelling, and Creizenach are of one accord in finding in Chapman's *Monsieur D'Olive* (c. 1606), though without recalling Falstaff or Addison, either; also they agree in thinking him one of the most diverting figures in Elizabethan drama. What is more, even "in the way in which these extremes are made to meet in him," adds Sir Adolphus,[27] "lies the originality of the character." For the likeness to Falstaff is one not at all of substance but only of artistic—of comic —conception and method, and it goes farther than the compound mentioned. He is, as Rhoderique and Mugeron agree in thinking,[28] a rogue. And he is of course much more of a dupe or gull than Sir John; but like him, "he uses his droll wit," as Mr. Schelling says, "with an imperturbable confidence in himself; and even when gulled into heading an embassy which is never sent, loses neither his temper nor his ready presence of mind."[29] Falstaff as an ambassador? More probable, but less comical, than as a captain! But Ward, Schelling, and Creizenach read no more than is printed, and take the data of the play at face value —not discounting them or discrediting them as the Morganns do with Falstaff and (in the opposite direction) with

[26] For the natural attitude, from the time of the ancients, cf. my *Shakespeare Studies,* pp. 444-49. In the Middle Ages and the Renaissance much was made of the *belles responses;* and even in wit Aristotle's principle applied—"a courageous man ought not to allow himself to be beaten." (*Rhet.* I, ix, 25.)

[27] Ward, *English Dramatic Literature* (1899), II, 439.

[28] End of Act I.

[29] Schelling (1908), I, 399.

the other characters,—and agreeably meeting the comic expectations of the dramatist, not thwarting them or insisting upon any pet psychological predilections of their own.

6

To this Mr. Charlton is more given than Morgann himself. With him it is "the *seeming* discomfitures in his attempt to make the robbery on Gadshill a tale of his valour"—"his *seeming* cowardice at Shrewsbury"—"though the round after Gadshill may *seem at first view* to have gone heavily against him";[30] and the moral values and judgments attaching to Falstaff's conduct here and to his treatment of his victims are almost completely upset. What the critic says of Sir John might almost be said of himself as a critic: "The difference between truth and falsehood is in an irrelevant order of reckonings." (P. 22.) In my last discussion,[31] answering Professor Kittredge's "not a coward *in fact,*" I quoted Wordsworth's saying, that "the appropriate business of poetry" is to treat of things not as they are but as they appear; and Archer's, that "the stage is the realm of appearances." In speaking of such novels as James's Mr. Percy Lubbock says much the same: "Below the surface, behind the outer aspect of [the hero's] mind, we do not penetrate; this is drama, and in drama the spectator must judge by appearances."[32] That is, the surface meaning in a play is the real meaning except where there are pretty perceptible indications (rather than "secret impressions"!) that it is not.[33] And this of Chapman's or of Shakespeare's is actual, not quasi, drama (for the stage and for a promiscuous audience), in which secrecy, pro-

[30]Pp. 22, 26; and cf. passages where the critic insists that the laborious humorist lays the traps and creates the predicaments himself, pp. 19, 29.

[31]*Shakespeare and Other Masters,* p. 355. Cf. above, p. 197.

[32]*Craft of Fiction* (n.d.) p. 162.

[33]Cf. *The Monthly Review* above, note 2: "The obvious meaning is most probably the true one." Cf. Halliwell-Phillips on Hamlet (1879), p. 13; or ask any good actor or producer.

ducing perplexity—"the first end of a writer is to be understood," says Dryden (and how much truer of a dramatist,
a comic one!)—would be woefully out of place. D'Olive
is plainly called a gull and a knave by those in the play
who ought to know, and in the action he as plainly so
appears. Likewise Falstaff is plainly called a coward and
(in various terms) a knave by those who ought to know,
and in the action he as plainly so appears; and I do not see
how in a theater, which, not the closet, is the only proper
place of judgment, there could be any other opinion.

In moral matters, above all (drama is not as life!), appearances are important. In comedy, as much as in tragedy,
the moral standard and ideals acknowledged by the author
must be the same as those acknowledged or understood by
the audience; the words "honour" and "coward," "valour"
and "discretion," and the corresponding conduct and deportment, must bear the same meaning for both. And contradictory values, such as Morgann, Bradley, Cazamian,
and Charlton[34] discover prevailing in the play, would be-
wilder and exasperate any audience, and any reader who
knows the stage. As I have elsewhere argued,[35] Iago must
actually be the terribly wicked man that is apparently depicted—Johnson at the time ironically called on Morgann
to prove him the contrary, not dreaming, in his day, that
some day others would!—or the audience and the author
would be at cross-purposes, their judgments and sympathies
run in different channels, and the emotions of pity and fear
not be directed or even aroused.

In comedy such a spirit of comprehension and concord
is quite as important. The emotions aroused are of a different order; there is generally much less sympathy with
the leading characters, and as in Molière, there may be an
(easy-going) antipathy instead; but there must at least be
sympathy with the author. Otherwise there will be no
laughter. In both Molière and the comic Shakespeare the
characters are, in Aristotle's phrase, not (as in tragedy)
"better," but "in some respects worse than men as they are."

[34]Pp. 14-15, 22, 24, 46: Cf. Bradley above, note 17.

[35]*Shakespeare and Other Masters,* pp. 27-28.

That is, Molière, like Ben Jonson, deals with men who are the incarnations of vices or foibles, or of ruling passions and fixed ideas. So does, in some measure, Shakespeare when not romantic, as in Falstaff and Shylock, Malvolio and Bottom. Both alike (and also Jonson and Aristophanes, Plautus and Terence) in securing comic effect observe or appeal to a standard of propriety and morality which is, more exactly, that of their audience and their age, but, essentially, that of any audience, any age. One main way leads to laughter, a piquant contrast between the character or the situation and what is normal—between vice and virtue, folly and wisdom, and (a difference *not* "irrelevant," witness liars on the comic stage before the Eastcheap knight and later!) between the false and the true. And for that—for laughter—the way must be open, the approach quick and sure.

So it is even with the artificial comedy of the Restoration, from Etherege to Congreve. The passage in Bradley already quoted is an echo of Lamb's essay:

They [these comedies of manners] are a world of themselves almost as much as fairyland. . . . They [the characters] seem engaged in their proper element. They break through no laws, or conscientious restraints. They know of none. They have got out of Christendom into the land—what shall I call it?—of cuckoldry— the Utopia of gallantry, where pleasure is duty, and the manners perfect freedom.

But as I have elsewhere endeavored to show, Lamb in making clear that the Restoration drama was a world in itself went too far as he contended that "it has no reference whatever to the world that is." The philosophy or code of conduct in this Utopia of gallantry is comical because it is so free and so gay; but also, as Lamb would forget, because it is so bold, bad, and different—because so wittily but also so startlingly phrased.[36] It has effect or meaning only as it is thrown into contrast with the normal morality

[36] My *Shakespeare Studies*, p. 52; above chap. IV, p. 57–8. And cf. Chesterton, subsequently, but independently, *Generally Speaking* (1929), pp. 205–7, to same effect; Auden (cited below, p. 274), p. 89.

(if not of the coterie audience) of English society in the background.[37] The code of the period of course needs no expression; and here the Saturnalian spirit of rebellion against the code, in those who nevertheless acknowledge it, takes, as in all ages, the form of wit and laughter. The witty epigrams of Etherege and Congreve were amusing because they were shocking, like Oscar Wilde's in his artificial comedies:—"Divorces are made in Heaven";—"in married life three is company and two is none." And like those of Shaw in his similar comedies, even when he is veiling a truth in his paradox.

7

Not that there is much of this Saturnalian rebellion in Shakespeare or in Molière, who are more popular, more conservative, but in whom as clearly and more directly the social conscience asserts itself. And in all those earlier dramatists mentioned, as well as in Jonson, there is more than in Shakespeare of the method of criticism and satire. By them the miser or the coward, the hypocrite or the pretender, is made comical but seldom witty, or humorous, or agreeable. With them is no doubt or indulgence: every stroke must count. There, at any rate, must be no considering of extenuating circumstances like that by Morgann and his followers; no allowances for the disreputable fellow's evil associations, his corpulence and age.[38] The comic social conscience is unsparing; it is only in real society and about genuinely "historic" characters that we may be virtuously bid remember "He is what the dear Lord made him." And then to laughter how disconcerting it is!

Shakespeare, on the other hand, though, like Molière,

[37]This matter of immediacy in the effect and of unanimity in the response as necessary in drama, Mr. W. P. Eaton has recently insisted upon anew in an article "The Plight of the Dramatist," in *Harper's* magazine, March, 1941. Surely every dramatist remembers the principle; just as nearly every critic, once started on a detective trail of original theory, forgets it.

[38]*Shakespeare Studies*, p. 482.

he is not James's ideal novelist, "entirely purged of sarcasm," is more nearly so,—and his comic characters are
generally witty and humorous, fantastic, or verbally eccentric and grotesque. Speech and poetry count for more than
with Molière or any of the others; situation (though, as
we have seen, for much) for proportionately less. As I have
elsewhere said:—

In the presentation of them there is somewhat the same method
as that already considered in tragedy—that of lyricism, as when
the wit of Mercutio, Beatrice, and Falstaff effervesces in fantasy;
and that of self-exposure, as when the corpulent coward descants
upon honor or discretion, or Dogberry and Aguecheek show themselves to be asses even in saying and repeating that they are. The
laughter, like the terror, is often for its own sake, even at the
cost of character. There is the lyricism also of witlessness and
nonsense, as not only in Dogberry and Aguecheek but in Shallow
and Silence, Launce, the Athenian mechanicals, Cloten, Trinculo
—"But art thou not *drowned,* Stephano?"—and in Falstaff when
at his story of the knaves in buckram and Kendal green. Folly is
not lashed but given the rein; the laughter is not "thoughtful" or
scornful but indulgent and wholehearted.

The particular indulgence before us, however, after the
order of Morgante, Pantagruel, Prince Hal himself, and
even Frank Harris, is not for the misdeed but for the misdoer; and not because so the dear Lord made him or mismade him, either, but because of his wit and merriment,
his ingenuity, geniality, and infinite variety. There is no
misdirected, bewildering sympathy, no condoning or explaining away. Otherwise, the ingenuity of the misdoer
would be only that of the misunderstood, and however
clever, not inherently funny.

In fact, instead of explaining and justifying himself, Falstaff, when on the battlefield facing death, like Benedick
when facing matrimony, like Sganarelle when avoiding a
cuckold's duel, and like many a medieval comic character
in a plight besides, only exposes himself, banters and rallies
himself,[39] by implicit reference (as he must do) to the com-

[39]Cf. *Shakespeare Studies,* pp. 457–67; *Shakespeare and Other
Masters,* p. 349.

mon moral standard of us all. And the medieval poets, still
less purged, still less faithful to reality, were even more bent
than Molière and Le Sage (and Shakespeare of course)
"on getting their fun out of the spectacle."[40] Of this
method, as found, traditionally, even in Voltaire, Stendhal
says that *c'est par trop contre nature qu'un homme se
moque si clairement de soi-même.* Falstaff not only is butt-
and-wit-in-one but makes a butt of himself. (But conventionally, not psychologically, as above, in the hands of the
Morganns; genuinely, not by a masochistic feint.) The
difficulty for us lies, partly, in the use of soliloquy, common
in both Shakespeare and Molière, and also their predecessors, as if one were addressing a second person, and, originally, in the comic character's improbable self-betrayals,
such as the Wife of Bath's and the Pardoner's: but difference in technique should not be enough to turn banter into
sympathy, and for an open mind it is even today no difficulty at all. When a warrior on the eve of battle cries "I
would 'twere bedtime, Hal, and all well," or, again, "What
is honour? A word," and in the thick of it, "Give me life!"
and "The better part of valour is discretion," thereupon
to fall flat before his enemy and to stab a dead hero obviously and even avowedly for fear he may come alive,[41] why,
we none of us need to have done reading in medieval farces
and fabliaux or anywhere else adequately to understand it.
He is both a butt and a wit at the same moment, and only
literary critics (or rabid pacifists)[42] would not understand it.

[40]The observation upon Molière and Le Sage, contrasting them
with Marivaux, is Brunetière's, quoted by W. A. Gill, *Fortnightly
Review,* LXXXVI (1909), 691.

[41]"Zounds, I am afraid of this gunpowder Percy, though he is
dead." Part I, V, iv, 123.

[42]In Shakespeare, as in the Bible, people have found their own
opinions; and England and America, now coming out of a Fools'
Paradise where they have dallied or slumbered for more than half
a century, will presumably soon be disposed to demand a little
evidence for such statements as this in one of the latest books on
Shakespeare, the poet of chivalry: that he left Falstaff out of
Henry V because his "philosophy" might so easily make the fighting scenes "seem ridiculous and pitiful."

8

Mr. Charlton (whom I dwell upon because the latest of these and so highly praised) has introduced an innovation, and a complication, though scarcely an improvement, into the Morgann and Bradley "transvaluation of values." Falstaff is not only to be treated as a real person but also as the hero of a comedy. As such, he must "survive." Consequently, he cannot follow the dictates of honor, and (as consequently) he cannot be a coward. Here is the same confusion as is to be seen above: who killed Jack Falstaff (literally or metaphorically)? The Prince, the dramatist, or he himself? To be sure, the theory (which I have touched upon already)[43] provides the critic with a formula, however specious, for exoneration. "Give me life!"[44] takes on a conveniently new significance; the rascal both survives and (through two dramas), at the cost of others, prospers! And the more sordid and scabrous role in Part II is thus to be looked upon but as a bit of biography, the rogue's natural and actual degeneration, which we must accept. Yet one moment it is Falstaff's "falling away" or "incompleteness"[45] and the author's consequent "grief" and disillusionment; the next it is merely the author's cynical bitterness and revenge. This, by way of *The Merry Wives* as well as of Part II, is carrying the "historic" metaphor prodigiously far.

Is there not, in a matter-of-fact world, a simpler, more natural explanation? Shakespeare and Dickens are not alone. In the comedy of the Renaissance, as in that of the ancients, there is still a sense of justice or retribution, if there is little enough in comedy or tragedy, either one, today.[46] In Part II Falstaff goes from bad to worse, as

[43]*Jahrbuch,* article cited, pp. 55–56.

[44]Charlton, pp. 20, 22.

[45]*Ibid.,* pp. 30, 31, 45.

[46]Cf. Professor O. Elton (*Modern Studies,* 1907, pp. 115–17) as he criticizes Raleigh's interpretation of *Measure for Measure* where the critic makes too much of the dramatist's sympathy and tolerance.

a successful rascal does in life and may with artistic propriety, therefore, in fiction. There has been continual indulgence; there has been little or none of such corrective laughter as in Molière. The fat knight's wit has carried all before it, and he himself has flourished like a green bay tree. Hence this practical correction, so belated; hence, too, the heavily moral quality of it—the Chief Justice and the Fleet! Propriety, probability, both the King's reputation and public decency, for that matter, and even the rules and spirit of chivalry, to which last Shakespeare and his audience were not, like the Falstaff critics, strangers,[47] demand something of the sort. Though Morgann and his highly respectable successors deplore it, Shakespeare, in his none-too-respectable theater, feels constrained to offer it. That is not greatly to his credit as an artist, but there are other things in Shakespeare that aren't; and it is quite to his credit as a man. Is it not equally to his credit, moreover, or else to that of criticism, that the confusion should thus discontinue between fact and fiction, and that Shakespeare and his creatures should no longer be at loggerheads with one another? Life itself may not be "what you make it," in fact, it generally is not; but your work, so far as worth the considering, is.

9

Since writing the above I have come upon Professor Kittredge's last words on the subject, page xiii in his sep-

[47]Cf. W. H. Schofield, *Chivalry in English Literature* (1912), pp. 217–18: "It shows a strange misunderstanding of Shakespeare's purpose . . . to worry because Prince Hal, when he became king, banished from court 'this tutor and feeder of [his] riots' until such time as he should reform. The *Order* expressly directs: 'When any noble prince . . . hath in his court or his company, wicked knights that never finish to admonish him that he do wickedness,'" and so on. Professor Herford, Professor Charlton's discerning predecessor, who himself says that Falstaff's finest jests are rooted in dishonor and breach of trust, quotes the discerning Fluellen, who would seem here to be Shakespeare's mouthpiece: "Harry of Monmouth, being in his right wits and good judgments, turned away the fat knight with the great-belly doublet," *Henry V*, IV, vii, 48.

arate text of *Henry IV*, Part I (1940). And to this great
scholar every student of our early literature owes profound
respect. But he is an authority in matters of scholarship—
language and text, source and influence—rather than of
criticism; and though not the humblest of spirits, he would
not himself have encouraged the notion, widely prevalent
among our Ph.D.'s, that he was an oracle. Here, I cannot
but say, Professor Kittredge is mostly reproducing Morgann
in his irrelevant distinctions and "finespun deductions," as
his contemporaries Johnson, Stack, and Davies called and
thought them.

In the robbery, then, Falstaff himself does the practical
joking; whereas that it is the Prince and Poins is made as
plain as a dramatist can make it. And to turn tail when
robbing (which is different from fighting) is not cowardice;
whereas to the Prince and Poins and everybody else in
Eastcheap, in their ethical simplicity, it never even occurs
that it isn't, including, very clearly, as we have noticed
above, Falstaff himself. Would any spectator at the Globe
have entertained or tolerated that distinction, or Jonson,
Molière, or Rabelais, or, for that matter, Chaucer? Notice
is taken of the fact that Shakespeare has given him the
name (but slightly changed) of the Sir John Fastolfe of
his previous drama, *Henry VI*, Part I, who there plays a
coward's part; thus labeling him for the audience, but as
Professor Kittredge seems to think, thus not at all "perplexing" them. Of Poins's prediction, of which Falstaff
knows nothing, fulfilled to the letter, with roaring and
sweating and fears of himself being robbed thrown in, the
critic takes no account. "The point of the jest [of which
also Falstaff knows nothing] lies, not in his taking to his
heels, but in his upbraiding the Prince and Poins for cowardice and thus enabling them to turn the tables; for it
was he who ran—not they." Except for the last clause, that
would be news to both the stage and the audience; and at
the Globe surely neither, in such a matter, required guidance. Of his subsequent embarrassment, after this (in
comedy) unparalleled triumph of self-sacrifice, the critic
again takes no account. And, in the same uncritical fash-

ion, he finds the fat knight passing "the test of courage" at Shrewsbury. " 'But,' objectors [he says] repeat, 'he did run away once upon a time.' True, but not from battle." True, but there he does something decidedly worse. He falls flat, plays "possum," then stabs the dead heroic Hotspur to claim the honor of having killed him. That, which Professor Kittredge, ignoring the stabbing, calls a "stratagem" (though Falstaff himself does not), would, for the audience, and in those days of chivalry only still more than in these of skepticism and pacifism, mean dastardliness and nothing short of it. He filches the "bright honor" he has pretended to scorn. And as for speaking of him, like Morgann, as a "veteran," and "when the time comes for action," as "always where he ought to be, in the center of the field,"—where duty calls or danger!—why, by the same process of "deduction," the great scholar would be in a fair way to whitewash most of the cowards of the Renaissance theater, English, German, French, and Spanish, as well as Parolles.[48] He judges the character by the implications instead of (as the spectator should) by the positive impression. The assumptions underlying the *miles gloriosus* or the *Capitano Spavento* he seems unable to accept, though, without thinking—without seeing them—an audience would, even today. Instead, he firmly remembers that in life cowards do not go to war, or if driven to it do not become captains; and that still less do they slip into dangerous proximity to such as "the Prince or the doughty Douglas or the heroic Percy," or profit by it in reputation if they do. Yet he ignores Falstaff's repeated confessions of discomfort in that precarious position—"I would 'twere bedtime . . I fear the shot here . . . Give me life"; and where else, or how else, in the theater, could be got the telling contrast, the full comic effect of that disreputable quality which in Falstaff till Morgann arose nobody had any difficulty in perceiving —neither Dryden nor Johnson, with whom (at one in such a matter of simple sense) I, at least, should tremble to differ—and which, since then, those who, like Sir Edmund

[48]See my *Shakespeare Studies,* pp. 431–36, 452–55, 457–65, 477–78.

Chambers and Tolstoy,[49] have kept their senses in their simplicity find, as Courthope found it, "absolutely transparent"? The improbability the great scholar does not see; but only, I think, because he does not see its purpose.

1943

[49]*Tolstoy on Shakespeare* (N. Y., 1907), p. 70.

CHAPTER XIII

All's Well *and* Measure for Measure

OUR POETS as they turn to criticism, even our dramatists and novelists, are, happily, more in accord with the early and the ancient critics than with our own. Knowing whereof they speak, they hold that the greatest literature is—though not of course in equal measure, nor to quite the same effect —for everybody, and for every time; and generally also— which is the correlative—that drama and even the novel at its best are primarily or ultimately emotional, more concerned with situation and poetry than with the portrayal of character. Wordsworth, Grillparzer, Arnold, Henley, Stevenson, Yeats, Santayana, Drinkwater, Maugham, Quiller-Couch, whether consciously or not, lock hands with Aristotle, Longinus, Milton—"simple, sensuous and passionate"—with Dryden and Goethe. The first eight I have cited to this effect elsewhere.[1] Mr. Maugham says of genius that "its appeal is not to this type of man or to that type, but to all men."[2] It is by that, according to Longinus, that you know him for a genius (vii, 4). Sir Arthur Quiller-

---

[1] In my *Shakespeare and Other Masters.* Mr. Somerset Maugham is quoted more at length above, chap. XI.

[2] *Summing Up* (1938), p. 76. Cf. Emerson, p. 388, *infr.* note.

Couch says of Shakespeare that "he wrote for all of us; and he wrote so that an ordinary man follows almost every one of his plots with anxiety and interest. This explains why our ordinary man so often shows himself so much sounder a critic of Shakespeare than the philologers."[3] (Menéndez y Pelayo, as we noticed in a previous chapter, says much the same of Cervantes.) And Stevenson in his "Gossip on Romance" and his "Humble Remonstrance," to which both Henley and Yeats seem to be indebted, writes as follows:

Situation is animated with passion, passion clothed again with situation. Neither exists for itself, but each inheres indissolubly with the other. This is high art; and not only the highest art possible in words, but the highest art of all, since it combines the greatest mass and diversity of the elements of truth and pleasure. (South Seas Ed., XIII, 139.)

Now in character-studies the pleasure that we take is critical; we watch, we approve, we smile at incongruities, we are moved to sudden heats of sympathy with courage, suffering, or virtue. But the characters are still themselves, they are not us; the more clearly they are depicted the more widely do they stand away from us . . . (P. 142.)

It is sometimes supposed that the drama consists of incident. It consists of passion, which gives the actor his opportunity; and that passion must progressively increase, or the actor, as the piece proceeded, would be unable to carry the audience from a lower to a higher pitch of interest and emotion. (P. 154.)

The characters may come anyhow upon the stage: we do not care; the point is, that, before they leave it, they shall become transfigured and raised out of themselves by passion. It may be part of the design to . . . depict a full-length character, and then behold it melt and change in the furnace of emotion. But there is no obligation of the sort; nice portraiture is not required; and we are content to accept mere abstract types, so they be strongly and sincerely moved. (P. 155.)

All alike are persuaded that, though to ennobling or enlarging effect, passion is the thing, emotional identification or contagion. And for that there must be ready understanding

[3]New Cambridge *Measure for Measure,* p. xx.

—"imaginative understanding," says Sir Arthur, "rules all drama";[4] and he might have added all poetry too, though for that it is an understanding not, of necessity, so broad and instantaneous.

This being the case, the interpretation of Shakespeare, or, say, Sophocles (neither of them, in Ben Jonson's words, "of an age but for all time") should be in the universally human terms in which, for the most part, they are conceived and expressed. On the one hand, we should not commit anachronisms. Our present-day idiosyncrasies—such as our pre-occupation with character as a psychological entity and the source of the action, or our interest in a central idea or thesis—should not interfere. But neither should we be pedantically historical. In adjusting ourselves to what in the Elizabethan was of his time we should not, as we have seen in previous chapters,[5] interrupt the instantaneous effect of his highly popular art with the application of Elizabethan physiology or any other technical learning. Nor with the application of history, either, least of all a hypothetical spiritual history of the time or biography of the dramatist.

2

The problem comedies,[6] as they have recently been called, *All's Well That Ends Well* and *Measure for Measure,* have suffered in such ways. They have been, even since Sir Walter Raleigh's and Professor Lawrence's books appeared, considered "gloomy," "ironical," "cynical," and "pessimistic," as in the mood of the so-called "dark period" of the great tragedies (and therefore, in part, dated as written then), a period which used to be connected by the biographical interpreters with the Dark Lady and the execution of the Earl of Essex, but of late (more soberly and

[4] *Ibid.*, p. xxxv.

[5] See chaps. IV, VII, as well as XIV.

[6] In the book with this title (The Macmillan Co., N. Y., 1931). By this, Professor Lawrence would, of course, not convey the notion that they are like the problem plays of Dumas *fils,* Ibsen, or Pinero, that they are *drames à thèse.*

prosaically, but still quite conjecturally) by Sir Edmund Chambers and others, with a physical and even mental breakdown in the poet; or, more loftily, with a "spiritual crisis" or "some process akin to what in the language of religion is called conversion, which left him a new man,"[7] ready to write *The Tempest*. Before that even Professor Wendell, who was not among those who clung to anachronisms or perpetrated them anew, had discovered a Calvinistic contempt for an evil world pervading *Measure for Measure* and "a profound sense of sexual evil" pervading both that and the earlier comedy. If the reader will bear with me I will repeat some immature words written more than thirty years ago,[8] which, incidentally, may serve to remind him of the situation in the plays:

. . . as Mr. Raleigh observes, "if the humorous scenes, in which most of the corruption comes to light, are needed only to present without disguise or extenuation a world of license and corruption, why are they humorous?" . . . A Vienna given over to carnal pleasure is demanded by the story—to provoke the Duke to revive the old law of death. The morality to which Shakespeare adheres in presenting this is but the rough-and-ready, conventional morality of the England of his day. The upper classes—Claudio and Juliet, as well as Angelo, the Deputy—are judged by it; the young pair confess and repent roundly and without reserve. Love does not count. The lower classes, on the other hand—the bawds and their various hangers-on—though they and Angelo are the really vicious ones, are treated, with Elizabethan amplitude, as matter for gibe and jest. Like the *homme sensuel moyen* even today, Shakespeare looks askance at the lady for her prank and laughs at the maid; and, like Chaucer and the Elizabethan novelists, he enjoys saying more of either than his conscience warrants . . . as appears, indeed, if nowhere else, in the character of the novice Isabella, "a thing enskied and sainted," who is shocked into virtuous rage by her brother's prayer for life at the cost of her compliance, but who acts out that part, by means oi the substitute Mariana, even to the point of crying aloud the loss of her virtue in the market place. And as for *All's Well*, "the cynical

[7] Lawrence, p. 226, quoting Sir E. K. Chambers, in 1929.

[8] *Modern Philology*, April, 1910, "Anachronism in Shakespeare Criticism."

irony of a modern Frenchman" and "the miserable mystery of earthly love," which Mr. Wendell finds in it, are ideas incompatible with the indecent conversation in which, in the first scene, the heroine engages with Parolles; with her businesslike method of taking possession of a husband; and with the dearth of passion —except for simple aversion in one case and frank affection in the other—evinced by either her husband or her. In the intention of the author, it seems to me, there is no cynical irony, no miserable mystery, for there is no disillusionment, or strife of passion, but the most unquestioning, unreluctant acceptance of the ways of the world and the flesh. What irony there is, is of the simple theatrical sort, such as arises from the heartless rebuff given the heroine by the man she worships at the moment when she seems to have won him: the lust which she later discovers in him neither surprises her nor for one moment deters her. (III, v, 71f.) Still less is there occasion for [Dowden's] sentiment concerning "Helena's sacred boldness in assuming command over Bertram's fate and her own," or her "healing of the spirit of the man she loves": and from the hour that she receives his letter— "When thou canst get the ring upon my finger, which shall never come off"—her character is left to shift for itself, that, for the story's needs, by hook or by crook, she may fulfill the stipulations thus set by Bertram for securing him as a husband in spite of himself. The dramatic complication is solved from without, not from within, by an answer to a riddle. In both comedies story carries it with a high hand. Gloom or bitterness over sexual evils, if the poet felt it, does not loom large enough to spoil the mirth and sport which these furnish, and ideas on the subject hardly put in an appearance at all.

Even Sir Walter Raleigh's objections did not put a stop to this irresponsible speculation; on the contrary, the tragical, biographical tendency was in some quarters only accentuated, exacerbated. In 1921 an anonymous writer in the *Times Literary Supplement* wrote of the "pure cynicism" in *Measure for Measure* and the "self-torturing mood" in *All's Well*.[9] In 1929 Sir Edmund could still be writing of "profound disillusion and discouragement" in this period, which is also that of *Timon of Athens,* saying that the dramatist "whips himself" (self-torturing again) "to an almost incoherent expression of a general loathing

[9] Quoted by Lawrence, p. 68.

and detestation of humanity." And in 1932 Professor J. D. Wilson, eagerly taking up with the "nervous breakdown," finds *Measure for Measure* to be proof that about 1603 Shakespeare was in a mood "of self-laceration [self-torturing!], weariness, discord, cynicism and disgust," and "quite obviously believed in nothing."[10] (From Calvinism to that!) Also, reviving the Essex business, he, in this same "biographical adventure," ventures into history as well, and sees a "shadow [lying] across the land, the shadow of the tomb, and the air thick with the breath of corruption," the accession of James I ushering in "a period of cynicism and gloom, self-indulgence and crime." As I said before in answering Miss Ellis-Fermor,[11] who somewhat shares these devastating views, I am content to leave such matters of their national history and biography both (and no doubt Mr. Lawrence would join me) to Englishmen, but preferably to Professors Sisson and R. W. Chambers,[12] who confront the reckless myth-makers with evidence, and above all with their own lack of it; and to the English scholar and poet Lascelles Abercrombie, who says that Shakespeare's career is "only intelligible as the career of an artist." Some recent critics, on the other hand, with no particular biographical or historical bent or prepossessions to satisfy, have not been so sympathetic with the poetry as Coleridge and his followers, and turning against the heroines celebrated by them, have, except for single scenes, spoken of the two plays disparagingly.

Into the breach, accordingly, Mr. Lawrence has stepped, in his *Problem Comedies* (under which name he includes *Troilus and Cressida* and *Cymbeline*), and with great learning and fine tact has applied the historical method.

[10]*The Essential Shakespeare, A Biographical Adventure* (1932), pp. 36, 113, 117, 122.

[11]*English Literary History,* March, 1939, "Recent Elizabethan Criticism."

[12]British Academy Lectures: 1934, "The Mythical Sorrows of Shakespeare"; and 1937, "The Jacobean Shakespeare." The latter, by Chambers, is a complete refutation: of my own discussion, *Shakespeare Studies* (1927), pp. 80–85, neither writer was aware.

This he has done not only in clearing up misunderstandings, but also in justifying the dramatist, his heroines, and his art here in general; and he has rightly insisted on the importance of tradition, the expectations of the audience, the dramatist's concern for theatrical effect, and the conventional necessity in Renaissance comedy, according to both practice and critical precept, of a happy ending. But (history again, though of another sort!) in so doing he, in my opinion, takes (or rather, keeps) too much the point of view of a medievalist, or is, as Mr. Middleton Murry says, as an historian "too positive";[13] he does not sufficiently distinguish between traditions literary or learned and dramatic or popular, and some of the conceptions he applies would, I think, not be familiar to the Elizabethan audience. Moreover, he and Sir Walter both find here more of the problem or of casuistry than (as I think) there is, and less of comic effect. On the latter subject Sir Walter, as quoted above, seems to have only the low-life scenes in mind.

In the discussion certain principles, I think, by this time perhaps not unfamiliar to my readers, should guide us. History has a place here—and Mr. Lawrence would no doubt agree with me—only in so far as the Elizabethan audience, the Elizabethan art, differs from ours. In all art, but particularly the drama, as both W. L. Courtney and Croce have recognized, "What is not expressed does not exist." Or as the Frenchman saw it before either of them, *En art il n'y a que d'exprimé.* Whatever is expressed, on the other hand, is important; indeed, all that is important —to the audience of Shakespeare's time, at least—is expressed. Otherwise, the drama would be no drama.

3

First, as for *All's Well.* Mr. Lawrence's opinions may be thus summarized, partly in his words, partly in my own: that Helena was meant to be wholly noble and heroic, and fully justified in her conduct; that the audience would have accepted these "tricks" [such as the getting of the ring and the substitu-

[13]*Shakespeare* (Macmillan Co., N. Y., 1936), p. 250.

tion in bed] without question; that Bertram's sudden change of heart at the end was a convention of medieval and Elizabethan story, which must be expected to follow Helena's triumph; that there is no suggestion of their being unhappy hereafter; and that the blackening of the character of Bertram and the disagreeable qualities of the Clown and Parolles are for dramatic contrast and dramatic motivation (p. 38).

"Wholly noble and heroic, and fully justified"—Mr. Lawrence thinks so because of a few stories (besides that of Giletta of Narbonne in the *Decameron,* ninth novella of the third day, here Shakespeare's source), in which a woman so devoted and cleverly persevering is sympathetically presented. It is, he says, a Virtue story; and Helena, so far, is like the patient Griselda of Chaucer and the Fair Annie of the ballad.[14] However, apart from Boccaccio's, there are only two stories similar to Helena's at the point that is (nowadays at least) most objectionable, the deceiving of the man into physical intercourse, which he has from the first refused; and these are a Turkish and an Egyptian, which we have no reason to think were known in England. Besides there is little evidence that the Elizabethan theater welcomed these medieval stories in which one virtue, such as wifely devotion or patience (or as friendly generosity) is celebrated somewhat at the cost of others. Dekker, indeed, with collaborators, wrote a *Patient Grissel;* but his similarly patient Candido is in full possession of the other important virtues, and of much shrewdness, common sense, and humor into the bargain. His Grissel is pretty submissive and (in the medieval sense) exemplary; but so in this matter is her father, and throughout it is made clear that, on the one hand, her brother is not so, and that, on the other hand, the Marquis, her husband, is only trying and proving her. This married pair, moreover, are contrasted with the farcical Gwenthian and Sir Owen, the shrew and her would-be tamer. Male supremacy was, of course, still everywhere acknowledged—then, and for long after, involved in the actual *mores*—but unless Shake-

[14] *Op. cit.,* pp. 49–52.

speare's *Taming of the Shrew* also implies a medieval attitude or revival, I do not see that his *All's Well* does. As Mr. Lawrence himself honestly notices, "there is, at the end, no formal recognition of Helena's devotion and cleverness,"[15] such as there is in Boccaccio. Not her heroism, nor the question whether it was heroism, either, but the striking situation, was what attracted the dramatist.

It is a well-known and natural practice—and with us today even as with the Greeks—for an audience to accept sympathetically a new rendering of an old and familiar story however improbable or aloof from the contemporary customs. Dekker, however, sagaciously took Patient Grissel for his title—the audience came expecting patience, nothing else or less. And Giletta is not in the title before us, nor in the text, either, and we have no reason to think the story was widely familiar in Shakespeare's day. As a mere matter of fact, it is treated quite differently. If in Boccaccio it is a Virtue story, in Shakespeare it is a romantic one. There is no evidence that Shakespeare or his audience, either, had any interest in medieval virtue, or in so peculiar a one as this; but both, as his and all other Elizabethan drama shows, had great interest in romance.

My own opinion is that Helena is made, not "wholly noble or heroic," but lovable and admirable (as the leading lady in romantic comedy, or tragi-comedy, which this play is) ; and not by means of any medieval tradition concerning extremely persevering wifely devotion, but simply, as so often in Shakespearean and ancient drama, by the generous and unreserved expression of their admiration on the part of the best characters—the Countess, the King, Lafeu— and both by her deportment in general and (especially) by her sentiments and speech, poetically so potent, before and also after her dubious undertakings. The propriety of these is not doubted or debated as in a true problem play it certainly would be. They but make the situation—contrasting with the delicacy of her deportment and sentiments and throwing them into relief. Like most of Shakespeare's

[15]P. 50.

heroines, and more than Othello, Hamlet, Lear, and (except to his wife!) Macbeth until the slaying of the King, she is the object of no criticism; and (something remarkable) she has the young man's mother wholly on her side, both before and after her choosing him, against the young man himself. Her following Bertram to Court, therefore, and asking for his hand as the reward for her healing of the King, can be prompted (as it is) by the spirit of high romance. With him she has been brought up; and what is in her own heart bids her expect to find the like in his. At first she thinks him too far above her. But at last such love, "religious" in its adoration, takes on the proportions of a faith,—

> Who ever strove
> To show her merit, that did miss her love?

In this she is, I think, not heroic or specially medieval or (of course) virtuous, but only as romantic as Julia, Viola,[16] Imogen, and Helena of Athens are in seeking out the objects of their desire; and as most of Shakespeare's maidens are in avowing their love—Silvia and Rosalind, Desdemona and Miranda, even taking the initiative—all against the dictates of decorum. She belongs in the same company with Shakespeare's maidens who—in play after play, and in *The Merchant of Venice* three of them—go to the length of putting on boys' clothing; but also with the heroines in Italian and Spanish novelle and comedies, in Ariosto, Spenser, and the medieval romances, even within the borders of countries where the code of propriety for women was far narrower and stricter than in England.[17] It is in the literature of the stricter countries for that matter—of Greece itself—that high romance most flourishes.

High romance is [as I have said elsewhere] not propriety carried to extremes but overridden . . . Propriety—reticence and reserve—are excellent things, but above all as a measure; and

[16]In the play as we have it there is little left of this, except at I, ii, 29, "He was a bachelor then"; and at II, iv, 113-24.

[17]Cf. my *Shakespeare Studies,* chap. ii, especially pp. 43-44.

the love that breaks their bonds—perfect love casteth out fear—
is stronger.[18]

The more highly romantic because (as thus we are made
to see) more deeply, recklessly in love; and it is this, presented so attractively, that is meant to warrant for us
Helena of Roussillon's undertaking. But it is not altogether
for the effect upon the audience (mainly men) or upon the
readers (either men or women dominated by men's taste);
there is even some realism in this romanticism; and Hugo
is right as he says in presenting the loves of Marius and
Cosette: *le premier symptôme de l'amour vrai chez un
jeune homme, c'est la timidité; chez une jeune fille, c'est la
hardiesse.*

The rebuff she gets only engages us more completely on
her side. Bertram's reasons—her station and her poverty,
which no one else remembers against her—discredit him;
and the King, Lafeu, and the Countess (again) are on her
side, not his. It is the situation, as Stevenson says, that
counts; and the sympathy is Helena's now more than ever.
Bertram might naturally and justifiably have rebelled
against being thus peremptorily disposed of; but nothing is
made of that ("what is not expressed does not exist"), and
simply according to the postulates or premises of the story,
not to any medieval, still-living tradition, I think, the King
—and Helena—are within their rights. In any case Bertram
should at least have felt a throb of gratitude. There is, however, no trace of any; and (situation again!) "the general
enlightenment, as Professor Herford observes, gives to Bertram's resistance an air of stolid obstinacy."

Her rebuff she takes in the finest spirit; and the improbability in what follows, as later she accepts the challenge of
the riddling conditions he lays down for taking her to his
arms, is mainly incidental to the working out of a comic
(that is, a non-tragic) denouement. Certainly Helena's part
in that is not to be reckoned against her. Comedy in Elizabethan times, especially romantic comedy, ended happily;

[18]My *Shakespeare's Young Lovers* (1937), p. 51; and for Greece
see above, p. 81.

and still more peremptorily than Molière's does, and the
modern novel, with a marriage; in Elizabethan times,
moreover, as earlier and later, too, there was something of
the same delight in ingenious intrigue that is to be found
in Italian comedy and *novella.* This artful or deceitful fulfillment of riddling conditions or prophecies in the denouement is like that in *Cymbeline, The Winter's Tale, Macbeth,* as well as the legend of Tannhäuser, besides the
medieval stories of sexual deception referred to by Mr.
Lawrence. It is at this point in the last named, though on
the part of a woman already living with her husband, that
there is the similarity asserted; but for the audience it is
quite enough that the conditions, as laid down in the Boc-
caccian story, are now plainly stated before them. Without
any medieval *milieu,* a Renaissance, or a Shakespearean,
comedy, filled, as by Scaliger's definition, with intrigue
(*negotiosum*), and preparing for a happy ending,[19] would,
especially at this late stage in the action, demand that the
conditions laid down should be fulfilled. The mere logic of
the action, as so far conducted, would demand it. Here, too,
it is not a matter of virtue, I think, or any that an Elizabethan audience would recognize. It is, again, the spirit
of high romance in the heroine, which has overridden the
previous obstacles to her love—so far, indeed, the undertaking is quite in keeping with her character—and which
must not be daunted now. In fact, this taking of another
woman's place at the rendezvous with the man to whom
one is outwardly married is, however little to our present-
day taste, only carrying the romantic overriding of the dictates of decorum to the limit. And the simple but coarse
or robust audience undoubtedly relished not only the solv-
ing and fulfillment of the riddle but also this further contrast—between a fine and delicate character and so indeli-
cate a situation. It is some such effect of contrast as this,
I surmise, that the dramatist produced and the audience

[19]Scaliger, *Poetice,* I, 3: *Comediam igitur sic definiamus nos,
poema dramaticum, negotiosum, exitu laetum, stylo populari.* And
Scaliger is not so much prescribing as recording.

accepted when Helena early in the play is involved in indecent conversation with Parolles, and when Isabella, in *Measure for Measure,* is, somewhat similarly, with Lucio. For like Desdemona, who listens to Iago's ribaldry on the quay, Helena and Isabella do not talk indecently themselves. Helena, however, is more deeply implicated; and if the impression of her purity is not a little troubled in the process, it is owing to Shakespeare's giving to her, as to Desdemona, a motive or excuse. Desdemona is covering over her anxiety, "beguiling the thing I am," as she awaits Othello's arrival from the stormy sea; and Helena converses so readily with Parolles because of his association with the god of her idolatry. This is Gothic art, of which we shall see more. Coming after one heartfelt soliloquy and before another, the colloquy is both indecent and comical, both pathetic and ironical, as they talk of virginity, the defending of it or the losing of it "to one's own liking."

The sudden change of heart in Bertram at the very end is, as Mr. Lawrence says, in the original story; and is also, (in keeping with the conventional denouement for Elizabethan comedy, or tragi-comedy, such as this) a necessary consequence (and completion) of Helena's triumph. Moreover, as usual in Elizabethan comedy—yet not because it is a Virtue story[20]—this is without any suggestion that their afterlife would be unhappy. Such sociological or psychological implications or questions would interfere with the present happiness and the finality of effect. The blackening of Bertram's character, however, particularly by his conduct in the previous part of the final scene, is another matter, and the most regrettable in the play. He is here a cad, a coward, and a liar as well as an adulterer—why should Helena desire him? As Mr. Lawrence observes, the intended adultery itself is an indispensable part of the plot. And the other misconduct was added, he thinks, to make more plausible Bertram's rejection of Helena and his incapacity for understanding her finer nature, to explain his

[20]Lawrence, p. 52: a convention of the Virtue story "that they live happily ever after."

willingness to commit adultery, and to create added sympathy for the heroine. "In Boccaccio's day, when adultery was sanctioned, no such explanation of Bertram's act would have been necessary."[21]

"Are these explanations really satisfying?"[22] asks Mr. Murry; and one must agree, I think, that they are not. Thus Bertram is madè more plausible (but less acceptable) by Helena's being made less plausible and less acceptable both. What palliates her persevering to the end is that to his worst meanness, which comes out in the final scene, she is not a witness; and the only excuse for this worst meanness is the fact (which Mr. Lawrence also recognizes) that it adds to the scene's dramatic effect. As he squirms and lies and slanders he prolongs the denouement and adds to the stagy excitement. That's about all one can say for him.

And about all that saves Helena here is the tardiness of her arrival, and the curtain; the audience which has witnessed denouements like those of *The Two Gentlemen, Much Ado,* and *Cymbeline* may well expect no deeper significance in this. Not much concerned (or expected to be concerned) with the mere implications of conduct generally,[23] they are still less so near the close. And she comes in late, the curtain falls soon. Presumably of Bertram's recent meanness she has not heard; but if now confronted with it she could no doubt do no better than answer like Mariana in *Measure for Measure,*

I crave no other, nor no better man.

It is appropriate therefore that for her who is the heroine the question should not be raised.

The objection to the medievalism in *All's Well* is much the same as to the deadly sins and the Elizabethan humors as incarnated in Shakespeare's tragic heroes; or to the Parcae in the Weird Sisters; or to "courtly love"[23a] in *Romeo.* It is the ever-valid objection in the theater to mere erudi-

[21]*Ibid.,* pp. 35, 62.   [22]*Shakespeare* (1936), p. 250.

[23]See my *Shakespeare and Other Masters,* pp. 14–24.

[23a]Out of place even in the *Fairy Queen,* cf. *Journal of English and Germanic Philology,* xli, 459.

tion, to the technical or the esoteric, to a tradition that is merely literary or learned, not dramatic or popular. As the best critics since Coleridge have generally recognized, the Sisters have the imposing quality and much of the important function of the classical Fates, but, for emotional, theatrical effect, also most of the ways and features of the familiar Elizabethan witches; while Hecate, who in the third and fourth acts appears with them, is by the best authorities supposed, not only for such reasons but because of the style and rhythm, to be an interpolation. So Romeo's love for Rosaline, which vanishes on Juliet's entry at the ball, has indeed some symptoms of the *fine amor*—solitariness, wakefulness, groaning, sighing, and languishing, under the trees and in the moonlight; but all that, together with the affected poetizing in conceits, and in contrarieties or oxymorons (which, however, is, and for the Elizabethans would seem to be, in the style of the sonneteers whom they knew rather than the troubadours whom they didn't know) the audience would readily and properly take to be the love of love, or mere lovesickness, without any dependence on medieval literary lore. They have no history of literature or culture at their disposal, or if they had, how would it advantage the play? Is this satire or burlesque, then, or a sympathetic treatment? The audience would not quite know—a sorry condition for an audience. In any case Romeo has violated the chief article of the chivalric code, unfaltering constancy; even simple, readily recognizable lovesickness is more to his credit. And high romance, which also needs—and then needed—no explaining, is more to the credit of Helena.

4

Much that has been said of *All's Well* applies to *Measure for Measure*. This too is not a tragedy but a comedy, that is, a very Elizabethan one, a hybrid. And Professor Lawrence is right about Mariana's betrothal as furnishing some warrant in popular opinion for the substitution of her for Isabella; about the final marriages and pardons as being within the conventional expectations; and about the maneuvers and deceptions practiced by the Duke, particularly in the final scene (like those of the King, assisted by Diana, in the corresponding scene in *All's Well*), as being for theatrical purpose and excitement. And he is right in defending the character of Isabella against our present-day prejudice, of course, as he was in defending that of Helena.

But while the Duke and Isabella may not because of their ruse be open to the charge of "moral laxity," they must—that is, if their conduct is to be taken as at all the expression of their characters—be open to that of some indelicacy, a noticeable perfunctoriness, in their conception of marriage. Even formally and legally, there is still something to be desired; and it is to make amends that Angelo, after the disclosure, is at once ordered off the stage:

> Go take her hence, and marry her instantly. (V, i, 382.)

That is, "make an honest woman" of her; and so made by such a man, in intention, as the Duke himself knows, not only a virgin-violator and a murderer, but a hypocrite, and (having broken faith and given orders for Claudio's death from fear of revenge)[24] a cowardly cheat besides! The Duke, Isabella, and Mariana herself seem to think both marriage and the consummation of it to be her due, as the good people in *All's Well* think they are Helena's. It must be remembered, however, that this is not wholly Elizabethan or medieval, either. We ourselves, not so long ago, used to hear that an engagement was as sacred as marriage, resolutely to be kept even though discovered to be a mistake, or though made by the man when not quite responsible, in his cups. One must be a man of his word, not let a lady down.

Both the Duke and Isabella, of course, are endeavoring to save Claudio (though always within the limits of the improbable story), and to force Angelo to do Mariana justice; yet there is no evidence that I see for Mariana's falling in with their purposes, as Professor R. W. Chambers finds,[25] to save him. Shakespeare might easily have indicated such a motive, and why, then, didn't he? Evidently

[24] IV, iv, 33.
[25] Pp. 32, 45.

(situation again!) because that would have lowered Isabella in our opinion—would have played into the hands of the critics (if ever he thought of any) who, from Hazlitt's day to the present, complain of her "rigid chastity." As for this last, Professor Wilson, who says that at this particular time Shakespeare "quite obviously believed in nothing," must here at least admit that he still believed (if too narrowly) in a little something; and that his audience, though at this "period of cynicism, self-indulgence and crime," believed in it too, not fancying a Monna Vanna such as Whetstone, the source, had, under Italian influence, presented. To a really cynical dramatist and audience, interested in problems, how much more interesting and striking a situation that would be—which Shakespeare thereby, ordinarily eager for such, unhesitatingly forgoes! And it is only because, like her, he and his audience believe or can believe in chastity as more than a brother's life (II, iv, 185) that they can accept the fierceness of her denunciation.[26]

The denouement, however unsatisfactory as a social document, is quite in harmony with the rest of the play. The forgiveness of Angelo is, apart from the requirements of a comedy, owing to his penitence, which appears in his repeated outcry for death as his punishment. (V, i, 376–79; 480–83.) This, though it does not make reparation to the psychology, does so to the emotional impression; and all the more because it is in keeping with what he had said to Escalus, the other Deputy, at the outset:

> When I that censure him do so offend,
> Let mine own judgment pattern out my death,
> And nothing come in partial. (II, i, 29–31.)

He has at least the virtues of consistency and courage. And the pleading of Mariana, who, like a woman, declares,

> I crave no other, nor no better man,

[26]Cf. Professor Oliver Elton, *Modern Studies* (1907), pp. 113–17, where the great scholar objects to Raleigh's magnifying Shakespeare's tolerance and sympathy somewhat at the expense of his morality, his spirit of approval or disapproval.

and that of Isabella, who (though a nun, perilously like a woman too) confesses,

> I partly think
> A due sincerity governed his deeds,
> Till he did look on me,—

both of these make the pardon, though not more plausible, more acceptable, if still, for us, not by any means enough so. Nevertheless, according to the Duke's formal and perfunctory principles, not as in life but as in the play, it is about the only thing he can well do. Having bedded her with the villain and married her to him, how can he but heed Mariana as she cries,

> O my most gracious Lord,
> I hope you will not mock me with a husband.

Even Isabella is here consistent, for she yields to Mariana's entreaty only when besought and, besides, she must remember how recently she has herself pleaded the cause of mercy before this judge, now judged. She has more virtues than one; and is not rigorous when rigor is of no avail.

Medieval justice, however, which Mr. Lawrence here invokes, has, I think, no bearing.

> . . . the Middle Ages knew but the two extremes . . . When the condemned criminal is pardoned, the question whether he deserves it for any special reason, is hardly asked; for mercy has to be gratuitous, like the mercy of God.[27]

That is like the medieval virtue at the expense of other virtues,—of wifely devotion as in Griselda, and of friendly generosity as in the stories of handing over to a friend one's own sweetheart, or of devotion as in the stories of saving a leprous comrade by dipping him in the blood of one's own child;[28] and if much in favor among the people as a whole at any time, such an attitude is not likely to have

[27]Lawrence, p. 117, quoting Huizinga.

[28]*Amis and Amile*, et cetera, Lawrence, pp. 23–24. The handing over of the sweetheart (as in *Decameron* X, 8) comes into *The Two Gentlemen of Verona*, indeed, but only in the denouement again, for the momentary sensation and to bring about the disclosure of Julia's identity.

awakened much sympathy in the Elizabethan theater. In general Shakespeare's notions of justice are like ours, as well as those of his age;[29] but like those of other dramatists in his own day and earlier, not strictly so in comedy, especially, as Mr. Lawrence also notices, at the denouement. There the leading likable characters, at least, though faulty, are, by marriage, "dismissed to happiness." Ordinarily in Shakespearean and other Elizabethan comedy there is no such villain; and ordinarily such as there are do not appear in the denouement to trouble it, having fled like Don John in *Much Ado,* or dropped out, after getting their deserts, like Shylock; but Angelo, like Bertram, and like Iachimo in *Cymbeline,* is in the denouement as an essential figure. To justice, moreover, acknowledgments have been made; and it is only after much pleading by those who have suffered injustice, and after the appearance of Claudio, supposed to have been executed, that the sentence of death is recalled.

5

The principal alterations in Whetstone's story are (apart from the substitution of the betrothed at the rendezvous with the wicked judge instead of Isabella) : the changing of the latter into a nun, and the disguising of the Duke (or King) into a Friar, who, playing Haroun-al-Raschid, becomes the chief intriguer and motive force in the play. In general they heighten the dramatic excitement but also they conduce to comic irony, which allays, by commingling, the tragic tone.

Of the Duke's psychology, Mr. Lawrence rightly thinks, little or nothing can be made: neither a coward nor a shirk, as others have thought, he serves to produce complications and resolve them. He is a stage figure, mainly. In a real sovereign much of his maneuvering and deceiving, even though good in the long run may come of it, would be inde-

[29]A father's authority, and a husband's too, were then, of course, stronger; but only, for the obvious reason, as warranted by the *mores* of the time, not by the medieval, nor (which some scholars of late have endeavored to prove) by the classical as known to Renaissance scholars.

fensible. But it is chiefly owing to him, unreasonable and
unplausible, sensational and stagy as he is, that the play is
both interesting and exciting and yet, as we shall see, not
too much so for comedy. Since we are in the secret of his
disguise, and quite aware that he knows all that is going
on, we are, when we need to be, reassured. Mr. Lawrence
calls him a puppet; and so he is, as the dramatist manipulates him; but he is also, as Mr. Murry says, "a power."[30]
The situation has been so prepared for that when he, as
the Friar, known, even in that character, by those on the
stage to know so much, is stripped of his disguise, he in the
very act of appearing accuses Angelo of all his secret iniquity:

> O my dread lord,
> I should be guiltier than my guiltiness,
> To think I can be undiscernible,
> When I perceive your Grace, like power divine,
> Hath look'd upon my passes. (V, i, 371–75.)

Mariana, of course, here serves to relieve Isabella of the
opprobrium of falling a prey to Angelo's lascivious treachery; but why is Isabella thereupon made a nun? Both
changes are, like the disguising of the Duke, meant, though
in different ways, to produce in the action a greater effect
of compactness and also of comic irony—external irony
(that is), not, to be sure, any at the heart of the play or in
the background, not the "Romantic" sort, of pessimism or
disillusion. The play must be kept a comedy. By the deception practiced upon him, Angelo, who, betrothed like
Claudio, had cravenly and brutally deserted Mariana because of her losing the dowry, is now put in exactly the
same position (though on a far lower moral level) as the
condemned Claudio, who, by mutual agreement with his
fiancée, had postponed the actual marriage to secure the
dowry, lying in other hands.[31] And by his disguise the Duke

[30] P. 258.

[31] Professor R. W. Chambers (*op. cit.*, 1937, p. 34) thinks there
is the difference of publicity in favor of Angelo's and Mariana's
betrothal. He is right if the "denunciation of outward order" (I, ii,
152) means that, not marriage.

is continually hearing, and comfortably or uncomfortably participating in, discussion favorable or unfavorable of himself; which also (and decidedly) lowers or counteracts the tragic tone.

As a nun, Isabella makes, in a sense, a more exciting (though in another sense a less dramatic) situation of both the proposal and also her refusal, before Angelo and then Claudio in prison; and, besides, she thus gives a more urgent occasion for Mariana's being sought as a substitute. But she thus also furnishes a contrast such as I have touched upon in the previous drama, though here much more fully developed, and apparently ignored by the critics,—one grimly comic, and often somewhat ironical too. A nun receiving such a proposal, or having it urged upon her, a saint unlawfully desired by a saint—"O cunning enemy!" cries Angelo after her first appeal, meaning, of course, the Devil,

> that, to catch a saint,
> With saints dost bait thy hook! (II, ii, 180–81.)

And the preceding portion of the scene is given the same ironical turn through such remarks as these of Isabella's, which touch him up a bit though without her knowledge:

> If he had been as you and you as he,
> You would have slipt like him. (II, ii, 64–65.)

> but man, proud man,
> Dress'd in a little brief authority,
> Most ignorant of what he's most assur'd,
> His glassy essence, like an angry ape,
> Plays such fantastic tricks before high heaven
> As make the angels weep. (II, ii, 117–23.)

> Go to your bosom;
> Knock there, and ask your heart what it doth know
> That's like my brother's fault. (ii, 136–37.)

Even with her words, she herself, unaware, now does the knocking. And in the previous scene, II, i, 9–16, Escalus, the other Deputy, demurring to such ruthlessness, has gingerly raised the same question—whether Angelo had never felt such infirmity, in his own person. To which, in the *hybris* of self-righteousness, he replies,

> 'Tis one thing to be tempted, Escalus,
> Another thing to fall;

which he is just on the point of doing.

The comic quality of the later scene, with Isabella, is heightened by the presence of Lucio (incongruous companion and adjutant!) and his humorous remarks. Certainly, high-pitched though it is, it is kept nevertheless from being tragic. The next, between the holy Sister and the saintly judge alone, takes on a comic cast, again, through his hypocrisy and his crafty coming out into the open. And the greater—the famous—scene, between the nun and Claudio, is kept from being too tragic for comedy in somewhat the same way as the first between her and Angelo,—through Claudio's making such an appeal to her, the nun, and through our knowledge that the Duke is overhearing it.

In herself, moreover, she is well constituted to serve for the comic contrast—is made not too much of a nun. She is not squeamish, finicky, or sanctimonious; and while she does not participate in the gross talk about her, she does not take much notice of it, either. She serves for a contrast without herself being compromised, and also without jarring upon us. She does no lamenting or grieving over sexual or other sinfulness in Vienna—that in the play is a matter left to the Duke and the Deputies: otherwise, she would not serve for the comic effect and would clash with the humorous scenes noticed by Raleigh, "in which most of the corruption comes to light." If the contrast between the dazzling purity of Isabella and the impurity roundabout her were not a little broken or blurred, the play would approach the aborted tragedy that many of the critics have taken it to be. As she is—not too good for this world—on hearing of the plight Juliet is in because of Claudio, all she says is "O, let him marry her"; and she goes through the necessary arrangements with Angelo for the rendezvous according to the Duke's directions, with (as she reports the matter, but well that it is only reported) no apparent shrinking. Most remarkable of all, at the city gates it is she herself, the nun, that brings the charge of his ravishing and murdering--the effect, because of our inside knowledge, is not tragic!—and with clamorous clearness. Sturdy, downright, and direct, "heroic and noble," she is not, however, —for that again would interfere with the comedy—delicate, pathetic, or tender. She loves her brother but—"There spake my brother,"[32]—heroically. When before those words, on her arrival in the prison, he asks what comfort, this is the way she produces it:

> Why,
> As all comforts are; most good, most good indeed.
> Lord Angelo, having affairs to heaven,
> Intends you for his swift ambassador,
> Where you shall be an everlasting leiger;
> Therefore your best appointment make with speed,
> To-morrow you set on. (III, i, 55–61.)

Bitterness outstrips tenderness; and as Claudio inquires, "Is there no remedy?" she replies, facing the facts,

> None but such remedy as, to save a head,
> To cleave a heart in twain.

So, when towards the close of the scene he pleads for life at her expense, she calls him a "beast," tells him " 'tis best thou diest quickly";[33] and when she hears Angelo has been his death, is not plunged in despair, but is for "direct action," as she might call it:

> O, I will to him and pluck out his eyes!

Her own, as Lucio notices a moment later, are "red"; but we are not permitted to take that much more to heart than he does. And it is with such vehemence that later she

[32]III, i, 86.

[33]Professor R. W. Chambers (pp. 41–42) is of the opinion that Isabella's "fierceness is the measure of the agony of her soul." I do not think her "hard as an icicle," like Miss Ellis-Fermor and others; but if Shakespeare had meant any such self-laceration, or such wreaking of herself on Claudio, he would have given the Duke, who overhears, some word of comment, or given her an aside. Such a mood, also, is not in Shakespeare's vein.

clamors for justice at the gates. In keeping with this abrupt vigor and incisiveness of speech is even her method of entry and approach:

> [*Within*] Peace, ho, be here!
> DUKE. The tongue of Isabel . . .
>   *Enter* ISABELLA
> ISAB. Ho, by your leave! (IV, iii, 110.)

So, before that, in the prison scene:

> [*Within*] What, ho! Peace here, grace and good company!

A vociferous, ironical nun! She is almost a Major Barbara.

The irony, as I have said, is external. It resides mostly in the situation of Angelo, though heightened by his relations to Isabella and Mariana, and in the parallel and contrast with Claudio; but also in the whole death-dealing venture of reform, which is preposterous, and, of course, in the deception and misunderstanding occasioned by the Duke's disguise. And this irony, the comic contrast of the votarist of Saint Clare, at the center of the sexual discussion and action, and the humorousness of the low-life scenes (Pompey, Froth, Lucio, and the constables) in which nature and rude sense assert themselves—all these effects or qualities are in keeping with one another. Whereas such irony as springs out of the bottomless skepticism imagined by Professor Wilson, or that "corroding atmosphere of moral suspicion" which, for Sir Edmund Chambers, "hangs about the play, leaving one not absolutely certain whether Isabella has not had her ordeal and in her turn failed, and whether the treatment of the Duke as Providence is not ironical,"[34] —either of them would be out of keeping indeed.

As for the irony in the reform, the Duke, or rather Angelo, has, of course, in the character of a Draco, gone prodigiously far. The vice, says Lucio (and the humorous spirit of the play bears him out)—"it is impossible to extirp

[34]*Survey* (1925), pp. 214–15. Raleigh himself speaks of Shakespeare's attitude in this play as "critical and ironical" (though sympathetically so); but is taken to task by Elton for it. See above, note 26.

it quite till eating and drinking be put down"—; even the Provost says "all sects, all ages smack of it, and he to die for't!" Isabella herself, who abhors it, but says so little about it, asks Angelo,

> Who is it that hath died for this offence?
> There's many have committed it;

while the Deputy, said by Elbow the constable not to abide a whoremaster, his blood, according to Lucio, being very snow-broth, turns out the greatest offender. Claudio, on the other hand, picked out to suffer death for it, is the most venial one, having been betrothed like Angelo—"upon a true contract . . . she is fast my wife"—and both he and Julietta avow their love. Everybody but Angelo, either good or bad (though to keep the tragicomic tone not much is said about it), esteems them and sympathizes with them; and the reformation has been a fiasco. But as usual in Shakespeare, there is, at the end, no moral, and, throughout, nothing approaching a thesis; for the Duke and the Sister, marrying, seem, quite properly, though absent-mindedly, to have abandoned, he the business of reform and she the ascetic ideal.

6

Now the qualities or arrangements at which we have just been glancing contribute to the effect of what is—even otherwise—a tragicomedy, still less than *All's Well* a problem play. No question is raised, no "casuistry" is engaged in, no "dilemma," whether intolerable or tolerable, is put.[35] At three points, to be sure, there might have been—the proposal by the judge, the substitution of Mariana, and the forgiveness of the judge at the end; but as we have seen, the last is promptly disposed of according to the expectations of comedy, and the other two as promptly, without hesitation or discussion, according to those of the conventional morality, whether of that day or this. By his deviation from his source, as also we have seen, Shakespeare has made

[35]Cf. Lawrence, to the contrary, p. 211; Raleigh, p. 164.

the play even less of the problem kind that it had been, turning the heroine into a nun, for whom such a sacrifice of honor was quite impossible, and substituting at the rendez-vous a woman who had upon the judge what was then considered, and popularly still is, a lawful claim, and who in the sequel, as the heroine herself is in the source, is further righted by matrimony. In fact, the moral rigor in the heroine—the want of a problem—is, as we have seen and are to see, what some unsympathetic contemporary critics complain of.

A tragicomedy, as, more or less, all of Shakespeare's comedies, and his tragedies too in some measure, are! With him and other Elizabethans the decisive difference between comedy and tragedy lies in the conclusion: though in comedy it is an unhappy and inharmonious effect if before that the tragic element gets the upper hand or rises anywhere to the heights. So the deeper and more poignant feelings of Isabella, Claudio, and Juliet are left in the background. And the tragicomedy now before us differs from such as *Much Ado* and *The Merchant of Venice,* besides the play last under discussion, only in that the ambiguous tone or tenor is more continuous. The cloud of suspense concerning Claudio and the Deputy, though now and then thinning, does not quite clear up till the very end. The comic contrast in the role of Isabella is fairly constant, and the Duke is ever at hand, either by our confidence in him to diminish our anxiety or else by his intriguing and deceiving to heighten it. He not only withholds from Isabella the truth concerning her brother's fate to the end but two or three times deliberately falsifies it. What is more, he and some of the other characters keep touching on the danger, and then on the circumstances, of decapitation. The Duke plays his part of Friar for all it is worth; acting as if Claudio's life really depended, and very insecurely, upon the will of Angelo, reconciling him to death in prison, and, after the judicial countermand that turns out a treacherous and bloody command, as if this had been carried out. Even with the Provost he has arranged only for a delay, which keeps the audience uncertain and alert.

What is most remarkable is the harping upon heads and beheading. This is painful to us, and yet not tragic: because of the tone of what has preceded—and because of the Duke's knowledge—we do not believe Claudio's head is to fall. Indeed the terrible or the horrible on the stage when the main trend and prevailing tone are comic or ambiguous, and when eventual disaster, because of what has preceded, is (as in *Much Ado* and *The Merchant of Venice*) improbable, itself tends towards the comic or greatly heightens the comic effect under way. Charlie Chaplin in his cabin balancing on the edge of a precipice gives us tremors but without terror or tears. So the judgment scene in *The Merchant of Venice* should really be neither tragic nor pathetic, though skirting either. And the comic trend here in Act IV of *Measure for Measure* is uninterrupted even as it is (or should be) in the Venetian judgment scene; where the scales, the whetting of the knife, and the eager but grotesque vindictiveness of the avaricious usurer only heighten the comic effect as, with the twitting of Gratiano and the ironical pronouncements of Portia, the tables are turned upon him.[36]

The jocular spirit in the scenes now before us, as in those already mentioned, itself reassures us, or would reassure the hardy Elizabethans at least, who could see heads on London Bridge any day; and this is a little like the comic tinge given to Isabella's speech and role. "Come hither, sirrah," cries the Provost to Pompey (who had been a bawd) at the very beginning of a "humorous scene" (IV, ii), somewhat like the earlier ones that deal with prostitution and lechery; "can you cut off a man's head?" And the heads are, it appears, to be Claudio's and that of Barnardine, a nine years' prisoner. Then comes Abhorson, the executioner, who, however, craves a more reputable assistant. The Provost, though, bids Abhorson "provide his block and axe for tomorrow at four." Then the two prospective victims are called, whereupon Claudio enters (Barnardine will not rouse himself) and is apprised. Hard upon his exit comes the Duke (as Friar); then the pretended countermand and

[36]Cf. my *Shakespeare Studies* (1927), pp. 316–18.

the consequent arrangement for the "delaying" of Claudio's death and for substituting Barnardine—to shave the head and tie the beard and thus pass him off for Claudio. "Off with Barnardine's head," cries the Friar. But, in the next scene, the Bohemian, on being summoned, casually, by Pompey—"Master Barnardine! You must rise and be hang'd, Master Barnardine"—roars out from within, "Away, you rogue, away! I am sleepy." "Pray, Master Barnardine, awake till you are executed, and sleep afterwards." But "Is the axe upon the block?" then demands Abhorson, lest we should forget it, as the unaccommodating culprit appears. And the Friar, though finding the man unfit to live or die, exclaims, as the rogue incorrigibly refuses to consider the matter, "O gravel heart, after him, fellows; bring him to the block." Yet immediately thereupon he tells the Provost that to transport him in the mind he is, were "damnable" (and we may add, intolerable); so they substitute for the substitute a notorious pirate, off stage. "Quick, despatch, and send the head to Angelo." "Here's the head," says the Provost, entering in a moment; "I'll carry it myself." And when Isabella, a few moments afterwards, comes in, the Friar tells her it is off and sent.

That is stagy and tricky, not only sensational but (though forbearing) a little barbarous; and also it is rather out of proportion with the main dramatic subject: but in the mere commixture of tragic and comic it is not out of keeping with the rest of the play. As we have noticed in the Isabella scenes the tragic effect is somewhat counteracted by Lucio's running comments and her own saintly garb and condition, or by this together with her free-and-easy speech. In several other scenes Lucio has slandered the Duke (when disguised) to his face, as a whoremaster. And in the long exciting scene of the denouement these comic or ironic elements appear together again and also separately, Lucio now slandering the Friar to the Duke as his slanderer, thus doubling his own guilt. Then, the Duke having left the stage and (as the Friar) re-entered, Lucio eagerly recognizes him—"Here comes the rascal I spoke of . . . This is the rascal"—thereupon accuses him again, and, amid insults, helps pull off his hood. Yet even this his self-exposure is not ironical enough—he, too, in conformity with the rules of comedy, and also with the Duke's notions of justice, already sufficiently manifested, must now marry, but a whore.

That, likewise, is pretty strong for our regenerate taste, but not too much so for the Elizabethan; it is comic not merely because of the poetic justice upon the obscene and slanderous Lucio, but also because of the prevailing tone of the denouement, which is comic, certainly, though not entirely so. The Duke knowing all, and all going, as we know, by his arrangement, we are free to be amused by the mystifications and ironical surprises,—not only at Lucio caught in his own trap, and at Angelo in his, but also (if robust enough) at the nun so loudly insisting on the loss of her virtue with no one to believe her, and at the humorous Duke meanwhile indignantly siding with Angelo, calling her, because of the imposture, "this wretched woman," and Mariana, "pernicious woman, compact with her that's gone." By the various means of comic deception—prevarication, impersonation, and disguise—the Duke, Isabella, Mariana, and Friar Peter play upon the others, to bring Lucio, but above all Angelo, to the point of a bigger and bigger ironical repercussion; and the Duke also plays even upon his partners, though this is to happier effect. It is certainly a better, because a two-sided, role, that Isabella takes up as she accuses Angelo, under the misconception that he has been the death of her brother, and more in consonance with her conduct before this and with the tragicomic tenor of the whole drama. There is a bitterness or indignation in her deception; and even because of that her forgiveness, still in ignorance but in acknowledgment of his penitence, takes on nobler proportions. The cruelty to Lucio, moreover, is no stumbling-block to the audience, just as it would not be to an audience of males and congenial females today. The court of Louis XIV laughed at George Dandin and Arnolphe, deceived husband and lover, as the Théâtre Français does still; and Castiglione in the celebrated Book of the Courtier (1528), among the many examples of acceptable wit in high life, presents the following:

It is also pretie when one is touched in the verie same matter that he hath first touched his felowe. As Alonso Carillo beeinge in the Spanish Court and having committed certain youthful parts that were of no great importance, was by the kinges commaundment caried to prison, and there abode for one night. The next day he was taken out again, & whan . . . he entered into the chamber of presence that was full of Gentilmen & Ladies, and jestynge together at this his imprisonment, maistresse Boadilla said: M. Alonso, I took great thoughɩ for this mishap of yours, for al that knew you were in feare least the king would have hanged you. Then said immediatlye Alonso: Indeed, maistresse, I was in doubte of the matter my selfe to, but yet I had a good hope that you would have begged me for your husband. See how sharpe & wittie this is. Because in Spain (as in many other places also) the manner is, whan a manne is lead to execution, if a commune harlot will aske him for her husbande, it saveth his life. (Hoby's version, *Tudor Transl.*, 1900, p. 184.)

The audience at the Globe, certainly, was no more delicate or courteous than the courts of Spain and of Urbino. In fact there are other such marriages on the Elizabethan and Jacobean stage.

If, by the way, the gruesome playing upon our nerves for sensation and for comic effect is owing to the "cynicism" or "morbidity" of this period of Shakespeare's development, we must remember that there is much the same thing in *Cymbeline* and *The Winter's Tale*,—after the poet is "a new man," according to Sir Edmund, or, according to Dowden, after he is out of "the depths" and "on the heights." In Act V, scene iv of the earlier play the Gaoler bids Posthumus get ready for death, and the two joke at length together about hanging and sleeping much in the vein of "and sleep afterwards" in Act IV, scenes ii and iii of *Measure for Measure*. So, in the denouement, Cymbeline, still deceived by their disguise, orders his sons and their guardian off to death; and in *The Winter's Tale*, Leontes, in his lunatical jealousy, orders wife and child to the fire and even threatens Paulina with it. We likewise are in no danger of taking all this too seriously—such is the tone of these scenes and of what has preceded—but no doubt the Elizabethans, with their stronger nerves, now and then (the taste is Gothic!) grimly or excitedly laughed, like even us at a Chaplin play.

7

The above considerations, if accepted, exclude the possibility of accepting Sir Edmund Chambers' opinion of the two heroines, to which Mr. Lawrence properly objects. In the article on Shakespeare in the Britannica, Sir Edmund says of them that Shakespeare here "drags the honour of womanhood in the dust"; and in the introduction to the later play it is Isabella's "white soul through the mire." For him the irony is not external—*All's Well* is "drenched" in it, and in *Measure for Measure* "the searchlight of irony is thrown upon the paths of Providence itself." The dramatist is an "idealist disillusioned"; "sin, which was human, has become devilish," and "the engineer of the reconciliation is surely a cynic."[37]

That the eavesdropping, intruding, maneuvering Duke seems to Angelo a Providence does not make it incumbent on us to take him for that or a "travesty" of it, either; or if so, what a frightful cynic William Shakespeare has really —but so suddenly—become! Mr. Wilson would then be right, which Sir Edmund (fortunately) does not too often take him to be. That Isabella is so foully entreated he does not definitely show, and indeed—"white soul"!—he seems not to have quite lost faith in her. Here the irony is for him not quite all-dissolving, as in Mr. Wilson's "wrapt in her selfish chastity," or as in Miss Ellis-Fermor's "not by any means such a saint as she looks . . . hard as an icicle." But with Helena "the meanness of the device to which she stoops . . . is a measure of the spiritual straits to which the instinct of sex has reduced the noblest of women." For Sir Edmund, then, it is truly a problem play, a modern one, with Mr. Wendell's "cynical irony of a modern Frenchman" and "miserable mystery of earthly love." Which is very strange in view of the fact that there is no inkling of this in the text and the young lady everywhere meets with

[37] *Survey* (1925), pp. 210–11.

the highest approbation. I wonder if Sir Edmund ever reflected on the titles *All's Well That Ends Well* and *Measure
for Measure,* together with *Much Ado about Nothing.* Do
they not all three seem frivolous—cynically frivolous—mis-
nomers—unless we remember the nature of Shakespearean
and Elizabethan tragicomedy, with its improbable, essentially tragical complications bundled out of the way by
equally improbable, conventionally cheerful solutions? For
us is the much ado about *nothing?* does all end *well?* is
there measure for measure? In the text of this last comedy
it is made abundantly clear that Angelo is getting the
"poetic justice" which Sir Edmund denies by the marrying
and the sentencing to death, to be saved only by Claudio's
reappearance;[38] that the preceding comedy does not "end
well" there is no suggestion; and in *Much Ado,* in the
golden days before the direly cynical period is conjectured,
so suddenly, to have begun, the conclusion is quite as
morally superficial and esthetically conventional as in either
of the other comedies, with the marrying of a cousin
"veiled," but guaranteed to be "almost the copy of my child
that's dead," who then turns out to be Hero herself. But
perhaps cynicism and irony were put into the titles too; and
Shakespeare's stock of either began to accumulate earlier
than has been imagined, and not so suddenly, and all England, including the audiences at the Globe (not mystified or
troubled, either, by the titles) was cynical besides. And then
in Shakespeare there must be the "Romantic Irony" which
I have said there wasn't,—all-enveloping, all-penetrating as
in the modern Frenchmen or Ibsen; and at the end "some-
one is laughing," as (so a few have thought) when Fortinbras declares Hamlet, if he had lived, would have made a
great king. And then, as the Clown in *Twelfth Night* puts
it, and as too often is the case in criticism, "Nothing that
is so, is so."

[38] V, i, 405–21, 495–501; and Lawrence, pp. 114–15.

8

However that may be, and however much my own irony
here may miss fire (even as this of the latter-day Shakespeare for nearly three centuries has done), there is no
denying that all-in-all, as Sir Arthur Quiller-Couch aptly
says, Whetstone's, though the earlier, is a more rational
story. In it there is no substitution, by means of "the holy
Isabel." The King is merely a judge of appeal, not a busy
manipulator. The heroine herself is married to the man
who wrongs her, and pleading for his life, secures it; the
King when condemning Promos (or Angelo) does not, as
the Duke does, know her brother is still alive, and the latter,
for love of his sister, "saves Promos' life at the hazard of his
own." Whetstone's, says Sir Arthur, might easily be made
out to be the

more rational story—as it is—and therefore the better—as it is
not. It is, on the contrary, tedious, flat, stale and unprofitable;
whereas *Measure for Measure,* for all its flaws, is alive, interesting, exciting, in parts powerfully—even terrifically—moving;
and the secret of its difference lies in its poetry—in that and
in nothing else.[39]

Such is often the case with Shakespeare when compared
with his sources; so in *All's Well* Shakespeare misses even
more than the rationality and coherence of Boccaccio. But
"nothing else" is a bit strong, though in *Measure for
Measure* there is great poetry, no question:

> O, I do fear thee, Claudio, and I quake,
>
> .   .   .   .
> O Isabel!
> What says my brother?
> Death is a fearful thing.
>
> And shamed life a hateful.
>
> Ay, but to die, and go we know not where;
> To lie in cold obstruction and to rot . . .

[39]New Cambridge *Measure for Measure,* p. xvi.

Such outcries are highly poetical; but they are intensely dramatic, too. And as in fact we have already seen, there are poetry and drama elsewhere together, though particularly in the utterances of Isabel, Claudio, and, to a less degree, of Angelo and the Duke. But here, as generally in Shakespeare's plays, there is not a spirit of poetry, such as there is in Racine and Sophocles, pervading and informing the whole. Of all Shakespeare's plays, *Othello,* perhaps, comes nearest to that. There is, however, as we have seen above, what is more important for a stage play, a predominant dramatic tone. The ambiguous tragicomic tone prevails; and the audience knows what to expect, how to respond. The Elizabethan, that is to say; an audience simply and frankly receptive, not concerned, as part of a present-day audience is, with implications or motives, with anything such as we can call psychology. "Alive, interesting, exciting"—poetical too—no more than that did the audience ask. And even at the greatest periods of drama no more than that, I think—though often, as here, they got considerably more—did they ever ask.[40]

1943

[40]Since writing the above I have come upon Professor H. B. Charlton's discussion of the "Dark Comedies" (*Shakespearian Comedy,* 1938). Like most critics, including the present writer, Mr. Charlton is better at contradicting previous criticism than producing his own. He convincingly overthrows the charge of cynicism by comparing the dramatist with his sources at points where he has diverged. But he then proceeds to find problems that are as little connected with the text or the course of the action as the central ideas he had found in *A Midsummer Night's Dream, The Merchant of Venice,* or the story of Falstaff. (Cf. *Shakespeare-Jahrbuch,* 1938, "Recent Shakespeare Criticism.") "Is there not a sort of irrational reason in instinct?" (*Troilus and Cressida*); "the illimitable capacity of human instincts to serve the noblest purposes of human nature." (*All's Well*); "What is goodness?", and so forth (*Measure for Measure*).

CHAPTER XIV

The Realistic and the Unrealistic in King Lear

Le théâtre parle fort et parle haut.
HUGO, *Preface to* Lucrèce.

IN THE *Review of English Studies,* January, 1942, there is an article entitled the "Two Techniques in *King Lear"* which here serves for my point of departure. That is, I am not reviewing the article, nor considering the opinions except where they come within my present scope. I should like to say of these, however, that in general they are not infrequently to the point, though sometimes they may seem newer and more original than they really are. As happens to many of us, the difference between Professor Watkins and a few of his forerunners sometimes lies in the expression.

Whether there are more than two techniques, and not only in this but in most other poetic tragedy, is a question we need not argue; I for one can more readily accept a dual division if with no such limit set, and if also not under the headings "psychological realism" and "symbolical stylization." That point too we need not stop to argue, though the reasons for the difference will soon appear. Even "realistic" and "unrealistic," which I prefer, are inadequate terms. In prose, and on a conversational level, Shakespeare is often poetical, not being able or willing to hold himself down. And the unrealistic may or may not be stylized (as Lear's words after his final entry, are not, though on a pinnacle of poetry); or if it is, it is in a fashion that may or may not contribute to the emotional effect, like Romeo and Juliet's dawn-song of parting after their wedding night, on the one hand, or the family's lamentations over Juliet, taken for dead, on the other. But the only stylization or want of realism we need to consider is, of course, that which does contribute to the emotional effect, on Aristotle's principle (*cap.* 25) when he speaks of impossibilities as "justifiable if they serve the end of poetry itself—if (to assume what we have said of that end) they make the effect of some portion of the work more striking." The word "symbolical," moreover, Mr. Watkins uses where I should think he would use "allegorical"; indeed, symbolism or allegory, either, he generally finds where I think there is none. And as for "psychology," all that I can discover in Shakespeare is (not so technically or pretentiously) a greater or lesser degree of external truth to character, according to the opportunities or exigencies of drama.

2

At the very outset Mr. Watkins finds symbolical stylization, and not only in the exalted and extravagant expression (which is stylization, indeed) but even in the recurring issue of the King's stipulated "hundred knights." At the outset "the poetic quality of [Lear's] anger and emotion," he thinks, "is out of proportion to the realistic motivation" (p. 17); which charge applies, presumably, to the first scene as well as to the subsequent quarrel with Goneril. As also others have noticed, there is, when we consider the interests of realism, and perhaps, too, of the best effect, insufficient provocation for the rage and the curses even when we allow for a regal and paternal authority and privilege unknown today. Moreover, Mr. Watkins is properly (though not decisively, see p. 24) disinclined to fall back upon Lear's "arrogance" or "irascibility," "egoism" or "vanity," as the explanation, although that more notable figures in criticism than he or I have done. And as properly, on the other hand, Mr. Watkins does fall back upon the passionate poetry of Lear's speeches; but not so rightly upon a symbolism in the matter of the hundred knights. As this, with the repetition, becomes between father and daughters the bone of contention, more is meant, he thinks, than meets the ear.

The theme reaches its full development in the last scene of the second act, shortly before the King rushes out upon the heath. "By this time," Mr. Watkins says (here justly enough), "the pain of Lear's growing recognition of what is being done to him and the terrible momentum of his two daughters' persecution have become so great that questions of motivation and responsibility, legitimately felt in the first act [his first three scenes, I would say] do not arise." (P. 18.) And the stylization appears as (the daughters vying with each other in the whittling down of the number of his retainers, and Lear turning from one to the other while they do this) the scene, near its end, comes to a climax. In the development of the theme there is, certainly, a want of realism: but there is stylizing, not symbolizing, as I take it.

3

The "growing recognition" and "the momentum," however (before taking up the particular scene in question), are, as I think, not quite sufficient whether for the previous dramatic movement or for effectual support to our sympathy with the King. And while arrogance or any other of the "tragic faults" above mentioned would motive his conduct, they would tend to diminish the sympathy; would help out the psychology but impair the emotional impression. Moreover, nobody on the stage suggests any such shortcoming. And psychology and emotional impression alike would be damaged by those present-day scholarly favorites, the deadly sins and the humors. In his own nature Lear is not a prey to wrath; as Othello is not to jealousy, or Hamlet to sloth, or Macbeth to ambition or false courage and true fear.[1] It would not do if they were. "Abstract the sympathy," says Gissing of Dickens and it is far truer of drama; "substitute cold observation [or bookish pseudo-science, which would be worse], and we should have a truth, perhaps, but wholly uninteresting. It is only by the vehicle of emotion that life can be translated into art."[2] But unlike these other heroes, Lear is under no external, exonerating influence, villainous' or fatal. Consequently, for sympathy and motivation both, the dramatist must depend on other devices. Such are (apart from the stylization, already noticed, and the exalted and violent expression, according to tragic convention, also for emotional effect), such are, I say: the familiarity of the primitive and improbable initial situation as it appears in the chronicles and the older drama,[3] in ballad and folklore; the poetical individuality of utterance (and that leaves no doubt of the sympathies of the dramatist, which are not in some little measure, as a few critics think, with Goneril and Regan); the manifest malice and ill will of the two daughters, despite the want on their part of positive aggression, together with their hypocritical affection from the outset and the genuine devotion of everyone else to the King; and (for motivation so much of a fault there must be) Lear's own highhanded ways. As for the first, the *märchenhaft* division of the kingdom, according to the professions of affection (an integral part of the old story), is, as the postulate, made more acceptable by being placed at the beginning, which is next best to being before it, where Aristotle would rather have had it (*cap.* 15); and the King's calamitous anger, also a

[1]See above, pp. 139–43; Miss L. B. Campbell's *Tragic Heroes,* passim; and Professor Schücking, below. And Lear becomes unrecognizable as a tragic hero in the hands above all of Mr. J. W. Ashton (J. E. G. Ph. 1932, 530) as he deals with Charron's four occasions to wrath: 1, weakness of spirit; 2, malady of mind, jealousy, ambition, covetousness; 3, lust, vain niceness, or self-love; 4, curiosity. All in Lear!

[2]*Immortal Dickens* (1925), p. 214.

[3]Geoffrey of Monmouth, et cetera; and the dramatic version, *The True Chronicle History of King Leir,* et cetera, c. 1594.

necessary part of the story, properly comes, not as in the older drama, but near the beginning too. As Raleigh says in answer to the question why Cordelia did not humor her father a little, "if she had been perfectly tender and tactful [which except with her sisters she elsewhere always is] there would have been no play." Also there would have been none had Lear not become so angry.[4] But once the action is well started this mere irascibility diminishes and gradually disappears; even from the first scene on, and increasingly, it is accompanied, and restrained or reined in, by remorse for Cordelia and "throes" of anguish and tenderness not only for her but for the other daughters. Against Goneril in the fourth scene of the tragedy he is unnecessarily violent (but as after his treatment of Cordelia he must be, else the action would flag, the audience be disappointed); and though in his hasty work, or in recasting the earlier version, the dramatist makes the malignant Goneril furnish too little actual provocation, he is here again depending on the familiarity of the story,[5] as he was but (for a later day at least) should not have been in the matter of the motive for Hamlet's madness and Faulconbridge's grudge against the Archduke of Austria. Moreover, the outcry against Goneril and Regan both, at the end of the much later scene, in the second act, which is now in question, is not nearly so atrocious and yet not any the less dramatic or at all disappointing; for the King's passion has deepened and widened, and his continually growing fear of madness both accentuates the tragedy and allays the effect of what revengeful spirit is shown. He has even, despite appearances, been desperately seeking excuses for Regan and Cornwall. And of late, and still more hereafter, another device is employed. As often with Shakespeare, it is not with him so much a matter of "interesting" us—not at any rate of showing in present-

[4]*Art and Artifice in Shakespeare,* p. 140; Raleigh, *Shakespeare* (N. Y. 1907), pp. 134–36, "His plays open with a postulate"; Granville-Barker *Prefaces* (1st ser., 1927), p. 146. Actually the division is already accomplished before the play opens, whereas in the old *Leir* it is not, and the rage appears late in the third scene.

[5]See the old *Leir,* III, i, Perillus' account.

day fashion how or why the fault arose—as of winning us, by added and accumulated traits that adorn or redeem the hero in our eyes.[6] Such are his affection for the Fool, his consideration for Poor Tom, his remorseful remembrance of Cordelia. And this all, surely, is no work of analysis, no "study in wrath" or in any other passion.

4

To consider some of these points more narrowly, still deferring the matter of stylization and symbolism in Act II, scene 4. Above all, the play gets started right. "The burden of a tragedy," says Sir Edmund Chambers, like the best of the critics, but like some of them also in not consistently remembering it, "is always an emotion, not an idea, which is for comedy; and the object of drama is not to depict character for its own sake but always by the help of depicted characters to effect the transference from author to audience of emotions or ideas." (*Survey*, pp. 74, 135.) By that Sir Edmund means something very different from what he later says of King Lear: "absorbed, as a true egoist, in his own emotions"; "the disillusion of a sentimental egoist" (pp. 243–44); or of Hamlet at the end, "the poor heap of ineffectual ideals and fantastic loyalties is borne away upon the bier" (p. 190). As I have suggested above, it takes the poets to set the critics right; and Mr. Auden has spoken of both the Pagan and the Christian artists "presupposing that their audience . . . would recognize the hero of tragedy as what they would like to be, and the rascal of comedy as what, perhaps, they were but would rather not be."[7] But those words the critics would no doubt forget as they even do Aristotle, not only as he continually insists that the tragic hero, though not faultless, "should first and foremost be good" (*cap.* 15), "better than the ordinary man" (*cap.* 15), or "than the men of the present day" (*cap.* 2), "coming to misfortune through some error of judgment" (*cap.* 13); but also (and most regrettably) when he says that

[6] *Shakespeare and Other Masters*, p. 275.

[7] *Commonsense*, March, 1941.

"pity is occasioned by undeserved misfortune, and fear by the misfortune of one like ourselves" (*cap.* 13).[8] By the present tragedy, at all events, those emotions in the audience are rightly aroused and directed. This hero has a fault, to be sure, but, like Othello and Hamlet, no deep and serious one. Despite the improbability at the beginning the first scene has been greatly admired, by the best judges, too, and so different as Sarcey and Granville-Barker; the former, after admitting that the scene is not *vraie, d'une vérité réelle et bourgeoise,* but insisting that it is *vraie d'une vérité idéale,* and that Molière has such scenes, of which *l'idée s'en dégage avec une clarté si merveilleuse que tous les hommes les emportent dans leur imagination,* dilates on the swift and gripping action:

. . . *jamais drame ne s'est ouvert d'une façon plus simple, plus grande et plus saisissante à la fois. Songez au temps que demande la moindre exposition de pièce, et considérez qu'ici vous entrez au vif du sujet, sans préparation d'aucune sorte: que du même coup vous comprenez et l'action qui s'engage, et les caractères qui vont la soutenir, et l'idée générale que l'auteur met en oeuvre, et vous serez ravis d'admiration.* (*Quarante ans de théâtre* [1900] III, p. 352.)

For there is something of French or Greek art in the condensation (the scene represents seven in the old play) and in beginning considerably later than the action has begun. But otherwise no art could be farther from the French. As I have said elsewhere:

. . . most of the motives in the anonymous *King Leir* or the other sources are dropped and none but superficial and obvious ones retained or provided. There are no ulterior ones, such as the King's undertaking to play a trick on Cordelia in order to induce her to marry a British prince and stay at home, or Goneril's and Regan's jealousy and hatred of Cordelia and desire to discredit

[8]There can be some difference of opinion about the meaning of "good," which may possibly be "above the common level"; but scarcely when he says "better than the ordinary man," or "than the men of the present day," and particularly when he says (*cap.* 13) "not pre-eminently virtuous and just," by which he means, of course, though good, not faultless.

her, or Cordelia's desire to test her father and rebuke her sisters. Such explanations and complications would interfere with the intensity and momentum of the scene; and a still greater interference would be the motives inferred or invented by modern critics, such as the King's own vanity or senile debility or "slothful" and "voluptuous" craving for a life of ease, or Goneril's and Regan's previous "sufferings from their overbearing and hot-tempered father."

On second thoughts (which at the theater, however, if you are swept along, you are not free to entertain) the scene is illogical and contradictory; yet, again, only to heighten the effect. In the old play, more outwardly logical in the conduct of the story and therefore preferred by Tolstoy to Shakespeare's,[9] the daughters are asked what they would do for their father rather than how much they love him; but that, though more sensible (and therefore preferred by another Frenchman, Jusserand), is not so emotional, nor is it in keeping with the still older story, as in Geoffrey of Monmouth. In the old play, again, the kingdom is not divided, into three equal parts, already: nor does the King, as in Shakespeare, hand over her share, unmathematically, to each of the elder daughters as she responds, without waiting to hear them all; nor, as he addresses Cordelia, offer the prospect of a third "more opulent" than those of the others: but by this arrangement, as in Geoffrey again, there is something to do—on the stage still more important than in a story—after each reply, holding the situation while Cordelia looks on and murmurs to herself, and the King, having reserved the richer portion for her, is by the rebuff more deeply wounded.

Certainly it is an emotional, an enthralling and rapidly moving scene, both the exposition and the complication being effected in that brief space, not, as usual, in no less than an act. As not in the old play, the improbable and unreasonable questioning comes in without being proposed or noised abroad beforehand, but as if on the spur of the moment, and is quickly disposed of. And as not in the old

[9] Cf. Croce, Ariosto, Shakespeare, and Corneille (n. d.), p. 286: "preferring minute prosaic details to sublime poetry."

play, our concern is now not for Cordelia, who, by her marriage, is at once provided for, but wholly for the King. He is in the wrong, but it is love, not vanity, that has made him cast his daughter off; she and Kent, both banished, think only of him, while the other daughters, the cause of Cordelia's misgivings, are clearly meditating mischief against him. Moreover, when next he appears, he shows that he is troubled about what he has done, as he takes on Kent in disguise for a servant, and hears from the attendant Knight how he himself is being neglected in the household and of the Fool's having pined away since my young lady's going into France. And this feeling quickly and steadily deepens.

If for no other reason, indeed, we should, from the outset, be on the King's side because of the principle brought to light by Watts-Dunton,[10] which explains, as De Quincey's comments (however poetical) do not, the effect of the knocking at the gate in *Macbeth*. The point is that though they too are in the wrong—and infinitely deeper, of course —we have identified ourselves with the thane and his lady and are startled along with them. "The identification of the spectators' personality is with the active character"; particularly when sympathetically treated, as the murdering pair (but especially Macbeth) certainly are, but with slenderer claims for such treatment than Lear.

It is on such principles, then, and by means of such dramaturgy that questions of motivation and responsibility in this last scene of the second act fall into abeyance; but above all because the regal and paternal wrath has been diminishing and been giving place to grief, remorse, and tenderness. It is not deeply rooted in his nature—he is not the angry man by temperament—and he endeavors to suppress it:

> I'll forbear;
> And am fallen out with my more headier will . . .

Of this is true what Professor Mackail says of Macbeth's ambition, "as soon as it has set the action going it has served

[10]*Harper's* magazine (1906), p. 818. Cf. Schiller, *Grund des Vergnügens: wir zittern vor dem Fehlschlag derselben Plane, deren Vereitlung wir . . . aufs feurigste wünschen sollten.*

its purpose, and is dropped."[11] And in both tragedies the purpose was to precipitate the complication, get the action started. "It is mainly for the sake of the action," according to Aristotle, "that [Tragedy] imitates the personal agents." (*cap.* 6.)

In this case the fading away of the faulty trait is to the effect particularly important: as we have seen, there is no fatal or villainous influence to bear the burden as there is in *Macbeth, Hamlet,* or *Othello.* Like Aristotle, Dryden thinks the hero must be virtuous if he is to be pitied;[12] and of his *All for Love* he observes what equally applies to Shakespeare's tragedy on the same subject: "That which is wanting *to work up the pity to a greater height* was not afforded by the story; for the crimes of love, which [Antony and Cleopatra] both committed, were not occasioned by any necessity,[13] or fatal ignorance, but were wholly voluntary."[14] No more than the greatest, as I have said before,[15] "is the Restoration dramatist content with character its own fate, as in life—and criticism." No more than one of the greatest even in our day, Thomas Hardy, who says that "the best tragedy—highest tragedy, in short—is that of the worthy encompassed by the inevitable. The tragedies of immoral people are not of the best."[16] And still less would any of these have the character a "study," in any fault, mortal or venial. But in the tragedy before us the pity does rise to the height, and because there is a struggle of an external sort, a passion steadily rising.

[11]*Art and Artifice,* p. 106; J. W. Mackail, *Approach to Shakespeare* (1930), p. 22.

[12]"Grounds of Criticism in Tragedy" (preface to *Troilus and Cressida*).

[13]*Necessitas,* of course.

[14]Apology prefixed to *The State of Innocence.*

[15]*Art and Artifice,* p. 64.

[16]Quoted by Katherine Anne Porter, *Southern Review.* Summer, 1940.

5

Now the stylization in the fourth and last scene of Act II
(the point withheld) definitely contributes to this effect.
As the King breaks with both daughters, cries out upon
them, anticipates madness, and rushes out upon the heath,
into the tempest, the action, as we have noticed, reaches the
climax; and the part of the scene that is in question,—that
is, the latter part, but still before the absolute rupture, when
he turns, repulsed, from one daughter to the other,—is
stylized in the sense that, not a trait of character, but the
emotional motif of his forlornness and abandonment is presented, and is developed to the limit—even at the character's expense—as he falls back upon Goneril, whom he had
cursed and at the sight of whom on her entrance, a few
minutes before, he has appealed to the heavens. And this
turning from one daughter to the other as they beat him
down on the terms of their hospitality is a summary and
psychologically unplausible, but yet effectively theatrical,
way of showing how Lear has reached the limit of endur-
ance—precipitating the rupture—leading us up to the
climax quickly and directly.

In the formal development of the motif, though not
in its function, it is like Richard's wooing of Anne, who is
now burying her father-in-law, though his blood, like that
of her husband, is on Richard's head. Standing by the coffin, he persuades her, still more improbably than Iago does
Othello, though, like him, in one scene. But there is greater
resemblance to four or five other situations: Valentine
handing over Silvia, out of friendly generosity, to the re-
pentant Proteus; Macbeth momentarily faltering in his
bravery when Macduff declares that he was not born of
woman; Claudius, despite the telltale dumb show at the
outset, sitting through the performance of the *Murder of
Gonzago,* and yet, after all, giving himself away as in anger
and alarm he cuts it short; Falstaff persevering in the exaggerations of his lies about the knaves in buckram and
Kendal green, though checked and rallied by the Prince;

and Albany and Edgar forgetting the fate of Lear and Cordelia, at the denouement of the tragedy now before us. The scene in *The Two Gentlemen* (also in the denouement) is not well developed; the scene in *Henry IV,* Part I, is comic, not tragic; but in all alike there is the securing of an emotional effect at the cost of realism. For such conduct, Falstaff is ordinarily too clever; Valentine, too fond of Silvia; Claudius, too hypocritical and cunning; Macbeth, too brave and desperate; Albany and Edgar, both too concerned and also too well aware of the peril that impends. Yet without Hal's ironical interruptions the attention of the audience would not be so sharply focused on the exaggerations and contradictions, (though to the psychologizing critic Falstaff thus seems to be only pretending to brag). Without Hamlet's dumb show the performance would be less suddenly alarming to the King, but less interesting to the audience. Without Macbeth's momentary faltering the effect of the prediction's coming true could not be made so evident, or that of his bravery—"Lay on, Macduff!"—in rallying itself in final defiance. Without the two hundred and fifty lines of distracting events, and three or four reminders after Albany's demand for the captives, the audience would not be at the highest pitch of anxiety when Lear enters with Cordelia dead, in his arms.[17] And so now with Lear's ignominiously turning from daughter to daughter and back again (stylized but saved from absurdity by the style!), till Regan hisses, "What need one?"—without that we should not see so directly how low in fortune the King, his very wits ready to topple, has fallen.

But the closest parallels are another in *Macbeth* and one in *Romeo and Juliet.* The former is the scene where Malcolm, unplausibly slandering himself, evades accepting Macduff's proposals to recover the crown of Scotland, and Macduff as unplausibly believes him, swallowing each charge that is brought until his cup runs over, but then at the last crying out, "O Scotland, Scotland," even as Lear does to Regan, "O, reason not the need!" In both incidents there are the clearly marked stages of development leading to the

[17] *Art and Artifice in Shakespeare,* p. 142–43.

climax of exclamation. The other parallel is the scene at the dance, when Romeo first sets eyes on Juliet, falling in love at sight. The outcry here comes at the beginning.

> O, she doth teach the torches to burn bright,
>
> .   .   .   .
>
> Did my heart love till now? Forswear it, sight!
> For I ne'er saw true beauty till this night.

But here there is more of the stylized, the formalized, than in either of the scenes last discussed. The outcry is in rime; and so, on both sides, is the wooing, which takes at the beginning the form of a sonnet. Even the sentiments, externally, are formal. This pair are not, like the others, dancing; but in their courting, with their exchange of compliments it is as if they were. It is contrary to psychology, as I have said elsewhere—contrary to nature, as well as the knightly principle of constancy—that in the presence of Juliet the romantic, high-souled Romeo should forget Rosaline at once and for good and all; but that he should do so throws his love for Juliet into bold relief. And this unrealistic formality is a simplification, a substitute—a subterfuge, indeed—for an analytical transition, which would take many minutes, if it could be managed at all. Yet the main thing, the emotion, is not missing, if the psychology is. At the end there is another outcry, for the tongue of Juliet now:

> Go, ask his name.—If he be marrièd
> My grave is like to be my wedding-bed.

In all cases, improbability, whether, as an essential part of the story, inherited with the source or deliberately contrived, is, when well managed, not so much a liability as an asset; not so much a shortcoming to be covered over as an opportunity to be exploited. Aristotle and Longinus but also Corneille—*les grands sujets doivent toujours aller au delà du vraisemblable*—together with the wisest modern critics have recognized the principle, even as the poets have always practiced it. This is particularly true of the fundamental improbabilities which have been the attraction, for the first hearers and for the later poets, in all the greatest stories of the world, from that of Adam, Eve, and Satan down,[18] especially those which involve a supernatural control or villainous intrusion. Naturally—out of his own jealous or suspicious nature—no such passions could develop as do, by the convention of slander, in Othello, who kills her whom he still loves, not in hatred, but as an act of justice, because he believes her, not basely suspects her, to be false.[19] Of these stories the greatest in artistic achievement is, of course, where the improbability is (so far as may be) disguised or poetically justified, as in that of Othello again. Iago's success in misleading and ruining a noble and unsuspicious nature is made plausible not only by his actually extraordinary cunning in the process but also by his impeccable reputation for honesty and sagacity with not merely Othello but everyone else in the play. And what in Iago's and Othello's language is by Mr. Watkins called stylized is not such as that of Lear and his two daughters in the bargaining, or that of Romeo and Juliet in the wooing, but, equally removed from that of reality, is sublimely passionate poetry besides. Thus the purpose of the improbability, to serve the end of poetry itself—which is to fire the imagination and rouse the emotions—is far more completely achieved.

6

As for the hundred knights, so often spoken of—so insisted on, and rejected—that is, I think, only a natural simplification and concentration, stylization but not a symbol. To bring in other grievances would clog the action, burden the exposition. In general there is no symbolism in Shakespeare, and allegory (then quite obvious too) only for moments, such as (in *A Midsummer Night's Dream*) the lines about the "fair vestal thronèd by the west," and the Induction to the second part of *Henry IV*, with Rumour on the stage. The only approach to symbolism that I ever noticed

[18]See the list in my *Art and Artifice in Shakespeare*, p. 2. Cf. also chap. XI above.

[19]Cf. my *Shakespeare and Other Masters*, pp. 201–2.

(though there must be others) is where Cleopatra, about to apply the asp, murmurs:

> Now no more
> The juice of Egypt's grape shall moist this lip,

which is more than wine. Mr. Watkins takes Bradley to task for his understatement as he speaks of "a mode of imagination not very far removed" from that in the Morality plays and in *The Faerie Queene.* Instead, Mr. Watkins might well have imitated him. In *King Lear* and *Macbeth,* as Herford, Dowden, and Sir Edmund have observed, there are larger, higher issues than in the other tragedies,— "forces external to men are brought into question." But this does not mean that the literary method is at all like that in Spenser. Surely Goneril (p. 23) is not a "symbol," unless the meaning of that word is to be stretched beyond all recognition, and then the other villains of either sex would also be; her blunt, brutal, rough-and-ready individuality is easy to perceive, and she is humanly consistent enough, psychological enough if you will.

Nor is the Fool (pp. 20–23) a symbol, either. He does serve as "a dramatic and poetic device," but is not "virtually a personification of the bitter truth tormenting Lear," or "a dramatization of what is really going on in Lear's mind." I wonder if Mr. Watkins is of those who think the ghost is a symbol or personification of what is going on in Macbeth's mind, or Brutus's, or Hamlet's. There is more reason for that (though little enough) than for this conception of the Fool. It is natural for us, who take little stock in the supernatural, or at least in superstition, to turn the ghosts, the Weird Sisters, Ariel, and even Caliban into symbols;[20] but it is a different matter, without the slightest clue in the text—such as invisibility or vanishing—so to treat any of the regular dramatis personae. Apart from the interpolations, as at the end of Act III, scene ii, the Fool has as much individuality in his speech as most of the characters;

[20]See my *Shakespeare and Other Masters,* chap. 8, *The Tempest; Shakespeare Studies,* chap. 5, "The Ghosts."

and in speech, as I have elsewhere endeavored to show, lies most of the virtue of Shakespeare's characterization anyhow. To be sure, we know nothing about him, his past or his present connections (though that is true of other characters in this play and other plays), and we are not told what becomes of him (though not of the King of France, Cordelia's husband, either) at the end. But that if a real person he is "a monster of sadism" because of his harping on Lear's follies, is beside the point. Conventionally in the drama, as actually in the courts or castles where he was kept, the Fool was "all-licensed" and had "as large a charter as the wind to blow on whom he pleased."[21] This one, moreover, is pathetic, and sympathetic, as no other fool in Shakespeare is; and is, as a half-wit, looked upon as fairly irresponsible, like a child that says clever and pointed things not realizing how they hurt. In point of irresponsibility he is, in effect, both on the stage and in the theater, like Hamlet playing mad, as he hurts Ophelia by his disrespectful treatment of Polonius or by the improprieties addressed to herself. And (as has been noticed by others) the wit and wisdom at the King's personal expense are, for the most part, early in the play, when there is, to the Fool's mind at any rate, some hope of helping him. Certainly the spirit of what he says, as the audience will not fail to notice, is friendly, solicitous; there is no "taunting" (p. 21) that I myself can see.

7

Still another matter of unrealistic technique is the "self-dramatizing" which Mr. Watkins finds in Lear, as frequently in Richard II, and (at the last) in Othello. He quotes Mr. Eliot as the latter speaks of Othello's "cheering himself up" and "turning himself into a pathetic figure, by adopting an aesthetic rather than a moral attitude . . . He takes in the spectator but the human motive is to take in himself." (P. 24.) This attitude Mr. Eliot relates, as Mr. Watkins notices, to the Stoicism derived from Seneca. I

[21] *As You Like It,* II, vii, 47–49.

have three times[22] called attention to the troubling and
damaging effect this interpretation has upon the noble
and heroic impression, surely intended—an interpretation,
which, naturally enough, has led Mr. G. W. Knight to his
still more damaging conception of Othello as a sentimentalist, who "loves emotion for its own sake, luxuriates in it,
like Richard II." Could there be a better (or worse) example of psychology applied and tragic fault determinedly
discovered? Of this final speech Mr. Eliot himself says (and
according to his own principles he should therefore have
stayed his hand) : "It is usually taken on its face value as
expressing the greatness in defeat of a noble but erring
nature."[23] For once into the nineteenth and twentieth centuries the right tradition had survived—then, by one of the
pre-eminent critics, to be rejected! On the stage all coin
passes at face value, unless there is something to indicate
that it is counterfeit; otherwise, what of the audience, who
must think and feel as one.

Mr. Watkins does not, moreover, discriminate between
self-dramatization and self-description; nor between what
is meant for morbid self-consciousness and what is not. In
Othello's final long speech there is self-description only, no
posing or play-acting at all. Partly this is a matter of
drama's not having yet been completely developed out of
the epical and lyrical—from the absolute to the relative
method; and often elsewhere in Shakespeare, as in Aeschylus, Sophocles, and Euripides for that matter, the heroes
and heroines speak frankly of their own goodness, as the
villains do of their own wickedness, in a fashion contrary
to nature. The dramatist is concerned with the attitude of
the audience—intent upon directing their opinions and
arousing their emotions—rather than with the speaker's
individual point of view. Even in monologues to be read
(for which the right impression and full emotional response
is not so immediately important) as in Ovid's, or Tennyson's, or that of Propertius in the mouth of Cornelia re-

[22]*Poets and Playwrights,* p. 59; *Art and Artifice,* pp. 173-74,
Shakespeare and Other Masters, p. 210.

[23]*Selected Essays* (N. Y., 1932), p. 110.

turning as a ghost to her husband, *Desine, Paulle,* the speakers are, if taken as transcripts, unnaturally conscious of their own beauty or virtue. It is Browning that contrives to dispense with the method; and by contrasts with another character in the background (or with the occasion, or with the speaker's profession) as well as by the complications and involutions, the emphases or suppressions, of his utterance, the poet, in such monologues as *My Last Duchess, Andrea del Sarto,* and *The Bishop Orders His Tomb,* secures for the speaker a point of view more nearly his own, and conveys, or rather suggests to us, his special moral or immoral quality. The bad one now may speak well of himself, though still he gives himself away. This method, however, requires close, yet enlightened, attention in the reading. Some critics, either too penetrating or too undiscriminating, actually side with Ferrara against his Last Duchess; and it is even because Shakespeare gives Iago a little relativity—letting him speak well of himself and (to Roderigo) ill of others—that he has by the critics been made out to be better than he is, to the extent of being a "prince of good fellows," with "hardly any malice in him."[24]

It is not a matter of Seneca's philosophy but Seneca's (and other ancient) dramatic technique. In fact the technique is somewhat like that in painting, and not only in Shakespeare's own time but even today. Often people look out unnaturally at the spectator instead of at each other, as in Frans Hals's Young Couple in a landscape (Amsterdam, *Ryksmuseum*), who, according to a critic, seem to be saying, "See how happy we are!" Othello here is more humanly dramatic than that. The primitive technique is handled with great tact and deftness: he is true to his character and to the situation as well. He has already gone through the agony of grief and remorse; and as he is about to die, he himself must see (which the dramatist would have also the audience see) that not out of his own nature, but deluded and entrapped, he had brought Desdemona

[24]Cf. above, pp. 213, 229 and *Shakespeare and Other Masters,* pp. 27–28, 260–61.

and himself to ruin. As I have said before, "he must now at the last think a little well of himself even because he has thought so ill; and what can be more tragic?"

Richard, on the other hand, both describes himself and plays a part,—pities himself, dallies with melancholy fancies, nurses sorrow, embraces despair. No audience can in the long run fail to distinguish between him and Othello or Lear, though in part the technique is similar. He himself speaks of "the sweet way he was in to despair," and not only friend but enemy comments on his frailty.

Lear, though both describing his emotional state and now and then dramatizing himself, is certainly not to be put in the same category. Even in the fifth scene he has a presentiment of approaching madness, which continually deepens; and whether true to psychology or not, that, in such a matter, is a more effective way—

> O let me not be mad, not mad, sweet heaven!

. . . .

> O, Fool, I shall go mad!—

a far more effective way than through any comment from others. And by the madness self-dramatizing is warranted. Mr. Watkins (pp. 9, 24) is not justified in comparing Lear's with Richard's, as in the mock trial of Goneril and Regan (Act III, scene vi) and in his faltering, appealing words about himself when he gropes back to sanity (Act IV). The only moment in Lear's histrionism that I find "disconcerting"[25] is (again) in the fourth scene of Act II when, kneeling, he ironically plays out before Regan his begging of forgiveness from Goneril. "Good sir, no more," is the answer, "these are unsightly tricks"; and us they affect as we read and imagine them (if I am not mistaken) somewhat the same.

8

Professor Schücking, also, is much troubled by the self-description, or self-dramatization; though, like one or two of his recent predecessors, he previously recognized, in gen-

[25]There is, however, something like it in the earlier scene with Goneril, I, iv, 246–57.

eral, the technical nature of it. But he belongs to the antiquarian school, touched upon above, who read Shakespeare
historically (as they think), though in the light of the
labored, fantastic learning, the pedantic science of the time,
forgetting Aristotle (again) both in the matter of the
goodness of tragic heroes and also of their coming to misfortune undeservedly, by some error of judgment. Which
principles are in keeping with the practice both of the Hellenic poets and also of Shakespeare, though those poets he
had not read nor (like them as well) Aristotle himself. It
is but owing to the essential nature of high tragedy that
there is this similarity in their art and this consonance with
the primary criticism, based upon it; and Professor Schücking and his fellow scholars are not truly historical as, relying
upon their own (necessarily fragmentary) acquaintance
with the *Zeitgeist*, rather than, like Aristotle, on an experience of the plays, they make out Shakespeare's tragic heroes
to be diseased or abnormal, "slaves of passion," or "addicts
of passion" as the German calls them, a prey to one or
another of the deadly sins or a study in melancholy, choler,
or fear. Really, and after all, they keep to the nineteenth-
century closet-drama principle of the *hamartia*, and of the
action proceeding, distressingly or depressingly, from the
character, with a full-dress contemporary psychological
make-up, but with the deadly sins and noxious humors
taking the place, unhappily, of those traits and passions
which are our common human heritage. (Or perhaps they
are more like the twentieth-century Freudians, with their
heroes laboring under a fixation or a complex.) Thus our
Shakespeare becomes more foreign to us than a Chinaman
or a Jap. And the contrast, instead of being between the
hero and the situation, or between character and conduct,
or between hero and fate or villain (the influence of either
of whom Professor Schücking pretty much ignores),[26] lies,

[26]As with Jonson's Catiline too (*British Academy Lecture*, p.
11), where he dwells upon the perverse and mad desire to wipe
Rome from the face of the earth as a sample of extravagance in
Elizabethan tragedy, without taking account of Sylla's Ghost,
which directly inspires it.

as in many a modern play (to be sure), within the hero's
own bosom; but it takes the form of an antithesis or paradox, such as that presumed in Macbeth—"fear of his own
courage"—himself (the hero!) being "a moral coward and
for a while a henpecked husband."[27] Could any German
audience, so studious and analytical but (as we nowadays
understand) so heroic, all blood and iron, all hoping to be
spared the ignominy of dying in their beds, put up with a
tragic hero, a Nordic general and king, so little of a hero as
that? Thus another of the greatest tragedies has (like Hamlet, with his self-deceptions, long since) been turned, in
effect, into a comedy. In Lear, however, all that the critic
finds "paradoxical" is the division of the kingdom,[28] which
would seem to be really no more than a contrast between
character and conduct.

Yet, like the other antiquarians, Professor Schücking considers Lear, as he does the other tragic heroes, to be diseased
or abnormal, beset by a deadly sin or a "humour." Death
on the stage—the hero's at least—must be the scriptural
"wages of sin"; and in Lear that is his irascibility, of course.
"On this fundamental trait Shakespeare based the whole
character."[29] Hence, since according to the Elizabethan
physiological psychology, or pathology, "the anger of the
choleric man is necessarily proportionate to his self-esteem,"[30] Lear's self-dramatization is no external, technical
affair. If Miss Campbell and Professor Schücking have in
mind merely the regal and authoritarian manner, they
surely will remember that on the Elizabethan stage, and
in Shakespeare as in Marlowe, kings were a little above
the level of mortals, and were properly expected, in Sir
Roger de Coverley's phrase, to "strut." But evidently they

[27]*British Academy Lecture,* p. 22. This "hazardous antithetical
character construction" as Professor Schücking (properly!) calls it,
"favoured by the style of the time," really began, as I show in
chapter XVI, with the closet drama of Byron. And there the paradoxes are plainly expressed, do not need to be laboriously laid bare.
[28]*Ibid.*
[29]*Character Problems* (N. Y., 1922), p. 178.
[30]*British Academy, Shakespeare Lecture* (1938), pp. 26–27.

have more in mind, and at this point ("vanity," "egoism," "sentimental egoism") the antiquarians lock hands with the unhistorical, but decidedly less inhuman, psychologists. Yet if Aristotle is right in saying that pity is occasioned only by undeserved misfortune, and fear by that of one like ourselves; and Dryden in saying that it is "absolutely necessary to make a man virtuous if we desire he should be pitied" —and who can doubt that right they are?—what is to be made of a hero so little heroic, so contemptible or pitiful? These scholars might (again) have remembered Aristotle where he says (*cap.* 15) that "the poet . . . in portraying men quick or slow to anger . . . must know how to represent them as such and at the same time as good men, as Agathon and Homer have represented Achilles"; or at least they might have done so to the point of leaving out the "self-esteem."

Far, then, from entertaining the notion of this condition as superficial or temporary, Professor Schücking is unable to accept that of a "purification" in him, as presented by Bradley[31] and others. Though philosophers and psychologists, the last-named, at least, keep to the text better than this hoplite of philological scholarship, and perceive the spiritual development in the King, out of anger and impatience—"You heavens, give me that patience, patience I need," II, iv, 274; "No, I will be the pattern of all patience, I will say nothing," III, ii, 37—into a new regard for others, especially the poor and houseless like (now) himself, along with a clearer perception of Cordelia's character and the wrong done to her, and of the difference between the false and the true, the just and the unjust. Nay, as Mr. Granville-Barker, without any philosophy but quite in keeping with the tenor of the tragedy, conceives him, Lear experiences not only purification but spiritual aggrandizement, and passes from "personal grievance to the taking upon him, as great natures may, of the imagined burden of the whole world's sorrow." But Professor Schücking refuses to admit that "Shakespeare associates compassion for the poor

[31]*Shakespearean Tragedy* (1908), pp. 284–87. Granville-Barker, Preface to *Lear*, p. 171.

and wretched with a higher moral standpoint. We know the social sense was very little developed in him."[32] And Lear in his clearer perception of shams and frauds the critic takes to be but following the beaten track of the melancholy type; for with this "humour" the old man is burdened as well as his deadly sin. So, instead of regeneration, there is physical and mental degeneration; and the change in him in the fifth act, as he no longer gives sign of vindictiveness or resentment, "is really contrary to his nature, is due to the state of physical decrepitude into which he has fallen." (P. 188.) And that to me is distressing, humiliating, rather than tragic,—"contrary" to both his nature and the text.

How does Professor Schücking come to "know" of Shakespeare's "social sense" except from his plays; and is not this one of them? Since melancholy is not there mentioned, the old King could have thus developed in perception of character from his experience with Goneril, Regan, and Cordelia; and in perception of justice, from the realization of his own injustice and his experience of that at the hands of others. And how does Professor Schücking come to know so much about the spirit of the age that he can securely declare a writer to be "sinning against it"[33] because of refusing to believe with him Hamlet to be "a study in melancholy," or tragedy to be essentially a study at all? He forgets Goethe as well as Aristotle:

> *Was ihr den Geist der Zeiten heisst,*
> *Das ist im Grund der Herren eigner Geist.*

In literary argument nowadays the *Zeitgeist,* of which we can know so little, is a great resource; though lately in danger of being supplanted by the "unconscious," of which we can know still less. In any case, Professor Schücking, with his Lear a study in wrath, is not perceptibly thus improving upon the play; and in keeping the character consistent up to Act V, or just before it, and then making of him "a different person" (p. 189) he is not conceivably serving either psychology or dramatic art.

[32]*Character Problems,* p. 186.
[33]*British Academy Lecture,* pp. 15, 22.

9

How little psychology applies to the great role appears, if from nothing else, simply from the fact that having lost his sanity because of his two wicked daughters' cruelty he does not lose it again at the death of the other, to whom he was cruel and who was good. And why not? Because in the tragedy there had been enough of madness, whether real or pretended; and because in madness the highest tragic and pathetic effect cannot be attained, as here at the end it should be; where, moreover, the function of comment upon the wider implications of the tragedy, the injustice in the world, can no longer be so profitably performed.[34] Lunacy, even Lear's, is less supremely moving than tragic sanity may be, is too capricious and grotesque. But though internally thus inconsistent (for a man once mad is by even a lesser calamity likely to be made so anew), externally he is, as before this, consistent enough. Of no character of Shakespeare's are Pope's words truer: "had all the speeches been printed without the very names of the persons, I believe one might have applied them certainly to every speaker." There is no mistaking him, in this sentence or that, for any of the other characters in Shakespeare, here or elsewhere. And even internally he is not "another person." At his last entry, though not crazy, not disordered or incoherent, he is evidently stricken and shattered. After his first outcries and lamentations he turns away from Cordelia: in him, as in the audience, nature demands relief, and he relapses, diverges. He tells the others of her voice, for which he has been listening, "ever soft, gentle, and low." Then, as if she were still alive, he speaks of his killing "the slave that was a-hanging thee"; and when the officer says, " 'Tis true, my lords, he did," he turns again, and boasts of the things he has done in the past. As, now, he looks about, he, uncertainly, recognizes Kent; and vaguely, perfunctorily responds to questions or remarks by others.

[34]Cf. Theodore Spencer, *Shakespeare and the Nature of Man* (1942), p. 137.

"He knows not what he says," Albany whispers aside. Then, without being noticed, while the others are making arrangements for his comfort and the ordering of the state, he reverts to the body of Cordelia, which he seemed to have forgotten. "O see, see," cries Albany, and again Lear's agony fills the stage and the house.

> And my poor fool[35] is hang'd. No, no, no life . . .

It is a great tragic effect, the conclusion and consummation of a natural but, when we remember, far from psychologically consistent development. He is like Othello at the close, who also seems for the moment to have forgotten the dead, yet turns to her as he dies. Still Othello is, and has been, in full possession of his faculties; with him now there is a reaction, too, but a less far-reaching, more normal one, not so startling. And the difference between the scenes is in keeping not so much with any psychology as (what is expected in drama) simply with our imaginative and emotional impression of each hero's previous conduct and experience, and with what is to come. Othello kills himself: it is the death of Cordelia that kills Lear. His mind, though stricken, has not broken; but his heart is about to break.

10

The situation is, as I have said, improbable; yet, though itself in a certain sense stylized, and, like the final passion of Othello, adapted (with two outbursts and an interval) to the needs or limitations of both actor and audience, the language is scarcely so, but (highly poetical as it is) mostly simple, and Lear's is so even to the point of homeliness. Often the finest effects are where the realistic and the unrealistic, the probable and the improbable, do not alternate but thus meet and combine. But in the greatest tragic poetry both are present, as the ancients (poets or critics, either) well knew; as, also, the poets of the Renaissance knew, though the critics not so clearly. Corneille, of the

[35]A colloquial endearment: it is impossible that (as some people still think) he should mean the jester.

wingèd critical words, was, of course, a poet; and Dryden, like him, was also a man of sense. So to him I leave the next to the last word, as spoken in the *Defence of Dramatic Poesy*. Of a serious play he says:

this last is indeed the representation of nature, but 'tis nature wrought up to a higher pitch.

to affect the soul, and excite the passions, and above all to move to admiration, which is the delight of serious plays, a bare imitation will not serve.

and reason suffers itself to be so hoodwinked, that it may better enjoy the pleasures of the fiction.

But the last word of all, in such a matter, must be left to one of those who, in literature at least, have been the devotees of reason. Lanson, asking (and answering) a little like Voltaire and Saint-Evremond before him, the question why the French classics seem to some a little fettered or petty, he replies that it is because they were so bent upon being true to life:[36]

Et si Shakespeare les dépasse, c'est parce qu'il a mis de plus dans son oeuvre que le simple vrai, le vrai certain et connaissable.

1943

[36]*Hommes et livres* (1895), p. 360.

CHAPTER XV

Source and Motive in Macbeth and Othello

The best tragedy—highest tragedy in short—is that of the worthy encompassed by the inevitable.

THOMAS HARDY.

SHAKESPEARE, of course, has, like the Greeks—unlike the Bourbon French—no *règles*, neither rule nor formula. But for all that, why in *Othello* and *Macbeth,* two of the great tragedies that are not histories and that apparently are not in any measure *rifacimenti* of previous plays, does he, in the matter of motivation, deviate so widely and so similarly from his source?

I

What in *Macbeth* he has omitted and what substituted Sir Arthur Quiller-Couch has made admirably clear, but has not considered the reasons for this or the similarity of procedure in *Othello.* In Holinshed's Chronicle there is the suggestion that, cut off by the nomination of Malcolm as successor to the throne from his own expectations, Macbeth had for his usurpation "a juste quarell so to do (as he tooke the matter)." The crown was then not strictly hereditary, and "by the old lawes of the realme, if he that should succeed were not of able age to take the charge upon himselfe, he that was next of blood should be admitted."[1] "Did Shakespeare use that one hint, enlarge that loophole?" asks Sir Arthur. "He did not."

> Instead of using a paltry chance to condone Macbeth's guilt, he seized on it and plunged it threefold deeper . . .
> He made this man, a sworn soldier, murder Duncan, his liege-lord.
> He made this man, a host, murder Duncan, a guest within his gates.
> He made this man, strong and hale, murder Duncan, old, weak, asleep and defenceless.
> He made this man commit murder for nothing but his own advancement.
> He made this man murder Duncan, who had steadily advanced him hitherto, who had never been aught but trustful, and who (that no detail of reproach might be wanting) had that very night, as he retired, sent, in most kindly thought, the gift of a diamond to his hostess.
> To sum up: instead of extenuating Macbeth's criminality, Shakespeare doubles and redoubles it. (*Shakespeare's Workmanship* [Holt, N. Y., 1930], pp. 19–20.)

And yet Macbeth is the protagonist, the hero, with whom as such, for the right tragic effect, there must, naturally, be some large measure of sympathy. So, having thus put him much farther beyond the reach of our sympathy than in the original, what does the dramatist then do but (indirectly) bring him back within it—in general, by the power of poetry, in particular, by the exhibition of the hero's bravery and virtue at the beginning, by emphasizing the influence of the supernatural presented, and of his wife's inordinate ambition distinctly mentioned, in the source.

There are additional devices which Sir Arthur dwells upon, such as the flattening of the other characters—that the hero and heroine may stand out in high relief, to absorb

[1]*Boswell-Stone's Holinshed* (1896), p. 25. Sir Arthur's quotation, preceding, is curtailed: "for that Duncane did what in him lay to defraud him of all maner of title and claime, which he might, in time to come, pretend unto the crowne."

our interest and (presumably on the principle considered in the preceding chapter) our sympathy also; and such as the keeping of the murders, as the ancients do, in the background, off the stage. "There is some deep law in imaginative illusion," says Watts-Dunton,[2] "whereby the identification of the spectator's personality is with the active character in most dramatic actions rather than the passive." We share the emotions, the perturbations, of Macbeth and his Lady, as even of Clytemnestra and Phaedra, because they are the impassioned doers and speakers, constantly in the foreground; and it is with their ears that we hear the owl and the cricket, the voices in the castle and the knocking at the gate. And still more clearly than in the veiling of the horrors the method is that of the ancients. The central complication—the contrast—is that recommended by Aristotle,[3] the *good* man doing the dreadful deed, though not unwittingly, nor quite unwillingly either. As with the ancients, again, he is under the sway of fate; for the Weird Sisters and his Lady—"burning in unquenchable desire to beare the name of a queene"[4]—together amount to that.

This, of course, is not what we ordinarily call motivation, not psychology. For both—the narrative or external motivation and the internal—there was, positively and negatively, better provision in Holinshed—not only the "juste quarell (as he took the matter)" but also "the feeble and slouthfull administration of Duncane,"[5] no treachery or violation of the laws of hospitality in the killing, and the just and efficient rule (for ten years) in the sequel.[6] *La carrière ouverte aux talents,* and Macbeth had the justifi-

[2]*Harper's* (November, 1906), p. 818. Touched on in the preceding chapter and in note 10 there.

[3]*Poetics, cap.* 13, 14.

[4]*Boswell-Stone's Holinshed* (1896), p. 25.

[5]*Ibid.,* p. 32. Cf. p. 20: "At length, Macbeth speaking much against the kings softnes and overmuch slacknesse in punishing offenders." . . .

[6]*Ibid.,* p. 32: "he set his whole intention to maintaine justice and to punish all enormities and abuses which had chanced," etc.; "made manie holesome laws and statutes for the publike weale."

cation of Napoleon, of Cromwell. But not Shakespeare's Macbeth.

Nor is this what we call drama, either, as it is ordinarily practiced today. It is as in Aristotle,—situation first and motivation or psychology afterwards, if at all. The effect is emotional, with which psychology or even simple narrative coherence often considerably interferes. To Schiller's neglect of careful motivation, and in a day of psychology and philosophy both, Goethe even attributes his superiority on the stage.[7] Shakespeare sometimes neglects it because it can be counted upon as familiar; sometimes, as with Hamlet's feigning of lunacy and Lear's dividing of the kingdom, because, the motive in the old play not being a good one, it is better that it should be omitted or only hinted at; but in Macbeth the omission is for a positive purpose, and the contravention of psychological probability is so as well. Here, as generally in Shakespeare, *Coriolanus* being only a partial exception, character is not its own destiny, the action is not exclusively derived from it. For Shakespeare "a human being" is *not,* as in Galsworthy's words or as in his own and his fellows' practice, "the best plot there is." To his minor characters the words better apply. The hero's conduct, at the heart of the action, is often not in keeping with his essential nature but in contrast with it.

Manifestly, and, if not forthwith, certainly upon a moment's consideration, by all the motives prompting or circumstances attending the murder of Duncan that have been omitted, the big, sharply outlined, highly emotional contrast in the situation of a good man doing the deed of horror would be broken or obscured. If Macbeth had been thwarted or (to use Holinshed's word) "defrauded," as having, at this juncture, a better title to the throne than Malcolm, or had thought himself better fitted to rule; or, again, if Duncan had not borne his faculties so meek and been so clear in his great office, as in the tragedy but not the chronicle he is; why, then, Macbeth's conduct in killing him would have been more reasonable and more psychologically in keeping, to be sure, but less terrible, less truly

[7]Eckermann (Castle), I, 400.

tragic. Even if Duncan had been less affectionate and generous, less admiring and confiding, still the hero's conduct
would have been less truly tragic! There is positive need
of "the deep damnation of his taking off." For the tragedy
is of the brave and honorable man suddenly and squarely—
fatally, too—turned against the moral order. Sir Arthur
compares him to Satan about to engage in the temptation:
"Evil, be thou my good." Or "Fair is foul and foul is fair,"
as the Weird Sisters have it, which Macbeth on his first
appearance echoes—

> So foul and fair a day I have not seen.

And that situation, no question, is a contrast big and sharp
enough.

Sir Arthur does not, indeed, pause to take notice how
unpsychological the change here is. Others besides fallen
archangels have so turned about, but evil they do not continue to call evil. Macbeth so does. He has scarcely a word
of ambition beforehand, not a word of delight in the power
when attained. As Mr. Firkins and even Mr. Bradley have
noticed, it is the deterrents that he dwells upon, not the
incentives; it is the spectral bloody dagger that he sees, not
a glittering crown; it is "withered murder" that he follows
to the chamber, not the call to sovereign sway and master-
dom. In horror he commits the crime, even as he is to
remember it. There is no satisfaction but only torment in
the thought of it. The conscience in him, before and after,
is that of a good man, not that of the man who can do
such wickedness; first the voice of God, then either that
or else—"accuser of mankind"!—the devil's.[8] It is Macbeth
himself that considers the "deep damnation," and neither
before nor after does he deceive himself, as the good turning to wickedness necessarily do. But the contrast is kept
clear and distinct; and the emotional effect—that the whole
world has acknowledged.

If, on the other hand, Shakespeare had kept to history,
to reality and psychology! If he had followed Holinshed—
made more of Macbeth's grievances, dilated on Duncan's

[8] Cf. below, chap. XVI.

unfitness and his own fitness to rule, without bringing on his head the blood of an old man, asleep, his benefactor and guest! If he had dwelt on reasons for committing instead of not committing the crime! And if afterwards he had expressed the psychologically natural or appropriate opinions upon his own conduct, excusing or palliating it, perhaps even justifying it! If in short Macbeth (and his Lady, too, who invokes the powers of evil at the outset and is tormented by conscience at the end) had acted more like the human beings we know of; why, then we should have had decidedly less of contrast and excitement, of imaginative and emotional power generated and discharged, of poetry and drama.

2

The treatment of the material in *Othello,* probably an earlier play, is somewhat the same. In Cinthio there is no warrant for introducing the supernatural; but in Shakespeare's hands the villain takes the place of Fate—of the Weird Sisters and the Lady—and more completely than is usual in the tragedy of the Renaissance. He is a devil in the flesh, as Booth played him, as Coleridge and Lamb implied, and George Woodberry, J. J. Chapman, Lytton Strachey, John Palmer, not to mention others, have put it explicitly.[9] Iago himself practically acknowledges it in the soliloquies—"Hell and night," "Divinity of hell! when devils will the blackest sins put on"—and on that point apparently he and Othello at the end are agreed:

> If that thou beest a devil, I cannot kill thee—
> > [*wounds* IAGO]
> I bleed, sir, but not kill'd.

Before that, to be sure, the Ancient is misapprehended by everybody; yet as Fate, as master of the show, he is holding nearly all the strings of the action in hand, and leading

[9] For their opinions see my *Shakespeare and Other Masters*, pp. 233, 238, 243–44.

both heroine and hero to destruction. In the victim now, not the victimizer, is the great change; but from good to evil only under a complete delusion—"be thou my good" he neither says nor thinks, and the prince of villains himself has no need to say it. For again, as in *Macbeth,* the motives are dispensed with. The Ensign of the *novella* is deprived of the internal incentives to his wickedness, and the Moor relieved of the traits which might have provoked or somewhat warranted it.

As Professor Wolfgang Keller notices, the villainy is "better motived" in the source. That is, more plausibly, more realistically. Not a devil in the flesh, a "black angel," as Mr. Chapman calls him, Cinthio's Ensign is still of "the most depraved nature in the world" (*della più scelerata natura che mai fosse huomo del mondo*). But as such he has provocation enough. He is a rejected suitor, and really suspects the Captain (Shakespeare's Cassio) of being the favored one. Against both him and the lady he has a grudge; his love for her is turned to the "bitterest hate"; whereas in the tragedy his love for Desdemona and her intrigue with Cassio are, like Cassio's and Othello's with Emilia, pretexts and afterthoughts. There he has need of these. His genuine reason for resentment is against Othello, but only for promoting Cassio above him, and against Cassio (incidentally) for being promoted. In soliloquy, as always in drama, the truth will out. "I hate the Moor," he mutters,

> *And it is thought* abroad that 'twixt my sheets
> He has done my office.

And the next moment the pretext is made still plainer: "I know not if't be true, but I for mere suspicion in that kind will do as if for surety."[10]

So the Ensign is deprived of his motive as much as the Thane of Glamis—as much as Richard III of his, which was ambition, or as Goneril and Regan of theirs, which was

[10]Cf. *Shakespeare and Other Masters,* pp. 236–38, for the way that his suspicions become convictions.

envy,[11]—but without an external Fate to relieve him of the burden of his iniquity. He carries it indeed, like the Weird Sisters, lightly enough; and the Aristotelian contrast of the good man doing the deed of horror is presented in his victim, who, however, unlike Macbeth, is guilty only of a mistake in judgment—the *hamartia*—and is far from uttering Satan's cry. Othello never loses our sympathy, as Macbeth, despite the poignant presentation of his sufferings, cannot but in some measure do.

What is almost quite as important to the emotional effect —to the steep tragic contrast—as the apparently unmitigated wickedness of Iago, is, as in the Caledonian tragedy, the nature of the victim and the circumstances of the crime. As we have seen, Shakespeare's Moor has changed places with his wife in the villain's enmity. Love turned to hatred is too ambiguous and appealing a passion—it is that, moreover, into which the Moor himself is precipitated, and, as Strachey observes, the villain's must not be anything of a parallel. For the contrast, again, it must not be. Moreover, though Cinthio's Moor is given some noble and attractive traits, especially at the outset, Shakespeare's is both there and throughout on a far higher level of intelligence and feeling. He is not a stupid dupe or a vulgarly vindictive cuckold. He is not the man to call the informer in to do the killing, or the concealing of it afterwards. For his own safety, Shakespeare's, unlike Cinthio's Moor, shows no concern. Nor is there, for that matter, the slightest evidence in his conduct or his utterance, nor in the woman's either, of the love Iago suspects between him and Emilia—no more than there is in Iago's own conduct or utterance, indeed, of his own love for Desdemona—though of late there has been a fairly prominent critic to say there is.[12] That would

[11]In the old *King Leir*, envy of Cordelia's beauty, cf. E. E. Kellett, *Suggestions* (1923), p. 38. For Richard, cf. Brandl, *Shakespeare* (1937), p. 120.

[12]It is of course not enough to urge the probabilities upon us— that a healthy and vigorous soldier of the time would lead "a *man's* life," and that Emilia was none too good for taking up with him. As I have repeatedly reminded my readers, no character in fiction has a private life, beyond the reach of the writer, which a character

be like thinking, with some Germans, that Hamlet had
betrayed Ophelia, for which, to be sure, there is a little
evidence, though far from enough; or with some Frenchmen, that Lady Macbeth as, reenacting in memory the deed
of blood, she whispers, "to bed, to bed! there's knocking
at the gate . . . to bed, to bed, to bed," she, having enticed
her husband, is now for rewarding him. On the contrary,
the black man is made the grandest and noblest of Shakespeare's lovers; and it is only through Iago's overwhelming
reputation for honesty and sagacity, the impenetrableness
of his mask together with the potency of his seductive arts,
that he is led astray and succumbs. For the highest tragic
effect it is the great and good man that succumbs. Like
other supreme artists, Shakespeare has here created his own
world, which holds together. Like Corneille (*les grands
sujets de la tragédie doivent toujours aller au delà du vraisemblable*) Goethe holds that *in den höheren Regionen des
künstlerischen Verfahrens, hat der Künstler ein freieres
Spiel, und er darf sogar zu Fiktionen schreiten.*[13] This
Shakespeare boldly does. No one else sees through Iago, including his own wife; so Othello, for not seeing, is no gull
or dupe. In the matter of the Ancient's cleverness in ma-
neuver and also of his success in hypocrisy the English is
a little indebted to the Italian writer; but the Ensign's wife
does see through him and only for fear of him holds her
tongue.

3

In both *Macbeth* and *Othello*, then, it is the whole situation that is mainly important, not the character; it is the
reciprocal matter of motivation (whether present or missing), of defects or qualities in both victim and victimizer
together. Here lies the chief point of the present discussion.

---

in a biography or history, on the other hand, has, not being the
writer's own creation. And in Shakespearean drama, as in the ancient or the classical French, none has the "past" or the "love life"
that is more readily expected, and so more easily suggested, today.
Cf. chap. VIII, above. [13]Eckermann, April 18, 1827.—I hope
Corneille here does not go beyond the endurable.

What if Shakespeare's Macbeth and Duncan had been like
Holinshed's, or like Henry IV and Richard II, or like
Cromwell and Charles I? And as I have elsewhere said,
"How the scope and stature of Iago's wickedness (and of
Othello's virtue) would be limited by any adequate
grudge!"[14] How they would be also by a credulous or suspicious nature—a predisposition or a psychology—in the
hero! Against that Shakespeare has guarded not only by
Iago's impregnable reputation and by his all-prevailing arts
but also by Othello's own reputation for capability and for
virtue. (A world of reputation and circumstance here, not
of motive!) Before the temptation begins, as in *Macbeth*,
but much more fully and felicitously, the Moor has not
only in his own right but through the admiration of everybody (and here even of the villain) been firmly established
in our good opinion and our sympathies. So with Desdemona, too, and she is not deceitful or supersubtle as Mr.
Shaw would have her, not enough so "to strengthen the
case for Othello's jealousy"; the dramatic preparations are
emotional, not analytical and psychological, primarily for
the situation, not the character. And both women, Emilia
at the last and Desdemona once the action is well started,
are shocked at the discoveries they make in their husbands.
But she is justified, when hers gives signs of jealousy, in
being unable to believe it; "not easily jealous" he himself
says (where a Shakespearean hero, or his best friend, is
expected to know and everything comes to light) at the
end. Even Iago, hearing that Othello is angry, exclaims,

> and is he angry?
> Something of moment, then. I will go meet him.
> There's matter in't indeed, if he be angry.

And in the fourth act, when the jealous rage is fully upon
him, Lodovico, newly come from Venice, is moved to wonder and to grief.

> Is this the nature
> Whom passion could not shake? whose solid virtue
> The shot of accident nor dart of chance
> Could neither graze nor pierce?

[14]*Shakespeare and Other Masters,* p. 245.

"He is much chang'd," Iago coolly, and still not super-fluously, replies. So he is, until, in the last scene, by Emilia's disclosures and Iago's self-betraying resentment, he recovers something of his old stately and generous self.

Macbeth too is changed, but for once and all. Othello had suffered from an overpowering delusion, and has just now, he thinks, performed an act of justice. Macbeth, not deluded, has come under the dominion of evil, his "eternal jewel given to the common enemy of man." Neither change is probable. In neither is there much of what can be called psychology. In life neither person would really have done what he did. In both tragedy and comedy, however, that is not exactly what is to be expected: for a Henry IV, a Cromwell, we should turn to history, not the stage. What is expected is what from life we do not get—enlargement, excitement, another world, not a copy of this. And that airy edifice, an imaginative structure, is the emotionally consistent story or situation as a whole,—the conduct of characters both active and passive, perhaps also a motiving both external and internal, but in any case an interplay of relations or circumstances as important as the motives themselves; not to mention the apportionment of emphasis or relief whether in the framework or the expression, the poetry that informs both, and the individuality of the speech, which, real, though poetical, leads one to accept and delight in the improbable things said or done. "It is when their minds (those of the audience) are preoccupied with his personality," says Dr. Bridges of Macbeth, "that the actions follow as unquestionable realities."[15] Not merely, that is, when the actions proceed from the character; and the convincing quality of the speech is only a participating element in the consistent overpowering imaginative and emotional effect of the whole.

4

"In tragedy and comedy both," I have said elsewhere, "life must be, as it has ever been, piled on life, or we have visited the theater in vain." It is not primarily to present

[15]*The Influence of the Audience on Shakespeare's Drama.*

characters in their convincing reality that Shakespeare and
the Greeks have written, nor in an action strictly and wholly
of their doing, but to set them in a state of high commotion,
and thus to move and elevate the audience in turn. And
here I fall back upon the authority of Mr. Santayana, a
philosopher (but also a poet and critic) who, without my
knowledge until of late,[16] expressed, though from a different point of view, similar opinions before me:

> Aristotle was justified in making the plot the chief element in
> fiction; for it is by virtue of the plot that the characters live, or,
> rather, that we live in them, and by virtue of the plot accord-
> ingly that our soul rises to the imaginative activity by which we
> tend at once to escape from the personal life and to realise its
> ideal. . . .

And as the eminent critic proceeds, he maintains that
poetry is not

> at its best when it depicts a further possible experience, but when
> it initiates us, by feigning something which as an experience is
> impossible, into the meaning of the experience which we have
> actually had.

And that is partly because "in the theater," as the producer
Mr. Robert Edmond Jones has assured us, "the actual thing
is never the exciting thing. Unless life is turned into art
on the stage it stops being alive and goes dead."[17] It is by
the excitement that the meaning is brought home to us.
And that is true, as in the next chapter we shall see, even
without a stage or without poetry, as in Dickens, who, according to Chesterton, "could only make his characters
probable if he was allowed to make them impossible."

1943

[16]*Poetry and Religion* (1900). Cf. my *Shakespeare and Other
Masters*, p. 369. The passage here quoted is as in the *Works* (Scribner, N. Y., 1936) ii. Cf. my "Plot and Character," to appear.

[17]*The Dramatic Imagination* (1941), p. 82 (quoted by W. W.
Lawrence, *Modern Language Review*, October, 1942, p. 424).

CHAPTER XVI

Heroes and Villains: Shakespeare, Middleton, Byron, Dickens

IN A RECENT BOOK on Shakespeare[1] which I value not only because it is well written but also because, among still other reasons, it follows in the wake of Johnson rather than Bradley, there is a tendency, in both thought and expression, that I consider not true to Johnson or to Shakespeare himself. The paradoxical, I mean. Of Hamlet Mr. Mark Van Doren says: "He has been called the best of men and the worst of men. One judgment is as just as the other." (P. 190.) So he says of Othello that he "is both the best and the worst of men; he is both superior to passion and its slave." (P. 225.)

That, so far as the phrasing is concerned, is in the spirit of the present-day highbrow criticism; but so far as the dramatist's characterization itself is concerned, it is in the spirit of Byron and Victor Hugo, of the Terrific novels and Schiller's Räuber, with their magnanimous bandits, high-thinking pirates, or maternal Medusas, who, in varying proportions, are both angels and also demons, and in structure

[1]Cf. my *Art and Artifice in Shakespeare* (1933), p. 21, for examples. And as another, L. L. Schücking, *British Academy Shakespeare Lecture* (1938), *passim.*

are incarnated contradictions, "embodied antitheses, pre-meditated paradoxes." Such are the Giaour, the Corsair, and Lara, Valjean, Javert, and Frollo, Hernani, Gomez, and Lucrèce, Walpole's (and Byron's) Manfred, Beckford's Vathek, Schiller's Karl Moor and Schweizer. Extremes and extravagances of love and hatred, of cruelty and tenderness, of egoism and magnanimity, of pride and (but rarely!) humility, of ruthlessness and remorse! *"Etes-vous mon démon ou mon ange?"* asks Doña Sol of Hernani, and no answer is needed. So Amalie cries out to Karl Moor, *"Mörder, Teufel, ich kann dich Engel nicht lassen."* Not that Mr. Van Doren's Hamlet and Othello have the same traits or features as these later characters; but theirs they have in similar combination and by a similar method—sharp and continual contrast, and that logical rather than psychological or dramatic. This is not in the spirit of the traditional conventions operating in either Shakespearean tragedy—supernaturally instructed vengeance and feigned madness in the one or villainous contriving and persuasion in the other. Coleridge's principle, the balance or recon-cilement of opposite or discordant qualities, applies to a poem, of course, as well as to a drama, and for that matter to architecture and the plastic arts as well as to the oral; but by Mr. Van Doren, if he is thinking of it at all, it is applied without much regard (I cannot but presume) to differences in medium. He ignores the primacy of plot, of situation, in Shakespearean drama (as in the ancient) when compared to modern drama or to the novel; and derives the action from the character. "The evil in *Othello* is more than an atmosphere. It is a force, and its origin, like the origin of everything else in the tragedy, is the char-acter of the hero." (P. 225.) "Nothing that is in Iago," he says again, "is absent from Othello." (P. 228.)

Thus Iago becomes, instead of the antagonist, the anti-hero, almost a phase of the hero, his Mr. Hyde; and the hero himself, instead of depending on an agency like the villain (or the ghost or fate in *Hamlet, Macbeth,* and an-cient tragedy) for being brought to the point of doing the "deed of horror," does it out of his own nature and of his own accord. Thus the contrasts which Shakespeare intended, that between the hero and the villain, and that (less external and entire) between the character and the action, are obliterated, and another, likewise between good and evil, is established within the bosom of the hero alone. And thus the healthy, romantic Elizabethan audience are left with two very bad men on their hands, and no hero at all.

2

This shift of the interest—of the contrast—to be sure, corresponds to the shift in modern drama, the action of which is supposed to proceed (mainly, not as with Mr. Van Doren, wholly) from the character. And that in turn is in keeping with the spirit and method of French classic drama—of Corneille and Racine—rather than the Elizabethan and the Hellenic, though the inner conflict there, as in modern drama and novel both, is not extravagant and paradoxical as in Byron and Hugo. It is in these that hero and villain are merged—and in our contemporary Shakespeare criticism. Particularly, here, under the sway of Freudian antithetical, paradoxical psychology—Miss Bodkin has the same notion of Iago as Mr. Van Doren— though in Ibsen too there is something of it, the antithesis and paradox being more prominent, however, in dialogue than in characterization. To the Elizabethan drama all this is foreign and disturbing; but, towards its decadence, the development was in that direction. Whether there was anything of a struggle or not, the evil arose, more than before that, out of the character, not from fate or a villain; though (as often in art) the conventional, traditional structure lingered on, sometimes without its original function, sometimes with the function disguised. Of Middleton, one of the greatest of this later period, Professor Herford observes: "His habitual occupation with depraved types becomes an artistic method: he creates characters which fascinate without making the smallest appeal to sympathy, tragedy which harrows without rousing either pity or terror, and language which disdains charm, but penetrates by remorseless veracity and by touches of strange and sudden power."[2] That is fine, though (as it seems to me) somewhat overstated.

Passion, not character, and (in effect) sympathy or pity and terror, not veracity, as the great critics agree, from Aristotle, Cicero, and Longinus down, are what in tragedy is all-important; and in Middleton's *Changeling* the universally admired scene, that between Beatrice and De Flores (III, iv), is one in which something of the conventional, unrealistic method still asserts itself. The action does not proceed strictly from the character, so far as Beatrice is concerned. Though otherwise clever enough, she suffers from the same sort of "stupidity" that has actually, but unjustifiably, been complained of in Oedipus and Othello. In this, as in the previous, colloquy with the villain (which should share the honors), it is psychologically improbable that, hiring the ugly dependant to kill her fiancé in order to have her heart's desire, she should not suspect the price she shall have to pay. But Leigh Hunt, Swinburne, and Arthur Symons, I fancy, would have been startled by William Archer's[3] complaint that the author had not "arranged things so that Beatrice could *reasonably* expect her hired assassin to be content with his money-wage." To have done so would have ruined the situation, would have cut short the later palpitating approach of the fair murderess to the point of her tragic outcry:

> Why, 'tis impossible thou canst be so wicked
> Or shelter such a cunning cruelty
> To make his death the murderer of my honour.

Here there is passion rather than psychology; emotional—dramatic—effect rather than truth to life; and the character somewhat in contrast to conduct instead of being its source. In her impetuous and imperious desire, she has not dreamt of a man, so far removed in station and person, as so far presuming, though, if flesh and blood, a woman as clever as she would have done that. It is "wickedness," it is "cruelty," a startling surprise, with an ironical contrast

[2] *Dictionary of National Biography, sub* Middleton.
[3] *Old Drama and the New* (Boston, 1923), p. 97.

in the utterance of it, "worthy of the greatest dramatist that ever lived," says Swinburne, which by more adequately realistic preparation would have been dulled and reduced.

Rightly to respond to Middleton, as to Shakespeare, we must of course take the point of view expected by him. It is upon the situation, not the psychology, that both dramatist and audience are intent, upon the bigness of the danger looming before the lady, not upon the improbability of her failing to see it. And the technique, the manipulation, contributes to that end. Middleton has arranged, or contrived, better than Archer thinks. The latter objects to "the gallant young gentleman of the source" being replaced by the "hideously ugly and ruffianly retainer" (though that makes the prospect of her falling into his clutches both more terrible and, in her own eyes, more unimaginable) ; and he wrongly takes De Flores' feeling for her to be "a combination of lust and hatred," adding that she knows it. From his soliloquies and asides, and from the *double entente* thus illumined, we know as she—to her intellectual credit, therefore—cannot, that "soul and body," as Swinburne has it, he is "absorbed by one consuming force of passionately cynical desire." Moreover, her very dislike and mistrust of him, which for a modern reader may make her subsequent conduct only more improbable, are given the contrary effect.

> The next good mood I find my father in
> I'll get him quite discarded. (II, i, 94.)

And, the next scene, this is in the back of her mind as she employs him. In her exit speech she mutters to herself:

> I shall rid myself
> Of two inveterate loathings at one time. (II, ii, 145.)

All this is, of course, dramaturgy, not realism, and still less is it psychology. No doubt heroine and villain, both, might have been made more plausible, as by her having been more engrossed with her purposes and by his having not so continually betrayed his own; but—*optique du théâtre!*—both he and she then would have been less exciting to the audience. Here it is as with Othello and Oedipus. We in the audience must see the cards Iago or Fate is playing against them; the heroes should not—and must.

In the *Changeling* there is little rousing of pity or terror because the leading character, though there is a villain, bears the burden of responsibility as hero or heroine in Shakespearean or ancient tragedy seldom does. This is in the decadence of tragedy; and when tragedy flourishes, attaining to its highest effects, sympathy is indispensable. Shakespeare's masterpieces could never have held his audience if they had been "studies" such as modern scholars make of them; and studies like *Hedda Gabler* and *Borkman* awaken less sympathy than Hugo's passionate paradoxes. But these in turn cannot vie with *Hamlet* or *Othello,* at which the audience can easily tell hero and villain apart. In Hugo the passions are developed in their extremity, as they are in Shakespeare and the ancients, and not in Ibsen; yet at such cost in probability and moral confusion that the sympathy is continually interrupted or troubled. However, the improbability of fatal or villainous interference is there replaced by the greater improbability of the character as its own fate, its own enemy, to the point of bringing about a tumult in emotion and incident as portentous as in Shakespeare. It is in Ibsen, though by a different method from Middleton's, that there is the penetrating and fascinating but remorseless and alienating veracity.

3

Later developments are so vast a subject that I can only pick out one or two points that occur to me as relevant to my previous discussions. In the novel, which can be a study and yet despite that hold the solitary reader who chooses it, there is no such need of condensation, of heavily colored contrast; and in the novel, as we know it, the action proceeds more plausibly from the character. But not altogether, as I have recently shown, in *Le Rouge et le Noir* or in *Tess of the D'Urbervilles;*[4] and at least two good nov-

[4] See above, chap. XI.

elists and critics, Stevenson and Gissing, celebrate the "dramatic novel," in which passion rather than character, and sympathy rather than faithful observation, prevail.[5] De Foe, moreover, the pioneer, a reputed realist and certainly in many regards an unquestionable one, is, despite (or perhaps because of) his sordid, humble, often ignoble subjects, as intent upon sympathy as any dramatist. And he has something of the Elizabethan method of opposition between good and evil. There are tempters, and not of the wholly internal sort. There are no villains, but there is, pretty frequently, the Devil, who lays a snare for Moll or puts the notion into her head; and in that novel as well as in *Roxana* and *Colonel Jack* there are subordinate characters, such as "my governess" and Amy, who (though not devilish) somewhat take his place. It is these that bear the brunt of responsibility; it is these that, like Shakespeare's villains, are in their wickedness naïve or comic, not the heroes or heroines, with whom sympathy must be kept. And one thing that contributes to this effect is the telling of the story in the first person. People who judge themselves so honestly, and deplore their own want of virtue or moral sense, relieve the hearer or reader of the need to judge.

Not that there is in these any deep feeling of sin. "De Foe's sense of evil is so evidently that of a formalist," says Mr. MacCarthy, a little exaggerating, "that we have all the excitement of moving in a wicked world without the unpleasantness of coming into contact with a single wicked person."[6] "A formalist," like Dante, who for one fault thrusts otherwise excellent people like Francesca, Brunetto, and Ulysses, deep down in the Inferno; "without the unpleasantness," for these are the milder shades of Purgatory; in short, here too are the great advantages, without the disadvantages, of evil-doing in story (though on a humbler, prosier level) as I have repeatedly exhibited them in Shakespearean and ancient tragedy.

And not only is the standard of morality a fixed one; it

[5] *A Humble Remonstrance,* South Seas Ed. XIII, 149f; *Immortal Dickens* (1925), p. 214.

[6] *Criticism* (1932), p. 222.

is also clearly and frankly recognized and acknowledged by the wrongdoer himself, as by Macbeth, King John, and the others, even beforehand.[7] Conscience is still of the traditional and supernatural sort, external and unequivocal. "I did what my own conscience convinced me at the very time I did it," says Roxana, "was horribly unlawful, scandalous, and abominable."[8] Beforehand there is no self-deception, and little or no self-exculpation afterwards. Though there are tempters, there are no temptations, which, as Stevenson, complaining of Tolstoy's *Power of Darkness*, reminds us, "are beautiful." Though Moll's and Roxana's motives—poverty, avarice, vanity, amorous passion—are laid bare, this is not so done—particularly with the last-named, which a Flaubert or a Balzac would have amply and alluringly presented—as to make their conduct (however more exciting) more intelligible. On the sexual subject De Foe keeps within the limits of a statement. It is (to compare the small with the great) as with Macbeth's ambition, which, apart from the mere statement, is supposed sufficiently to appear from his conduct: quite unpsychologically, though dramatically, it is the deterrents, not the incentives and seductive imaginings, that occupy their thoughts. And it is, again as with him, an external rather than internal struggle, against a conscience that is a still small voice from above (beforehand), from below (afterwards), not from within— a certain fearful looking forward unto judgment, not repentance. So it was, generally, in Elizabethan times, and Beaumont and Fletcher's Evadne, unwilling to kill her king asleep (as Hamlet to kill his when praying) lest she should "rock him to another world," which is heaven, wakens both him and "his evil angel, his sick conscience," that he may die in sin. Not in salutary sorrow for it. Moll and Roxana, both, are troubled and even tormented as they remember their crimes and misdemeanors (the former word they honestly prefer) ; but though for those persons whom they have made to suffer they are sometimes a little sorry (and more

[7] See my *Shakespeare and Other Masters* (1940), pp. 27–28, 34; *Shakespeare Studies* (1927), pp. 349–55.

[8] *Roxana* (ed. Brimley Johnson, n.d.), pp. 34 *et seq.*

so than Macbeth and his Lady), it is not to the point of amends, of turning over a new leaf and making restitution.

And there is the same mythical, mystical conscience in Richardson's Lovelace[9] and the heroes and villains (the distinction between them, as not between Shakespeare's, is obscure) of Walpole and his successors on the stage or in the novel, of Byron and Hugo. It fits in with the whole antithetical scheme, now arising, as hero and villain merge: remorse without repentance, but in souls (unlike Moll's and Roxana's) too great to repent, as Byron says of the Corsair[10] and Lara, and as the poet Campbell said of Lady Macbeth. At this point (remorse or impenitence, either) the tradition is not that of Aaron, Richard, and Iago, who are conscienceless, in love with evil, but of Marlowe's Mephistopheles and Milton's Satan—grand, romantic figures, with a grievance but not without compassion, with a love or devotion though perhaps turned to hatred, and with other virtues though thwarted and distorted, themselves being not inclined to evil but thrown back upon it, melancholy not merry, solitary not convivial, witty or bitter not comic. The Marlovian or Miltonic tradition was almost unavoidable in the process of welding the two antagonistic natures —villain and hero—together: but the main underlying purpose of this was to recover for the novel and the stage the motive power and the passionate abundance and striking contrasts of the Elizabethans. A taste for realism, fostered by the novel, now required that the action should proceed from the character. So hero and villain were commingled, instead of the hero falling into fate's or the villain's snare. Some of the supernatural machinery—ghosts, omens, and marvels—lingered on; but with little artistic result, and external fate gave place to the villain-hero's fatalism. The conscience, indeed, is the point of greatest resemblance to the true Elizabethan hero; but there is no danger of mistaking the Byronic figure for either that or anything in

[9]"A thousand vultures in turn are preying upon my heart," *Clarissa*, viii, letter 59.

[10]II, x: "impenitent remorse"—"the weak alone repent"; *Lara*, II, xix.

nature. The chief aesthetic effect is owing to the fire of the presentation, and to the poet's making a mystery of (what indeed by the nature of the situation he could not satisfactorily reveal) the hero's past, the secret of the unholy mixture, the injury that had so "warped" him,[11] the curse upon him, which he in turn brings on those he loves.[12] *Ténébreux, fatal, amer*, says Lanson[13] of the Byronic, Hugoesque hero; *il sort on ne sait d'où, il passe enveloppé d'un triple prestige de mystère, de crime, et d'amour:*—there is no such single figure in Shakespeare or in really popular English tragedy. And yet of a judicial conscience the hero has need, not for his psychology, with which it is incompatible, but for the stage, or (however poetical) a stagy tale or novel.

4

Dickens, though he was pretty far from being the "dramatic" novelist of whom Stevenson was dreaming, had perhaps come nearer to him than any other of Stevenson's time. As everyone knows, he was hugely interested in the theater, now and then trod the boards himself, and has many theatrical and (sometimes) melodramatic traits in his art. No one in the nineteenth century, moreover, on the realistic and comic side, came so near to Shakespeare. Chesterton in contrasting him with Thackeray says that he

[11]*Corsair*, I, xi. In this characterization, as well as the indebtedness to Milton, Mr. Logan P. Smith has anticipated me, *Milton and His Critics* (1941), p. 49; but cf. *Shakespeare and Other Masters*, p. 279, and others before us.

[12]Of the curse brought upon her whom he loves, the chief example is Manfred. But also in the form of a curse, or brand of Cain, the ancient fate, sometimes inherited, comes to life again, as in *C.H.*, I, lxxxiii, 8–9; III, lxx, 8–9; IV, xxxiv, 6; *Lara*, I, xviii. So in the terrific novels before Byron; and even in *Redgauntlet* (1824), the horseshoe on the brow and the doom that the valor of the family should be fruitless.

[13]*Histoire* (1898), p. 964. How much also of Schiller directly or of Chateaubriand too there may be in this (cf. E. Estève, *Byron et le romantisme* [1907]) M. Lanson does not stop to inquire; nor can we.

"writes realism to make the incredible credible";[14] and exactly that is what for some years I have been endeavoring to show that Shakespeare does, though more in poetry and tragedy, as in *Hamlet* and *Othello*. Yet he did it in prose and in comedy, too. *Les grands sujets de la* comédie, Corneille might have written, remembering Aristophanes, *vont toujours au delà du vraisemblable*. Thackeray is very truthful; Dickens is more original and entertaining, as Major Bagstock is than Major Pendennis. Chesterton insists upon the unreality of Paul and Florence Dombey . . . the utter reality of monsters like Stiggins or Mantalini.

Dickens could only work in his own way, and that way was the wild way. We may almost say this: that he could only make his characters probable if he was allowed to make them impossible. Give him license to say and do anything, and he could create beings as vivid as our own aunts and uncles.[15]

Art, as Mr. Santayana conceives it, "is the response to the demand for entertainment, for the stimulation of our senses and imagination, and truth enters into it only as it subserves these ends."[16] And for the likes of Sairey Gamp, as Gissing avers, one must go to the very heights of world literature, to him who bodied forth Dame Quickly and Juliet's nurse. Not that he thinks there is direct imitation of either Shakespeare or reality.

No painful observer of her class, could, by mere faithfulness, have transferred to paper this thick, gurgling flux of talk; knowing the lingo, we recognize it upon her lips, but at the same time we know that we never before listened to Mrs. Gamp; fortune never led us into this odorous presence. . . . (*Immortal Dickens,* p. 127.)

[14]*Victorian Literature* (Henry Holt & Co., N. Y., 1923), p. 125. Cf. Gissing, *Charles Dickens* (Dodd, Mead & Co., N. Y., 1898), pp. 110–11, where independently a similar point of view is taken and Bagstock is contrasted with Major Pendennis; and for the next citation, Chesterton, *Charles Dickens* (1907), p. 187.

[15]Reprinted by permission of the publishers, Dodd, Mead and Company, Inc.

[16]*The Nature of Beauty* (Borgum), p. 81.

With Sairey and Falstaff I have dealt in another chapter; and these are also alike, and representative of their authors, in that so much of their vitality resides in their speech. By that we know these and other Shakespearean or Dickensian characters, rather than by their conduct, which may be improbable, or than by the analysis, which, if there is any, is often summary or dull. "The best of his creatures," Professor Elton says of Dickens, "whether on the greater scale or the lesser, whether Pecksniffs or Gargerys, are triumphs of style rather than of character-drawing."[17] No third author in English or perhaps in the world has successfully distinguished and differentiated so many characters, in so large a measure, by their vocabulary, accent, cadence, and rhythm, by "the tone of voice, the trick of utterance." What Pope said of printing Shakespeare's dialogue without the name-tags would apply equally well to the novelist. He himself "declared that every word spoken by his characters was audible to him"—as every word spoken by his own must have been to Shakespeare, and so to us should be, even in print.[18] And in general it is the same sort of speech —impetuous and riotous, fanciful and highly colored. "Great draughts of words," Chesterton says of Dickens, and of Shakespeare it is still truer, "are to him like great draughts of wine—pungent and yet refreshing, light and yet leaving him in a glow."[19] For though Dickens wrote only prose and Shakespeare mostly drama, of both alike Professor Elton's remarks about Dickens hold good, "a pas-

[17] *Survey*, 1830–80 (1920), ii, 217.

[18] This is, of course, a common illusion of the artistic imagination, which fairly objectifies itself; like Michelangelo's setting his figure free from the marble as he carves it or Rousseau's removing of veil after veil from the landscape as he paints it; it is not any justification for the inartistic delusion of the critic that the character takes the bit between his teeth and runs away with his author, saying and doing things—getting drunk, even—without the author's permission or knowledge. It is, however, justification for the critic, reading with the same spirit that the author writes, in so using his inner ear and eye, not depending mainly on analysis. Cf. my *Shakespeare Studies* (1927), pp. 260–61, 117–27, and my treatment of Morgann's "historic beings," chap. XII, above.

[19] *Charles Dickens* (N. Y., 1907), p. 124.

sionate creature, ever straining towards the lyrical."[20] In tragic or contemplative vein as well as the comic this applies; but what they had most in common they had in common with their England. It is the lyricism of fantasy and grotesquery, of witlessness rather than of wit, of nonsense rather than of sense.[21] There are Falstaff in his bragging and Pistol in his swaggering, as well as those delicious idiots, Shallow and Silence, Dogberry and Verges, Aguecheek, Launce, Cloten, Trinculo, on the one hand; and there are, on the other hand, Sairey and Betsy, Dick Swiveller and the Marchioness, Toots and Susan Nipper, Cuttle and Bunsby, Pecksniff and Chadband, old Willet, the Micawbers, Bailey Junior, Mould the undertaker, and numerous other revelers or flounderers with words and notions. For "the English," as Hazlitt noticed before Dickens had as yet risen above the horizon, "are the only people left who understand and relish nonsense. We are not merry and wise but indulge our mirth to excess and folly."[22] And it was after Hazlitt, in Dickens' own time, that nonsense came pure and neat, with Edward Lear and Lewis Carroll.

Nothing can justify this extreme relaxation, Hazlitt continues, but extreme tension; and while Dickens does not, like Shakespeare, presently take our breath away in following "his eagle flights" nor (at other times) "make the cordage of our hearts crack," "justification" he does provide. There is plenty of tension; there is plenty of high excitement, though not always truly tragic or pathetic; and for one thing, as Chesterton observes, Dickens "certainly created a personal devil in every one of his books."[23]

These villains, too, are Shakespearean, not Byronic, neither Miltonic nor Marlowesque. They are not grandiose villain-heroes; and like Shakespeare's own, have little or nothing in common with the real hero of the story. The legerdemain of antithesis or paradox is over; and like

[20]*Survey*, 1830–80, ii, 216.

[21]*Shakespeare and Other Masters*, p. 38.

[22]"Merry England."

[23]*Charles Dickens* (1907), pp. 285–86.

Shakespeare's, they have "no redeeming points." There is none, as Chesterton says, in Squeers, Monck, Ralph Nickleby, Bill Sikes, Quilp, Brass, Mr. Chester, Pecksniff, Jonas Chuzzlewit, Carker, Uriah Heep, Blandois, "or in a hundred more."[24] And why none? Chesterton infers that Dickens "wished to have an obstreperous and incalculable enemy. He wished to keep alive the idea of combat, which means, of necessity, a combat against something individual and alive." So did Shakespeare, as well as his audience, and Dickens' public, much greater than Byron's; or rather, they did not wish it, but so to have it was in harmony with their way of thinking about the world and with their way of imaginatively imparting or receiving emotions.

Though more like Shakespeare's than are any other modern villains, those of Dickens have, however, as Chesterton says, "a peculiar and vigorous life of their own." They are no imitations. They are like Shakespeare's—in their originality. Without redeeming point, they attract, and by their abounding vitality and ingenuity, their wit and humor, their unmistakable individuality as it appears in their speech. Like Shakespeare's, moreover, they are merry— romantic melancholy, for novel readers, had had its day— or in their gloom they are likely to be grotesque. Morose people, on the other hand, Dickens, as Mr. Santayana elsewhere remarks, "made wicked, not virtuous in their own way, so that the protest of his temperament against his environment never took a radical form nor went back to first principles. He needed to feel, in his writing, that he was carrying the sympathies of every man with him." And all that is like Shakespeare too. Quilp, though as a dwarf he might be expected to be bitter or disillusioned like Scott's Black one, has, as Chesterton puts it, a "kind of hellish happiness, an atrocious hilarity that makes him go bounding about like an india-rubber ball."[25] So he is more like Richard III, the hunchback.

At one point, however, Dickens resembles the Romantic, Terrific school—the external conscience. Shakespeare gives

[24]*Charles Dickens* (1907), pp. 285–86.

[25]*Ibid.,* p. 286.

none to his demons—Aaron, Richard,[26] Iago—but only to evildoers such as the Macbeths and (on their deathbeds) to Cardinal Beaufort and Cymbeline's Queen. In the Gothic romances not only the villain-heroes have it, but also the villains almost unrelieved, like Mrs. Radcliffe's Schedoni. Not that the Dickens villains are too great, too proud, for real repentance, but too disinclined—at that point, indeed, too natural. What they had done they had wanted to do, and like most criminals have no disposition to regret till— and then not sincerely—under the influence of a priest or under the shadow of the gallows—in Dickens not often even then.

That the conscience-smitten evildoer is not "sorry" Dickens makes as plain as De Foe or Byron; and sometimes, as in Bradley Headstone and Jonas Chuzzlewit, there is not even this supernatural remorse but only the fear of discovery. Oftener, however, it is the mysterious spiritual retribution, and on the deathbed "the horrors," as in Magwitch's story: "So Arthur was a-dying, and a-dying poor, and with the horrors on him" (chapter 42); or as at the bad end made by Fagin: "He grew so terrible, at last, in all the tortures of his evil conscience that one man could not bear to sit there eyeing him alone; and so the two kept watch together." (Chapter 52.) And long before the final earthly reckoning some of them, like Bill Sikes and the steward Rudge, are "haunted" by the figures of their victims.

Poe,[27] in his review of *Barnaby Rudge*, complained of the steward's suffering the sting of conscience—so many years and so keenly—as inconsistent with the brutality of his character. Yes, if the conscience is what Poe, evidently, takes it to be; but if it is the external, supernatural sort, time does not count, or the sting would grow even sharper toward the end. And really, if psychology is to be considered, that thought might lend greater weight, on the other hand, to the objections of some candid critics to the spiritual torments of the Macbeths the night of the

[26]Except momentarily, on seeing the ghosts.

[27]*Works* (1914), vii, p. 73.

murder, before the deed and after. Time and reflection, more naturally, might bring not only remorse but repentance—when weary of the crown, not when ruthlessly grasping for it. (This psychological advantage Dickens deliberately rejects not only by the continuance of the brutality but also by making Rudge turn a deaf ear to the pleadings of his wife for a change of heart before his death.) Be that as it may, "the hypersensitiveness of Macbeth and Lady Macbeth," as Mr. Chapman has it (or, in other words, their consciences thus unplausibly intruding), "is one of Shakespeare's greatest strokes of genius."[28] His originality, however, lies, as is usual with the greatest dramatists (or other artists, for that matter) only in doing better what others had done well or indifferently before him, and in availing himself of the conceptions, the prepossessions and prejudices, already established in the minds of the public. It is so that the greatest emotions are aroused, the biggest effects produced. Now this external conscience is a resource of tragic horror and terror, and in Christian times to a higher degree than in the ancient.[29] "It is a bodying-forth of unearthly fears and more than mortal misery."[30] It extends the scene, as with Dante, and more certainly and terrifically than with the ancients, beyond the limits of the grave. And of itself it creates an emotional situation, the character being, so far (and the hero of course still farther), superior to his conduct, in contrast with it. It is one of the chief devices for making the assassin as the leading figure endurable. Moreover, to complain of the sensitiveness of the Macbeths and (*a longo intervallo*) of the Steward is to complain of the initial postulate or premise of the struc-

[28]*Glance toward Shakespeare* (1922), p. 71; *Shakespeare and Other Masters,* p. 34.

[29]For this external, supernatural conscience is not Christian exclusively. "And even if any [wrongdoers] think themselves well fenced and fortified against detection by their fellow men, they still dread the eyes of heaven, and fancy that the pangs of anxiety night and day gnawing at their hearts are sent by Providence to punish them." (Cicero, *De Finibus,* I, xvi, 51.)

[30]*Shakespeare Studies,* p. 352, and compare the whole discussion, pp. 349–55.

ture—of the tragedy or the novel as a whole. And in
Barnaby Rudge it is, however improbable, no contemptible
story, this of the villain, himself thought by everyone, including the reader, to have been killed long ago with his
master, now haunting as well as haunted, continually visiting the scene and neighborhood (compare Dostoevski's
Raskolnikoff!), and especially on anniversaries of the murder, one of which nights the sexton (properly enough)
takes him for his ghost. (To keep the spirit quiet and afar—
requiescat!—are not death-day anniversaries still ceremonially observed by the Catholics, as by the pagans for ages
before them?) On the night of the storming of the man-
sion, as he looks in at the tavern and inquires about it, the
alarm-bell then sounding as it did when rung by his master
just before death, he gives a fearful cry and rushes away.
And it is in the ruins of the house that he presently is cap-
tured. The conscience that is a nemesis, the fire let down
from heaven, "his evil angel," the worm that never dies!
But psychologically inconsistent and fragmentary as this
all is, it is not, despite the traditional element, remote from
human nature; after a sort, it is simple, sensuous, and passionate; and the murder story as we have it serves for a
mystery in the background of the novel, as with a better
psychology it wouldn't.

5

In the realistic development which ensued what became
of the Shakespearean and the Miltonic-Byronic narrative
traditions, of satanism and the supernatural conscience?
The trend was still towards an action derived from the character; and with no longer a fate or a villain to bear the
burden of responsibility, was imaginative and passionate
elevation to be lost to the hero and force and scope to the
story? They were, pretty much. To keep the sympathy of
reader or audience the hero or heroine must now have
faults or defects that are petty, like pride or vanity, envy or
irresolution; sordid or mean, like forgery or destroying a
will; or inherited, like physical degeneration or syphilis; or

if the dramatist or novelist attempts bloodshed, as Ibsen, Hardy, and Stendhal sometimes do, he produces motives for it such as those in *Rosmersholm,* which however they explain leave us rather cold or unconvinced. So, as I have noticed before,[31] his chief recourse is to primitive life, with its abrupt, illogical transitions; or, above all, to the complications of sex. Here are faults that are less repugnant, and contrasts or contradictions, paradoxes or ironies that, unlike Byron's and Hugo's, are really plausible, fairly inherent. Thwarted love turns to hatred, though still love underneath. "His honour rooted in dishonour stood." But still are lacking the force and scope, the bigger dimensions and sharper contrasts, provided by the Shakespearean hero and villain. However, Iago's

> Hell and night
> Must bring this monstrous birth to the world's light

will not do; for there is no motive for it, only a trumped-up one. And Satan's

> Evil, be thou my good,

has for a motive only a fallen angel's defiance, because of his "injur'd merit." How, then, shall the requirements of psychology, in motivation, be satisfied and at the same time the demand for the imaginative and emotional effect of positive evil be met?

The further development of the Romantic movement, cultivating emotions and sensations to the limit, provided the answer: "Be thou my good" as the supreme sensation! This, the (also defiant) delight in adultery, incest, or sexual perversions, in blasphemy or profanation, in cruelty—sadism and masochism—or even murder[32] is psychological, though pathological, is only too natural and probable, though "unnatural" and morbid; and at last the demand

---

[31] Cf. *Shakespeare and Other Masters,* pp. 409–10, for a fuller discussion.

[32] Praz, *Romantic Agony* (1933), *passim;* and for the everyday deportment see F. L. Lucas, *Decline and Fall of the Romantic Ideal* (1937), chap. ii.

for motivation and excitement together is met. The answer
is far from satisfactory, to be sure; and it was no doubt
partly accidental. These late Romantic writers, Gautier,
Flaubert, Baudelaire, Verlaine, Huysmans, Barrès, Wilde,
Swinburne, D'Annunzio, with Chateaubriand before them,
often were looking into their hearts to write, drawing upon
their own experience. Their extravagances in this kind are
like theirs in everyday speech and conduct, dress and demeanor. Yet they were also endeavoring, as artists should
and must, to be interesting; and it must be admitted, they
are. In the drama, by the nature of the case, they were not
so free with their innovation—public decorum or the authority of the state was in the way; but in plays such as
Salomé and novels such as *Salammbô* and the *Tentation
de Saint Antoine* and in lyrics such as the *Fleurs du Mal
(dans le mal se trouve toute volupté)* the writers could not
only spice the fare for an ordinary jaded taste but also
actually provide (in comparison to what there had been
of late) an enriched intellectual and artistic quality. Most
of those mentioned above are great writers. But they alien-
ate sympathy, and offend the moral judgment, as no one
ever did before. By the mere closeness of their approach to
reality they do. There had been incest before, as between
Milton's Satan and Sin, and in Walpole's *Mysterious Mother*
and Shelley's *Cenci*, but only to heighten the horror; and
as in *Laon and Cythna* and *Parisina,* but not for the sharp-
ening of the parties' own sensations. And the failure of realism as it thus reaches out for the larger and more powerful
effects of the nobly conventional art of Shakespeare, Milton, and the ancients, justifies moderns like Goethe and (if
they may be mentioned together) Hauptmann and D'Annunzio as they fall back upon the legendary stories such as
the early poets employed, and perhaps also,—incidentally,
—those critics who cannot conceive or interpret the conventional but noble art as if it were not such.

6

Above I have twice dealt with Macbeth, and now I wonder whether there and in previous discussions[33] I have sufficiently answered the objections of the critic Gourmont (though after making them he magnanimously himself declares them not worth answering) :

mais l'esprit demeure insatisfait, parce que les caractères incertains ont plutôt donné ce qu'exigeait d'eux la logique des situations que ce que demandait la logique de l'esprit.

On voit l'ambition et le crime naître en même temps dans le coeur de Macbeth, sans que rien nous ait préparés à admettre cela. De fait, on le voit, on ne le comprend pas.

Avec Shakespeare tout est possible et je crois qu'il a eu moins d'intentions profondes qu'on ne lui suppose, et qu'il s'attardait moins à la vérité psychologique qu'aux surprises de l'action.

La scène de la tache et du somnambulisme n'est pas moins saisissante ni moins artificielle. Rien n'est encore expliqué et on a peine à admettre qu'une femme si hardie dans le crime soit si profondément déprimée, aux jours mêmes du triomphe.

The first and the next to the last passages are strikingly in harmony with one in *Some Remarks on the Tragedy of Hamlet*, 1736, with which Shakespearean criticism really began and, on that particular aspect, nearly ended: "he studyd more to work up great and moving Circumstances to place his chief Characters in, so as to affect our Passions strongly, he apply'd himself more to this than he did to the Means or Methods whereby he brought his Characters into those Circumstances." And the second and the fourth express dissatisfaction with the psychology presented in both hero and heroine,—a conscience more prominent than the overwhelming passion, a temptation that does not allure.

Not only is M. Gourmont himself not convinced, but his

[33]*Shakespeare Studies*, index, *sub* Gourmont; and *Promenades Littéraires* (1912), iv, pp. 312, 314, 315–16.

objections vanish, he says, at the thought—it is Shakespeare's. That means more than most similar avowals, of which there have been plenty. For Gourmont is a great critic, and is a Frenchman; and here, if our notions of either are correct, he is ceasing to be either. Yet he still keeps the essential quality (in critics, paradoxically, the rarest), that of perfect candor. He still "sees the object as in itself it really is." He would rather go no farther than go wrong, rather give up criticism than betray it. Like the greatest of philosophers, he knows—and confesses it—when he does not know.

1942

CHAPTER XVII

Browning's In a Balcony

THERE is an interesting difference of opinion, of which I have only of late become aware, concerning the value of Browning's closet drama *In a Balcony* as well as the interpretation of it. In 1940 I had written of it as follows, at the conclusion of a discussion of the tragic situation, involving conventions or postulates, in both the *Oedipus Tyrannus* and *Othello:*

Browning the psychologist, the impressionist before his time, achieved what is perhaps his greatest situation, in *In a Balcony,* after a really similar fashion, at equal cost to probability, when Constance persuades her frank and noble lover Norbert, out of love for him and gratitude to the Queen, to declare to their mistress that all his service has been prompted by his love for her. The improbability lies not only in the success of the deception but also in the willingness of Constance and Norbert to take the risk; nor is it overcome by all Browning's careful preparation and motivation. The improbability, the deception, is, as in *Othello* (and indeed in the *Oedipus*), the price still necessarily paid for a superbly ironical *contretemps* such as that when the Queen, who, though married, has never known love, rushes to Constance, apparently for confirmation of the news, but really to tell her what

love is like, bid her once the time comes give up everything for
it, and, when Constance reminds her of obstacles in the way, cry
out, as if not to her but to the stars,

> Hear her! There, there now—could *she* love like me?

> Hear her! I thank you, sweet, for that surprise.
> You have the fair face: for the soul, see mine.
> I have the strong soul: let me teach you here.

Les grands sujets de la tragédie, says Corneille, himself not always remembering it, *doivent toujours aller au delà du vraisemblable.*

Of the situation thus secured Mr. Arthur Symons, as I
then knew, had a high opinion, and as I have later found,
Professor C. H. Herford. The former, writing in 1886 (re-
vising in 1906), says of it: "passionate and highly wrought,
to a degree never before reached, except in the crowning
scene of *Pippa Passes.*" And he thus condenses the latter
part of the story:

His [Norbert's] aim, all the while, though unknown, as he
thinks, to her, has been the hope of winning Constance, the
Queen's cousin and dependant. He is now about to claim her as
his recompense; but Constance, fearing for the result, persuades
him, reluctant though he is, to ask in a roundabout way, so as to
flatter or touch the Queen. He over-acts his part. The Queen, a
heart-starved and now ageing woman, believes that he loves her,
and responds to him with the passion of a long-thwarted nature.
She announces the wonderful news, with more than the ecstasy
of a girl, to Constance. Constance resolves to resign her lover, for
his good and the Queen's, and, when he appears, she endeavours
to make him understand and enter into her plot. But he cannot
and will not see it. In the presence of the Queen he declares his
love for Constance, and for her alone. The Queen goes out, in
white silence. The lovers embrace in new knowledge and fervour
of love. Measured steps are heard within, and we know that the
guard is approaching.[1]

"Each of the characters," Symons continues, "is admirably delineated"; Norbert, "honest, straightforward, single-
minded, passionate," presenting the strongest contrast to

[1]*Introduction to Browning* (1906), Dent, London, p. 133.

Constance's feminine over-subtlety. She is "peculiarly wily for goodness, curiously rich in resource for unalloyed and inexperienced virtue." Does then her proposal to relinquish Norbert in favor of the Queen show her to be lacking in love for him? Is she "noble and magnanimous" or "radically insincere and inconstant"?

Her love, we cannot doubt, was true and intense up to the measure of her capacity; but her nature was, instinctively, less outspoken and truthful, more subtle, more reasoning. At the critical moment she is seized by a whirl of emotions, and, with very feminine but singularly unloverlike instinct, she resolves, as she would phrase it, to sacrifice herself, not seeing that she is insulting her lover by the very notion of his accepting such a sacrifice. Her character has not the pure and steadfast nobility of Norbert's but . . . it is genuinely human.

In the matter of postulates or premises Professor Herford, in 1905, anticipates me, though his are not the same.

In its social presuppositions this community belongs to a world as visionary as the mystic dream-politics of M. Maeterlinck. But those presuppositions granted [that love is the absorbing preoccupation of this society and that for a brilliant young minister to fail to make love to his sovereign is a kind of high treason], everything has the uncompromising clearness and persuasive reality that Browning invariably communicates to his dreams. The three figures who in a few hours taste the height of ecstasy and then the bitterness of disillusion or severance, are drawn with remarkable psychologic force and truth. . . . One of them, the Queen, has hardly her like for pity and dread. A "lavish soul" long starved, but kindling into the ecstasy of girlhood at the seeming touch of love; then, as her dream is shattered by the indignant honesty of Norbert, transmuted at once into the daemonic Gudrun or Brynhild glaring in speechless white-heat and implacable frenzy upon the man who has scorned her proffered heart and the hapless girl he has chosen.[2]

Concerning the artistic value of the Queen's character there seems to be little difference of opinion, but plenty of it concerning that of Constance, upon whom the situation depends. Of her, however, Herford thinks still more highly

[2]*Robert Browning* (1905), Blackwood, London, pp. 144–45.

than Symons. "Between these powerful, rigid, and simple natures stands Constance, ardent as they, but with the lithe and palpitating ardour of a flame. She is concentrated Romance." (P. 146.)

A very different judgment is Mr. Stopford Brooke's, in 1902.[3] He finds the "lying" of Constance "unendurable"; and her self-sacrifice, "supposed by some to be noble, done in pity for the Queen," he takes to be not that but "more like jealousy."

No one, I suppose, believes her motive is wholly pity; it is, much more, love for Norbert, which stands steadfast when the Queen comes to her for confirmation; yet to this critic himself "Constance, even as a study of jealousy," is quite unsatisfactory. "The situations she causes are almost too ugly." Her lying is to be explained or excused "only by the madness of jealousy, and she, though jealous, is not maddened enough by jealousy to excuse her lies." And "jealousy has," he acknowledges, "none of these labyrinthine methods; it goes straight with fiery passion to its end. . . . But it may be a study by Browning of what he thought in his intellect jealousy would be. At any rate Constance, as a study of self-sacrifice, is a miserable failure. Moreover, it does not make much matter whether she is a study of this or that, because she is eminently wrong-natured." And presently he roundly declares her "radically false," and though Norbert is "radically true," is of the opinion that after their momentary outburst of love at the end "nothing could be better for them both than death."

In general, Brooke is not by any means the equal of Symons or of Herford as a critic; and at this point, where not only the others agree but also Browning himself, with whom, as Mr. De Vane says, the poem was a favorite, Brooke might almost be ruled out of court. But in aesthetic matters, as not in the scientific, the opinion of the humblest (and Brooke is of course not that), if it is considered an honest opinion (and Brooke's is surely that), deserves attention. A poem, obviously, like any other work of art, depends for its value, as for its meaning, upon the purpose of the

[3]*Poetry of Robert Browning* (Crowell, N. Y.), pp. 340–43.

artist, but also, and as much, upon its effect. And that is not merely the effect produced in the highest circles.

Why, then, is not the word of Brooke, who is possibly nearer to the common man, for whom, as Wordsworth and other poets loyally say, the poet writes, as good as that of Symons and Herford? For several reasons it is not.

First and foremost, Brooke has not at the outset yielded himself frankly and freely to the spell, as the common man, reader or spectator, either, would do. *Laissons-nous aller de bonne foi,* Molière begs us, *aux choses qui nous prennent par les entrailles.* If the critic had responded generously and adequately to the situation between Constance and the Queen after the latter gets the news, he would have found the justifications for the violations of probability, the answers to his troubled questions.

Second, the critic does not realize, or else not remember, that not only here but in general, as in the *Oedipus* and *Othello,* improbability, at the outset, is the inescapable price of the supreme situation; that, as Corneille says, the great subjects go beyond the probable. This does not mean the mere "marvelous" of the Renaissance critics—incidents or achievements that are beyond the range of experience— but passions that are. As I have said elsewhere, "Even if life were different, and itself afforded such good situations as those of ancient myth or poetic invention, still it would not do. In great drama they would therefore have to be better, that is (again) improbable—though not *within* the drama, of course, even as such situations in great drama, are not now."[4] If not big, and (though probably) improbable, who cares to see or read them?

Third, the critic does not sufficiently value the principle of Aristotle, fully confirmed by poetic practice, that plot or situation comes first in importance, not characterization— the play of passion on the stage or in the story, which rouses the emotions in the audience, not truth to life in either character or circumstance, which satisfies their intellects.

That is, the critic is wrong not because he is wanting in

[4] *Art and Artifice in Shakespeare* (1938), p. 163.

delicacy of discernment but because he is confined within a formula—realistic, psychological, and moral. The improbable—the conventions or presuppositions—he fails to recognize as the price paid for a bigger, higher effect than the probable, as the approach made to a world of passions beyond the probable; and though with far less fidelity to the text, he, like Mr. Arlo Bates, who thinks Constance is learning a lesson in love, endeavors to do away with them, to psychologize them. He cannot then enter into the passions, for in his own person he has not paid the price and lacks the warrant. His expectations and prejudices interfere with the natural, emotional response to them, and he does not bear in mind the critical principles by which they would be neutralized. In fact, if he were not troubled by the expectations and prejudices, he would not have much need of the corrective principles, would readily grant the improbable presuppositions and take instinctively to the auspicious method of approach. "Poetry," the late illustrious W. P. Ker observed, and in an essay on this same poet, "is its own interpretation." "The best one can do," he adds, "and it is no dishonourable office, is to get the right point of view, to praise in the right way."[5]

Little praising, as is apparent above, has Brooke done here, whether rightly or wrongly; and as I cannot but think, he has not got the right point of view. He has not appreciated—that is, not responded to—the poetic or dramatic power brought to bear; nor has he comprehended the author's meaning or purpose. The tragic tension of the colloquy between Constance and the Queen and the exaltation of the lovers when their pretenses are abandoned and their fate is upon them, leave him cold; and the charming impulsiveness of Constance and the haggard passionateness of the Queen do not convince him of their reality. Instead of praising he has done what Molière thereupon begs us *not* to do: *ne cherchons point de raisonnements pour nous empêcher d'avoir du plaisir.* Indeed, revolted by the duplicity and moved to incredulity by the self-sacrifice, he

[5]*Collected Essays* (1925), i, 277-78.

does what no reader and still less any critic should do, goes behind the returns—questions the word of the author as if the characters were real people, not fiction—to discover a new motive, of which in the text, where alone their whole existence lies, there is not the slightest inkling. Bates has some basis for his theory: Constance has learned at least to know Norbert better when, near the end, she murmurs, half to herself,

> . . . as if you were a man.
> Tempting him with a crown!

But it is contrary to all the evidence that she should have been sounding either him or the Queen. In which case her duplicity would be even greater, for then she would have been deceiving Norbert too! Generosity that really is jealousy? In life that is to be found, no doubt; but the fact does not now concern us unless this is of such sort here in the play. Brooke is yielding to the present-day critic's taste for the paradoxical, or else for the subconscious, whether it is in the play or not. And nevertheless, in vain! For from the above it is sufficiently apparent that with his hypothesis the critic is dissatisfied himself.

Not that the fragmentary tragedy under discussion keeps up, in between, to the high level of the Queen's colloquy with Constance and that of Constance with Norbert at the close. There is a further improbability (though a heightened tension) in Norbert's not realizing the situation—the peril—they are in when he re-enters; and there is too much philosophy or morality on his lips and too much ingenuity on hers, both before they kiss farewell (in which business they are caught by the Queen) and after. Nor is it that as a whole the little tragedy is quite popular, immediately effective, like Shakespeare in his own time, or is meant for the "unaccommodated man," however "common." Browning is here, as elsewhere, now and then a little difficult or esoteric. The main trouble, to be sure, is that our spectators or readers are, like Brooke, so realistic and psychological in taste or bent that the ancient dramatic conventions of persuasion and deception are not now so acceptable as in Shakespeare's

day; though this flattering sort, practiced upon a love-
hungry woman, is inherently much more plausible than
that upon Othello. Even the "presuppositions" that Mr.
Herford notices are not made so clear and conspicuous as
some readers or spectators would require. That function
of the courtier as a lover, expounded in Castiglione, and
that fiction of the statesman as in love with the Queen
(marrying a substitute only by her permission), exemplified
at the court of Elizabeth, are matters now more familiar
to the learned. And so with the duplicity. It would offend
others, no doubt, than Brooke (though perhaps less deeply);
but not the readers of ancient, medieval, and Renaissance
poetry, where love and pity, as here they do, conspire.

With many a reader, nevertheless, and far more with the
spectator, love and pity, without any erudition, would suffice. To the spectator, yielding, as he should do, to the main
dramatic current, to the charm to which Norbert himself
here yields, even Constance's "unloverlike" taking of such
chances would not give offense. Considerations which are
not suggested to the audience, says Mr. Courtney of drama
in general, are considerations which do not exist for them.
Spectators live more in the moment, under the spell (if
there is one) of the dramatist and the action, and, so far,
are almost as frankly and unreservedly receptive as hearers
or readers in medieval times, when in fiction such self-
sacrifice by either sex was common. There is the story of
the maiden who offered her life's blood to save the leper,
finely dramatized since Browning's day by Hauptmann;
there is the story of Gisippus in Boccaccio (as of Valentine
in *The Two Gentlemen of Verona*) who gives up his betrothed out of devotion to his friend.[6] All three are, like
the patient Griselda story, examples of the medieval carrying of a virtue to extremes; but the invention is similar to
that in the legend of Faustus or in ancient myths like those
of Oedipus, Orestes, and Prometheus, producing material
for drama, not for psychology. Here, to be sure, it is the
men that, to us, upon reflection, seem unloverlike; but is

[6] Cf. Professor W. W. Lawrence's *Shakespeare's Problem Comedies,* pp. 23–24, etc.

not Norbert so as well, in taking up, however unwillingly, with Constance's proposal? And is not Der Arme Heinrich? His chief advantage with the spectator, like that of a Faust, or an Oedipus or a Phaedra, lies in the familiarity of the improbable story. Not to cavil or call in question would the audience, thus attracted, be sitting there.

Nor, even in this unfamiliar story, would the duplicity give the ordinary spectator offense. Indeed, on psychological grounds the dramatist has somewhat provided against that. Near the outset—the proper place—he has reinforced the presupposition that the minister may be serving the Queen for love of her by letting Constance insist upon a distinction between the sexes, founded in fact—"women hate a debt as men a gift"—and upon the superior wisdom of the women. In other words, women hate to pay; they want to give. Men hate to receive; they want to earn, deserve. Women feel the debt, but would pay it without seeming to do so, generously, beyond the bond. "I owe that withered woman everything," Constance avers; yet, in the same breath, she would have it that the tactful way is the sole way not only to keep the Queen's favor but also to win her permission.

This proceeding, then, has some warrant both in nature and also in expediency, or enough for the premise to a play. In any case, this lying, tragic in outcome, is magnanimous, is meant to bring happiness—"Love, she is generous!" Constance mistakenly cries—to all three concerned. "Just," as a man is, she apparently does not think her; and this is to be a compliment—though regrettably similar to most of the compliments we give, if not receive. Constance herself has no qualms, nor has Norbert, despite his own truthfulness and straightforwardness. At no time has he such a feeling as Brooke, that life with such a woman would be impossible—"a fatal split inevitable." Her duplicity, like her unloverlike treatment of love, is, though more prominent than his, overshadowed by her daring, her gallantry beforehand and her gameness afterwards. And the spectators, swept on by the action, by the passion, would remember only—and not then halt like a Hegel, to weigh the value of them in the scale of eternal justice—the devotion and the pity, however mistaken. Her love, as Symons says, we cannot doubt. She is alive, and even for that reason also in her conduct convincing—alive by her perceptibly individual accent; and at no time is she so convincing as when she shows her love:

> Oh my heart's heart,
> How I do love you, Norbert! That is right.
> But listen, or I take my hands away!
> You say, "Let it be now"; you could go now
> And tell the Queen, perhaps six steps from us,
> You love me—so you do, thank God!

Thus, surely, our doubts should be forestalled; and if any arise out of the recklessness of the venture, by her ecstasy at the recovery of what has been abandoned—they are scattered. Now, as before this, with the Queen alone, she is no longer ingenious, but reduced to the simplicity of outcry and repetition.

> Con. Feel my heart, let it die against your own!
> Nor. Against my own. Explain not; let this be.
>   This is life's height.
> Con.   Yours, yours, yours!
> Nor.   You and I—
>   Why care by what meanders we are here
>   I' the centre of the labyrinth? Men have died
>   Trying to find this place, which we have found.
> Con. Found, found.

For it is even to reach the labyrinth—to achieve the big situation, with its ironical contrasts and tumultuous passions—that the improbabilities are incurred; and it is by the preliminary impact of these, together with the convincing individuality and fascination of the characters, in their speech rather than in any psychology, that we are reconciled to them. And if, in this age of realism, the two great contemporaries, Dickens and Balzac, draw, as Saintsbury says, "with unerring faithfulness" the characters which they have themselves created, not imitated, how much truer is that of their still greater contemporary! For he has at command also another, a readier, still more time-honored, means of access to the passions, beyond the *vraisemblable,* —and what but poetry?

When that fails, the situation suffers. Yet no one, so far as I am aware, has objected to the very last word of the play, on the lady's lips:

> Con.   There's the music stopped.
>   What measured heavy tread? It is one blaze
>   About me and within me.
> Nor.   Oh, some death
>   Will run its sudden finger round this spark,
>   And sever us from the rest!
> Con.   And so do well.
>   Now the doors open—
> Nor.   'Tis the guard comes.
> Con.   Kiss!

In itself the word sounds flat and prosy; indeed, it is too much by itself, alone. By the phrase "And so do well" it is a little supported and enriched; and no doubt Browning would have us now remember that farewell kiss which betrayed them to (and saved them from) the Queen. That meant separation; this means—no less!—reunion. My ear, however, misses that meaning in its fullness, the appropriate passionate, tragic depth of tone. Elsewhere, at the important moments, it does not. For though a psychologist and (in goodly measure) a realist, and also a forerunner of the verse of today, Browning was decidedly something more and better. And "all poetry," he once wrote to Ruskin, is the problem of "putting the infinite into the finite." He certainly then had in mind details such as are here in question; yet, pretty certainly, also larger matters, the situation and the total structure. He must himself have known that he began with an improbability, and (however little he may have paused to consider the question) known why. For he was a poet, not unlike the greatest. Far less than any novelist did he imitate, reproduce.

1942

CHAPTER XVIII

Psychoanalysis in Criticism: Dickens, Kipling, Joyce

We may take it as settled that one virtue of style is perspicuity . . . our speech unless it makes its meaning clear will fail to perform its proper function.

ARISTOTLE, *Rhet.* III, ii.

I have sometimes thought that the most acute and original-minded men made bad critics. They see everything too much through a particular medium.

HAZLITT, *On Criticism.*

In a very real sense, what is wanted is the simple critic, who would be in truth the most subtle critic.

CHESTERTON, *Fancies versus Fads.*

FREUDIAN PSYCHOANALYSIS frequently—if indeed not always—is ill advised as it takes to literary criticism. That is true, whether the author or his characters are the subject, though particularly when the latter; and still truer when the literature belongs to earlier times. This is not so much

339

—though that is enough!—because the author himself, his scientific contemporaries, or his unscientific public had not heard the bad tidings out of Vienna. It is rather because the critic, knowing so little of the author's life and inner nature, necessarily falls back upon his artistic work, which is, of course, not fact but fiction; and, in the second place, because in those earlier times, indeed pretty far into the eighteenth century, the character, in both drama and novel, was often not the only or indeed the principal source of the action. The hero or heroine, swayed by fate or trapped by a villain's guile, seldom brought low merely by a "tragic fault" within, kept, and was intended to keep, at least the sympathy, if not also the admiration, of spectator or reader. Even in more recent great work—Hardy's and Stendhal's, as I show in chapter XI—the situation, its emotional effect, is, now and then, the primary consideration. And as for the other matter, however much we may know of the writer's life and inner nature, *il n'y a que des rapports incertains,* as Gourmont observes, *entre la vie d'un homme et son oeuvre, entre sa conduite et celle qu'il impose à ses personnages.* Often like dreams, the writing "goes by contraries," as with the glorification of the practical man by Kipling, noticed below, or of the adventurous by Scott and Stevenson.

As an example of Freud's influence on criticism I am taking not the worst but, as far as I know, one of the best of his disciples, and one of the most reputable critics in America. Three or four reviewers of his latest book, *The Wound and the Bow,* have said as much as that or more; one of them even congratulating him upon his knowledge of psychoanalysis as to criticism nowadays (a commentary on both that and our art!) indispensable. It may therefore seem indispensable to the criticism of his criticism; but I hope I know at least enough about it to suggest that here or there in literary work it has no rightful place, and with all the better warrant now that it no longer has so much of a place as it had in psychology.

Since Mr. Wilson is learned, and reads Greek, as most American critics nowadays, apparently, do not, we may

begin with him even at the Freudian beginning, with Oedipus (supposed to have the complex now named for him)
and Sophocles. After German philosophy had done its work
with tragedy—with Sophocles and Shakespeare—German
psychology necessarily took its turn; and however it may be
with him in Shakespeare, in Sophocles Mr. Wilson seems
to be under the influence of both. On his philosophy I
cannot dwell—the idea that in the *Philoctetes* "genius and
disease, strength and mutilation, may be inextricably bound
up together," and that consequently the bow would be
useless to the Greeks without the owner.[1] The old story provides both a title for the book and a connecting thread for
the studies, ancient and modern; and (quite remarkably)
support for the Freudian's idea "that works of art are born
out of a conflict in the writer himself, due perhaps to some
painful experience in early youth, which haunts him, even
when he thinks he forgets it."[2] I can, however, find no
basis for either the philosophical or the psychoanalytic conceptions in this tragedy of Sophocles or, indeed, in any
other. Here, as elsewhere in Sophocles, it is as Goethe said,
a good dramatic situation that the dramatist found all
ready, an opportunity for debate and the passions: if Philoctetes were not needed as well as his bow, and had not to be
powerfully persuaded, there would be—would have been—
no drama.

In the *Oedipus Tyrannus,* on the other hand, it is, for
Mr. Wilson, a matter of psychoanalysis only, according to
and directly after Freud. The present King of Thebes, the
reader will remember, had, in endeavoring to escape the
fulfillment of the oracle that he was to kill his father and
marry his mother, unwittingly done both, and is now fear-
fully facing the disclosure. Mr. Wilson judges that Freud
has named the complex properly, since Sophocles had not

[1] *The Wound and the Bow* (1941), pp. 289, 294. Quotations are
by permission of Messrs. Houghton, Mifflin & Co., Boston. The
quotation from Chesterton at the head of the chapter is by permission of the publishers, Dodd, Mead & Company, Inc.

[2] Desmond MacCarthy, review of Mr. Wilson, Sunday *Times,*
March 29, 1942.

only dramatized the legend "but had exhibited the suppressed impulse behind it in the speech by which he makes Jocasta [his consort] attempt to reassure Oedipus," telling him that it was not uncommon for men to dream about sleeping with their mothers (p. 290). And the critic proceeds to show how elsewhere, in Electra and Antigone, Sophocles presents "abnormal" character and conduct.

Neither Wilson nor Freud, who quotes Jocasta before him, sees that her words import only the insignificance of such dreaming, both in her own opinion and very probably in the dramatist's, though at a time when dreams less common meant, in story at least, almost as much as oracles. Certainly—for the King and the Queen, the dramatist and the audience alike—they meant nothing psychological. At this point, as the context shows, she and her foundling husband both are thinking of his mother as the Queen of Corinth, without suspicion of Jocasta herself; she is only poohpoohing his fears; and that with either matter—incest of any dreamer with his mother or of Oedipus with his own—there should be involved a suppressed impulse or repressed desire is a notion as remote from the mind of either character, and also of the dramatist, as the pole. A desire? If but for dramatic reasons only—for the very situation—there must be none. This is one of the biggest situations, and sharpest contrasts, in all tragedy; and its effect in the theater even today, and in the reading as well, is due to the passions developed in the gradual disclosure, the unmitigated terror or horror and the unhesitating pity produced both on the stage and in the house. For Freud, indeed, who thinks this is not like other tragedies of fate (and certainly in his hands it isn't) the effect is owing to the fact that

. . . the oracle laid upon us before our birth the very curse which rested upon him. It may be that we were all destined to direct our first sexual impulses toward our mothers, our first impulses of hatred and violence toward our own fathers; our dreams convince us that we were.[3]

[3]*Interpretation of Dreams* (1933), p. 255.

Not all of us, in fact or conviction, either, though this notion that consciously or unconsciously most sons hate their fathers and most daughters their mothers infects our present-day criticism; and after reading a passage like that, or what Freud says of Hamlet[4] and of the Mona Lisa, one wonders at his reputation, and wishes, at any rate, he had kept his hands off literature and art. Like most psychologists, historians and sociologists, but worse than most of them, he treats either as a document or exhibit. In the first place, what is the point of the psychoanalyst if Oedipus, under the sway of the complex, the impulse to love and marry his mother and to hate and kill his father, thereupon marries or kills, as he does, a person whom he takes for an utter stranger, killing the man before seeing the woman and not knowing before or after the marrying that she was his mother, he his father, she the dead man's wife? And in the second place, if the complex, or the tendency, is in all of us, how, then, in the drama can the right tragic effect of terror (or horror) and pity be produced? The sympathy, indeed, might then be not much impaired; but the terror and admiration would be. By the secret or unconscious inclination—by a psychological problem—the situation would be unduly troubled and complicated; and that, as Sophocles or any other Greek conceived it, is one of perfect innocence, to make an acute and total contrast,—the just and high-minded hero fleeing from his destiny, from both father and mother, *not* (like one with a complex) meeting and (though in horror) embracing it. It is the moderns, as we saw in chapter XVI, that go in for paradoxes. The whole point of the tragedy is that in ignorance he both

[4]"Hamlet is able to do anything but take vengeance upon the man who did away with his father and has taken his father's place with his mother—the man who shows him in realization the repressed desires of his own childhood." (P. 258.) Various others have taken up this (to me) utterly preposterous notion of Hamlet's identifying himself with his uncle and echoing the treachery within himself. (Cf. Miss Bodkin, *Archetypal Patterns* [1934], p. 12, f.) As for the Mona Lisa, the analyst reconstructs not only the painter's sexual aspirations and frustrations but (of course) his mother's.

kills and marries,—and by that very fact there is no evidence that he has a "complex" at all.[5]

Treating Sophocles as he does, Mr. Wilson, were he to take up Shakespeare, would surely approach his characters in the same "clinical" or detective rather than emotional and poetical fashion; and like too many nowadays, would apply also to them the Freudian psychology, or else the Elizabethan doctrine of humors, in any case discover a "tragic fault," with similar damage to the effect. In discussing the *Antigone*,[6] as he complains of the "new humanists" and their ethical philosophizings, for which they think to find support in Sophocles, he says something that, like the Shakespeareans, he too little himself remembers in dealing with that play and the *Oedipus* and the *Electra* as well. "Sophocles is essentially a dramatist." Yes, and obviously—even superficially—one, or else, indeed, but a poor one. "It seems to me plain," he however in all soberness declares, "that in Antigone Sophocles was consciously presenting a case of what we should call nowadays a brother-fixation." An obsession, this desire of hers to secure the repose of her brother's spirit! That is, here is more of Freudian psychology, and so much the less, therefore, of tragedy. (Which, particularly the Hellenic, is "simple, sensuous, and passionate," and has little to do with psychology of any sort.) Thus she becomes a figure of curious interest, not of reverent and passionate; and that is really for comedy. As Sophocles conceives her, and as any attentive audience, even at present, would understand her, she has chosen, tragically, to obey the laws of heaven and of her own heart rather than the dictates of the King, who would leave her brother's body to the fowls of the air. For the Greeks the burial rites were as much of a sacred duty as (including confession

[5] Since finishing the chapter I have found Chesterton saying the same: "It was the whole point of Oedipus that he did not have the Oedipus complex." (*Come to Think of It*, Dodd, Mead & Co., N. Y., 1931, p. 62.) Many others, not psychologists, must have said or thought it. "Nobody familiar with the Greek play would ever have used that Greek parallel"—but here Chesterton's memory betrays him.

[6] The *New Republic*, December 3, 1930, pp. 69-70.

and absolution) for the Catholics ever since. And she has chosen sisterly love and piety, though at the cost of death, unwedded. Is all heroism now "abnormal," a fixation or a complex, or some other equivalent "psychological disorder," and tragedy the transcript of it, all genius bound up with disease? To Mr. Wilson, as to many other critics nowadays, nearly every leading character, every notable author, is a "case"; for which, however, there is a diagnosis.

Mother, brother, and (for Electra) a father, each the object of a perverted passion! Yet for some reason Mr. Wilson eschews the Electra-complex, though apparently accepted as the feminine equivalent by Freud. Perhaps a little to lighten, or vary, the Atlantean burden of morbidity upon the prehistoric Theban and Mycenaean families and the Sophoclean text, he calls the daughter "schizophrenic" (split personality) instead.[7] (For always it is something wrong with hero or heroine, not the villains or the world!) Schizophrenic, for she can both weep over the urn supposed to contain her brother's ashes and also prepare for the murder of their mother! But the mother had killed their father and rejoiced at the reported death of Orestes himself. Vengeance upon her is the daughter's duty and desire, as the burial is Antigone's, though not, like that, forbidden by the ruler; and what is "abnormal" here, as there and in the *Oedipus,*—as for that matter, in a Shakespearean tragedy—lies in the situation, not the character.[8] There is certainly no disease, no want of balance, either; but, though not a clash with authority (or fate) as in Antigone, there is a contrast—that the good daughter should thirst for her mother's blood. And a contrast with Orestes, who does—yet abhors to do—the killing; but since that is of his mother, not a Freudian father, his skirts are clear, the Oedipus question cannot be raised—no analysis is attempted.—Let us pass on, however, to stories and situations nearer our

[7] *The Wound and the Bow* (1941), p. 291.

[8] Cf. W. H. Auden, the modernist poet (whose opinion Mr. Wilson would respect, as not that of Jebb or other Victorian classicists), *Commonsense,* March, 1941, "Joyce and Wagner."

own day and doings, or to the authors whose lives or inner natures are supposed to explain them.

2

In Dickens and Kipling both, according to the Freudian formula, their boyhood is all-important,—the debtors' prison where Dickens' father lay and the blacking-factory where the boy worked, in the one case, and the rigorous and narrow-minded relatives with whom Kipling and his sister lived, in the other. And no doubt these "painful experiences" did leave their mark upon both the man and his writing, though whether so deep or (to our fallible eyes) so discernible the reader must judge. As indeed most of us do, Mr. Wilson discovers what he was looking for; and Sophocles, for us all, had no boyhood.

Because of his past and his poverty, Dickens is, for Mr. Wilson, a sort of Ishmaelite in the Victorian world: by his interest in villainy (which, however, is not explained, and by his conjugal difficulties, which are not, either) he is doubly so; and here the Freudian psychology is again at work, though more apparently in the novelist's latter days. His public readings of Bill Sikes's murder of Nancy are an example. "Dickens obviously derived from thus horrifying his hearers some sort of satisfaction." (P. 95.) A sort of sadism, it would appear; and "the scene was perhaps a symbolical representation [Freudian phrase!] of his behavior in banishing his wife." This is rather extraordinary, even with the "perhaps" and for all that we nowadays see in the newspapers about "mental cruelty." May not his "satisfaction" have been no more than that of most successful readers or actors, in the biggest response he got? In any case, Mr. Wilson dwells unduly on the reading as "an obsessive hallucination," for Dickens was now no longer quite himself. The performances began in October, 1868; in June, 1870 he died.

Likewise the critic makes too much of *Edwin Drood,* the "sinister" detective story, his last and unfinished work. Cut off, now, from society by his separation from his wife and his taking up with Ellen Ternan, Dickens "has discarded the theme of the rebel and is carrying the theme of the criminal . . . to its logical development." The choirmaster who murders his nephew is, according to the Freudian formula again, the author in disguise. An artist, smoking opium, he leads a life of imagination apart from men. Is he a villain too?

. . . All that sentiment, all those edifying high spirits, which Dickens has been dispensing so long, . . . has all this now grown as false as those hymns to the glory of the Christian God which are performed by the worshiper of Kali? . . . But it will not be the innocent Pickwick [etc.] whom we are now to meet in jail; nor yet the wicked Fagin, Dennis, or Rudge. It will be a man who is both innocent and wicked [paradoxes again!] . . . the old hierarchy of England . . . has made him accept the ruling that he is a creature irretrievably tainted; and the mercantile middle-class England has had its triumph, too. For the Victorian hypocrite has developed—from Pecksniff, through Murdstone, through Headstone, to his final transformation in Jasper— . . . into an insoluble moral problem which is identified with Dickens' own. (Pp. 101-3.)

Like "symbolical," "identified" is a Freudian word. "When Jasper announces . . . that he devotes himself to the destruction of the murderer he is preparing for his own execution . . . So Dickens, in putting his nerves to the torture by enacting the murder of Nancy . . . has been invoking his own death." (P. 103.) Did he, then, want to die? Did he think himself hypocritical or tainted?

From a social outcast—the Marshalsea and the blacking!—to the moral! And still it is the social! How Dickens himself and this temporal "hierarchy" get into the story, is beyond my understanding; and most Freudian identifications, as we shall see, are more complimentary to the self involved.

3

Mr. Wilson's treatment of Kipling is not so Freudian, but still clinical, if fictional is not a better word. "Baa, baa, black sheep" the critic rightly considers a reminiscence, in perceptible measure, of the boy's experience, from six years old to twelve, in the household at Southsea; but to this childish resentment against Puritanical petty tyranny he attributes the mature Kipling's "ferocious antagonism" (as he calls it) against democracy. (P. 143.) The author's sister says that at this period he was in the habit of keeping up their spirits by "reminding himself and her that their guardian was of such low caste as not to matter." She was a relative of his father's: the word "caste," as well as the nickname for her of Kuch-nay, Nothing-at-all, seems only to be an echo from India. At any rate, one's social and political philosophy is hardly determined so early. Kipling's sister, Mr. Wilson notices, denies that the ordeal "produced in him any permanent injurious effects." (P. 110.) If, however, there were any, and this child must be father to the man, I should think the ferocious antagonism would quite as probably have been directed against tyranny, or aristocracy, instead.

Of Kipling's caste, family, or heredity, Mr. Wilson seems to be much more conscious than Kipling himself; which, of course, might well be the case, yet, without much evidence, he again makes use of the consciousness in opposite directions. As we have seen already and are still to see, this literary critic has a determined sociological and political as well as psychological bent; but what is to be made of the following analysis? Kipling's "want of faith in the artist's vocation" and his dedication of his "talents to the praise of the practical man" Mr. Wilson would attribute to "something vulgar in him, in the middle-class British way [the American intellectual radical must step warily here!] perhaps connected with the Methodist ministers who were his grandfathers on both sides." (P. 151.) And yet there is the "ferocious antagonism"; and earlier (pp. 118–19), the fact is mentioned that his father being a painter and sculptor and his mother's sisters having married two celebrated painters, Poynter and Burne-Jones, he was under artistic influences from an early age. Moreover, at school, he quotes Mr. Beresford as saying, "Kipling's attitude had been that of an esthete who disdains athletics and has no aptitude for mechanical matters" (p. 119)—he who wrote the "Bridge-Builders" and *M'Andrew's Hymn!* Also Mr. Beresford says that he could do nothing with his hands but write. The critic himself has heard of Kipling's admiration for a friend who managed to put a detached castor back under a chair. (P. 156.) Now his acknowledged artistic mastery of mechanical matters—"new rhythms, new colors and textures of words, for things that have not yet been brought into literature." (P. 157)—Mr. Wilson attributes partly to "pure virtuosity." That is, Kipling had an imagination, and got the subject up. Is not, then, his praise of the practical man, together with his delighted presentation of him and of all sorts of rough and active life, quite in keeping with this? *Tout écrivain se récompense comme il peut de quelque injure du sort,* says M. Valéry. *Comme tous les artistes, Byron et Shelley ne créaient que pour consoler de ne pouvoir vivre,* says M. Maurois. That, surely, is psychological enough, without further complication. Why, when the lad was already so impractical and aesthetical, and perhaps aristocratical too, drag in Methodist grandfathers and middle-class vulgarity?

Not even in the presentation of passion and suffering does Mr. Wilson allow the story-writer's imagination autonomy. He thinks that Kipling's pictures of suffering undeserved, and perhaps those of "obsessive horror with a sense of guilt," also have their origin in the childish experience at Southsea. Southsea is another Marshalsea, and more. "The only cases in which the obsessive horror is connected with any kind of guilt arc those in which a man is hounded to death by the vision of a woman he has wronged." (P. 166.) At this point, however, the critic hesitates, and his candor is disarming. Of this theme of betrayal he admits that "we do not know enough about his life" to connect it with a notion of the six-year-old boy that he had sinned against his mother; though it "has the appearance of having been derived from a morbid permanent feeling in injury inflicted by his experience at Southsea." Evidently, the critic would be better satisfied could he say a little more, but he doesn't.[9]

Would that analyst or biographer could oftener thus stay his hand! Imagine the Shakespearean if at Stratford or in the City something could be raked up to explain his "ferocious antagonism" against democracy—the Sir Thomas Lucy experience would, like the Southsea, point the other way!—or his interest in villainy! Or if it could be discovered that in his latter days he had been given to reading some of his murder scenes, which abound! Or that he too had had a boyhood, and a father to hate, a mother unduly to love! For the myth-makers need some basis, however slender, to work upon; such as has been lately found in Donne, who had a stepfather that he never mentioned and "whose misogyny may be sprung from his perverted love for his mother" and whose handwriting, moreover, "gives a hint of homosexual tendencies."[10]

4

Also Mr. Wilson, as he was predestined to do, has written of Joyce. Here indeed (though like the other critics, to be sure) he does stay his hand: Joyce is not the subject but the practitioner of psychoanalysis. Yet I see no reason in his

[9] In *The Intent of the Critic* (Princeton, 1941) Mr. Wilson writes as follows of *The Ordeal of Mark Twain:* "in which Brooks uses an incident of Mark Twain's boyhood as a key to his whole career. . . . He has himself since repudiated the general method on the ground that nobody but an analyst can ever know enough. . . . (P. 55.) Nevertheless, after acknowledging "the bad results" Mr. Wilson is of the opinion that "Brooks had hold of something."

Psychoanalysis has a devastating effect upon both analyzed and analyst. (The two Danubians, what they have done to the world!) In this same book (p. 104) Mr. J. C. Ransom speaks approvingly of Dr. Hanns Sachs, Freud's successor. In a row of slot machines which exhibited female nudity, one was neglected by the curious males, and that turned out to be the Venus of Medici. It was because she was beautiful, Dr. Sachs inferred; not, as any of the uninitiate would have done, because she was but marble instead of flesh and blood.

[10] *Times Literary Supplement,* March 27, 1943, p. 154.

case for reversing the process, unless it be simply that, like his critics, the writer himself was of the Vanguard. That, and his having a wife and children: otherwise, how he would have been pounced upon as a specimen of suppressed impulses or repressed desires and the consequent mental disorder! According to the Freudians, "Man sexualizes the universe";[11] certainly they themselves do; and yet no repressed or perverted celibate writer we know of has gone nearly so far as Joyce in that direction. Nearly every page bears the mark of it, and not the normal sexuality only but the aberrations as well. Nor is that all. His thought and narrative methods, his diction and imagery, closely resemble what of this we find in dreams and the similar states of waking fantasy or of lunacy. Here, for once, the Freudian (if he will take it) has full warrant; and in this case, I think, it is with some knowledge of psychoanalysis, but as applied to both writing and writer, that the book should be read. "The result is what the surrealists appear to aim at," says one reviewer, "an uprush of words or images from the subconscious imagination." That phenomenon is a mystery, or, rather a myth; and as easily to be refused credence as given. In any case Joyce spent sixteen or seventeen years on *Finnegans Wake* (and 1,600 hours on the episode *Anna Livia Plurabelle*), pertinaciously rewriting and complicating it. He was far from spontaneous, was conscious enough.

In part, certainly, this disorder is positively intentional. In *Finnegan* and to some degree even in *Ulysses* Joyce is presenting the dream state, or reverie, or drunken hallucination: and when not doing any of these, he is, as he tells his story from the leading character's point of view, still presenting, as immediately as may be, the uncontrolled and irresponsible flux and current, ebb and flow, of consciousness. But why, then, should the presentation and expression be not only irresponsible but nearly unintelligible, and not merely in part but in the whole? Books that deal with dreams should not be as formless, as incoherent and unintelligible as dreams. Cicero's, Bunyan's, De Quincey's aren't

[11] A. A. Brill, *Psychoanalysis* (1922), p. 117; quoting Kleinpaul.

nor (just as writings which deal with low life should not be, either the dialogue or the text, what Joyce's also are) in baffling dialect or *argot;* and even the direct discourse there, as good critics, like good writers, recognize, should only suggest the dialect or argot,—carry, as Sir Arthur Quiller-Couch says, the rhythm and the lilt, something of the word-order and the cast of phrasing, but little of the actually appropriate but generally incomprehensible vocabulary. The author of *Kubla Khan* himself observes that "a poem may in one sense be a dream but it must be a waking dream." For the first end of a writer is, as Dryden declared (though Aristotle and Jonson said it before him, and if less roundly, Addison, Wordsworth, Arnold, Sir Arthur, and no doubt many another after him) "to be understood";[12] and surely the world is not totally or irrecoverably different today, if the writers are. "The chief virtue of a style," Ben asserted, "is perspicuity, and nothing so vicious in it, as to need an Interpreter." And the second is to interest, to please or arouse. Indeed, if not to be understood, why write? If not understanding, how be pleased; or if inclined to riddles, how can one, as by poetry or other fine art one is supposed to be, be imaginatively and emotionally excited? The description or representation of "disintegration" or chaos must not itself be "disintegrated" or chaotic, nor of what is dull, tiresome, or disgusting, itself be dull, tiresome, or disgusting. Such unpleasant qualities should be only intimated. But in *Ulysses,* and still more in *Finnegan,* they are not: there is no curb put upon the leading character's consciousness (or unconsciousness) just as there is none upon his conduct, and little discernible direction given to it. And (which is worse) no curb upon the expression of it, but positive misleading given instead. The fetters (which really are the instruments) of expression—grammar,

[12]Quoted, against the "new poets," by Max Eastman, *The Literary Mind* (1931), p. 49. Page 93, he remarks upon Hart Crane's *The Bridge,* acclaimed by critics as one of the greatest poems of our generation, while they incidentally acknowledge that "they do not know what the poet is talking about." Another poem begins with a quotation in Latin. Asked what it meant, Crane replied: "I don't know what it means: I don't understand the language at all."

sentence-structure, punctuation, idiom and accepted word-order, the very words themselves in their associations as we have known them—are repeatedly, even continually, tossed aside; and coinages, distortions, and conjunctive (or disjunctive) malformations run riot, often beyond the speaking (or thinking) character's conceivable range. Not seldom the associations admitted are Joyce's own private property or experience, mystifying and confusing to almost any reader; and even to the learned one the accumulated literary and historical allusions, whether in character or not, and the words in divers tongues mingled or monstrously merged with the English, are, if decipherable, far from a pleasure. The creator now and then seems to be dreaming, or raving, as wildly and irresponsibly as his creatures are.

The mere fact of Joyce's predilection for the dream-state or fantasy should, in other circumstances, be enough to bring the psychoanalysts in swarms down upon him; but as Mr. Wilson himself notices, that is characteristic of the Symbolist school, to which Joyce in part belongs, and in Joyce I think it is mainly out of a desire to have scope for his own lawless and freakish bent. Certainly Freud in his *Interpretation of Dreams*[13] furnishes a very Joyce-like vocabulary from not only the psychopathic cases but also the normal. *Uclamparia,* for instance, which = eucalyptus + malaria; for the patient had been at a monastery in Italy and drunk of a liqueur made of the eucalyptus, planted there to overcome the disease. This is like the (of course) quite normal and wideawake but highly facetious Disraeli's "anecdotage" as incident to old age, and like the Christmas season as the "alcoholidays" which Brill[14] had read of in a short story; both, though used consciously, being in the style of the dreaming Finnegan's (or Earwicker's) "alcoherently." Such "condensations," as they are called, or portmanteau words, are represented to be characteristic

[13] (1933) pp. 285–89.

[14] *Psychoanalysis* (1922), p. 401. *Finnegans Wake* (Faber & Faber, London, n.d.), p. 40. This is cited hereafter by page numbers in the text.

of dreams: in these, as Freud says, "words are often treated as things, and therefore undergo the same combinations as the ideas of things"; and Brill tells[15] of a patient in that state endeavoring to reach a certain Likonor Bay, which was an amalgamation of words and images associated with a beautiful body of water by which she had spent the summer. It recalled, as, probing, he discovered, Locarno and Lugano, and the battle of Lucknow, a painting of which she had lately seen, and also "love, honor, and obey," in the marriage ceremony; for the lady was sexually baffled, of course. That sounds much like the interpretations already before us or yet to come. So Joyce himself, in *Finnegan,* exclaims, *"O foenix culprit"* over the moral downfall of Earwicker, the hero echoing St. Augustine's exclamation, *"O felix culpa,"* in joy over the fall in Eden because of the consequent institution of Salvation; which verbal perversion is owing to the Phoenix Park near at hand, scene of political murders. But the phoenix rises from his ashes, and counterbalances the "culprit";[16] and like a dreamer, though no ordinary one, the writer himself here invents and contrives.

In general, this ingenious but wrongheaded, irresponsible Irishman, though really not dreaming, not raving, is nevertheless, like a madman (such as King Lear) or like Edgar (who is pretending) and Miss Stein[17] (who is not), himself a prey to associations; and to those of words at the expense of ideas, and of the sounds of words at the expense of their

[15]Freud, *Interpretation of Dreams,* p. 285; Brill, pp. 95–98.

[16]Harry Levin, *James Joyce* (New Directions, Norfolk, Conn., 1941), pp. 157–58. I cannot stop to disclose all the complications, after Mr. Levin, and "how the four levels of symbolism are subsumed by a single phrase."

[17]From *How to Write* (Paris), pp. 14–15:

We will enjoy with and without that it is said that they do present well.

Buy me a present.

. . . . . .

Prevail.
Part of a mail.

meanings or of the context. What this last really is, to be sure, is generally difficult to ascertain or determine, but in *Finnegan* he puns (or echoes, transmogrifies, and "condenses") through 628 exasperating pages; and the portmanteaus, as we shall see, are often unquestionable examples of the mental infirmity in question, particularly the double-barreled perverted quotations such as "was Parish worth thette mess?" (*Finnegan,* p. 199), or "the flushpots of Euston [the railway station] and the hanging garments of Marylebone." Henri IV, Egypt, Babylon,—this wit is for its own labored or empty sake! Some passages, like the following from *Ulysses,* in the library episode, commended by Mr. Wilson, may have a dramatic justification such as he offers. John Eglinton is seen by Stephen, whose apprehension has been "heightened and blurred by some drinks at lunch-time":

Eglintoneyes, quick with pleasure, looked up shy-brightly. Gladly glancing, a merry puritan, through the twisted eglantine.

It is "Eglinton" and "puritan" that suggest *L'Allegro,* which is not beyond Stephen's range. Yet in both this book and *Finnegan* there is so much drunkenness or daydreaming —with also so many slightly relevant or comprehensible verbal and textual associations, often beyond the speaker's or thinker's experience, by way of remote languages—that we must take them mostly for Joyce's own. Besides, as we have seen, a book should be fairly intelligible, the train of thought not at every other turn jumping the track.

The abundant "identifications," also, seem to be dream phenomena. In Brill and Freud the dreamer or daydreamer continually identifies himself with another person, and thus disguises himself, and then has to be discovered by the analyst *not* to be the person read about in history or story, for instance (as it is with Bloom) not to be Jesus Christ.[18] But while in this earlier book the hero is also Ulysses, Elijah, and the Wandering Jew, in the later, Earwicker is, still more abundantly, Finnegan, Tristram, Adam, Michael,

[18]Brill, pp. 222–24, as Parsifal and Christ; 246, as Ibsen; 313–14, as Maupassant's Clochette; 326, as the emperor of China.

Humpty Dumpty, Napoleon, Swift, the early invading
Dane or Cromwell, Hosty the cricketer, even Pearse and
O'Reilly ("Persse O'Reilly," by way of "Erin," "earwig,"
and *"perce-oreille"*),[19] the Irish political martyrs. How
could such a notion as the last occur to this vulgar publican,
or to a patriotic writer, either, and what point is there if
it did?

And the narrative method, what there is! Jung, the psychoanalyst, affirms (and others will heartily agree with
him) that *Ulysses* has neither a beginning nor an end; that
it can be read both forwards and backwards.[20] That of itself,
to the normal, light-armed reader, though not to the
Joycean, is disconcerting; and Mr. Levin adds that he will
encounter allusions long before they are explained. Even
more baffling is the method of *Finnegan*. The very plot, says
Mr. Levin (p. 146),

is little more than a series of verbal associations and numerical
correspondences. A street number masquerades as a date, 1132, is
both the address of a misplaced letter and an entry in the annals
of the middle ages, the accession of St. Malachy to the primacy
of the Irish church . . . The temporal numbers twelve to four
seem invested with all the mystical meaning that Dante reserved
for the number three . . . We hear the bells of twelve churches;
we try vainly to make out whether the twelve members of the
jury we must face are the twelve customers with whom we got
drunk in the pub last night. The four walls of the bedroom speak
with the voices of the four evangelists, who are the spokesmen
of the four provinces of Ireland. . . .

All that, along with the acrostics and anagrams, rebuses,
palindromes, conundrums, and other verbal and literal
tricks, how mechanical and medieval in spirit, but not at
all in clarity! What story there is is really "circular": the
first sentence of the book is, remarkably, the conclusion of
the last. "A book," says Mr. Levin (p. 180), "must have
a beginning, a middle and an end; but a dream may be a
jumble of excluded middles." But is this, then, not a book?
Some of us have more than suspected it wasn't, yet Mr.

[19]Levin, p. 155.

[20]*Ibid.*, p. 95.

Levin and numerous other Joyceans have been laboring to make us think it was. Still, without the *Exagmination of James Joyce* (for all the discouragement in that title), "it is doubtful," Mr. Wilson confesses, "if the reader could have got the hang of the book at all"; and even before that, without Valéry Larbaud, Mr. Levin confesses (though as little embarrassed), *Ulysses* "could scarcely have been comprehended." "Nothing so vicious," quoth the downright Ben; but if the author himself does not see to his being "understood," the faithful follower must! And after the "Exagmination round this Factification for Incamination" there was still left prodigiously more to be done: after the Frenchman must follow Mr. Stuart Gilbert with his volume (on *Ulysses*, moreover, itself) of 379 densely printed pages (and its indices which cover even the soap and the potato in Bloom's pockets); for which thorough-going Joyceans were more grateful still. Funny, but really pitiful; for no one knows what a time they had had with their poet (as they call him) till into their hands fell a tome (the bigger the better!) that expounded him! A godsend, for though it was a load of exposition that they already carried, they must, in their bewilderment, welcome more! And then came *Finnegan!* What book that keeps up any pretensions to sanity (which some of the Vanguard's do not) could be farther from conformity to Coleridge's principle, but observed by the greatest in all ages: "Every work of art must contain within itself the reason why it is itself and not otherwise." A sobering consideration for the disciples should be that the two latter interpreters, at least, if not the Exagminators, had themselves to go, for what light they bring us, back to the master himself. There, however, is the advantage of the Joycean commentator over the Dantesque or the Shakespearean: his interpretation cannot (if his valuation may) be called in question.[21]

Still another characteristic of the dreamer or lunatic must be noticed, the unblushing Stone-Age interest in

---

[21]Mostly, but not wholly, I trust. The ingenuity of Mr. Gilbert in detail passes belief, even when attributed to a Joyce; and without Mr. Gilbert, it could never have reached the reader.

bodily functions, excretions and excrements, in mere sexual diversions and perversions. Yet Mr. Wilson thinks Joyce's artistic failure, so far as there is any, is due not only to his piling up and complicating personal and local allusions, but also "to a curious shrinking solicitude to conceal from the reader his real subjects."[22] The delicacy I fail, and I think many other simple folk will fail, to detect. The processes of elimination some of the more pronounced Joyceans openly delight in because as in no other writer (*teneatis risum*) they play the part that they do in life. Much of the grossness or lubricity, however, seems to be entirely gratuitous; and though some of it, particularly the homosexuality, is only suggested (for that in Joyce a little suggestion is quite enough!), the remainder, certainly, is ineffectively concealed. Without that and his blasphemies, indeed, would Joyce, in his later work, have any readers in the general public at all? Besides, both sorts of impropriety are evidently meant like the verbal distortions, to be comic, which, to much of the public he has, as to gamins and savages, they actually are.

With these, in fact, Joyce, not really a dreamer, still less a lunatic, shares the unregulated, uninhibited condition of mind. Availing himself of such license for his narrative, he delights in obscenity, in unbridled verbiage and word-coinage, as if a case of arrested development.[23] He is the twentieth-century Rabelais, though the gaulois, as one critic has said, himself followed the thought, not the word; but historically he is akin to the contemporary primitivists, who in verse, sculpture, painting, dance or music, emulate the Cambodians or the darkest Africans. His having a wife and

[22] *The Wound and the Bow*, p. 266.

[23] *Alice in Wonderland* and the other Victorian nonsense books, such as Lear's and Calverley's, reflect and appeal to the same childish taste, but expurgated. *Phallus in Wonderland* is the title of a poem cited by Mr. Sparrow (p. 128), thought by him to be under Mr. Pound's influence; but it would be a good epigraph for Joyce, and one wonders how, with the pun, it escaped him. In Lear and Calverley, moreover, the "portmanteau words," as well as the jabberwocky nonsense, are Joycean; but they are not numerous and require no study, no exagmination.

children is not what saved him with the Vanguard *littéra-
teurs,* from their psychoanalysis: he was too evidently one of
them, in both his science and his art. His primitivism or
barbarism goes farther and deeper, however, than that of
other writers of this persuasion, is more vigorous and natural. It is a case of retrogression, rather than of degeneration. There are evidences of the qualities above mentioned
in his earlier work, the *Portrait of the Artist;* even by the
Joyceans he is identified with Dedalus, and himself, apparently, was addicted to the elementary pleasures of foul
talk and dog-Latin. And in his later books he is also developing according to the principles of his clique or school,
which, except in his grossness and barbarism, gave him warrant to follow his bent. That is, as others have noticed, the
school of Mallarmé, of the symbolists or super-realists of
divers sects and names. The leader said that the poet *cède
l'initiative aux mots.*[24] Take care of the words, and the
thoughts will take care of themselves! And it is thus, roughly,
that the Age of Unreason, in which we still languish, began.

Rimbaud went farther:

I habituated myself [he writes] to simple hallucination; [and he
mentions some of them]. Then I explained my magical sophistries
by the hallucination of words . . . I ended by finding sacred
the disorder of my intelligence.[25]

Many of the other symbolists and later extremists skirted,
or even crossed, the confines of insanity, or else pretended
to do so. And M. Barranger, in 1931, declared that

Surrealism now aims at recreating a condition which will be in
no way inferior to mental derangement. Its ambition is to lead
us to the edge of madness and make us feel what is going on in
the magnificently disordered minds of those whom the community shuts up in asylums.[26]

And here in America some of us remember our first taste

[24]John Sparrow, *Sense and Poetry* (London, 1934), p. 23.

[25]Wilson, *Axel's Castle* (Charles Scribner's Sons, N. Y., 1931),
p. 272.

[26]Henri Barranger, "Surrealism in 1931," quoted by Sparrow,
op. cit., p. 31 (note).

of the Vanguard poetry of the last and the present generations, with their irresponsible, incommunicable broodings, their suggestions, evocations, or incantations, their startling and bewildering incoherences, their words and images treated as if they were the notes, the chords (or discords) in music, or the lines and pigments on a canvas. So too we remember the vacuous meandering prose of Miss Gertrude Stein. To all of this we have got accustomed now, however little we accept it. But Joyce and Miss Stein, though in comparison to some of the Frenchmen rather conservative, have, in the matter of keeping up the appearances of sanity, steadily deteriorated; yet the former is hailed as the greatest writer of the day. Few have the courage to question the reputation of either. If fifty or sixty years ago either had been brought by his or her relatives up before the appropriate tribunal, with *Finnegan* or *Preciosilla* as evidence—but it could not happen now. How many of us, though, after visiting an up-to-date art exhibit or conning an up-to-date anthology have echoed (or answered) Chesterton's question "Are they going crazy?"! But by 2039, I learn, it is expected that, at the present rate in the population as a whole, the right-minded are to be outnumbered. The Vanguard are better named than I had thought.

5

Joyce's prose is musical, or rhythmical, too, more happily so than Miss Stein's because less deficient in sense; but no one of these whom I have heard of has gone in so deep for the mental processes and expressions supposedly peculiar to dreams or to the wandering consciousness. Like the lady herself, "alone with English," like most of the symbolists, intent upon an individual and unique experience, and seemingly indifferent to that of an audience or public, he is, however, at bottom less indifferent than any of them, twists words or plays with or upon them for comic effect, to which a public would seem to be indispensable, and continually, relentlessly puns. Still, like the rest of the Vanguard, he is above all else recklessly intent upon originality.

For this, indeed, above all else he is praised—his genius is "creative," as we say,—and this quality appears in what is told, in the manner and order of the telling, and especially in the language. Often in consequence, the words are so original as, in effect, to convey nothing at all.

In a sense, to be sure, any great poet or prose-writer creates the language he uses, as well as the characters, the incidents and the sort of world in which they can take place; and the idiom not only for each of his creatures but for himself. That is, he avoids words that have been over-worked and have gathered associations uncongenial to his purpose, while into those he does avail himself of he, by his handling and ordering of them, puts a new life and meaning. But seldom (instead of continually!) does he coin words or mutilate them, still less murder them; and he does avail himself of the established associations when he profitably can. Then these are, indeed, his finest material. But the "new poet," the superrealist of whatever sort, more often shuns them, endeavors to brush them away, and consequently, since ordinarily they contribute to the meaning, he, so far, fails to convey any. Miss Stein (and apparently a good many others in both prose and verse), employing, for the most part, the words we have previously heard or heard of, nevertheless does her best to rid them of their meaning, as well as of any grammatical relation, and manipulates them as "merely vocal noises, out of which the artist tries to compose a pattern."[27] Joyce does not. Nor does he (seeking, as he is, comic effect and catching in his net every form of life, however low or questionable) so much avoid associations as (we have seen) fall a prey to them or turn them to vulgar or fantastic account. Too many associations he has (and too private and personal) rather than too few, once he is definitely discovered to have any. In his later development, still more bent upon perfect originality and novelty, he disarranges or misspells most of the words he does not quite recast. And he means to startle and amuse even by the familiar or vulgar, whether relevant or irrelevant, whether really novel or not. "Good morning,"

[27] John Sparrow, *op. cit.*, p. 25.

says Bloom, but under his breath, to an untidy acquaintance whom he meets, "have you used Pears' soap?" repeating the forty-year-old advertisement. But the well-worn sanitary salutation seems to have grown upon him; and it is "Work in Progress," I presume, as Earwicker babbles, with thickening pedantic allusions, about the Resurrection, "Guld modning, have yous viewsed Piers' aube?" (P. 593.) Work for the reader, certainly; whether progress for the writer— the reader, after the deciphering, will judge.

The gross and grotesque, the fantastic and phantasmagoric, the learned and facetious, are, undoubtedly, part— and a big part too—of the desired effect; but the utterly unintelligible really is not, or why did Joyce take the trouble to indoctrinate his interpreters, and when deferential complaint was made, tell Mr. Max Eastman "the demand I make of my reader is that he should devote his whole life to reading my works"?[28] He had a boyish, roguish delight in tricksy mystification; but even therefore would he be studied. Study, however, for fine literary effect, will not do; and not merely because time and attention are wasted, so that there is none left for appreciation. Interpretation will not do, either; not even an interlinear text for *Finnegan* (which, who knows, may be coming) as for a Greek or Latin classic. Literature and, still less, poetry (for by his followers Joyce's puzzles are taken to be such) are not like philosophy or science, which can be put into other words. The words in Joyce do not quite, as with Mallarmé, come first, but neither are they simply added or loosely attached; and a work of art that of itself, in its own day, to the author's own people, is unreadable, unintelligible (why in our late day must one say a thing so obvious?), is simply a miscarriage or abortion,—to the public addressed, at any rate, an impertinence, not a work of art. Of that the form, the expression, is part and parcel, and by being so arbitrary and freakish, personal and learned, labored, ingenious, and cryptic, inevitably impairs the effect. Intended to fire the

[28]Wilson, *The Wound and the Bow,* p. 266. There is no indication here that either Joyce or Mr. Wilson thought this monstrous or ridiculous, though Mr. Eastman may be depended on.

imagination and rouse the emotions, a work of art cannot do either thing if in itself a problem or conundrum; it alienates and repels the open-minded, healthy, and unindoctrinated public if, like *Finnegan,* it is at best a pattern of puns, but oftenest an intricate texture of murdered words and clipped or twisted constructions. And so it should do. A work of art that is baffling or annoying is a contradiction in terms, is only a work. Seventeen years!—a priori *Finnegan,* might well be suspect! "All art is a collaboration," says Synge, as well as Vernon Lee, Lascelles Abercrombie, and many another; it is the spontaneous, joyous collaboration of artist and public, with the history of art—the very nature of it—bearing the critics out. "It is never the first business of a poet," says Mr. Desmond MacCarthy, "to be original, or even thoroughly himself. Poetry is created also out of a stock of common experience, not all of it necessarily, either directly or acutely, felt by the poet—only present to his imagination."[29] Poetry, such as Donne's and Browning's, may be intellectual and subtle; it need not be so instantaneous and universal in its appeal as Homer's and Shakespeare's; but really to be poetry, there must be understanding of it (as for these poets there is) and (however severe and lofty it is) a pleasurable response. With that, novelty or profundity of content may interfere; but much more disastrously will interfere an obviously—freakishly and wantonly—needless difficulty in the expression. In Joyce, in his later development, the expression pretty nearly *is* the content. In all poetry, to be sure, the words are highly important and fairly irreplaceable; but in Joyce and his school they of late often really come first, as in Mallarmé. If replaced, there is, comparatively, little left. But that fact does not make the unacceptable style acceptable. And it is quite otherwise with the masterpieces of our literature or of the ancient, which are not structures so formless or empty, can bear translation, and even today, so long after, need little explaining. They were not the products of wrongheaded ingenuity. And they have an audience or public; to them mind and heart can still respond.

[29]Review of Stephen Spender, Sunday *Times,* March 8, 1942.

The Dubliner's writings, especially the latest, like those
of his spiritual predecessors, are decidedly esoteric; unlike
the classics, they are for a coterie, not for Dublin even; not
"a funferal," as he too confidently calls them, they are fun
for few; and yet his adherents and advocates, strange to
say, are mostly radicals and proletarians, though decidedly
of the parlor variety, in the *première classe*. Our highbrow
weekly and monthly press in America is, at the same time,
for the Unintelligibles and the Untouchables too. In both
art and life, to be sure, they all are revolutionaries; and yet
it is a curious phenomenon. They blow both hot and cold,
and the right hand knoweth not what the left hand doeth.
They profess the purpose of flinging wide the portals of
culture, which they shut. In the interests of "the forgotten
man" they are for turning the political, social and economic
fabric upside down; and at the same time they disparage
the literature that he could appreciate but (*contrā* William
Morris and Tolstoy both) glorify what is and will ever be
beyond him. They are for Joyce, Pound, and Stein, for
Crane, Cummings, and Crosby, and his fellow eccentrics
in this country as well as those whom Mr. Sparrow takes
account of in England. They have, of course, like Mr.
Wilson, a grudge against the Victorians, and exalt Donne
and Hopkins, whom, except here and there, the forgotten
could not read at all, to the detriment of Milton, and
Tennyson and Kipling, whom he could. If of Shakespeare
they are tolerant it is because of the criticism that has made
him, too, esoteric, though a quite popular playwright in
his own day and, in translation, popular everywhere outside
of the English-speaking countries now. And the critics who
oppose the Vanguard and compare them unfavorably with
the classics, they call old fogies or die-hard Tories, though
these are endeavoring to defend and preserve the common
man's literary inheritance. Indeed, as was perhaps inevitable, Joyce's very unintelligibility, his "malapropism," is
made out to be "the literary expression of social maladjust-
ment," just as "the boyish inscription" [childish, I would
call it] in a closet of Clongowes Wood College, *Julius
Caesar wrote The Calico Belly,* [which may indeed do well

enough for local color] "was a protest against things as they are."[30] Such philosophic profundity is beyond my reach: radicalism or humanitarianism, either, has, I think, nothing to do with the case. If this esoteric art,—this arbitrary jargon, with its mental eccentricity and isolationism, its farflung and intricately connected literary or wholly personal and private allusions, and its verbal formations interlarded with odds and ends from half-a-dozen foreign tongues—is so much better than the traditional or conservative, understanded of the people, why, then, the proletariat must, after all, still bow the knee before an aristocracy—that of art and prestige, however, instead of wealth and power —and hasten to get itself painfully and prodigiously educated or else now be left, with its high wages and abundant leisure, out in the cold. But as we have seen, it isn't better, nor so good.[31]

6

A lofty claim is put in by the advocates of Joyce, even by Mr. Levin in the passage quoted at the end of our discussion, for the immediacy of his effects. This (not in the sense of instantaneousness, of course!) is the ideal (in the abstract at least) of the Vanguard in both criticism and creation. They would have literature, like the novel, to be as the drama, without author—without comment or expo-

[30]Levin, p. 189.

[31]Since finishing this chapter, I have come upon a review of Mr. Levin's book (*New Republic*, September 28, 1942) by Professor Max Lerner, who is another of the "progressives" in politics delighting in progressive art. Objecting to the term "coterie-writer," applied to Joyce by Mr. Van Wyck Brooks (it seems) before me, he in the same breath insists that Mr. Levin's book is "necessary." And like many of the Vanguard critics (but, happily, not Messrs. Wilson and Levin) he is a coterie-writer himself. Not that he or they are like Joyce, however, except in being (though after a different, less intelligent fashion) unintelligible: *"Finnegans Wake* is the *purest distillation of the trends in Joyce's career"; "the tech-*nology of language and the geometry of symbolism"; "what we need is to take Joyce's sense of workmanship and the new worlds of symbolism he discovered, and weld them to the collective affirmations out of which we shall create our future." For that, in both art and life, the sensible must tremble!

sition—intruding or intervening. They would have the poem to be as their painting (but *not* as their music) with little content and no comment, and (though painting, even that of the superrealists, still has generally something of it) without the Aristotelian "imitation," just a thing of power and beauty, just a poem, in short. That claim may with some pitiful color of justification be allowed to Miss Stein, who, though incoherently—though pointlessly and recklessly—uses mostly familiar words; but not to Joyce. Or else, even more speciously, to those extremists also living on the European continent but more "alone with English," or like Harry Crosby (at times) still more alone without it, writing (instead of painting) like Andrea del Sarto, "from himself and to himself," whole poems without a single representative of the English vocabulary in them; but not to Joyce. As we have seen, he demands a hearing. Within the book he has little enough of comment on the characters or situations or incidents; but, as we have also seen, he would have a prodigious deal of it from without, brought to bear upon the book itself. Miss Stein we do not delight in or accept, but there are people, we are told, who are impressed and carried along by her meaningless rhythms; at any rate, they are not continually jolted, halted, or baffled. To her meaning is unimportant. *Finnegan* is, of those Vanguard books readable at all, the slowest reading, the least immediate or directly effective writing, I know. (Mr. MacCarthy, himself an Irishman, has met only one man who has read it through, Mr. Thornton Wilder; and he said "its real subject was original sin"! Like Horatio, "so have I heard and do in part believe it.") A method whereby so little of guidance and explanation is furnished and so much indispensably required, is "immediate" very fallaciously. The language, the medium itself, is not a language, not a medium but an obstacle. It is in the much-admired passage at the end of *Anna Livia Plurabelle,* a part of *Finnegan*—"beside the rivering waters of, hitherandthithering waters of"—that Joyce is more effectively immediate, and partly because, though grammatically more incoherent, he is verbally less unintelligible, less un-

readable, than is his wont. There is less of meaning intended and more of rhythm effected (as in Miss Stein), if
that is the ideal. The value of the passage, I myself, however, must think, is that, for once, rhythm and meaning
somewhat coalesce.

That, perhaps, is the main thing: they coalesce. Not all
poetry, of course, is wholly logical, coherent, or intelligible,
but it is readable, or singable; is not puzzling and bewildering, perplexing and vexing; does not cry out for a key or
an interpreter, or exasperate you even because it does.
Kubla Khan, such poems of Morris's as *The Blue Closet* and
Two Red Roses Across the Moon, as well as some lyrics
of Poe's, are examples of one sort; nonsense verses like
Lewis Carroll's and Edward Lear's are examples of another
sort, obviously on a lower level. But both sorts are of genuine and pleasurable poems, self-contained, conforming to
Coleridge's principle, mentioned above.

Mr. T. S. Eliot is said to have said that Joyce is the
greatest master of language in English since Milton.[32] With
all respect for the great critic and poet (though as the latter
and also as a critic he is somewhat open to the charge of
obscurity and irresponsibility himself) I must nevertheless
record my ineffective protest, and call the Irishman only
the greatest taskmaster. Like him (in their early days) even
the masters unquestioned, Chaucer and Milton and (still
more) Shakespeare—Swift, also, to whom the Joyceans
liken their idol, though rashly and precariously in view of
the difference between the way Swift wrote and the way he
lived and ended—are fascinated by words, and sometimes
dally with them; but he, unlike them all, both is a prey to
words and preys upon them. And Mr. Eliot (that, I myself
have seen) compares Joyce to Milton in the putting of
sound before sense, though it is with the meaning of the
latter only that he says he has to "wrestle."[33] This, properly
but yet surprisingly, the author of *The Waste Land* does

[32]Wilson, *The Wound and the Bow,* p. 255.

[33]English Association *Essays and Studies,* xxi, 1936. Mr. Eliot
contrasts him with Shakespeare and Dante (who else ever had to
"wrestle" with Milton as with them, particularly the former? Let

not at the time consider a virtue in a poet (earlier, like Donne, he "must be difficult"),[34] yet, amazingly, finds it in John Milton, not in James Joyce! It would seem that the critic had not only not yet finished *Finnegan* but not even fairly begun it; although, if with only *Ulysses* open before him, this must still be considered a partisan pronouncement. Milton, whose aim and achievement were, as the great Mackail[35] puts it, with the judgment of the judicious behind him, "perfection"; "whose workmanship throughout is such as had been in English poetry undreamed of, such as has never since been equalled, such as we cannot imagine ever being surpassed by any human skill"? Milton, "in the science of his art our one absolute master, like Bach in music"? Moreover, though there may be still greater heights for the poet in poetry itself (not upon the confines of music) as in Shakespeare, these words the greatest English poets and critics since Milton's day would echo or do, including folk so different as Arnold, Tennyson, Housman, and Wilde. And certainly Milton would not be a master of language at all if he could con-

---

Mr. Eliot but turn back to his schoolbooks, the vocabularies and pages of notes!). And contrasts him with Joyce, finding in the latter a similar dominating musical element, but here, apparently, and remarkably, not to the disadvantage of the sense. And with Dryden, because the latter more nearly "preserved the tradition of the conversational language in poetry." Of Joyce even in *Work in Progress* he says that he "always maintains some contact with the conversational tone." Yes, there is certainly no superhuman elevation; and in the later book the slang, street jargon, *argot,* and advertisements, the obscenity and blasphemy, are almost all that is left of the recognizable, the untransmogrified, in his vocabulary. There he must needs be understood!

[34] "The Metaphysical Poets" (1921). *Waste Land* appeared in 1922 and in the same year *Ulysses*. In the essay Mr. Eliot also says, "the poet must be more comprehensive, more allusive, more indirect, in order to force, to *dislocate,* if necessary, language into his meaning." He even says, still more sympathetically or prophetically, that to look into our hearts and write "is not looking deep enough." "One must look into the cerebral cortex, the nervous system, and the digestive tracts."

[35] *Springs of Helicon* (1909), p. 171. For Wilde see "The Critic as Artist."

tinually or even occasionally be tempted from the path of his thought by a fortuitous similarity of sound or will-o'-the-wisp of association, or could continually fail to use his medium for the conveying of the meaning he has.

No doubt Joyce's double-tongued utterance does, as Mr. Levin has it, widen the orbit of his phrase. For instance: "museyroom," the Vatican as "chalkfull of masterplasters" (p. 152), or "The Smog is lofting" (the smoke and fog are lifting). (P. 593.) But about as the orbit of his phrase was widened by the first late riser that combined the words, like the meals themselves, in "brunch." So Mr. Padraic Colum (the poet!) who shares the Joyceans' passion for portmanteaus, admires Joyce's "Healiopolis" (Tim Healy, Mayor of Dublin, and the Egyptian sacred city) and "these *gretched* youngsters" (Gretchen, "with a sense of girlish delinquency"), because both words "combine two concepts"; but the principle of economy, thus seemingly respected, is really flouted. There are fewer words but greater friction and higher resistance, together with an irritated sense of cleverness thrown away. "Brunch" (when newly coined) had really the advantage: a joke, by its nature, is not a poser. The mere distortion, to be sure, of one's mother tongue—and Joyce is far, far from above it—is, though a cheap and simple, a widely comprehended way of being funny; but in Joyce the none-too-precious effect is generally spoiled by his ingenuity. His "muchwhat" and "longly" remind me of the "muchly" and "somewhatly" and "thusly" of my callowest schooldays; but though "biscuitfully"[36] (for "with a mouthful") presents no considerable difficulty and with some indulgent ears may pass, what is funny enough to be worth the work in "feetstoops" and "clamn dever" (the more venial "tear and wear" and "nothing or little" have been compared to children's turning their coats inside out);[37] or in "the first chapter of Guinness's" (the

---

[36]On "biscuits" he in two books rings the changes as commingled with "pax vobiscum" and "box of Jacob's biscuits" (a Dublin make).

[37]*The King's English* (1906), p. 217, under the heading "cheap originality." Another Joycean schoolboy prank: "solemncholy."

Hibernian intemperance beverage, and the joke is only in
the jingle) ; or in the conundrum: What opera resembles a
railway line? (the *Rose of Castille* is the answer) :—all to
be found in the Aeolus episode? And what is gained for
either his "orbit" or ours by "thuartpeatrick" (St. Peter,
St. Patrick, peatrick, or peatreek, and the rock) or by the
multiform hero shouting, as if, in military fashion, through
the Archangel's megaphone, "Array! Surrection. Eireweeker
to the wohld bludyn world!" [Whole old bleeding-bloody
world?] (p. 593) or by Sophocles' turning into "Suffo-
close," Shakespeare into "Shikespower," Isolde's "Mild und
leise" into a Dublin "Mildew Lisa," Mathilde Wesendonck
into "Muheeldy Wheesindonk," or Tristram himself into
"Treestone"? Of the esoterically much-admired *Anna Livia
Plurabelle*, where Treestone figures largely, Mr. Eastman says
that Joyce, before reading from it, told him that either two
people, or a rock and a tree, or the principles of organic
and inorganic nature, are talking to each other across a
river.

One of his learned commentators has since issued a paper to
the effect that it is the two sexes, male and female, which are
talking across this river: another maintains that it is two washer-
women; but I believe only what Joyce told me . . .[38]

Which was quite enough! A great latitude, however, is
obviously permissible in the interpretation, as in the composition before that.

And in the relevance! A prey to memory, to total verbal
recall, Joyce is a part of whatever he has read or heard,
however distant or incongruous. "We've heard it aye since
songdom was gemurrmal" (p. 251)—which itself is an
example. It rather seems to be related to the preceding
sentence ("But listen to the mocking birde to micking barde
making bared"); yet though Sodom and Gomorrah may,
as Mr. Levin thinks, be there, the phrase "cultic twalette"
of p. 344, which Mr. Levin (p. 159) quotes in this connection, is, both in itself and in the context, an infelicitous condensation, really meaning, I think, "toilet" only, and if
"Celtic," not "twilight" at all. In any case, what have these

[38]*The Literary Mind* (Scribner's, N. Y., 1931), p. 99.

cities of hoary ill fame, or their besetting sin, either, to do with singing? Moreover, while the passage quoted and apparently admired by both Mr. Levin and Mr. Wilson, "Nobirdy aviar soar anywing to eagle it [nobody ever saw anything to equal it]," p. 505, may, by Joycean standards, be somewhat justified by the preceding ornithological tenor again, it is not at all perceptibly by the succeeding: "But rocked of agues, cliffed for aye!" Ages? agues? Essential irrelevance is in *Finnegan* almost a principle. As Mr. Levin (p. 190) well puts it, "every sentence is a wilful divagation from the expectations raised by the last." If so be, any *are* raised. Mr. Levin has just been taking pleasure in the words about the Gracehoper's despair: "Was he come to hevre with his engiles, or gone to hull with the poop?" "Havre" merges with "heaven," "angels" with "engines," "Hull" with "hell," "poop" with "pope"; but, pray, is this, then, "a man" (to adapt Wordsworth's definition of a poet, surely not yet altogether discredited) "speaking to men"? Still, whether relevant or not (for the preceding and succeeding sentences are to me much more impenetrable) here is a sort of ingenuity; and even that I fail to find in many sayings like this: "Of manifest 'tis obedience and the.Flute!" (*Sic.*) Yes, *sic!* Could anything be more inept or inane? I myself much prefer the "Calico Belly," though that is not notably above the level of "Beer Crossing" on Minnesota forest roads instead of "Deer." Mr. Levin does not undertake to commend it; but you would think that in quoting it (p. 157), as he touches on Milton and original sin, he would have been inclined, if only that he might keep himself in countenance with the commendations he has been bestowing, now to shake his head.

7

Though I cannot help thinking there was something wrong with the man, it is not so much the sanity or sensibleness of Joyce that I am moved to question as that of the critics who eulogize him, or else my own. Creation must be granted some latitude, for genius, big or little, is to madness near allied; but criticism, surely, is not expected to be. And what makes me tremble for myself is only the superior poetic insight and sensitivity of such critics and men of letters as Mr. Eliot and others, already mentioned or not. On the other hand, nothing so reassures me as what they themselves say when they quit their generalities of encomium, and, in one of Joyce's happier phrases, "come nown ["now down," I surmise] from the asphalt to the concrete." By the "polyphonic phrasing" of "How hominous his house, haunt it?" (p. 560), which Mr. Levin (p. 189) musically elucidates, I am moved to wonder, indeed, but not as he is.

"Will he swagger himself out on's own eyes?"

or, in this case, ears? And even to the point of a flagrant offense against the Muse? Mr. Levin has, unquestionably, a sound and delicate pair of organs at his disposal; but rather than his senses he here trusts his wits, and upon Hugo's

Waterloo, Waterloo, Waterloo, morne plaine

he soberly holds

Walhalloo, Walhalloo, Walhalloo, mourn in plein (p. 541)

to be "a manifest improvement." (That, though it grieves, reassures me much.) It is the "condensation," again: "on the Belgian battle-field . . . [the phrase] heaps Valhalla, a war-cry, full mourning, and full morning" (p. 192). Double-barreled, high-powered prose, if indeed, since an "improvement," it is not rather to be called poetry! That, in English or any other language, "mourn in plein" means nothing, is to Mr. Levin, apparently, of no importance, does not for him break the emotional current, cut off the power. Nor does the nonsensical babble of the context, either: "I wegschicked Duke Wellinghof to reshockle Roy Shackleton." A partisan at present, Mr. Levin is all for "condensation"; though for Joyce "congestion, contraction, and distortion" would be nearer the mark. And the same bias, the same indifference to the intelligible and idiomatic appears in Mr. Wilson's comment[39] on the long passage about Swift's madness, not itself, supposedly, the utterance of a madman, beginning "Unslow, malswift, pro mean, proh noblesse," ending, "honath Jon raves homes glowcoma," and requiring of the reader, unguided, some particular and readily available knowledge not only of history, biography, and ancient poetry but also of the Greek, Latin, French, and German languages commingled, though of English not so much. Mr. Wilson, to be sure, is here, I am happy to say, not irrecoverably content. Mr. Colum,[40] however, apparently is so, as, full of praise for Joyce's "telescoping" and "activating" of words, he works out his twelve-line exegesis of an uncouth eight-line text, but leaving nearly half of the stumbling-blocks—and the worst of them, too—such as "duominous, muzzatinties and pew-millieu," still in the way, and (what is even more regrettable) offering no explanation for the obviously wide discrepancy between either exegesis or criticism and expression, as well as no reason for the choice of such expression in the first place: "and the oragel of the lauds to tellforth's glory." Oragel combines "organ" with "orgulous"—"proud" [why leave out the German *Orgel?*]; in that combination we have the swelling sound of the organ associated with "lauds" and "glory"; "tellforth's" is a bit of local knowledge—Telfords are the organ-builders of Dublin. "Massgo bell," moreover, two lines above, "gets people moving to mass," and "Massgo" also "recalls [why recall, though or how?] Moscow, a city famous for its bells." Mr. Colum is not joking. Indeed, as I said above, most of the mere interpreting and expounding of Joyce, unhappily, is true; and, if anybody, it is he himself that is joking, ponderously,[41] portentously, 628 pages of it, mostly of the deadly elaborate

[39]*The Wound and the Bow*, p. 261.

[40]*Yale Review* (March, 1941), p. 642.

[41]In Mr. Sparrow's last chapter, "Specimens," there are examples of criticism quite as incredible and perhaps not directly inspired.

sort—too obvious or too obscure. Mr. Paul Rosenfeld,[42] on the other hand, is content beyond all question as, after his labors upon the first two pages of *Finnegan,* including the now notorious thirty-two-syllable polyglot vocable for thunder, he cries exultantly: "Thus what seems gibberish at first glance, ultimately resolves itself into conglomerates of meaning." When before in history did literature in its own day, for its own people, seem gibberish at first glance, or thereupon resolve itself into conglomerates of meaning, whatever those entities may be? Is the reader, like the critics, no longer to trust his senses, his own eyes and ears? Evidently not, if he would not be old-fashioned.

What does even more than all that, however, to reassure me is the demand made for special privilege. Here now is the hated aristocratic principle asserting itself in art and criticism aggressively, even as it has done, some of these same revolutionaries bitterly remember, in life itself. Hitherto, since the beginning of the world, I suppose, until the time of Mallarmé and Rimbaud, the man of letters met his public (whether an aristocrat or a radical) democratically, halfway. He told a story that was recognizable and comprehensible as a story, with no need of a tome to give "the

---

[42] *American Mercury* (July, 1939), pp. 367–71. Here the writer has got into line after being taken to task by Faugh An-Ballagh Faugh, for his review in the *Saturday Review of Literature,* May 6, where he says the book "conveys or seems to convey a meaning," and hopes that "in future years the new language will grow less private." This Kelt with the nursery-tale name who, like Colum and Strong, is very mysterious, bids him understand that to appreciate the "polychromaticfugal effects" one must have been brought up a Jesuit or a high-church Anglican" (*ibid.,* June 3). Esoteric indeed, and Mr. Rosenfeld hath done what he could; but what is to be done with the Irishmen who, as writers and critics, thus conspire together to murder the English tongue and then, with the acquiescence of the other critics, take on airs? For not unnaturally it is in Ireland and this country that Joyce has greatest vogue; partly because of a want of tenderness for the tongue that Shakespeare spake; partly because of the "progressive" or revolutionary spirit; partly because of the highly colored low life, somewhat familiar; partly because of the widespread taste for the comic effect of distortion and (in this country) the influence of advertisers and politicians who thus endeavor to attract attention.

hang of it"; and (to his own delight as well as that of his hearers) in his native, hereditary tongue. But Mr. L. A. G. Strong[43] (for whom I have as genuine respect as for Mr. Eliot) bids us remember that "with Joyce words have always had a value in themselves . . . He has more than a poet's, more than a singer's, more than a priest's, sensitiveness to them." (How much sensitiveness to those he has inherited, my reader is now in a position to judge for himself, and may also wonder if Joyce's own reader was, or is not now, also supposed to have any.) We should permit him, then, "his ritual, his incantation,"—regular refuge, alas! or subterfuge, of the practitioners and defenders of the *art nouveau.* So Miss Stein "proceeds by incantation," according to Mr. Wilson,[44] in some absurd verses (as I cannot but think them, though indeed not her absurdest). And one thing that more than any other hinders our understanding is what but our way of reading, from left to right:

. . . if I keep my mind unfocussed and read a paragraph aloud two or three times, a collective meaning [conglomerate again?] grows before my mind—a whole picture. . . . We look at it first as a whole; then we come closer and study the details. . . . Joyce is asking the reader to unlearn something, to study a page as a picture and not as a series of logically connected images arranged in lines from left to right.

Picture-writing (primitivism again!), as with the earliest Egyptians and the Hittites! And is it to be from right to left, then, as with the Jews and Arabs, or from the bottom to the top, or upside down? Not even Joyce himself ever directly asked the public to do the like—not only study but start again to school, learn anew to read, be as scriptural "little children," in order to "enter therein." And is it not the *sine qua non,* and indeed the essential nature of art that it should take things as they are, though making the best of them; and should conform to the requirements of the medium, or meet the expectations and satisfy the taste of the public, though turning them all to its advantage?[45]

[43]*American Mercury* (August, 1935), pp. 433–37.

[44]*Axel's Castle,* p. 251.

[45]See the second sentence of note 46.

But still, if Joyce is our greatest master, and *Finnegan* must be accepted as a classic, as good as Milton or better, why, then the demand made for him is no more than his due. If Joyce may be permitted to change the ways of writing, we others must change our ways of reading, that is certain.

Mr. Strong, indeed, is not the only one. Three years before him a reviewer quoted by Mr. Sparrow (p. 152) had made much the same plea in behalf of a book by Mr. Auden, one of the younger but promising Unintelligibles:[46]

Read it as passively as possible, just as a body sensitized to words, without letting intellect interfere . . . Don't bother to think at first, just listen. Then it will all begin to stand out like the red cliffs of Parnassus.

And Mr. Ezra Pound goes them both one better: he would have us learn, not to keep from thinking (which is, I fancy, really more to the point), but to cerebrate after another, a quite novel fashion. Speaking for artist and critic both, he says that "we no longer need to think in terms of mono-linear logic,—the sentence-structure, subject, predicate, object, etc." Which "we"—namely, the intelligent Unintelligibles—certainly long since discontinued to do.[47] Nothing so discredits Joyce as the defending he has had, the claims that have been put up for him. Not, of course, that these reviewers or men of letters, either, are crazy; though one cannot but be reminded of Joyce's own words about Shakespeare's being "the happy hunting-ground of all minds that have lost their balance." The Dubliner, being obviously so

[46]Yet in *The Intent of the Critic* (1941), cited above, Mr. Auden blames the lack of communication between artist and audience upon the lack of communication nowadays "between all men" (p. 135). And (p. 146) contrary to the practice and the theory of his sect he says of his ideal critic: "He will see artistic freedom and personality as dependent upon the voluntary acceptance of limitations, which alone are strong enough to test the genuine intensity of the original creative impulse; he will distrust the formless, the expansive, the unfinished, the casual." As a critic Mr. Auden is far above the level of his reviewer.

[47]In my *Shakespeare and Other Masters*, p. 8; and pp. 3 to 10, I discuss further this matter of mystery-mongering and legerdemain in both art and criticism.

much more cryptogrammic and difficult, is, naturally enough, taking the place of the myriad-minded one, though for him (or his critics) no such demands were ever made. But since the minds now in question are not unbalanced, there must be some other reason for the admiration.

8

Why, then, such patient and humble industry and receptivity on the part not only of fellow authors but of great critics and scholars, who have known and really loved the classics, in weighing and considering—racking and cudgeling their brains over—ingenuities both so pedantic and so puerile? Why such delight in the piling up of bulging portmanteau words and preposterous, far-fetched puns? Is not life too short for that, the profit or pleasure too meager? But evidently these spirits have better wind and bottom, and can take more punishment, than the generality of mortals, for some of them have time and strength left for Miss Stein. I, for one, wonder at them as at those—for they are of those!—who pore over the crossword puzzles. Mr. Levin and Mr. Wilson alike themselves find difficulties, obscure and dubious points, in the subject matter of both *Finnegan* and *Ulysses,* which, after much rereading (my wonder waxes) as well as poring and pondering, they cannot clear up. And in view of such difficulties, as well as those in the expression, Mr. Levin, at least, sorrowfully concludes that Joyce "will doubtless go down in the histories of literature as the archetype of misunderstood genius."[48] As if even to that end he had not labored and striven; and for nearly a generation over *Finnegan,* continually rewriting and, as appears from the versions preserved, steadily and deliberately thwarting the understanding of it. Mr. Wilson, indeed, after considering the four states of a passage in *Anna Livia Plurabelle,* boldly but refreshingly confesses his own feeling to be "that he ought to have stopped somewhere between the second and the

[48]*Op. cit.,* p. 217; and yet, p. 220 he, like Joyce himself, is confident of "his eventual authority."

third."[49] Both critics, in fact, have too much reverence for form and style not to be a little uncomfortable with their unreadable barbarian; by both nature and training they are discriminating, and several times Mr. Wilson admits that in *Ulysses* and *Finnegan* alike Joyce has attempted too much.[50] Why, then, this self-effacing admiration, this self-lacerating toil?

I see no other reason than that it is a revolutionary age, that the critics like the writers are sophisticated and eso-teric, and that the spirit of innovation and ingenuity in poetry and prose, music, painting, and sculpture, under which the general public for more than two generations has suffered and smarted, has not yet spent its fanatical strength. Never have there been so many varieties of *art nouveau,* and even in poetry and prose. All forms and styles change, as to be effective they sooner or later must; but in the nineteenth and twentieth centuries originality or nov-elty itself has come, or endeavored, to be the style, that is, not, as this should be, the medium between artist and public, but between artist and coterie, or artist and critic. Rightly they abhor the dull and commonplace, the cheap and trite and facile; but they do not remember the distinction between that and the nobly simple, the universal, as in the Greeks and Shakespeare, as, for that matter, in Swift. And critic and coterie, both, rejoice in the "difficult" and exact-ing because, in art, though not in politics, they are, like the artists themselves, aristocratic and exclusive; and it isn't of course the industry that they are admiring (but Joyce is boasting of) as they dwell on the seventeen years or the 1,600 hours. Read *Finnegan?*—not everybody can do it, or delight in it, as we do,—forgetting that if it were such as others could a little, they should more imaginatively and emotionally themselves. Like the author, again, the critics, not to be outdone, are elated and infatuated by their own ingenuity. *This* is the "cultic twalette," in both meanings,

---

[49]*The Wound and the Bow,* p. 262. And yet, p. 263, Mr. Wilson speaks as if the main difficulty lay in the unfamiliar Dublin topog-raphy and Irish history.

[50]*Axel's Castle,* pp. 214–15 (211–12).

as Joyce, if not involved, would have been first to say. Their simple senses they do not deign to trust—nor their eyes or ears, and their common sense still less—as critics should. If the writing seems gibberish at the first glance or the second, they look sharp, put on their thinking-caps, roll their eyes inward, and, ultimately, "it resolves itself." But above all they are unduly impressed by the ingenuity of the artists. Joyce, in his ritual, has really cast a spell, as Mr. Strong would have him do; yet only upon minds ready-prepared and disposed to receive it. His originality overawes them; his daring inspires them; the exhibition of his dexterity and agility makes amends for or renders actually acceptable his hundreds of pages of verbal contortions and lingual acrobatics. All these critics think the Dublin pundit a genius of a high order. Of *Ulysses* Wilson says that it is a "supremely finished and disciplined work of art."[51] Just, I should say, what it isn't, though it is better, of course, than *Finnegan*.

With most critics the motive is oftenest not so much the vanity of the esoteric as the horror of proving an old fogy. They do not want to be caught missing a genius when he appears. So they are eager to follow a leader; and Mr. Bonamy Dobrée,[52] though by no means a humble unenlightened spirit, finds Mr. Wilson on Joyce "illuminating." He quotes him as saying that in *Finnegan* "we are in the region whence all languages arise." (How, pray, do we get there?) In *Ulysses* Joyce took us into the minds of his characters in a normal state of consciousness: "Here we are to be at one with their unconscious." "When we realize this," Mr. Dobrée continues, drolly and coaxingly, "the work becomes more comprehensible." He then takes "one of the simpler passages," the beginning of the Mookse and the Gripes,—"an easy passage," he tells us, which, comparatively, it is.

Eins within a space and a weary wide space it wast ere wohned a Mookse.

[51]*Axel's Castle*, p. 220.
[52]*Modern Prose Style* (Oxford, 1934), pp. 244–46.

"There is no difficulty about that, especially if we know a little German"; and then Mr. Dobrée proceeds in quotation for more than thirty lines: "The onesomeness wast alltolonely, archunsitslike, broady oval," et cetera, et cetera. "The object," he insists, "is to represent human existence below the level of consciousness . . . to make use of the new awareness of our being, made possible by the psychology of this century"; and Mr. Dobrée would not be left behind. But how, one wonders, does Joyce himself reach below that level, presumed to be unknown to him as well as us, or how is Mr. Dobrée able to judge of Joyce's success when he does? And how are we? This is the "uprush" that we heard of at the beginning: by this begging of the question any sort of nonsense can be palmed off upon us. And why should an Irish publican's "unconscious" or any other person's, even Joyce's own, as it becomes conscious, take on here, as indeed is its wont in *Finnegan,* a German, Italian, Latin, and (possibly) a Greek expression? If it does, we must, of course, accept it, as the internationalism of Nature, however unintelligible; but Mr. Dobrée even finds the expression "easy." I am not boasting when I say that I know more than "a little" of the first two languages; for, I confess, I here stumble a good deal, though partly because, as above, the foreign words are murdered as well as the English, and notice of the change of tongue is not always served on me by means of italics. In any case, if the deeps of our polyglot psyches contain treasures no richer than these which now lie before us, why, at such a cost, uncover them?[53] Hoax or humbug, which?

[53]Mr. Leavis cited below, note 59, says, on p. 213, of Joyce's medium: It may be the "Esperanto of the subconscious"; if so, the subconscious is sadly boring. On the same page Mr. Leavis, despite his progressiveness, falls foul of the wit and humor which the Joyceans openheartedly admire but at which I have caviled above: "An inveterate solemn ingenuity, and it is often the very willing pimp to a poor wit." Witty an Irishman is presumed to be; an American has a claim to humor; and I had begun to think I must be what both call "English." Yet who knows but Mr. Leavis may be, though a Cambridge Don, a Celt.

9

Original Joyce is, and a genius (possibly) besides, but not, pray, of a high order. How high, it is not for me, with a very limited knowledge of the contemporary novel and the current esoteric technique, to say. I am here only endeavoring to discredit and abate the exorbitant claims put in for him, particularly for his style. But since writing the above I have come upon Mr. Eliot's newly published "In Praise of Kipling's verse,"[54] which more happily reassures me, by its likeness instead of extreme unlikeness to my views. He seems now to have flung off the spirit of partisanship (which was that of partnership, a little, as well), and no longer exalts the "difficult." Among other wholesome and conservative opinions, he of the truly "great poet" says that "at his greatest moments he is doing what Kipling is usually doing on a lower plane—writing transparently, so that our attention is directed to the object and not to the medium." Of Joyce can that ever, for a moment, be said, or, in his latest work, is "the object"—the meaning—to the unaided eye often even discernible?

Yet though a prey to words and associations, he is, to be sure, as a manipulator of them remarkable. In *Ulysses* he has something of the faculty of Dickens for discriminating the speech of one character from another, Gerty MacDowell, for instance, from Bloom's wife. That really is a finer development of his admirable gift for pure mimicry, as of a nannygoat (Megegaggegg! nannannanny), of a horse (hohohohohoho! hohohohome!), of a bicycle bell (halty-altyaltyall!), or of a squeaking door (theeee!).[55] (The despised Aristotelian imitation, in its lower forms! But I generally find Joyce most enjoyable when most unmistakably intelligible.) He has, moreover, nearly as good an ear as Synge for the Irish accent, intonation, and idiom, sentence-structure and cadence: "What call had the redcoat to strike

[54]*Harper's* magazine, July, 1942.
[55]All from the Night-town episode in *Ulysses*.

the gentleman, *and he under the influence?*"⁵⁶ That is Irish,
has the ring. In fact, as with Dickens and Shakespeare and
most other English dramatists this is his main formative
means of characterization. (It has to be, in figures identified
with so many other personalities in history or fiction as
Bloom and Earwicker are.)

And he has a feeling for rhythm not only in the succession of syllables and as a means (again) of characterization,
but also (to give some shape and structure to the whole)
in the matter of repeated motifs. When, however, the
themes or motifs are purely onomatopoetic or symbolical,
with meanings intended but not appended, as with the long
series presented at the beginning of the Siren episode in
Ulysses, they pretty completely fail of effect, at least for my
insufficiently delicate ear. In reading Mr. Levin's list, with
the meanings furnished (pp. 99–105), only one, the theme
for the assignation, could I definitely and securely recognize and accept; in fact, because of the ordering, I got
mixed up, making, apparently, some wrong connections,
though even of that I am here and there not yet wholly
certain. I am like Mr. Eastman, not when he believed only
what Joyce told him, but when Joyce read him some lines
in *Anna Livia,* upon which themselves he had worked 600
hours and into which he had woven the names of five hundred rivers (he was curiously given to records and numbers), without Mr. Eastman's hearing the name of one. "I
have examined them patiently since and have not yet found
but three-and-a-half rivers."⁵⁷ What, I wonder, however,
would Mr. Eastman have done with the 496 others if

⁵⁶*Ulysses* (N. Y.), p. 586. Cf. Synge, *Playboy of the Western
World,* Act I: "And I'm thinking it's a queer daughter you are, if
you'd have me crossing backward through the Stooks of the Dead
Women, *with a drop taken.*"

⁵⁷*The Literary Mind,* p. 99. (So far as the numbers are concerned, one is reminded of the flowers worked into the Lotus-eater
episode and the ninety-five rhetorical figures worked into the
Aeolus episode, both in *Ulysses,* as of the actual lists of the hundred
and sixty-three names given to Anna Livia's "mamafesta memorial-
izing the Mosthighest" (*Finnegan,* pp. 104–6) and the eighteen
names compounded in Humphrey Chimpden Earwicker's own
(Levin, p. 155). This "universalizes" him, it is naïvely thought.

found? What would anyone do with them, or the other lists or catalogues that in *Ulysses* and *Finnegan* are to be found without such difficulty, unless he has time on his hands and, like Mallarmé, is "triste," and has read all the other books, *lu tous les livres?* Not everybody is ready to sit down, with Mr. Levin (p. 188), "by the waters of babalong"—"and laugh." Many of us too tenderly and bitterly "remember Zion"—Milton, and the English language as we have known it, and even Swift, when writing, at his maddest.

And when the recurring motifs are not symbolical or onomatopoetic, there is all too little of the structural effect that is sought. To give form and shape (again) to the often natural and piquant but uncontrolled flux of consciousness as well as to the plotless story, the rather aimless or pointless wanderings of Bloom and of Dedalus, Joyce has imposed on it the parallel of the wanderings of Ulysses, and also apportioned a set of repeated motifs, whereby in every one of the eighteen episodes is reflected not only one of the adventures of the Hellenic hero but also various other matters such as a color, an organ of the human body, and an art or a science. Besides, there are numerous other recurrences—allusions, echoes, reminiscences—and there is the litany of the daughters of Erin, rehearsing Bloom's experiences, in the Night-Town episode, into the bargain. Thus a musical development, approaching the symphonic in structure, is presumably attained, was certainly intended. Yet more than a somewhat musiclike structure is needed to produce with words an effect like that of music.[58] What of this repetition is really perceptible is to my thinking mostly forced and frigid or grotesque, too labored to be either poetical or funny. The various episodes in Joyce are about as similar to those in Homer as the Jewish advertiser himself is to the Ithacan king. There is, moreover, something crudely factitious and formal, mechanical or medieval (again), about the bodily organ, the color, the art or science

[58]Cf. the comments of one of the advanced critics and poets, Ronald Bottrall, *Determinations,* ed. by F. R. Leavis, 1934, pp. 193–94, on the attempts at counterpoint and musical harmony in Joyce and Pound.

thus regularly introduced; and also in the style or imagery
supposedly fitted to the occasion, the flowers worked into
the *Lotus-eater* episode and the ninety-five rhetorical figures into the *Aeolus,* as in the five hundred rivers impercep-
tibly running through the *Anna Livia Plurabelle.* And the
litany, a "recital" and "running commentary": —

> Kidney of Bloom, pray for us [*Calypso*]
> Flower of the Bath, pray for us [*Lotus-Eaters*]
>
> .   .   .   .   .
>
> Canvasser for *The Freeman,* pray for us [*Aeolus*]
>
> .   .   .   .   .
>
> Wandering Soap, pray for us [*Scylla and Charybdis*]—

that is to my poor pair of ears no more musical or amusing
than the counterpoint of the Siren episode discussed above.

As mere writing, Joyce, though he has undoubted abundance of material and imagination and plastic power, is,
I cannot but think, too unsatisfactory, often too arbitrary
and exasperating, for high art. His principle, when not
mechanical, is too often freakish, or both together. As his
most intelligent admirers, we have seen, acknowledge, he
in both of his chief books tells a story or presents a situation
that of or in itself is, despite much elaboration and precision, nearly formless and often unintelligible. The later one
and much of the earlier he has deliberately turned into a
continuous travesty of English grammar, idiom, and diction, as well as of the normal processes—the "monolinear
logic," the sentence-structure—of our human thought. And
that much-admired combination or amalgamation of nat-
uralism and symbolism in one piece of writing which is
Ulysses, whereby the real and the fanciful, the present and
the past, or thoughts spoken and unspoken or even unconscious, come tumbling one upon the heels of the other, as
in the Night-Town episode,—it is indeed an adaptation
of the cinema technique, with its fade-outs, flashbacks, and
close-ups, but is far from being so successful as on the
screen. There we can tell the difference between the present and the past, between fact and fancy, as here we often
with difficulty can. In short, while Joyce craves a reader he

rebuffs or punishes, baffles or torments him. He demands that the reader shall give up his life to studying Joyce, after spending his own life to make that necessary—or out of the question. Modern art, to be sure, is full of such egotism and arrogance—Whitman, Strauss, Strindberg, the Symbolists, Pound and Stein, and their variously aligned and denominated, still more willful and erring, descendants or adherents; but Joyce has quite as much of it as any of them. And as with the Symbolists and their followers, it is not merely a personal matter, either, or a matter of content, but a vice of expression, which, since a work of art, not of philosophy or science, is intended, plays havoc with the content as well as the technique.

10

Yet, as I suggested above, it is a natural (though all-too-natural) development, from *Ulysses* to *Finnegan,* as indeed from the *Portrait of the Artist* to *Ulysses;* and *Finnegan* is the consummation. That, I suppose, is Joyce's triumph (though I doubt if the delicate Mallarmé would have applauded it) by words over sense. To quote Mr. Levin once again (p. 184), from his exquisite piece of critical mythopoeia, in *Ulysses* there is as yet too much comment, too much meaning;

The drastic solution . . . is to subordinate content to form: . . . and confer complete autonomy upon words. They are now matter, not manner. Nothing could be farther from the fallacy of imitative form. . . . We are borne from one page to the next, not by the expository current of the prose, but by the harmonic relations of the language—phonetic, syntactic, or referential. . . . The mythological themes, recurring, varying, modulating . . . have a consistency of their own. When we have an index to them, we shall comprehend the book.

And again (p. 194), still more complacently:

Joyce, conceding the priority of the word to the thing, renews our perception of language as an artistic medium. . . . Turning from representation to presentation, he allows nothing to intervene between the prose of *Finnegans Wake* and the flow of the Liffey.

Joyce's last effort, in fine, is both his best and his worst. Consistency of tone is maintained: in *Finnegan* Joyce is consistently grotesque and unintelligible. There is a greater unity or continuity than in *Ulysses,* not in content or structure, of course, but in what may be called the serio-comic style, the double- or multiple-barreled wording, the boyish word-making and -destroying. A sort of concord arises out of the discords; a barbarous harmony is perceptible in the persistent fantastic travesty of sense and reason, of the decorous, the poetical, and the heroic. Not to the "object," however (as Mr. Eliot calls it), is our attention directed but now almost wholly to the medium; and what a tale—of the *art nouveau*—is this we have just been hearing! It is true enough, of course, just what Joyce endeavors to (but Mr. Eliot says the great poet does not) do; as one of his fanatical followers has it, he is "developing his medium to the fullest";[59] but surely Mr. Levin realizes, if Joyce and his particular coterie do not, that in literature "presentation" cannot quite replace representation; that only with the Ancient of Days *Am Anfang war das Wort;* and that such a harmonized presentation of words, as if of substantive elements, is illusory, chimerical, itself a myth. Even the critic, after his labors, seems to crave the index; though here, with the Liffey, as we have already acknowledged, between the author's prose and the "object" ingenuity has intervened less than usual. "Complete autonomy on words"—the cart before the horse, the effect before the cause! The literary medium cannot itself be the "object": still less, indeed, than a picture can be lines and colors without form, can poetry be words without meaning. There, as Pope has it, "splendour

[59]Quoted by Mr. F. R. Leavis, *For Continuity* (Cambridge, 1933), p. 207. This book and this particular essay on "Joyce and 'the Revolution of the Word,' " I regret not having seen until at the point of going to press. I still more regret the American Joyceans' not having seen it before going to press, for then I myself might not have had to go. Though not a conservative, Mr. Leavis yet keeps his balance and neatly exposes the essential charlatanry of *Finnegan* (or *Work in Progress*) and its organization as "external and mechanical."

borrows all her rays from sense." The dictum of Mr. Mac-
Leish

> *A poem should not mean*
> *But be,*

is an hyperbolical paradox, allowable in verse, as not in
critical prose (though here for once, I fancy, a poem of
MacLeish's *does* mean). Poe (*The Poetic Principle*) as he
celebrates the "poem per se," "a poem and nothing more,"
"written solely for the poem's sake," is by no means thinking of any without meaning, still less of one with meaning
but hard to get at. And as Mr. Eastman has said, all fine
art is to some extent and will forever be—and no invention
or sophistication can deliver us from it—an "imitation of
nature."[60] That, of course, is not mere mimicry (at which,
however, as we have seen, Joyce himself is excellent), and
Mr. Eastman, no doubt, as well as all the greatest critics
before the present hapless era of Unreason, would (if to
say that is not presumptuous) join with me in adding: All
literary art, however fine, to some extent conveys, or at least
somewhat depends upon, a meaning. And so would now
even the greatest in this era of literary and critical chaos;
for in the article above mentioned Mr. Eliot, speaking of
the dangers of musical analogies in discussing poetry, pronounces that "the music of verse [and prose he would no
doubt include] is inseparable from the meanings and associations of words." That is large-minded of Mr. Eliot as
both critic and poet; and what would he say when the
words have too few associations, or else (after the decod-
ing) too arbitrarily and confusingly many, for the meaning
to be, as from the beginning of literature it has been expected to be, of itself, in its own day at least, readily, and
either pleasurably or stimulatingly, perceptible?[61] With

[60] *Op. cit.*, p. 206.

[61] By implication Mr. Eliot has already answered. In the London
Sunday *Times* of November 1, 1942, the review by Mr. MacCarthy,
he is quoted as referring, before the Classical Association, to Shakespeare and Milton as "our two greatest poets,"—he, "thanks to
whom Milton had been deposed with remarkably little fuss," but to
the applause of the Vanguard. This defection may be the turning-
point, not in verse or "creative, high-powered," prose, perhaps, but
in criticism.

Swinburne, Shelley, Coleridge in *Kubla Khan,* it is another matter,—in a world of words, imagery, and music but the words all such as we know. "Nor does valuable originality consist in unlikeness to other men," says Emerson,—least of all to the poet's own hearers or readers.[62]

As for the future to which the Joyceans look so confidently, we shall endeavor to keep our faith in the race, to believe that the year 2039 is not to be the turning-point; that the Vanguard is not really the Vanguard and will not be able to make most of us read from right to left, or look at what passes for English as at a picture or a puzzle; that in short the style of *Finnegan* or even *Ulysses* is not to prevail. For if there should be no Restoration, and Reason be not to come to her throne again, what a world this then would be! Only for the lower classes would high-class reading be still a pleasure, an imaginative or emotional experience; but by that time, after the war, there are, the politicians say, to be none. There would be only lowbrows and highbrows; and then even the lowbrows—apart, with the past—would have, though still the easier time of it, not so much pleasure as they might.

[62] *Shakespeare; or the Poet:* "No great men are original," he has just said, despite his idealism and "self-reliance." So, in *Uses of Great Men:* "The true artist has the planet for his pedestal; the adventurer, after years of strife, has nothing broader than his own shoes." Or, as Lowell puts it, glancing at Whitman, "when a man *aims* at originality, he acknowledges himself unoriginal."

CHAPTER XIX

Milton a Romantic

THE WORD ROMANTIC is here used in the narrower sense.
It is not opposed to "classical" (as Dante, Shakespeare, and
even Milton himself may be to Virgil and Sophocles) but
to "neoclassical"; and it stands for the poetry of the Revival
—that of Scott, Wordsworth, and Coleridge, of Byron,
Shelley, and Keats. It does not include their medievalism
or adventurousness (though there is in Milton a little of
both); but their inclination to reverie and wonder, their
delight in the natural and instinctive (or the unconven-
tional or rebellious), and in the shadowy, the mysterious,
the spacious or distant for its own sake, and in particular
their general aesthetic bent, which turned things in themselves a little ugly or painful into things of beauty. Of this
last there is, of course, something in earlier poetry, even in
Virgil's and Homer's; but in none the Romantic variety that
is in Milton's. Upon the subject I have touched already;[1]
and my present undertaking is further to illustrate some of
the points there made, as well as to make new ones.

[1]*Poets and Playwrights* (1930), the essays on Spenser and Milton,
pp. 189–99, 289–93. Cf. John Bailey's *Milton,* pp. 101–2, 111,
where the critic points out passages penned as if by a Shelley or a
Keats.

The very manner and demeanor of the poet is Romantic, despite his classicism. His "dim intimations" and remote adumbrations are not in the vein of the classics or the classicists, of the Middle Ages or the Renaissance. As is well known, he does not delineate like Dante, as with a point of acid or of fire, but, after a bold, firm stroke or two, leaves the contours or outlines of the figure suggestively wavering and indeterminate. He does not trace boundaries or enclosures, as the ancients and both Dante and Spenser do; and ventures even beyond the skyline. Space is indispensable to him, and he takes to "Pisgah-visions" far and wide, from province to province. He delights in what is vague and vast, dim and shadowy, immense and mysterious. And he is not only in the ancient classical style a prophet or seer, but in the Romantic,—an "original genius," inspired (though not intoxicated), proud and authoritative (though not wayward or freakish), prominent in his narrative (though not intimate or confidential), and he is a freethinking rebel (though not a lawless one) in both politics and theology. Such, more or less, without the negative qualifications, are Blake, Coleridge, and Wordsworth; as such they regarded or presented themselves. Byron and Shelley had the pride, intimacy, and lawlessness. And they and Coleridge, like the painters Claude and Turner, rejoiced in perspective, depicted panoramas. It was much they had to say of the infinite; one of their favorite words is "unimaginable." And while their descriptive method is not that of Milton's abstraction and circumlocution, paradox and oxymoron, and figure or allusion accumulated, they have a good deal of this, and the contemporary (and later) Romantic painters have a similar cloudiness of effect.[2]

2

At the word Romanticism we think of Nature, and not as a setting or background but for her own sake. Milton's presentation is not, like Wordsworth's, mystical; but it is like his and that of other Romantic poets, mysterious and

[2]*Poets and Playwrights,* pp. 269–75.

aesthetic. That Romantic bent for turning the ugly, painful, or fearful into the beautiful; that delight in what is wild and superstitious, or dim and distant whether in space or time; that disposition generally to run to extremes of emotion and sensation; and whatever else it is that gradually gave words like *wild* and *weird, drear* and *dread, bleak* and *waste, lorn* and *forlorn, old* and *lone, faint* and *frail, pang* and *throe, awe* and *anguish, charm* and *spell, trance* and *swoon, magic, glamour,* and *enchantment*[3] a new or sweeter significance—all this fairly begins with Milton or Spenser and may develop from the former. Even his Hell is not horrible and terrible like Dante's, but mournful and sublime. There is no filth or stench; Sin herself is, as to be real she should be, not wholly hideous; and the prospect is relieved by vastness and variety, by light and shade. Twice, in Books both I and II, there is lofty music; in the description, it is more penetratingly beautiful than that in Heaven. And as for the earth, though he shows no such pleasure as Wordsworth and Coleridge, or Shelley and Byron in savage mountain scenery, more than any poet before him he delights in a landscape desolate and solitary, or darkened with superstitious or legendary associations. The use of superstition is illustrated below in the similes; and for such a landscape presented directly there is little occasion in the two epics and the *Samson*. But the fictitious and supernatural Hell and Chaos are made "bleak" and "blasted," and "wild" and "picturesque" enough, as in the passages cited below in connection with Satan; and when in Book II the fallen angels depart "on bold adventure to discover wide that dismal world." Any Romantic imagination, moreover, would have exulted at coming upon

> *the throne*
> *Of Chaos, and his dark pavilion spread*
> *Wide on the wasteful deep;*

or, in Book XI, upon the ruin of Paradise, floated down the river, to the gulf,

[3]For still others, see *Poets and Playwrights*, p. 193.

> *an iland salt and bare,*
> *The haunt of seals and orcs, and seamews' clang.*

"There let the wind sweep and the plover cry," as Tennyson has it, who shared the Romantic delight in a waste of land or sea. And this is to be found elsewhere: in the *Hymn on the Nativity,* "The lonely mountains o'er," by the sea; in *Il Penseroso,* the forlorn moon, "led astray," and the far-off curfew sounding "Over some wide-water'd shore"; and above all in *Comus,* with desolation and superstition blended in the celebrated passage about the

> *airy tongues that syllable men's names*
> *On sands, and shores, and desert wildernesses.*

No more than Coleridge himself did Milton believe in ghosts or specters, witches or portents, as Spenser and Shakespeare not improbably did; for that reason he was as free as Coleridge to employ superstition esthetically, like the institution of chivalry, as a thing antique and remote:

> *Such sights as youthful poets dream*
> *On summer eves, by haunted stream.*

And twilight, gloom, night itself, which to Spenser and Shakespeare were rather repellent, and even "hideous," were to him, like their spiritual accompaniment of melancholy, sweet, solemn, awe-inspiring, as they were to Coleridge and Shelley, Byron and Keats. Music for him was *not* "to drive away the dull melánchóly," as for Spenser, but, as in *Il Penseroso,* to uplift, enlarge it. Even of medievalism there is something in Milton, in keeping with his general esthetic bent. What was old and far away, and was already touched with poetry, was, despite his puritanism and rationalism, not easily resisted; and we find delighted references to it in *L'Allegro* and *Il Penseroso* and both the epics. One of his favorite epithets is the Virgilian post-positive, as in "prophets old."

3

All this, I said above, fairly begins with Milton and may develop from him. But not from him alone, of course, and (though English literature would not be as it is without him) certainly without him there would have been a Romantic movement. That was inevitable; and as a whole it did not with him really begin. His aesthetic bent by no means dissolves away realities, or gives experience a sweet (and in the end often bitter) savor upon his tongue, as it does particularly with Byron, Shelley, and Keats. For him Hell is still a place of torment; the earth, a place of struggle and trial. He has no hunger or thirst for the Infinite, in the right Romantic fashion; nor has he any thought of communing with Nature, or worshiping her, like Wordsworth or Keats, or blending his being with her, like Shelley. He has only a religious and an aesthetic interest, the latter kept firmly in hand. And the subsequent development of Romantic tendencies is tardy and gradual, and, if really continuous, long underground. Eighteenth-century sentimentalism is, in a sense, Romanticism before its day. Through the whole century, indeed, both the neoclassic age and the Romantic, the influence of Milton, in phrasing, meter, and verbal reminiscence, is, as is ordinarily acknowledged, fairly evident. But with these or other specific "influences" I am not here concerned. In the larger matters of style and sentiment, where the possibilities are so numerous, they are often highly questionable; and even when less so they are, if more striking and arresting, less deeply and permanently interesting than mere resemblances. These a little settle our shaken faith in the power of the imagination, both the poet's and the critic's, and in the identity of our human nature.

In my previous discussion I touched upon the manifestations of Romanticism in the minor poems; and to these I will not recur. Now I wish to take up the two epics in order, and point out, leaving the treatment of Time and Space for the next chapter, what strikes me as Romantic before its day. In doing so I shall endeavor to keep to resemblances that, once noticed, are fairly evident.

4

The villain himself is Romantically conceived; and hence the enthusiasm for him of Byron, Shelley, and Hazlitt. Here, as we saw in chapter XVI, there is actual influence. Satan is the first as well as the greatest of the "Satanic School," and (by way of eighteenth-century novel and drama of Terror) the lineal predecessor of Lara and the Corsair, Cain and Manfred, and many another in the Romantic age. Like them, haughty and dauntless, rebellious and defiant, ambitious and self-centered, and as conscious of his own wickedness as of his "injur'd merit," he is yet loyal to his comrades, compassionate towards the feeble, and melancholy both in his intercourse with them and in himself. Like them he is depicted by Milton's favorite devices for dealing with the supernatural, by hyperboles and abstractions, by antitheses and oxymorons or paradoxes. These classical epical devices, as I have noticed elsewhere,[4] are by Milton much more developed, are used, not as by Virgil, to give the effect merely of the elevated or superhuman, but of the supernatural and spiritual, of the moral and immoral in a complication, as well as of the vast and vague. The antitheses or contrarieties are required also for the situation, for the archangel newly fallen, as for the Byronic hero and villain combined into one. Like him, he is filled with "impenitent remorse"; but unlike him, being supernatural, is

> *from despair*
> *Thus high uplifted beyond hope.*

He is not, like the villain-heroes, sentimentalized. Not less than "archangel ruin'd," he must not yet be a devil nor on the other hand have our sympathies wholly with him. "Cruel his eye," but as he essays to speak before his assembled host

[4]See *Poets and Playwrights*, pp. 269–71.

> *Tears such as angels weep, burst forth . . .*

And for abstractions:

> > > > *care*
> *Sat on his faded cheek, but under brows*
> *Of dauntless courage.*

His place, moreover, befits him, depicted by an oxymoron too.

> > > *Yet from those flames*
> *No light, but rather darkness visible*
> *Serv'd only to discover sights of woe,*
> *Regions of sorrow, doleful shades, where peace*
> *And rest can never dwell, hope never comes,*
> *That comes to all.*

That, surely, is as "dim, shadowy, and unsubstantial" as even Hazlitt could have wished it; and so is this:

> *Seest thou yon dreary plain, forlorn and wild,*
> *The seat of desolation, void of light,*
> *Save what the glimmering of these livid flames*
> *Casts pale and dreadful?*

The words "forlorn" and "wild" have not yet arrived at their secondary Romantic signification, but they are approaching it. There is no ugliness, really.

In the description of Satan's person, I, 192 ff., there is not only the vagueness of manner, but also the legendary or superstitious in matter, which the poet takes to as a means of suggesting the supernatural, the intangible. "As whom the fables name of monstrous size"—"or that sea-beast Leviathan"—

> *Him, haply slumb'ring on the Norway foam,*
> *The pilot of some small night-founderd skiff,*
> *Deeming some island, oft, as seamen tell,*
> *With fixèd anchor in his scaly rind,*
> *Moors by his side under the lee, while night*
> *Invests the sea, and wishèd morn delays.*

Nature herself and the realities of zoology are too solid and substantial for his purpose: and when the poet does draw upon her as she is, it is a Nature remote as Imaus or the Ganges, or else herself veiled in superstitious or legendary lore. When the fallen angels spring up upon the wing they are likened to the cloud of locusts

> *That o'er the realm of impious Pharaoh hung*
> *Like night, and darken'd all the land of Nile.*

And when, for the first time since their downfall mustered before him, Satan confronts them, his glory darkened, he is compared to the Sun as it

> *behind the moon*
> *In dim eclipse disastrous twilight sheds*
> *On half the nations, and with fear of change*
> *Perplexes monarchs.*

So, near the end of this book, the spirits, voluntarily diminished in size, are as fairies

> *Whose midnight revels, by a forest-side*
> *Or fountain, some belated peasant sees,*
> *Or dreams he sees, while overhead the moon*
> *Sits arbitress, and nearer to the earth*
> *Wheels her pale course.*

It is the witching hour; and in the second book Sin, met by Satan at Hell-gate, is given the supernatural quality of the night-hag

> *when, call'd*
> *In secret, riding through the air she comes,*
> *Lur'd with the smell of infant blood, to dance*
> *With Lapland witches, while the labouring moon*
> *Eclipses at their charms;*

and Satan himself, as the combat with Death impends, is as a comet

> *That fires the length of Ophiuchus huge*
> *In th' Arctic sky, and from his horrid hair*
> *Shakes pestilence and war.*

So, though the *ignis fatuus,* or will-o'-the-wisp, readily lends itself, as a fleeting, mysterious phenomenon, to the poet's purpose, particularly at the Temptation, yet it is not without the malign coloring of superstitious hearsay:

> *He, leading swiftly, roll'd*
> *In tangles, and made intricate seem straight,*
> *To mischief swift. Hope elevates, and joy*
> *Bright'ns his crest, as when a wand'ring fire*
> *Compact of unctuous vapour, which the night*
> *Condenses, and the cold environs round,*
> *Kindl'd through agitation to a flame,*
> *(Which oft, they say, some evil spirit attends)*
> *Hovering and blazing with delusive light,*
> *Misleads th' amaz'd night-wanderer from his way*
> *To bogs and mires, and oft through pond or pool,*
> *There swallow'd up and lost, from succour far.*

Thus Eve is led, in broad daylight.

By such means Milton imparts to his supernatural creations not only moral qualities, foreign to Nature herself, but a dimness and unsubstantiality not otherwise attainable. And it is the same thing that was done by Romantic poets such as Coleridge, though generally in a different way. It is the same way here:

> *The water like a witch's oils*
> *Burnt blue and green and white.*
>
> *A speck, a mist, a shape, I wist!*
> *And still it neared and neared:*
> *As if it dodged a water-sprite,*
> *It plunged and tacked and veered.*

But for the most part Coleridge or Rossetti, having in the story human life (which Milton by the nature of the case, in his prehistorical epic, hadn't) as his point of departure and return, and as an ever-present basis of contrast, is able to use superstition, like Dante and Shakespeare, directly, and as it were dramatically, instead of by similitude, marking the transition by a voyage into an antipodean world or into a distant time, or by repeated misgivings and questionings—

And what can ail the mastiff bitch?

In *The Ancient Mariner,* indeed, it is rather Dante's method than Shakespeare's; the mortal is translated into the realm of the supernatural, which is made poetically real and vivid, instead of (at a distance) poetically unreal and vague. "As if it dodged a water-sprite,"—such impossible perils being here not beyond all conjecture. Still, by all these poets, though differently, superstition is employed to the same end. The element of dubiety and uncertainty Milton has also, not only (as above) in the parentheses "they say," "as seamen tell," or "dreams he sees," but also in his oxymorons or other contrarieties—"if shape it might be called, that shape had none." These, however, are the poet's own, descriptive, not dramatic.

Most Romantic of all Satan is in *Paradise Regained,* and particularly when detected by the Son:

'Tis true, I am that Spirit unfortunate . . .

"The low slow accents of the first two syllables," says Symonds, "the proud emphasis upon the fourth, the stately and melancholy music-roll which closes the line . . ." There we have the pathos, the pride, and the melancholy in perfect blending. That line Byron would delightedly have penned—had he had it in him.

5

Belial is of a less heroic mould, but is conceived more aesthetically still. Like Sin he is fair, and not like her only to the waist—

A fairer person lost not Heaven.

And would not Byron have been glad to pen that too with its unsettling implications? Such shadowy and dubious beauty, like the "withered" glory of the fallen angels assembled before Satan, the princely counsel yet shining in the face of Beelzebub, "majestic though in ruin," and the "faded splendour wan" of the apostate himself in Book IV, is much in the vein of Coleridge and Hazlitt, Byron, Keats, and Shelley. Belial has more of the spirit of reverie than Satan, common to the Romantic age:

> *for who would lose,*
> *Though full of pain, this intellectual being,*
> *Those thoughts that wander through eternity,*
> *To perish rather, swallow'd up and lost*
> *In the wide womb of uncreated night,*
> *Devoid of sense and motion?*

Healthy and vigorous, from death and nonentity he recoils, as Shelley and Keats and Chateaubriand at such moments would not; but he has the same bent for musing and for brooding over the abyss. *Il Penseroso* is not Keats's ode on *Melancholy,* or Coleridge's on *Dejection,* or Shelley's *Stanzas Written in Dejection, near Naples.* The doughty, tough-minded Puritan does not cherish or embrace his sorrow, or yearn to lie down like a tired child, or to cease upon the midnight with no pain; but, however it might have been as yet—"before Time was"—with his lusty Epicurean devil, he himself, manifestly, would have understood the later poet as he wrote

> *then on the shore*
> *Of the wide world I stand alone, and think,*
> *Till Love and Fame to nothingness do sink.*

"There never were, I think," says Chesterton, "men who gave to the imagination so much of the sense of having broken out into the very borderlands of being as did the great English poets of the romantic or revolutionary period; than [*sic*] Coleridge in the secret sunlight of the Antarctic, where the waters were like witches' oils; than Keats looking out of those extreme mysterious casements upon that ultimate sea."[5] None, that is, but Milton. After the lines

[5]*Victorian Literature* (N. Y., 1913), p. 20.

about the pavilion of Chaos quoted already come others
still more mysterious:

> *with him enthron'd*
> *Sat sable-vested Night, eldest of things,*
> *The consort of his reign.*

"Eldest of things," in that inverted foot is awe before something more imposing, more remote, yet touching us more
nearly, than perilous seas in faery lands forlorn.

6

Paradise, with the primitive and innocent pair in it,
would have been just the subject for a Romantic pen; but
it was involved in Milton's larger undertaking. Besides, he
is too puritanical and rigorous to make it quite to suit the
later taste. Adam and his mate are not so naïve as Blake
or Byron, in their very different fashions, would have them;
and their poet, not so unfettered or irresponsible. Milton
insists upon their nakedness, and doggedly defends it, until
it fairly seems the contrary of what he would have it be.
Adam is, moreover, so prodigiously and insistently saga-
cious that at times he becomes a bore. It is as he is tempted
that he is really interesting, and Eve herself in that situation
is still more so; yet both are attractive before that as they
speak of the beginnings of consciousness and of love. Here
the instinctive and the naïve, in true Romantic fashion,
come into their own. It is the first confidence, this retrospect of several days ago.

Eve tells Adam how she first waked from sleep, and hearing the sound of water, went and lay by the pool, and saw
a shape within the watery gleam, which (as she did) started
back and returned, with looks of sympathy and love. Only
by the voice of the angel could she now be led from it; and
when she saw Adam under a plane-tree, less fair, less ami-
ably mild, she turned away. He was a disappointment; till
he called, and seized her hand. And later Adam tells
Raphael how he himself had waked into being, and looked,

and wondered. He gazed awhile the ample sky; then sprang
up, glanced about and listened, ran and spoke.

> *And ye that live and move, fair creatures, tell,*
> *Tell, if ye saw, how came I thus, how here?*
> . . . . .
> *Tell me, how may I know him, how adore,*
> *From whom I have that thus I move and live,*
> *And feel that I am happier than I know.*

The last line particularly is in the Romantic vein:

> *We feel that we are greater than we know.*

And presently there is something more Romantic still, and
Wordsworth (or his readers at least) would have given
many a poem of his in exchange for this quintessential expression of love as "an unerring light and joy its own security."

Up hither, from among the trees appear'd
Presence divine. Rejoicing, but with awe,
In adoration at his feet I fell
Submiss: He rear'd me, and "Whom thou sought'st I am,"
Said mildly . . .

There, at last, the barriers against which the Romantic
spirit is ever beating fall away; "and the question and the
answer are one." It is as with the lovers in Romantic verse,
who, with one accord, sink into each other's arms, without
profession or confession. And what of Adam as he tells the
Angel, of the woman given to him, that

> *All higher knowledge in her presence falls*
> *Degraded; Wisdom in discourse with her*
> *Loses discountenanced, and like Folly shows.*
>
> (viii, 551 f.)

A Romantic paradox! As such, indeed, it is received by the
Angel, "with contracted brow"; and inexperienced Adam,
several days old, is at once set right.

7

Nevertheless Milton is not to be taken as frowning Romantic love quite down. Sir Herbert Grierson quotes Adam's words to Eve as he surrenders:

> *However, I with thee have fixt my lot,*
> *Certain to undergo like doom; if Death*
> *Consort with thee, Death is to me as Life;*
> *So forcible within my heart I feel*
> *The Bond of Nature draw me to my own,*
> *My own in thee, for what thou art is mine;*
> *Our state cannot be sever'd; we are one,*
> *One Flesh; to lose thee were to lose myself.*

And then he remarks: "That is the language of romantic love, but for Milton, the first, the primal sin,

> *whose mortal taste*
> *Brought Death into the world, and all our woe.*"

Which, strictly, literally speaking, may be true, yet Sir Herbert has just been saying, with fine perception, in reply to the Romantics Blake and Shelley and the modern psychoanalysts, that "neither consciously nor unconsciously" is Milton on the side of Satan; but that

in Milton the creative imagination and the critical intellect did not work in such harmony with one another as they have in some other poets . . . Milton is most a poet when his imagination, his creative power, works in most entire freedom from preconceived purpose—To justify the ways of God to men—or Biblical or ecclesiastical tradition.[6]

This principle, as I conceive it, applies to Adam as well, on whose side Milton is; though I should say that the difficulty lies not in the constitution of the author but in the subject. The justification of the Lord was, as it still is, impossible; the story as a whole, of the origin of evil, is incredible and unmanageable;[7] and, in a great poem, there

[6] *Cross Currents*, Chatto & Windus (1929), pp. 262–64.
[7] Cf. my *Poets and Playwrights*, pp. 278–81.

absolutely must be sympathy with the fated human pair. So now, on earth, in Eden, the poet, as we shall see more definitely in the final chapter, is slipping out of the trammels of Biblical and theological epic into the liberty of human drama. And this is the more dramatic even because the best there is in Adam is what, later, prompts him to share Eve's fate. Certainly now it is Romantic love demanding its own, in the words already quoted; also then it is a true cry of the heart, in

How can I live without thee?

and the dramatist would not have us pass upon this choice of All for Love and the World well Lost, here at the beginnings of both, in anything of a judicial spirit:

> *no, no, I feel*
> *The link of Nature draw me: flesh of flesh,*
> *Bone of my bone thou art, and from thy state*
> *Mine never shall be parted, bliss or woe.* (ix, 913 f.)

Better extinction with her than immortality without her. There, is a paradox again (though now not expressed); and (as we shall see, though more explicitly in the final chapter), it is in preparation for the conclusion, which is an approach to mortal life as we know it. This, in a great poem, like the very motive which prompts Adam, cannot rest under absolute condemnation.

Indeed the poet has gone farther than he needed to go for the bringing of the immortal pair down to the level of life as we know it; but not too far for our sympathy, or his drama. Before Adam's arrival, Eve, thinking of the consequences, has said to herself

> *Adam shall share with me in bliss or woe:*
> *So dear I love him, that with him all deaths*
> *I could endure, without him live no life.*

How can I *die* without thee? In her, to be sure, this is not the best there is; for partly it is jealousy, the thought of another Eve supplanting her, but it is reckless love again, and like that of the famous lovers of times to come. And never has she loved him so much as now, after he has stood the trial, choosing to incur Divine displeasure for her sake or death.[8]

That is rather upsetting to the theology. What is all-important, however, and is constantly forgotten, is not so much the intrinsic difficulty of the subject, as the fact forgotten too often, that Milton had an imagination, which, as with the other great poets, passes far beyond the confines of his actual sympathy or approval. He was himself no primitivist or anarchist, no satanist or antinomian; and no Romantic, either, in the thoroughgoing lawless modern sense. Like most great poets and other artists he delighted in noble imaginings, emotions, and sensations for their own sake more than his contemporaries; but his range was wider than that of his predecessors partly because the province of sensibility for both poets and also other men had meantime widened. He was thus no sentimentalist or sensationalist, for he was big enough in his other faculties to keep the balance even. And by his imaginative sympathy with Satan Milton, though in the presentation he takes up more completely with the demon's point of view, his "injur'd merit," is no more compromised than a Shakespeare with his villains.[9] Keats's words to Woodhouse (October 27, 1818) cannot be too often repeated: "The poetical character itself . . . has as much delight in conceiving an Iago as an Imogen. What shocks the virtuous philosopher delights the chameleon poet." Simply because of the open-sesame and safe-conduct of his imagination, Satan engages our sym-

[8]A recent fine critic of Milton whom I came upon only at the last moment thinks Eve guilty of murder. Adam, then, would be guilty, I should think, of suicide. But as the critic surely remembers, in the world of romance, of all for love, and, indeed, of poetry, matters are not so logical, and there is not a conclusion to every premise.

[9]No more than the reader necessarily is, in the imaginative re-creation. By a not unfriendly critic (E.L.H., 1938, p. 191) I have been charged with conniving at "antisemitism in the library" because while disapproving of the playing of the Jew that Shakespeare drew I favored the reading of him as such. Which would be like actually sharing the prejudice against the rabble, or that against the French as soldiers, in so far as for comic purposes Shakespeare availed himself of either.

pathy like Macbeth and even Richard III, on Watts-Dunton's principle referred to in chapters XIV and XV above,
as the leading and active character,—a sympathy constantly
restricted by the poet's own words of condemnation. And to
be kept out of "the Devil's party," where Blake would have
him, Milton need not be, as M. Saurat would have him,
actually both the Devil himself, in his pride and heresy,
passion and sensuality, and also his antagonist, who drives
him out. How deadly uninteresting, except to the psychoanalysts and the biographers, the epic then becomes; and
how confusing if, as the "lost Archangel," Milton asks his
"bold compeer,"

> Is this the region, this the soil, the clime . . .

he then "must have thought of the condition of the Elect."[10]
Milton and the Elect (*mon Dieu!*) in Hell! However, the
imagination can, of course, be compromising or contami-
nating (or else, which is more likely, quite absent, and this
then is the right place for the psychology and biography),
as it actually was, we saw in chapter XVI, for nineteenth-
century decadent Romanticism, particularly across the
Channel. "Evil, be thou my good!" cries Satan. But in defiance. Such as Baudelaire and Flaubert and their followers,
whether dramatically or in their own persons, say the same,
but for the evil's own sake, as heightening the flavor of the
aesthetic pleasure. This is in the spirit of sadism, or masochism, or other perversions, of which there is nothing at all
in Milton; just as there is no pleasure, either, in the painful
or the horrible or the ugly for its own sake—even Shelley's
lines on the Medusa would have made him shudder—to
his unjaded appetite. So, too, his delight in the distant and
remote has nothing in common with the exoticism which
is a cover for eroticism;[11] and the aesthetic transmutation
was only partial as he presented a waste of landscape, the

---

[10]*Milton, Man and Thinker*, p. 215, 220–21, et cetera. Cf. Miss
Bodkin. *Archetypal Patterns* (1934) pp. 222–24, who welcomes the
Freudian paradox, as in Hamlet hating his father, Iago the Shadow-
Side of Othello. See above, pp. 343, 309.

[11]Praz, *Romantic Agony* (1933), pp. 200–1.

infernal gloom, the shadows of superstition, or touched on the beauty of sin. The moral meaning and purpose he never neglected or obscured. The "iland salt and bare" at the head of the Persian Gulf, considered above, is the wreck of Paradise and human happiness, not a truly Romantic ruin; "darkness visible" is a spiritual torment, not merely a Rembrandtian study in light and shade; and the superstitions, used so subtly, are, though Milton does not believe in them, meant to suggest what is baleful and evil.

8

The most Romantic feature of the poem, however, is the conclusion. As a whole, to be sure, it is classical, in conformity, not only (as Addison and Johnson recognized) to ancient practice and precept in the epic, but also to the spirit of the ancient poetical practice in general. In accordance with the one, the outcome is not tragic; in accordance with the other, even in tragedy, it is quiet and consoling. In the true Greek spirit, Milton here, as in the sequel and *Samson Agonistes,* in *Comus* and *Lycidas,* and even in the separate books of the two epics, descends to a close. That is not, as often in our day, the climax. Still, he is too individual and independent wholly to suit the classical taste, or the neoclassical at least. Addison would have the poem end with

> *The world was all before them, where to choose*
> *Their place of rest, and Providence their guide.*

Of those lines which follow—

> *They hand in hand, with wand'ring steps and slow,*
> *Through Eden took their solitary way—*

he says that, "though they have their beauty, [they] fall very much below the foregoing passage, and renew in the mind of the reader that anguish which was pretty well laid by that consideration,

> *The world was all before them, . . ."*

Yet the close as Milton frames it has not only a beauty in itself but a fitness to all that had gone before. Without the subsequent two lines, the words "And Providence their guide" are too consolatory, too didactic; and "The world was all before them, where to choose their place of rest," too matter-of-fact. Milton would have the pair more meditative and pensive, more regretful and uncertain. The ending as Addison would refashion it is too solid and flat; Milton would have it a little up in the air. The man and woman are now for the first time "out in the world," and are neither dejected nor (as has been said, still more infelicitously) "elated." It is a mingled feeling.

The difference between the Romantic art and the classical at their best is apparent as we turn to the *Iliad*. The subject of the epic is the wrath of Achilles, and that ends with the burial and funeral of Hector, who, Achilles had vowed, was to have neither:

> Thus they held the funeral of Hector, tamer of horses.

The subsequent victory, the fall of the city and the death of the hero, are not recounted; but these matters are familiar, and in the present story they have been ordained by the gods and foretold by mortals. The fighting has ceased, it is made clear, only because Achilles has magnanimously yielded, and granted an armistice; and the hero knows of his own death at Ilium (which, with fame, is the alternative he had nobly chosen) through his goddess mother, and by the horse Xanthus and the dying Hector has been apprised that it is very nigh. So Adam and Eve know of their future and that of the race through the vision and prophecy of Michael. Both quiet and consolatory endings are suggestive. But here the outlines are firm and distinct. In both much is still to happen. But here there is no musing, or melancholy, or anything else that might be called a mood. The hero has retreated from view, not only his wrath but his vengeance satisfied, and "peace and consolation," matters of fact but still of poetry, lie imbedded in the story.

Now this musing, melancholy ending, with a look into the future or back at the past, and a mystery over all, is characteristic of the narrative poems of the Romantic age, like *Alastor, The Ancient Mariner, Michael,* and the story of Margaret in *The Excursion,* like *Lara, The Corsair,* and *The Bride of Abydos.* It is far better than that of any of these—quite free of moralizing sentiment, or the author's intruding person—and is concise and suggestive, the story still moving on. But it is in the true Romantic vein of giving a glimpse of Life (as in this later day it began to be called) behind what merely in itself is a trivial matter or occurrence, and of Nature, the world enveloping the individual.

Addison's strictures, then, with his misgivings, only reassure me: those of Richard Bentley and Mr. John Erskine, at first, do not. What Addison is objecting to may be only the Romantic; what the others are objecting to may be something else. Bentley—magnus Bentleius even the German philologists called him—was certainly a great scholar; ("he was no fool," says Professor Mackail, adding, drolly, yet not superfluously, "and he was the first scholar of his age") ; and Mr. Erskine is, ordinarily, a fine critic. Yet the one objects to the conclusion as it stands, and the other— he does not make it quite clear—either to that or to all the rest of the poem. Both do so on the score of logic and sense —hard and meager sense and logic, not the poetic. Our first parents, says Bentley, "were guided by Providence, and therefore needed not to wander; they were reassured by Michael's predictions, and so might well display an engaging briskness; while as for 'their solitary way,' they were no more solitary than in Paradise, 'there being no Body besides them Two, both here and there.' "[12] Now, if not before this, we see clearly why the two lines were added! And John Milton, I suspect, for all his faith and theology, knew that in life Providence was not so confidently to be counted on, and would not misrepresent its dispensations in his poem. Mr. Erskine,[13] keeping to the literal meaning,

[12]Quoted from Raleigh's *Milton* (1915), p. 157.

[13]For a fuller account of his opinions and my objections to them, see my essay, "Was Paradise Well Lost," *Poets and Playwrights,* pp. 203-9.

finds the conclusion, not melancholy, but "lively"—"indeed, they go out in excellent spirits"—"for the world before them they had nothing but zest"—and then (naturally enough) considers this sort of conclusion an afterthought. On the one hand, he ignores the inner meaning, the pensive mood and rhythm; on the other, he ignores those preparations (to be found in nearly every book of the poem) for a consolatory, though not cheerful, close, where good should be brought out of evil, and death change from a penalty to a remedy,[14] and even become "the gate of life."[15] If these be inconsistencies or contradictions, they are those, not only of *Paradise Lost,* but of theology, and (in part) of our common experience. They are the antinomies of existence, the paradoxes of verse. What then Bentley and Erskine are objecting to is, I suspect, nothing more or less than poetry.

Yet Romantic poetry is less rigidly logical or sensible than any that preceded it, and more of a stumbling-block to the wise and learned. To it such objections would more evidently apply; and I am loath to think that Addison, even with misgivings, would be for amputating anything that was like the poetry he knew of. Indeed, the mere fact that a poet and a scholar of the neoclassical age, both so deeply imbued with the spirit of classical poetry, should have thus agreed in caviling seems to indicate in the beauty of the lines, by the Romantic age acknowledged, something as yet strange and remote. Hazlitt, De Quincey, and Landor acknowledge the beauty eagerly: "The ending," says the last-named, "is proper and complete."

And I wonder if there is not here something else a little new to poetry, Romantic and even Pre-Raphaelite, in the highly significant repeated motif:

They hand in hand, with wandering steps and slow . . .

Mr. Charles Williams, before me, has remarked in print the echo from

[14]See *ibid.,* pp. 205–7; and *Paradise Lost,* III, 206ff; XI, 59ff.
[15]*Paradise Lost* XII, 571.

> *So saying, from her husband's hand her hand*
> *Soft she withdrew*

as she willfully separates in the morning; and that from

> *So saying, her rash hand in evil hour*
> *Forth reaching to the fruit, she plucked, she ate . . .*

But he fits it all into a philosophical meaning. To me it
seems a merely but highly poetical way of signalizing and
connecting important moments in the action, with a human
meaning. It is like the repeated "all our woe," in the second
line of the poem and, in the same position at the end of
the verse again, when Sin takes the key of Hell from her
girdle to unlock it, and when Eve is led by the serpent to
"the tree of prohibition, root of all our woe."[16] It is the
same hand, offending and forgiven, withdrawn and now
indissolubly linked; and is this not a poetic method of calling attention to a moment, or a feature, or an object, similar
to Rossetti's with the knife and the laugh in *The Last Confession,* and his staff and scrip in another poem, and William Morris's with the haystack in the Floods? Still, it
resembles more such repetition in the ancients, as in Sophocles and Homer; the Scaean Gate, for instance, whereby
Andromache would have Hector make his stand and at the
last he does so, awaiting Achilles, and whereby the victor
himself is to fall.[17] In Milton there is more of merely human
significance than in the ancients; but more of functional
effect than in the moderns, and that not so obvious.

9

Paradise Regained is generally in a severer and drier style
than the preceding epic; *Samson Agonistes* is (in form) a
Greek tragedy; and there is little that verges upon the Romantic in either. Yet in the sequel Satan, as we have noticed
already, reappears; and there is, besides, what, in so little

---

[16] *Poets and Playwrights,* pp. 247–48.
[17] *Shakespeare and Other Masters,* p. 392.

space, is perhaps the most enchanting of all revivals of medieval romance, the oft-quoted:

> *Fairer than feign'd of old, or fabl'd since*
> *Of fairy damsels met in forest wide*
> *By knights of Logres, or of Lyones,*
> *Lancelot, or Pelleas, or Pellenore.*

10

And which of the ancient classics was Milton's favorite? Strange to say, but as is generally acknowledged, Ovid, the favorite of Shakespeare (if indeed of the classics he knew any other), and of the Middle Ages, back to which our Romantic poets looked and from which, however transmuting the material, they drew. Not Virgil or Homer, either, though Milton had learned of both; and also not Aeschylus or Sophocles, but the more romantic Euripides. I do not know enough about the classics rightly to discuss the matter; but Milton shares with Ovid (as in his early Latin verses and his depiction of Adam and Eve) the delight in the amorous and idyllic, and (both there and elsewhere) in the forms of natural life and scenery, in light and shade, in the weird and strange, in the fabulous and mysterious, in the geographical and historical or legendary names which conjure up associations, and in the world of imagination merely for itself. And like Ovid again, Milton has the cosmical outlook, is interested in the beginning and the end of things, and takes to paradox and oxymoron in endeavoring to present such matters and others that are beyond the reach of experience—

> *Sea cover'd sea, sea without shore . . .*
>
> *Omnia pontus erant, deerant quoque litora ponto.*
> *(Met.* I, 292.)

In Milton, then, with his huge and cloudy imaginations, his lofty consciousness of his genius, and his delight in the dim and distant, in Nature, and—though not disproportionately—in sensations and emotions for their own sake, there are rather clearly perceptible anticipations of the Romantic age. But without its failings or delusions. Truth to him is not beauty, nor beauty truth; and the meaning is not blurred, the moral ideal slighted, nor, for all his suggestiveness, the architectonic purpose forgotten. He is a Puritan, is a classic. Nature or the past, the infinite or his own emotion, is for him no covert or refuge; and his genius, no warrant for caprice or extravagance.[18]

[18]In an article entitled "Give the Devil His Due," to appear within a twelvemonth, I reply to Mr. C. S. Lewis (referred to in note 8 above) defending both Eve and Satan.

CHAPTER XX

Time and Space in Milton[1]

TIME AND SPACE, these latter days, have greatly occupied the attention of the philosophers, and consequently the critics of poetry too. According to recent ingenious opinion (widely accepted in this country, it would seem, among the literary learned) Milton's conception of space was deeply influenced by the contemporary astronomy, and, through the use of the telescope, his imagination was transformed. I have of late demurred to this; and now before taking up the matter of his interest in time, I beg leave to summarize what I said of the other "category," so closely allied and involved.

Not only does such a transformation seem in itself inconceivable but the facts of the case are against it. In Milton's poems written before he went to Italy and saw Galileo there are far views and effects of perspective as well as in those written after; and our feeling that there is more of spaciousness in the later poems is mainly owing to the sub-

[1] This chapter is chiefly the latter portion of an article entitled "Criticisms Criticized," *Journal English and Germanic Philology*, October, 1942. I here leave out what has to do with Spenser; and, in the summary above, what is more controversial or of less general interest concerning Milton.

ject, which is, of course, the cosmos. Spaciousness and the effects of perspective are to be found not only in Ovid and Virgil but in Homer; and those in the painting of the seventeenth century, which began to appear in Tintoretto and the later Titian of the sixteenth, are no more certainly to be connected with the progress of science than, on the other hand, the want of them is in the Barbizon school and the Pre-Raphaelites of the nineteenth. Moreover, Milton does not, as is thought, differ widely in his cosmical conceptions from the ancient philosophers and poets. Ptolemy (as well as Cicero, Lucretius, Boethius,[2] and the sixteenth-century Bruno) even outdid the modern astronomers and Milton himself in notions of the magnitude of the universe, the velocity of the celestial bodies, the boundlessness of the void; and Milton has the same way as Lucretius and Ovid of describing the warring elements of the "hoary deep" or "the wild abyss,"—by negatives or privatives, by oxymoron and paradox, by abstraction and the adjective used substantively,—in fact, he distinctly echoes them, coping, like them, as best he may, with the inconceivable, beyond the reach of perception and of the telescope.

Now Milton's imagination has still more in common with the ancients. It produces a perspective not only in space but in time. David Masson once said, "Shakespeare lived in a world of time, Milton in a universe of space." Passing (for once!) Shakespeare by, I yet claim time (as in the preceding chapter I have practically done already) for Milton too. For the imagination, as for the memory, the corridors of time and of space intersect if they do not coincide, as they do with the Romantic poets, with Spenser and the Latins, not to mention their readers themselves. And with Milton most conspicuously, strange to say, in his earliest good poem, the ode on the Nativity; where the poet's

[2]References not in the article: Lucretius VI, 650–52; I, 958ff; II, 1048ff. *Somnium Scipionis*, 15, 16. For Boethius and other ancients see E. H. Blakeney's *Somnium* (1927), p. 45; Theodore Spencer's *Shakespeare* (1942), pp. 3, 5. Also, George Wither, *Britain's Remembrancer* (1627), Gutch's edition (1863), p. 129: "the world . . . but like an atom under me."

imagination circles far above and beyond the Child, amphibiously, in both elements. In *Paradise Lost* and *Paradise Regained,* alike, moreover, there are far-reaching perspective panoramas. This motif, so dear to Milton, comes down from Moses' vision of the Promised Land; but the geographical or traditional details are a blend of the sacred, merely descriptive method—"Jericho, the city of palm trees" —with the classical, which involves associations remote in time both present and to come. Milton here abounds in these, as also in his similes; and they are not rare in Virgil, Horace, and Catullus. To Marshall's edition of Horace a table of historical allusions is appended; and there are the mythological besides. And when the Romans travel or think of travel, it is pretty much as we do:

> *Sive per Syrtes iter aestuosas*
> *sive facturus per inhospitalem*
> *Caucasum vel quae loca fabulosus*
>   *lambit Hydaspes.*
>
> (Odes, 1, 22.)

> *Furi et Aureli, comites Catulli,*
> *sive in extremos penetrabit Indos,*
> *litus ut longe resonante Eoa*
>   *tunditur unda,*
> *sive in Hyrcanos Arabasve molles,*
> *seu Sagas sagittiferosque Parthos,*
> *sive quae septemgeminus colorat*
>   *aequora Nilus,*
> *sive trans altas gradietur Alpes,*
> *Caesaris visens monimenta magni,*
> *Gallicum Rhenum, horribilesque*
>   *ultimosque Britannos . . .*
>
> (Catullus, xi.)

The "storied Hydaspes," and the famous, the strangest as well as remotest places and peoples! And, like us, the Romans have memories as, like us, like Heine and Hugo or even the medieval pilgrims, they yield to the vernal impulse to wander, afoot or on the wings of song:

Ad claras Asiae volemus urbes. (Catullus, xlvi.)

Without time space is well-nigh meaningless, measureless, the infinite no better than the finite, like the empty heavens, the sea without sail or funnel; and alone under his dark pavilion, Milton's Chaos, the creature of his imagination, would have been imaginatively incomplete, but

> with him enthron'd
> Sat sable-vested Night, eldest of things,
> The consort of his reign.

There, in the phrasing and the rhythm, in the awesome shifted metrical accent on "eldest," and the superlative applied not to persons but to "things," is, if anywhere, Time the shadow, the specter, but, so to speak, as an additional dimension. So far, Milton's own thoughts, however it be with Belial's, "wander through eternity." His imagination, though towering, was balanced and normal, and after Italy as before.

In fact Milton takes very considerable account of time— on the surface at any rate he seems to make as much of it as of space. The mere map of it that he draws is as exten- sive—from eternity to eternity, from before the begetting of the Son to the ultimate Judgment and consequent purg- ing conflagration (xi, 900–01), with innumerable glimpses of world changes in between. And his feeling for time is perhaps as profound. In his historical sense and compass he is of course like Virgil, not Homer. The sin of Eden over- hangs *Paradise Lost* from the beginning, and the light of the atonement, of which there is a glimpse at the beginning, early rises to relieve the shadow deepening towards the end. What poet, moreover, so abounds in historical, or legendary, reminiscences? His similes are steeped in them. And by re- moteness in time the effect of remoteness in space is heightened for him—by grand and vague associations in the reader's memory, his vulture being on Imaus bred, his icebergs of Petsora, his bridge Hellespontic, his odors of Araby the blest—; his rivers are faraway and famous,— Abbana and Pharphar, not only Hydaspes but Choaspes, the "drink of none but kings"—; and when he beholds the multitudes scattered thick on the inflamèd sea, they are like the leaves that strow the brooks in Vallombrosa, or the sedge on the Red Sea coast in such a storm as when its

> *waves o'erthrew*
> *Busiris and his Memphian chivalry.*

So, when mustered on the shore, they are not less innumerable and formidable than all the giant brood of Phlegra joined to the opposing armies at Thebes and Ilium, and (familiar to the reader but ever enchanting)

> *what resounds*
> *In fable or romance of Uther's son,*
> *Begirt with British and Armoric knights;*
> *And all who since, baptiz'd or infidel,*
> *Jousted in Aspramont or Montalban,*
> *Damasco, or Morocco, or Trebisond;*
> *Or whom Biserta sent from Afric shore*
> *When Charlemain with all his peerage fell*
> *By Fontarabbia.*

Fable or romance, or faraway history, who has such a feeling for it as Milton, down to the day of Coleridge? Not Spenser certainly, who hadn't it in him to call up a vision so rich and rare as that in *Paradise Regained* (to the reader more familiar still) :

> *distant more,*
> *Under the trees now tripp'd, now solemn stood,*
> *Nymphs of Diana's train, and Naiades*
> *With fruits and flowers from Amalthea's horn,*
> *And ladies of th' Hesperides, that seem'd*
> *Fairer than feign'd of old, or fabl'd since*
> *Of fairy damsels met in forest wide*
> *By knights of Logres, or of Lyones,*
> *Lancelot, or Pelleas, or Pellenore.* (ii, 353.)

What poet, as in the body of that epic or on the margin of the earlier, ever so conjured up, even by the music he made

out of the names, either the medieval or the ancient world?
And this feeling for the opulent multitudinous mystery of
the past, like his feeling for space, which is indeed inseparable from it, Milton showed even in his early poems. As
in the *Hymn on the Nativity,* with its historical or legendary
retrospect and prospect and the central crisis:

> *No nightly trance or breathèd spell,*
> *Inspires the pale-ey'd priest from the prophetic cell.*

> *Peor and Baalim*
> *Forsake their temples dim,*
> *With that twice-batter'd god of Palestine;*
> *And moonèd Ashtaroth . . .*

and both there and in *L'Allegro:*

> *From haunted spring and dale . . .*

> *On summer eves by haunted stream;*

and in *Il Penseroso:*

> *And if aught else great bards beside*
> *In sage or solemn tunes have sung,*
> *Of turneys and of trophies hung;*
> *Of forests and enchantments drear,*
> *Where more is meant than meets the ear.*

Not to mention the mythical "airy tongues" in *Comus,* "that
syllable men's names on sands and shores and desert wilder-
nesses." Why, the past (as we saw in the last chapter), the
past romantic and mysterious—mythical or superstitious,
historical or legendary—was one of Milton's most precious
resources.

It is true that Milton has proportionately less of a feeling
for time than the later nineteenth century but he has also
less for space. "Carlyle's and Arnold's, Hugo's, Swinburne's,
and Hardy's constant sense of man's life as a drop or mote
in the abyss of eternity, is fairly foreign to him."[3] But so is
theirs for man's person in the bottomless void. John Milton,

[3] Cf. my *Poets and Playwrights,* pp. 293–94. In that discussion of
Milton I somewhat underestimate the relative importance of time.

le silence éternel de ces espaces infinis ne l'effraie pas. Of
time we know more than he knew; for us the world was not
framed 4,004 years before the present era. It is unlikely,
however, that he himself accepted the petty figure, after
looking backward with Lucretius as the latter denied the
eternity of creation, "which could not have despised the
mighty strength of immeasurable ages from infinite time up
to this present" (v, 377–79). The important thing is not
the geological and astronomical figures, for time or space,
either. On the imagination they have little immediate
effect, and the imagination (again) is all-important. It is
as with the Copernican astronomy. Carlyle and the rest can
have such a sense for infinity in space and time alike only
because their public has something of it themselves, and
men have been brooding over it in the generations since
Milton's day. Imagination is a two-sided, reciprocal, co-
operative function. Infinity has been borne in upon men,
and the poet's words that touch upon it can then strike
home. To Milton and his generation

man is immortal, is not, with his belongings, to be swallowed up
in what is no better than an instant in the gulf. He has a place in
the sun. Over the Puritan poet's eyes Eternity does not hang, as
it does over ours today, like the night. With scarcely a hint in
preparation Conrad can write of Daudet's characters and be at
once understood: "They are very near the truth of our common
destiny: their fate is poignant, it is intensely interesting, and of
not the slightest consequence." What is in the back of his mind
and of ours here furnishes the transition: indeed, it is upon this
dark groundwork that is spread the whole intricate texture of
our poetic thought.[4]

Time and space alike Milton does not so take to heart.
They remain for him more solid and external. The past is to
him more romantic than to Virgil and Horace, to Catullus
and Propertius, because it offers a longer vista of history
behind him, and (with chivalry as well as the legions and
the phalanges there) a more varied and striking one. But
essentially Milton's attitude is similar. "Think, too, of all

[4]*Poets and Playwrights,* p. 294.

the noble cities, the achievement of man's toil, piled high on steepy crags, and the streams that glide beneath those ancient walls"—

> *adde tot egregias urbes operumque laborem,*
> *tot congesta manu praeruptis oppida saxis*
> *fluminaque antiquos subterlabentia muros.*
> (*Georgics,* II, 155.)

And as Ilium, the ancient, collapses:

> *Urbs antiqua ruit, multos dominata per annos.*
> (Aen., II, 363.)

The sentiment of antiquity without its poignancy! Yet the following from Propertius has more of Romantic melancholy in it than anything in Milton that I can remember: "Alas! Veii, thou ancient city, thou too wert then a kingdom":

> *Heu Vei veteres! et vos tum regna fuistis*
> *Et vestro posita est aurea sella foro:*
> *nunc intra muros pastoris bucina lenti*
> *cantat, et in vestris ossibus arva metunt.* (IV, x, 25)

And now "the sounding of the shepherd's horn, and the reaping, over the citizens' bones"! For though a sponsor of the Romantic age and also a characteristic representative of the seventeenth century, Milton was the latter in still another sense—and, though a Puritan, more profoundly than many of his contemporaries—in being a classicist, but one of the heroic mould.

In some respects Milton belongs beyond the period of Propertius. Though he wrote *Il Penseroso* he would not delight in our latter-day enervating melancholy, and though as we saw in the preceding chapter he can find a beauty in what is waste and shadowy and forlorn, he does not take to the ugly, or the morbid, and still less, of course, to the horrible or the "poisonous honey" of the "flowers of evil"; certainly he did not know the Romantic Agony, nor even the right Romantic shudder. Also, though a Puritan, he was no Calvinist, no prostrate, clinging devotee, convinced of mortal depravity. Both his faith and his stout spirit support him, make him bear up and steer right onward. Hence time and space have upon him no desolating, overwhelming effect. He does not recoil upon himself, or brood, or pine, or wail. But he has feeling enough for their immensity.

CHAPTER XXI

From the Superhuman to the Human in Paradise Lost

ONE OF the greatest beauties of *Paradise Lost* lies, I think, in the gradual transition from the supernatural to the natural, in the felicitous approach and descent to the close. I have elsewhere[1] shown the twilight scene at the last, with its pensive mood and rhythm, the exiled pair looking forward but also backward, going hand in hand but with wandering steps and slow, to be appropriate not only to the situation—the end of Paradise, the beginning of life—but to all the rest of the poem. I there indicated a few of the many preparations for such a quiet and consolatory ending in the avowed purpose of God to bring good out of evil, make death not only a penalty but a remedy, and dismiss our first parents, though sorrowing, yet in peace. And I there hinted at the larger internal rhythm of the poem:

Twilight and dim horizons at the end—after the darkness visible and lurid splendors of Hell, after the glories of Heaven, after the sweet but unreal light of Paradise. At the beginning the towering passions of the devils and the ecstasies of the saints; the

[1]*Poets and Playwrights* (1930), chap. vii: "Was Paradise Well Lost?" and chapter XIX above.

naked and spotless purity of Paradise in between; and now the shame and sorrow, and love and hope, of frail humanity.

It is on this last subject that I wish now to dwell, endeavoring to indicate how, in the conception and presentation of the scene, of the character, and of the sentiments, the poet keeps proportion and propriety, and thus leads us, also, from Hell and Heaven to Paradise and then out into the world.

2

It is, of course, difficult to determine the purpose of an author in a long epic or novel which has taken years in the writing and has for years been borne in mind. His purpose changes, as in *Don Quixote;* his powers fail him, as in *Faust.* And this is especially the case with the expression. If Milton's purpose was, as I think, to adapt his style to the subject and scene, and gradually to approach the exquisite simplicity and chastened humanity of the close, how much of this may, in the upshot, be merely accidental, and owing to a decline in energy or a change in taste! These possibilities must be allowed for. Indeed, there is, in the later books, a drift (if ever the redoubtable Puritan drifted) to the style which prevails in *Paradise Regained.* There is something of the same dryness and conciseness, the same tendency to parenthesis, ellipsis, and a less dynamic rhythm.[2] But even in *Paradise Regained* these qualities are prominent only where Milton's imagination is not fully stimulated, and are there so frequently only because his imagination is less seldom aroused. They do not trouble us in the later *Samson Agonistes;* nor do they in the earlier epic. In the close of *Paradise Lost* there is no sign of them; and for our purposes, in this essay, they need not be considered further.

There is another rhythm in the poem than that above mentioned, still more a matter of equilibrium; I mean the

[2]For a finely discriminating account of this and other aspects of Milton's rhythm in *Paradise Lost,* see Professor Mackail's essay on Milton in *The Springs of Helicon* (1909), to which I am here indebted.

paradox or antinomy of good coming out of evil, of death not only a penalty but a remedy, and even the "gate of life." This, which has been thought to be an inconsiderate contradiction, the result of an afterthought, is really the specific problem of the drama, and an example of that "balance or reconcilement of opposite or discordant qualities" which Coleridge expected in a poem. Both as art and as reality the antinomy is in the end acceptable. The Lord does not contradict himself in that having pronounced death as a punishment he later declares it to be a relief. Death is both, we know. And such a reconcilement of opposites furnishes the essential structure not only of the greatest epics but also of the greatest tragedies and lyrics. We have only to recall great epics and tragedies of fate and free will like the *Iliad* and the *Oedipus, Macbeth* and *Othello,* and dramatic lyrics from Drayton's *Since there's no help, come let us kiss and part* to Patmore's *Azalea.*

And there is still another sort of rhythm involved with this, as the theme of woe yields to that of hope. I have elsewhere remarked[3] upon the second and third lines,

> *whose mortal taste*
> *Brought Death into the world, and all our woe,*

as a sublime wail for the sin of the world which echoes and re-echoes through the poem. The phrase "all our woe" is a *leitmotiv* which reappears, in the same prominent position in the meter, both when Sin takes the key of Hell from her girdle and when the Serpent leads the woman to the tree; and in the ninth book, that of the temptation, it recurs in changing form, six several times. Then, once the woe has really come, the theme subsides, and that of hope and reconciliation, touched upon even in the following line of the Exordium, "till one greater man restore us," replaces it. While the human pair were happy and guiltless, woe hung over them; once fallen, it is hope instead. There is thus

---

[3]Above, chap. XIX, and *Poets and Playwrights,* chap. ix: "Milton, Puritan of the Seventeenth Century." From this discussion is drawn also some part of the subsequent description of Milton's grand style, and of the contrast between him and Dante.

attained the contrasting "duplicity" of effect, and the richness of texture, that belong to great poetry and drama.

3

Something of the same time-honored principle, undoubtedly, prompted the poet as at the beginning he aroused sympathy and admiration for Satan. Whether the Devil be the hero or not (but of course he isn't) and whether or not it was intended that he should be (but of course he wasn't) Milton, if he was to pen a great poem on the subject and begin it at the point in the story that he had (and rightly) chosen, did but what must be done. Even Iago is made to win our admiration, and though Othello both does that and wins our sympathy besides, he appears at the outset, not, like Adam, late in the story, and is a great tragic figure, not, like him, a mere innocent. Man and woman, until much later, are only a pair of pawns; and Satan's true antagonist is the King of Heaven. But even so, Milton shows flexibility and tact. Satan degenerates and gradually loses our sympathy.[4] As he surveys the new world and then approaches the couple in Paradise, he falls more and more a prey to envy and hatred, jeers and sneers instead of breathing defiance and melancholy, and stoops to flattery and deceit. And when he returns in triumph he has recourse, in his vainglory, to stage-acting and melodrama. Rightly his greatness is abated and his luster beclouded as the sympathy is shifted to the tempted and misled. In his own nature and his primal dimensions, the demigod, though fallen, would overshadow the human pair. So far as they know, their tempter is only the Serpent.

But at first it is as he is—an archangel newly overthrown, his form having not yet lost all her original brightness, matchless but with the Almighty—that he, like his followers, must appear. They are Titans, as against the gods of Olympus; they are spirits of evil, in keeping with the vaster imaginings in the Psalms, the Prophets, and the Revelation, and with Milton's own. For the presentation of

[4] Sir Walter Raleigh denies this (*Milton,* 1915, p. 139).

the invisible, the seventeenth-century poet found the restricted limits and materialistic conception of Dante inadequate. He magnifies and dilates, circles about or adumbrates, where the Tuscan grapples or penetrates. To this end he has recourse to many rhetorical devices of the ancients, with a novel and mysterious effect. He employs abstraction and oxymoron, hyperbole and circumlocution, both in the speech of the beings themselves and in the description of them and their shadowy abode. Satan's

> *What reenforcement we may gain from hope;*
> *If not, what resolution from despair . . .*[5]

is a paradox or contrariety like the "darkness visible" and "if shape it might be called that shape had none," employed by the poet himself. Circumlocutions like "the sounding alchemy" for trumpets, and abstractions like "the grisly Terror" for death, abound. The fallen angels are thus and otherwise made lofty and indefinable in person and power, thought and feeling, movement and demeanor. Their deliberations are a ceremonial; their diversions a spectacle or adventure; their solace the pleasing sorcery of philosophy or a sublime concord of harp and voice (II, 527-70). And the wild and melancholy scene is a fitting background.

4

With this the whole stylistic and metrical effect, whether in the speeches or in the poet's descriptions, is in unison. There is the true sublime, elevation without inflation. Plain and simple words are not avoided, but all common or mean associations are. The imagery is drawn from legend, history, or the large, remote, and extraordinary phenomena of nature, frequently colored or clouded by superstition. And the metrical effects have a range and volume elsewhere unexampled in English poetry. This is the organ voice of England, and sooner or later every stop is touched. In short, as never before in the history of poetry, the classical and Renaissance prescription of the "heroic" and the "mar-

[5] *Paradise Lost*, I, 190-1.

velous" for the epic is observed; and everything is in proportion and in harmony in this world of shades and of woe.

It is so in Heaven, with bliss for torment, and light for
darkness, though, until the schism and the battle, with
rather too much of theology and theodicy for poetry and
drama. As is well known, Milton is less at home in the
ethereal regions than with the thunderous atmosphere and
bold chiaroscuro of Hell. But there is poetry in the adoration of the saints, drama in the combat, apocalyptic pag-
eantry in the triumph of the Son of God. It is the grand
style, again, unmistakably. Yet not only the art of the
theater but each of the others involving time is an "art of
preparations"; and even here, amid the communings of
the dual Deity, there is a note of tenderness and of interest
in the human life that is to be which, thus remotely, prepares us for the close. The expression of this, though still
noble and lofty, is simple, befitting the God who is to come
down to earth:

> *Father, thy word is past; Man shall find grace;*
> *And shall grace not find means, that finds her way,*
> *The speediest of thy winged messengers,*
> *To visit all thy creatures, and to all*
> *Comes unprevented, unimplor'd, unsought?*
> *Happy for Man, so coming; he her aid*
> *Can never seek, once dead in sins and lost;*
> *Atonement for himself or offering meet,*
> *Indebted and undone, hath none to bring:*
> *Behóld me then, mé for hím, lífe for lífe*
> *I óffer: on mé lèt thine ánger fáll . . .*[6]

If ever there was fit wording or intonation for the divine
love and pity, it is here.

The schism and combat are, of course, previous history,
relegated to Books V and VI in the tale of Raphael. Here
again is the organ, if not orchestral, music of Books I and
II. In Book III, where stands the above passage, and the
scene is Heaven, the range and volume, though appropriate,

[6]*Ibid.,* III, 227–37.

are necessarily somewhat reduced. There is no broad contrast; no strife or contention, for that is now over; and a voice tender and compassionate arises in this heroic Heaven. In Hell, for the minor key, there is only pathos, as the angels consider their own hapless fall.

5

Satan discovers Paradise; and here there is a change. The scene is sinless and idyllic like the two inhabitants; and the height and volume of tone are reduced. This too is no such living or such country as we know of, but the proportions of either are more within our compass. It is earth and man, though before the fall. Satan, soliloquizing, still speaks in a high style, but, to fit his degenerating character and his present undertaking, a style less elevated than in Hell; and Adam and Eve, in a tone proper to their surroundings, to their worship and their love. Their imagery is drawn from nature; the poet's own, from the lovelier aspects of mythology and Greek and Latin verse. And in his contemplations and reminiscences a vein of tenderness and pathos is laid bare, with exquisitely fitting accompaniment. The organ becomes the flute, or rather, it is the same instrument played with the softer stops:

> *Not that fair field*
> *Of Enna, where Proserpin gathering flow'rs,*
> *Herself a fairer flow'r, by gloomy Dis*
> *Was gáther'd, which còst Céres áll thàt páin*
> *To séek her thróugh the wórld.*[7]

It is such a harmony, and cadence, as is not to be found in Books I and II, or even in Book III, but somewhat like these others:[8]

> *Flów'rs of àll húe, and withoùt thórn the róse.*

> *whére thy abúndance wánts*
> *Partákers, and ùncrópt fálls to the gróund.*

[7] *Ibid.,* IV, 268–72.
[8] *Ibid.,* IV, 256, 730–33.

For, though the scene is Paradise, the Fiend is in it. And in the more heartfelt emotions of the human pair, though sinless still, there is something of the seriousness or sadness of tone that to Milton, as to most artists, is inseparable from happiness:

> *to give thee being I lent*
> *Out of my side to thee, nearest my heart,*
> *Substantial life, to have thee by my side.*[9]

Here already there is the throb of a mortal throat, and in Milton's Paradise there is no happiness unalloyed. At dawn they rise, and before the curse is come upon them they work. Of the bliss of idleness the Puritan has no conception or else no sympathy with it; and life as we know it is not afar.

It is a felicitous arrangement that this account of our first day on earth should include its close. Sunlight is not easily distinguishable from the light of Heaven; but twilight and the nightingale, the moon and the stars, are neither of Heaven above them nor of Hell under the earth; and are indissolubly associated with the mingled emotions of our common humanity:

> *Now came still evening on, and twilight gray*
> *Had in her sober livery all things clad;*
> *Silence accompanied, for beast and bird,*
> *They to their grassy couch, these to their nests*
> *Were slunk, all but the wakeful nightingale;*
> *She all night long her amorous descant sung;*
> *Silence was pleas'd; now glow'd the firmament*
> *With living sapphire: Hesperus, that led*
> *The starry host, rode brightest, till the moon,*
> *Rising in clouded majesty, at length*
> *Apparent queen, unveil'd her peerless light,*
> *And o'er the dark her silver mantle threw.*[10]

With that we are nearly at home, and the expression is serene and simple as the evening itself. Three shadowy

[9]*Ibid.*, IV, 483–85.
[10]*Ibid.*, IV, 598–609.

scenes in the poem linger in my memory: the "dismal situation waste and wild" at the beginning, this first sweet evening on earth near the middle, and the evening when Adam and Eve, out in the world, look back at their happy seat "wav'd over by that flaming brand." The three mark stages in the epic.

6

Next day, with the visit of Raphael, which is prompted by the pity of the King of Heaven, comes his tremendous tale of the Rebellion and the downfall of the angels, a warning against disobedience, in the Titanic style once again. This throws the innocence that precedes and the human frailty which follows the day after, into relief. In the difference of opinion between the man and the woman before they separate in the garden, the limitations of human nature, such as have already become apparent, more clearly assert themselves—without a weakness how can one fall? And with the temptation we are in the midst of life at once, the arts and wiles of the Devil awakening the vanity and curiosity, the jealousy and willfulness of Eve. The style is not wholly simple, for Satan is the chief speaker and this is the great moment of the story; yet he is in the Serpent, and is addressing a woman. The style fluctuates, as it should do, according to speaker, mood, and occasion; but on earth it never reaches the height of that in Hell or in Heaven. The poet himself enjoys more freedom, as when he likens the Serpent, leading the way, to the will-o'-the-wisp—

Hóvering | and bláz|ing with | delús|ive líght.[11]

For we must be reminded that he is more than bestial or human, and how he flickers and allures!

Epic grandeur must, and does, give place to drama. There is simplicity (and presently duplicity) enough in Eve, and this is fine and vivid. In Paradise, she is already fairly a woman of this world. Having dwelt on the whole

[11]*Ibid.,* IX, 639.

subject elsewhere,[12] I will here only point to the skill wherewith Milton avoids the danger of her now seeming a different person. In the dispute with Adam before she left him she is still irreproachable, though well-nigh a mortal female in her pique:

> *But that thou shouldst my firmness therefore doubt*
> *To God or thee, because we have a Foe*
> *May tempt it, I expected not to hear.*
>
> . . . . .
>
> *Thoughts, which how found they harbour in thy breast,*
> *Adam, misthought of her to thee so dear?*[13]

Yet how sweet and inveigling in wording and in rhythm! It is a sign of his love and faith that she should be permitted to "have her way"! And it is not so much her vanity and curiosity as her willfulness, and in particular her resentment against what seems to her the ungenerosity of the prohibition, that is her undoing. A very woman, she is centered in her affections and emotions: through them she falls, and once fallen she is to them a prey. Shall I tell him and share with him? Or rather not, the more to draw his love and render me more equal, and perhaps superior? But what if God have seen and death ensue, and Adam, wedded to another Eve, shall live with her enjoying, I extinct? A death to think!

> *So dear I love him, that with him all deaths*
> *I could endure, without him live no life.*[14]

And that is true, despite the blandishments and cajolery with which she approaches him and betrays him; and her feeling is sincere and unfeigned as for joy she embraces him, and

> *Tenderly wept, much won that he his love*
> *Had so ennobl'd, as of choice to incur*
> *Divine displeasure for her sake, or death.*[15]

[12]*Poets and Playwrights*, pp. 257–67 and chap. XIX above.
[13]*Paradise Lost*, IX, 279–89.
[14]*Ibid.*, IX, 832–33.
[15]*Ibid.*, IX, 991–93.

Through her vicissitudes her character is, as far as is possible, kept intact. She is still herself as, later, she retorts to the reproaches of the first of husbands for not staying at home:

> *Was I to have never parted from thy side?*
> *As good have grown there still a lifeless rib.*
> *Being as I am, why didst not thou, the head,*
> *Command me absolutely not to go . . .*[16]

But she is herself above all in her tenderness and repentance as she assumes the whole burden of fault, especially in the lines:

> *Forsake me not thus, Adam; witness Heav'n*
> *What love sincere . . .*[17]

> *Between us two let there be peace; both joining,*
> *As joined in injuries . . .*[18]

Her language is always a woman's, and this broken rhythm is that of a woman's pleading.

7

From the moment of temptation on, the speeches of Adam and Eve are, except for some of Adam's lamentations and upbraidings, simple in expression; but now all are more complicated in matter, as befits those of a many-sided human nature. They are now the voice of pathos or affection, wisdom or fortitude, hope or fear, as at the temptation they were that of resentment and deceit, vanity and an affection beyond measure. They have the complication, but (though more of that) not the energy and elevation, or the admixture of evil, to be found in those of the fallen angels at the beginning. Even the speeches of the Lord and of the Son are less exalted than formerly, being not those of wrath

[16]*Ibid.*, IX, 1153-56.
[17]*Ibid.*, X, 914-15.
[18]*Ibid.*, X, 924-25.

and justice but of mercy and compassion. And of the Deity things are now said that were not said before:

> *And thought not much[19] to clothe his enemies.[20]*

> *. . . yet this will prayer,*
> *Or one short sigh of human breath, upborne*
> *Ev'n to the seat of God.[21]*

(The verse itself is such a sigh.)

> *and in mind prepar'd, if so befal,*
> *For death, like that which the Redeemer died.[22]*

Here, considerably before its time, is the New Dispensation, which also is to preside over the exile. Of the world under it, good being brought out of evil (though not profusely), there is a vision vouchsafed to Adam and a prophecy from the lips of Michael. And for that mingled web, good and ill together, that complex of thoughts and emotions which makes up the situation at the close and represents human experience ever since, there are now continual preparations. Of such a nature are passages like these:[23]

> *but strive*
> *In offices of love, how we may light'n*
> *Each other's burden in our share of woe.*

> *new hope to spring*
> *Out of despair; joy, but with fear yet linkt.*

> *Thy going is not lonely, with thee goes*
> *Thy husband . . .*

> *Nor love thy life, nor hate; but what thou liv'st*
> *Live well; how long or short permit to Heaven.*

[19]That is, that it was not too much to do.
[20]*Paradise Lost,* X, 219.
[21]*Ibid.,* XI, 146–48.
[22]*Ibid.,* XII, 444–45.
[23]*Ibid.,* X, 959–61; XI, 138–39, 290–91, 553–54; XII, 473–76, 614–19.

full of doubt I stand,
Whether I should repent me now of sin
By me done and occasion'd, or rejoice
Much more, that much more good thereof shall spring.

but now lead on,
In me is no delay; with thee to go
Is to stay here; without thee here to stay
Is to go hence unwilling; thou to me
Art all things under Heav'n, all places thou,
Who for my wilful crime art banisht hence.

The last are from Eve's final words. A Romantic paradox
again, yet not like Adam's, touched on in chapter XIX
above. But love, the beginning, is now the end of all; and
though she is not happy, still less (as has been said)
"elated," in her and her mate at least good has come out
of evil, strength out of weakness, sweetness out of bitterness,
hope out of despair. And in those passages and others like
them in the last two books, there are both the conception
of life and something of the mood and utterance that we
find in

The world was all before them, where to choose
Their place of rest, and Providence their guide:
They hand in hand, with wand'ring steps and slow,
Through Eden took their solitary way.[24]

8

And hand in hand! In the preceding chapter we noticed
how the poet indirectly reminds us of its being the same
hand that had withdrawn and had plucked. And apart
from the fine suggestion thus achieved, the simplicity, the
reticence! "They left Paradise arm in arm" was once a
student's version—as for a promenade!

I have elsewhere remarked[25] a fine effect, attained by
Dante, of continual interplay, parallelism and contrast,

[24]*Ibid.*, XII, 646–49.
[25]*Poets and Playwrights*, pp. 281–89.

between life on earth and that in Hell, Purgatory, or Heaven. The earth, though not described or presented, is ever the *point de repère* of the story, and by way of the memory not only of the living men but of the shades. This, together with the impression of the spirits, human and superhuman, upon the visitor, and still more that of him upon them, is his chief and most fruitful means of presenting the spiritual world. In *Paradise Lost* no such effect of compression and volume was possible. There mortal life begins only at the end. But instead there are the effects of rhythm and equilibrium that we have noticed, and also those of progression and gradation. There are no such juxtaposition and interplay, but Hell and Heaven are intent upon the earth from the time of the fall of the angels; they there meet and contend with each other for possession of it; and though good on the whole prevails, human life, now beginning, is of their making. The last shadowy scene of exile, though another spirit informs it, recalls the first. There is, therefore, in keeping with this progress, an appropriate decrease in the magnitude, and increase in the complexity, of both the emotions and the expression, as we proceed through the great poem to its close.

1935

Index to Names and Titles

(Topics may be found by the Table of Contents. Unless dealt with frequently, writings are indexed only under the author, and characters under the writing. More important references are in italics. *N* is for footnote.)